Red Carpet Rose

A "Rose is Rose" Collection
by Pat Brady and Don Wimmer

**Andrews McMeel
Publishing**

Kansas City

Rose is Rose is distributed internationally by United Feature Syndicate, Inc.

06 07 08 09 10 BBG 10 9 8 7 6 5 4 3 2 1

ISBN-13: 978-0-7407-5700-6
ISBN-10: 0-7407-5700-8

Library of Congress Control Number: 2005936215

www.andrewsmcmeel.com

ATTENTION: SCHOOLS AND BUSINESSES

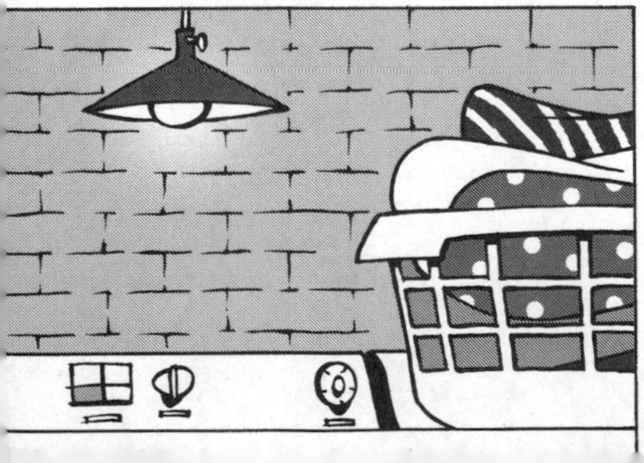

Other "Rose is Rose" Books from Andrews McMeel Publishing

She's a Momma, Not a Movie Star

License to Dream

Rose is Rose 15th Anniversary Collection

The Irresistible Rose is Rose

High-Spirited Rose is Rose

Rose is Rose Right on the Lips

Rose is Rose Running on Alter Ego

**FLIP THE PAGE CORNERS FROM FRONT TO BACK
AND WATCH BOTH SIDES TOGETHER!**

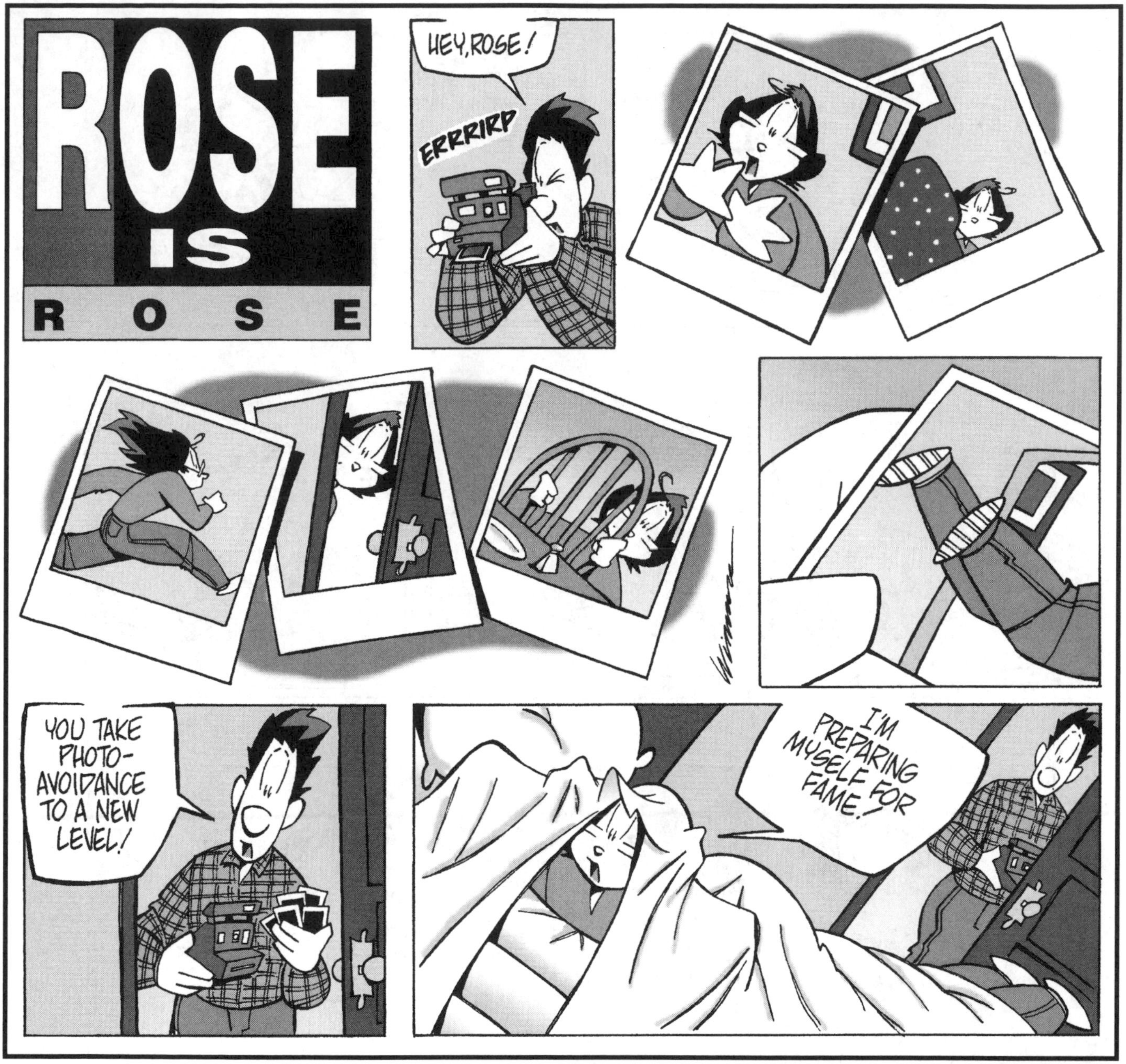
ROSE IS ROSE
HEY, ROSE!
ERRRIRP
YOU TAKE PHOTO-AVOIDANCE TO A NEW LEVEL!
I'M PREPARING MYSELF FOR FAME!

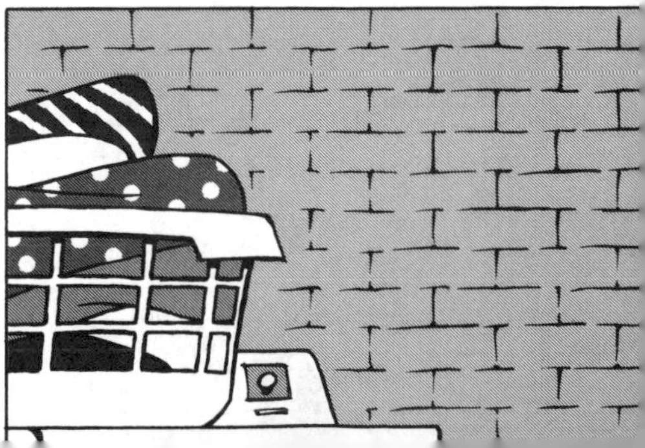

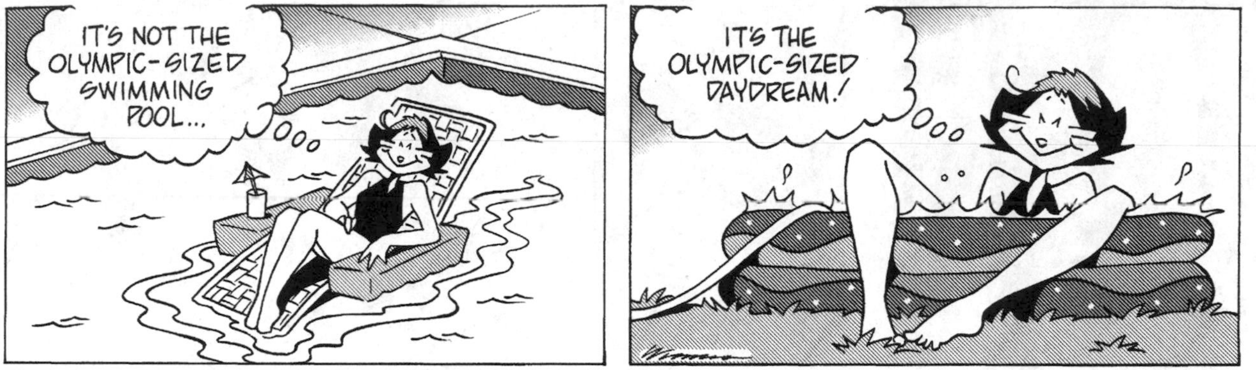
IT'S NOT THE OLYMPIC-SIZED SWIMMING POOL...
IT'S THE OLYMPIC-SIZED DAYDREAM!

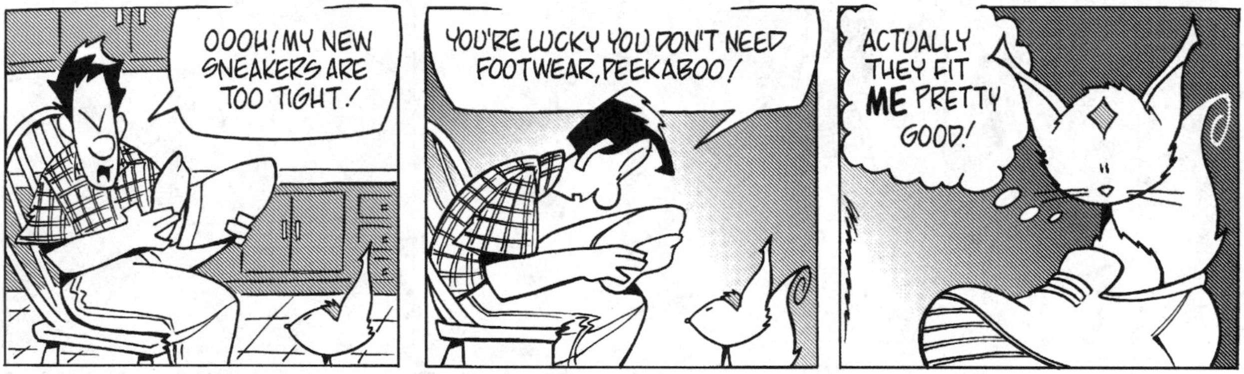
OOOH! MY NEW SNEAKERS ARE TOO TIGHT!
YOU'RE LUCKY YOU DON'T NEED FOOTWEAR, PEEKABOO!
ACTUALLY THEY FIT ME PRETTY GOOD!

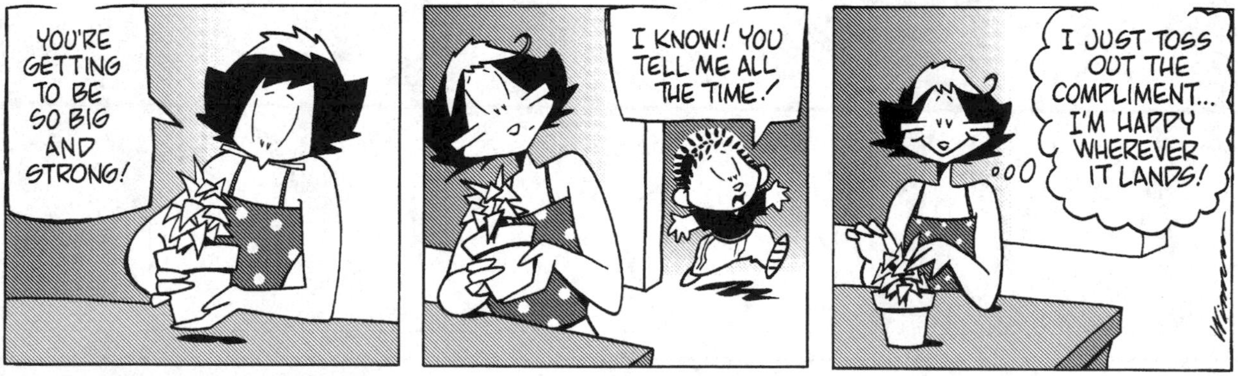
YOU'RE GETTING TO BE SO BIG AND STRONG!
I KNOW! YOU TELL ME ALL THE TIME!
I JUST TOSS OUT THE COMPLIMENT... I'M HAPPY WHEREVER IT LANDS!

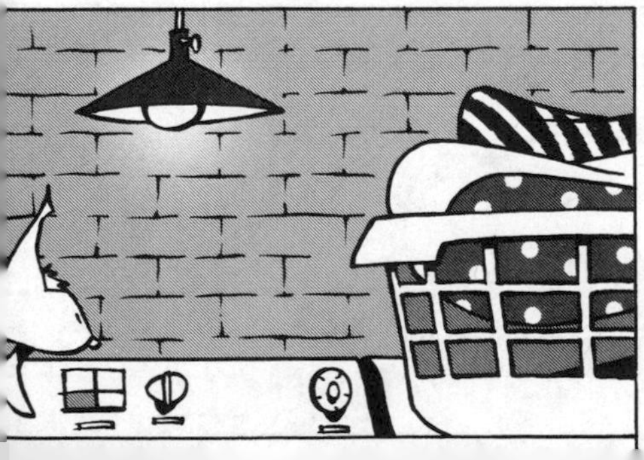

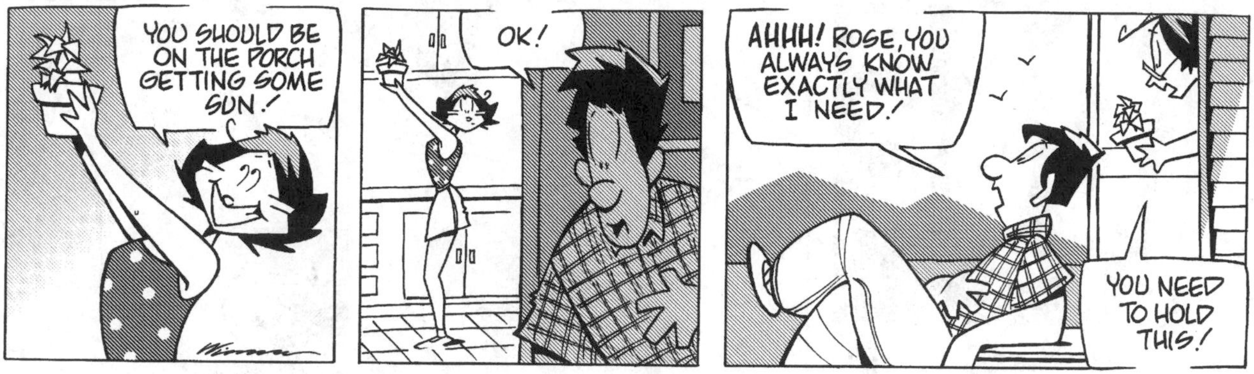
YOU SHOULD BE ON THE PORCH GETTING SOME SUN!
OK!
AHHH! ROSE, YOU ALWAYS KNOW EXACTLY WHAT I NEED!
YOU NEED TO HOLD THIS!

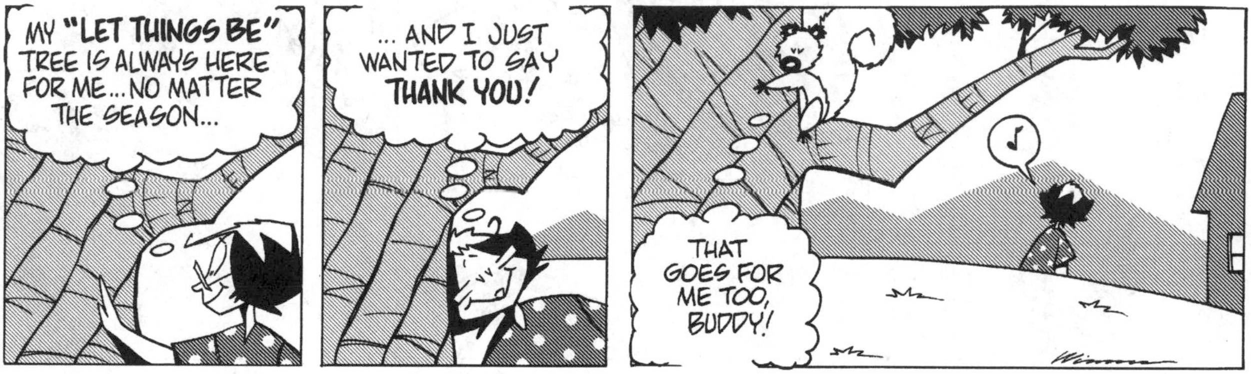
MY "LET THINGS BE" TREE IS ALWAYS HERE FOR ME... NO MATTER THE SEASON...
... AND I JUST WANTED TO SAY THANK YOU!
THAT GOES FOR ME TOO, BUDDY!

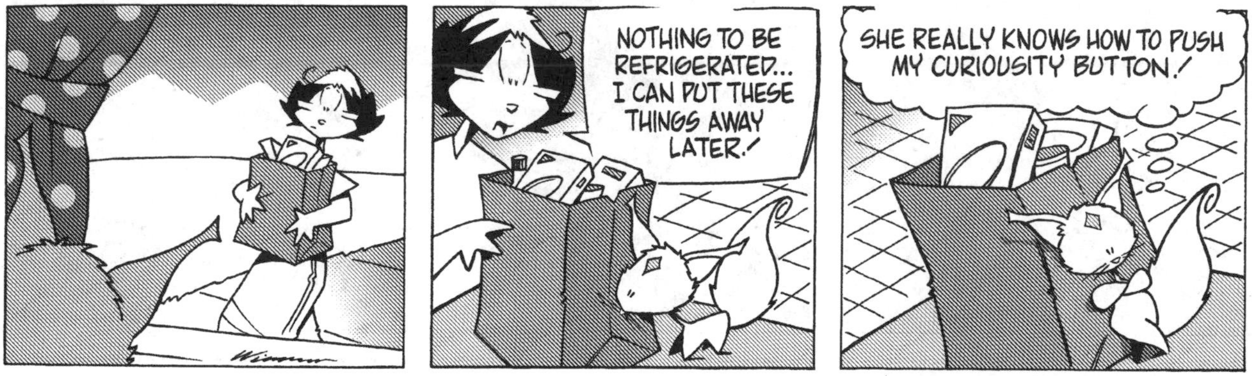
NOTHING TO BE REFRIGERATED... I CAN PUT THESE THINGS AWAY LATER!
SHE REALLY KNOWS HOW TO PUSH MY CURIOUSITY BUTTON!

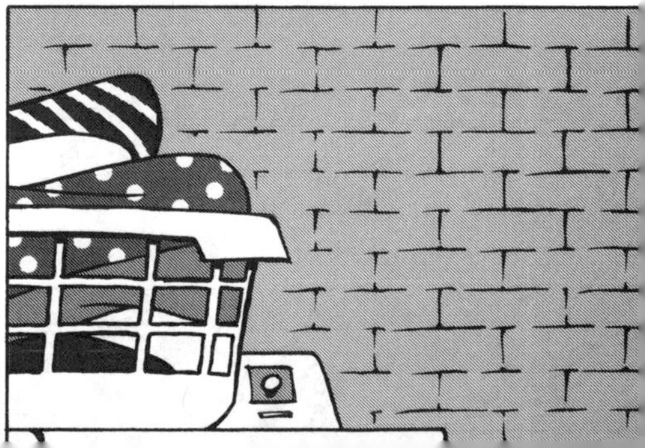

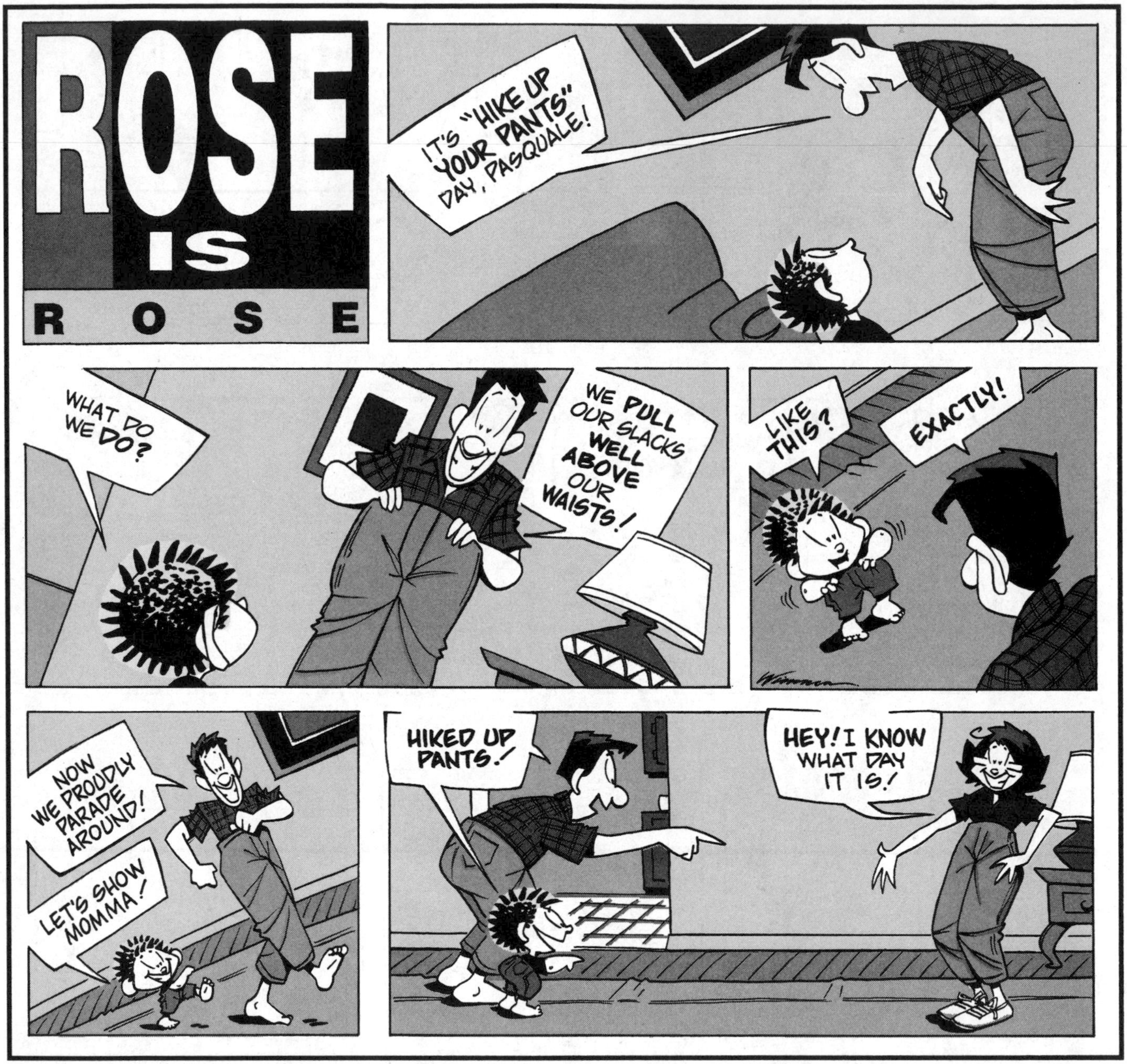
ROSE IS ROSE
IT'S "HIKE UP YOUR PANTS" DAY, PASQUALE!
WHAT DO WE DO?
WE PULL OUR SLACKS WELL ABOVE OUR WAISTS!
LIKE THIS?
EXACTLY!
NOW WE PROUDLY PARADE AROUND!
LET'S SHOW MOMMA!
HIKED UP PANTS!
HEY! I KNOW WHAT DAY IT IS!

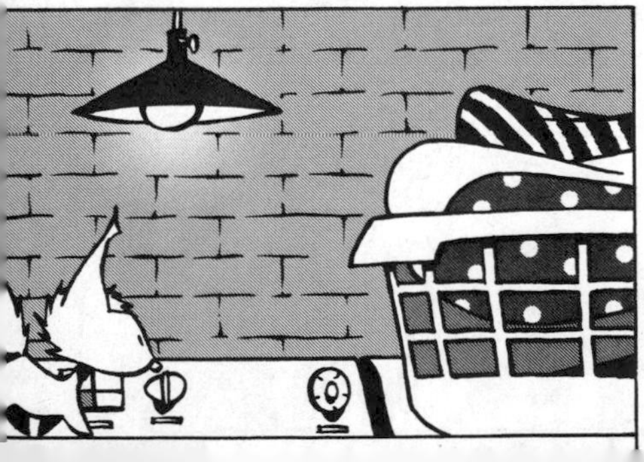

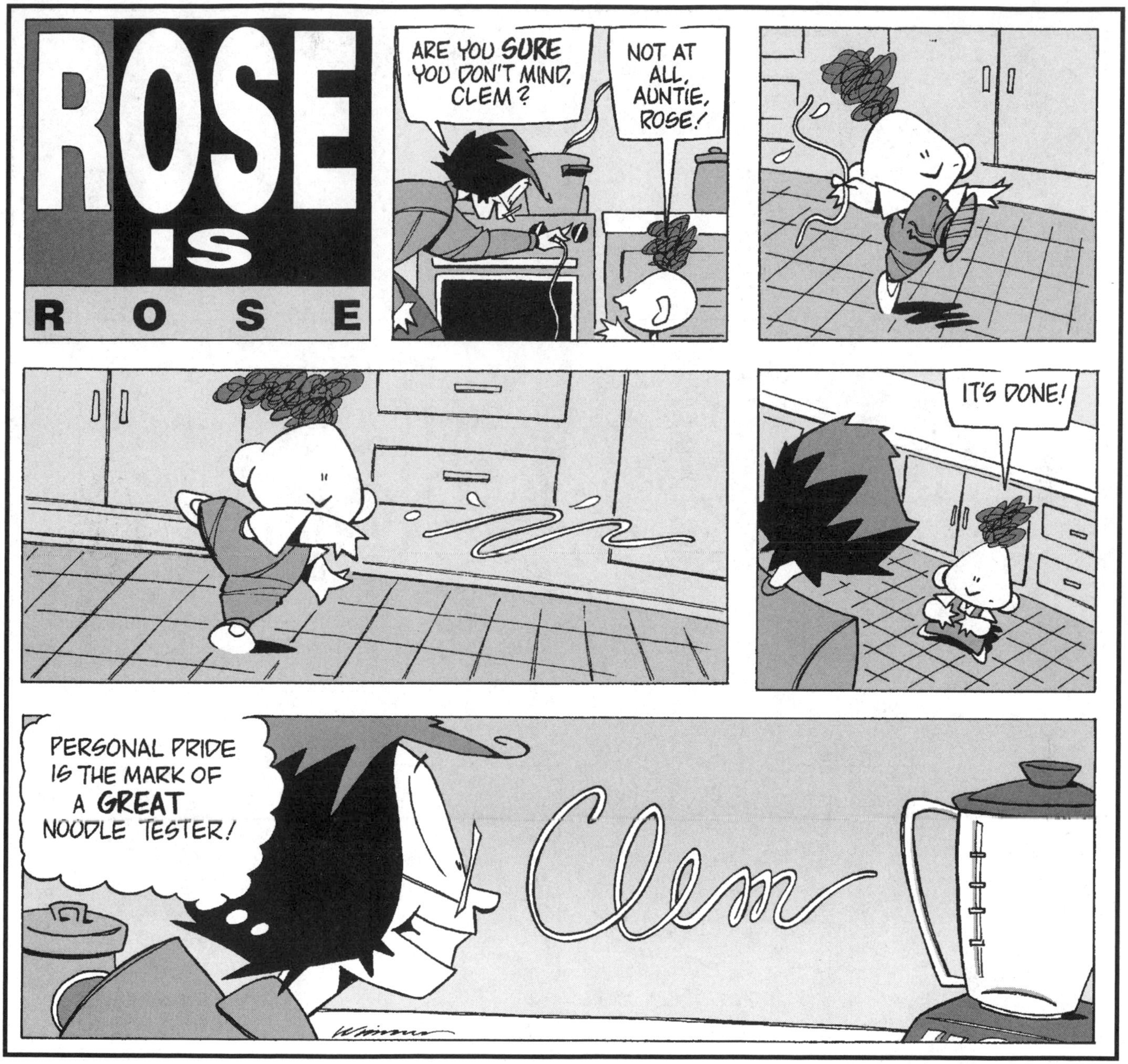
ROSE IS ROSE
ARE YOU SURE YOU DON'T MIND, CLEM?
NOT AT ALL, AUNTIE, ROSE!
IT'S DONE!
PERSONAL PRIDE IS THE MARK OF A GREAT NOODLE TESTER!
Clem

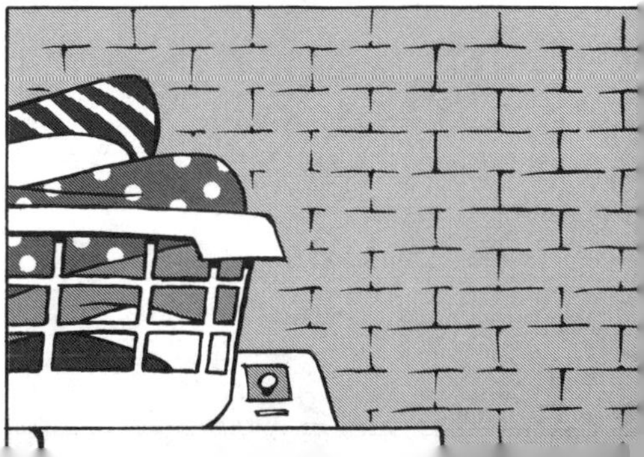

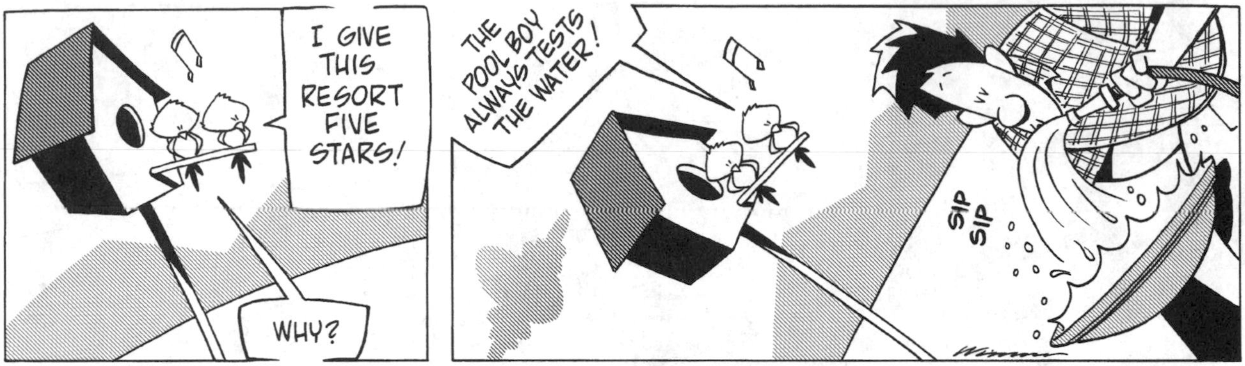
I GIVE THIS RESORT FIVE STARS!
WHY?
THE POOL BOY ALWAYS TESTS THE WATER!
SIP SIP

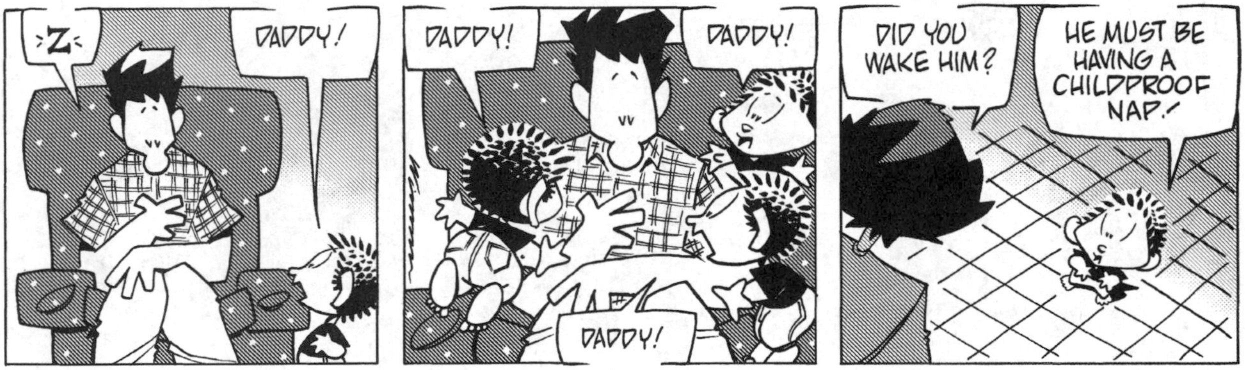
Z
DADDY!
DADDY!
DADDY!
DADDY!
DID YOU WAKE HIM?
HE MUST BE HAVING A CHILDPROOF NAP!

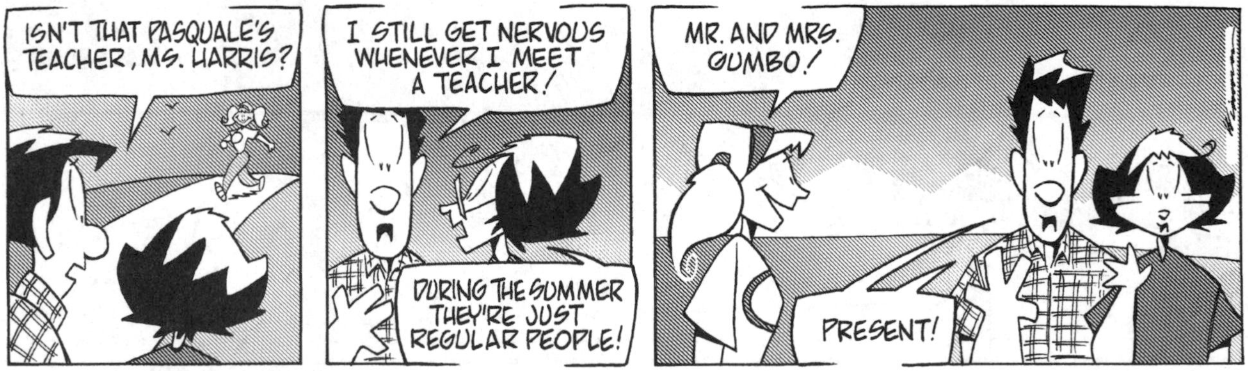
ISN'T THAT PASQUALE'S TEACHER, MS. HARRIS?
I STILL GET NERVOUS WHENEVER I MEET A TEACHER!
DURING THE SUMMER THEY'RE JUST REGULAR PEOPLE!
MR. AND MRS. GUMBO!
PRESENT!

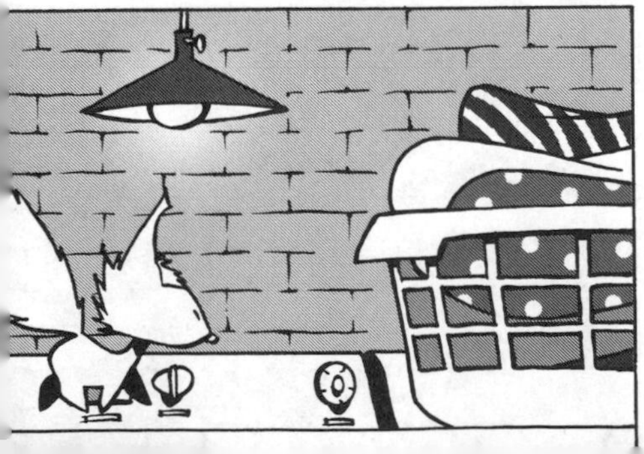

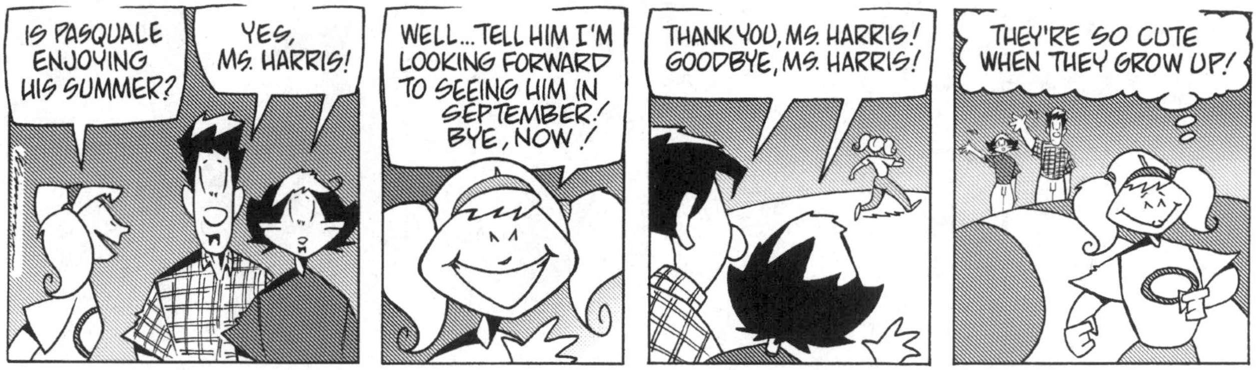
IS PASQUALE ENJOYING HIS SUMMER?
YES, MS. HARRIS!
WELL... TELL HIM I'M LOOKING FORWARD TO SEEING HIM IN SEPTEMBER! BYE, NOW!
THANK YOU, MS. HARRIS! GOODBYE, MS. HARRIS!
THEY'RE SO CUTE WHEN THEY GROW UP!

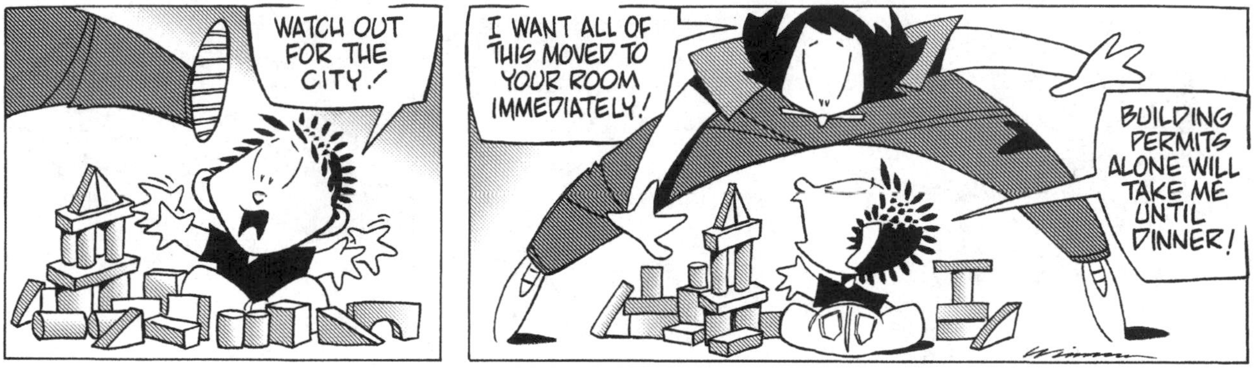
WATCH OUT FOR THE CITY!
I WANT ALL OF THIS MOVED TO YOUR ROOM IMMEDIATELY!
BUILDING PERMITS ALONE WILL TAKE ME UNTIL DINNER!

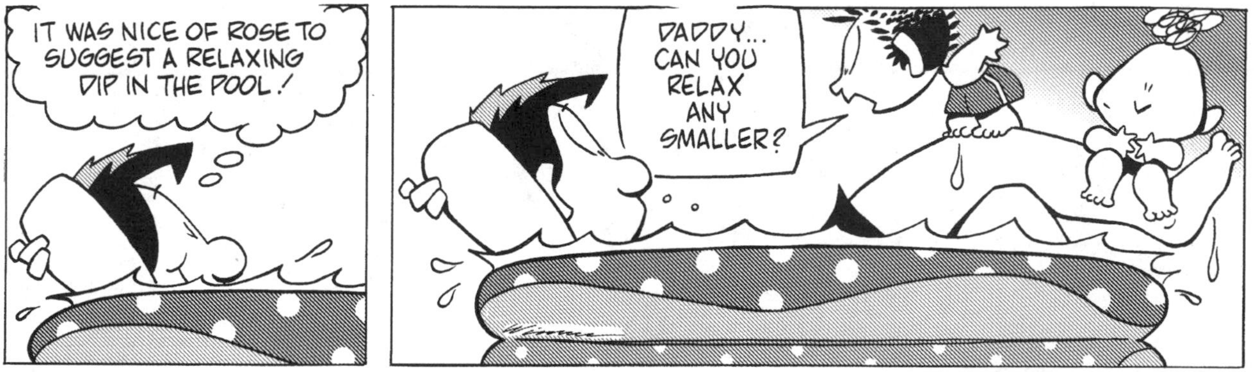
IT WAS NICE OF ROSE TO SUGGEST A RELAXING DIP IN THE POOL!
DADDY... CAN YOU RELAX ANY SMALLER?

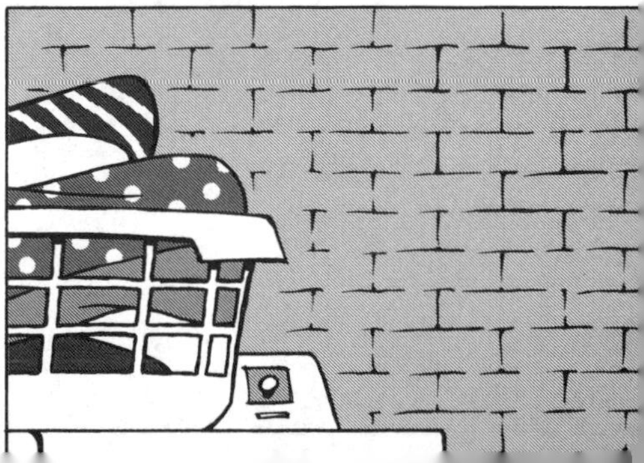

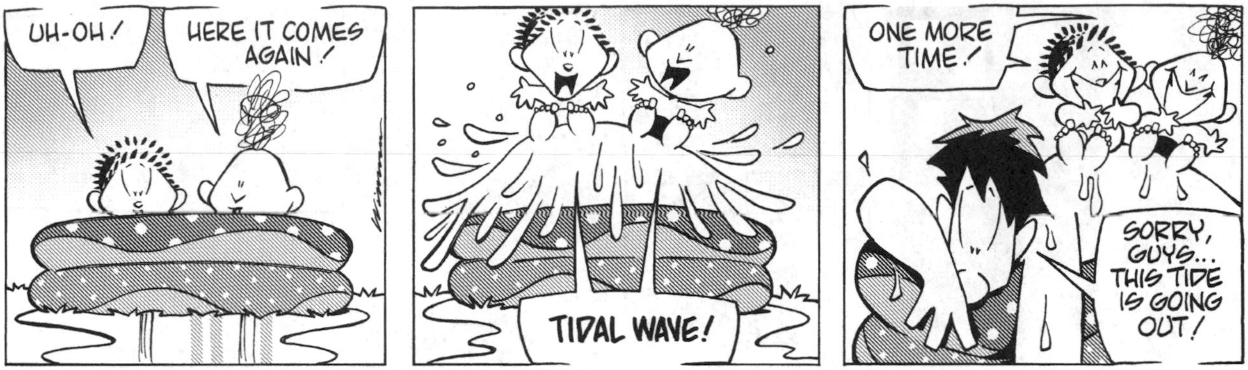
UH-OH!
HERE IT COMES AGAIN!
TIDAL WAVE!
ONE MORE TIME!
SORRY, GUYS... THIS TIDE IS GOING OUT!

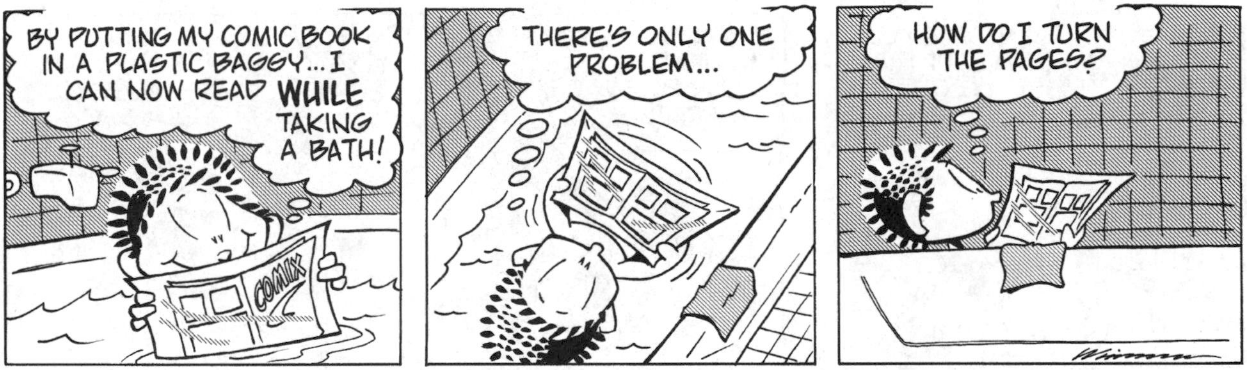
BY PUTTING MY COMIC BOOK IN A PLASTIC BAGGY...I CAN NOW READ WHILE TAKING A BATH!
COMIX
THERE'S ONLY ONE PROBLEM...
HOW DO I TURN THE PAGES?

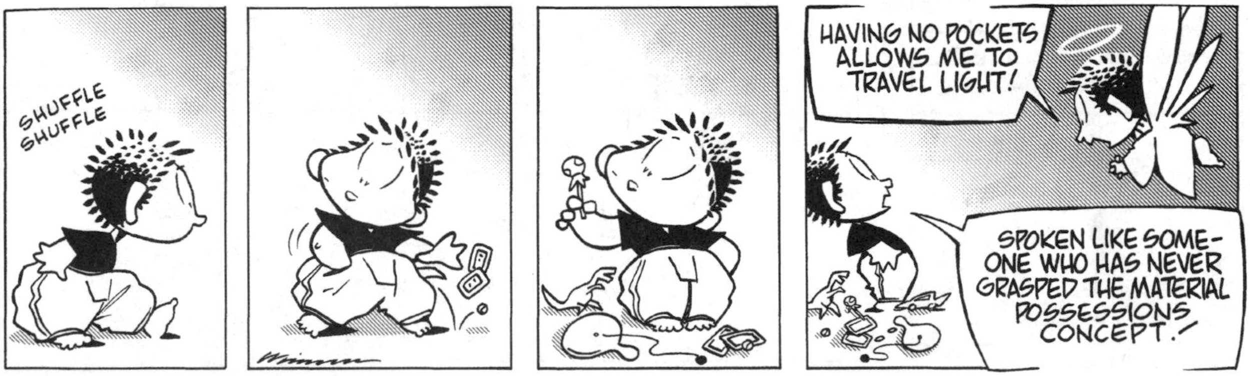
SHUFFLE SHUFFLE
HAVING NO POCKETS ALLOWS ME TO TRAVEL LIGHT!
SPOKEN LIKE SOME-ONE WHO HAS NEVER GRASPED THE MATERIAL POSSESSIONS CONCEPT.!

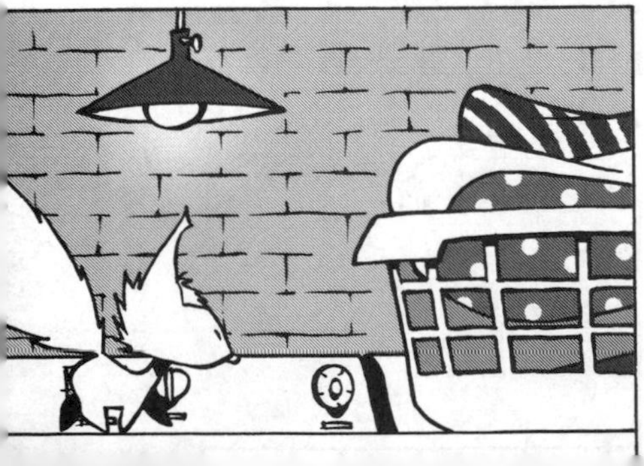

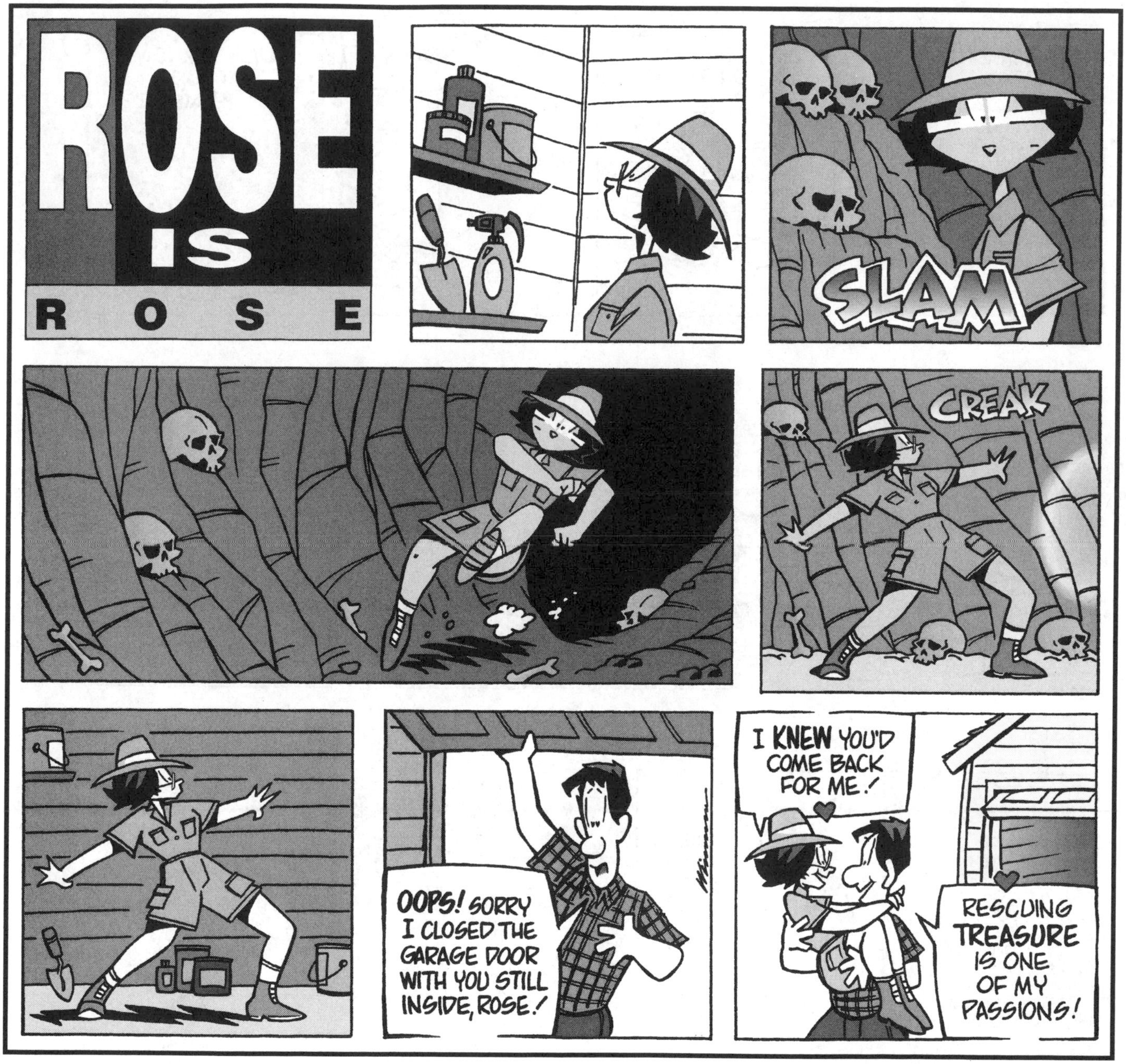
ROSE IS ROSE
SLAM
CREAK
OOPS! SORRY I CLOSED THE GARAGE DOOR WITH YOU STILL INSIDE, ROSE!
I KNEW YOU'D COME BACK FOR ME!
RESCUING TREASURE IS ONE OF MY PASSIONS!

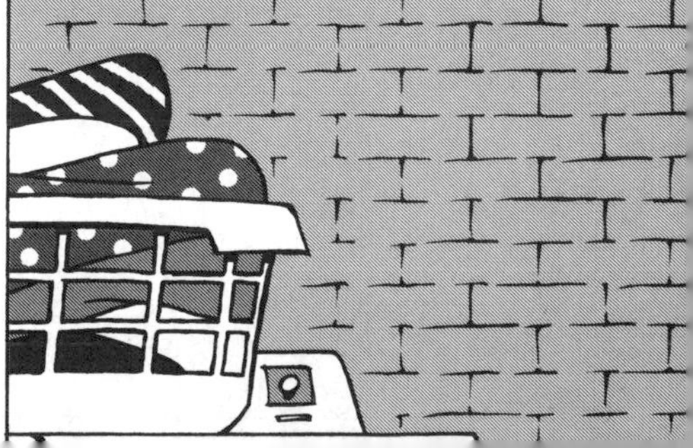

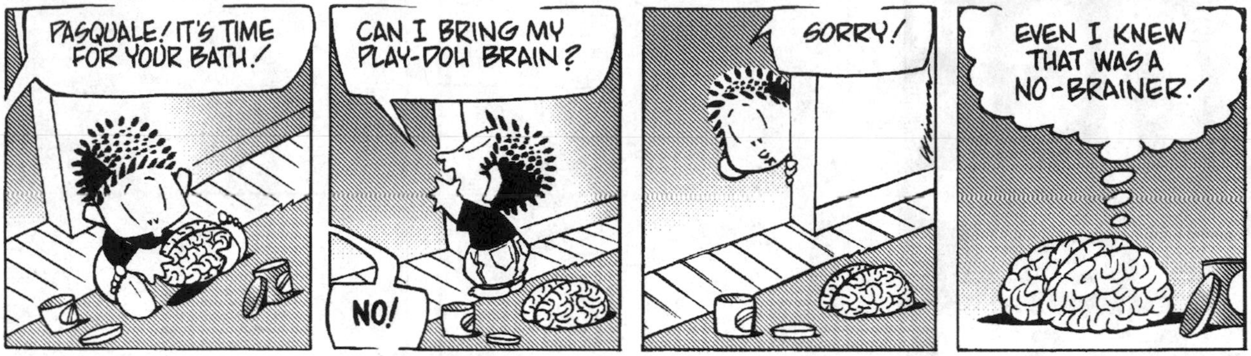
PASQUALE! IT'S TIME FOR YOUR BATH!
CAN I BRING MY PLAY-DOH BRAIN?
NO!
SORRY!
EVEN I KNEW THAT WAS A NO-BRAINER!

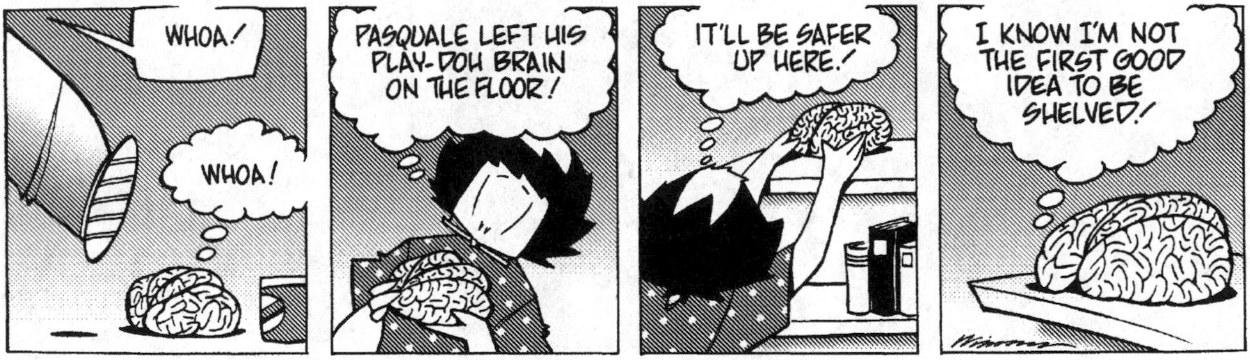
WHOA!
WHOA!
PASQUALE LEFT HIS PLAY-DOH BRAIN ON THE FLOOR!
IT'LL BE SAFER UP HERE!
I KNOW I'M NOT THE FIRST GOOD IDEA TO BE SHELVED!

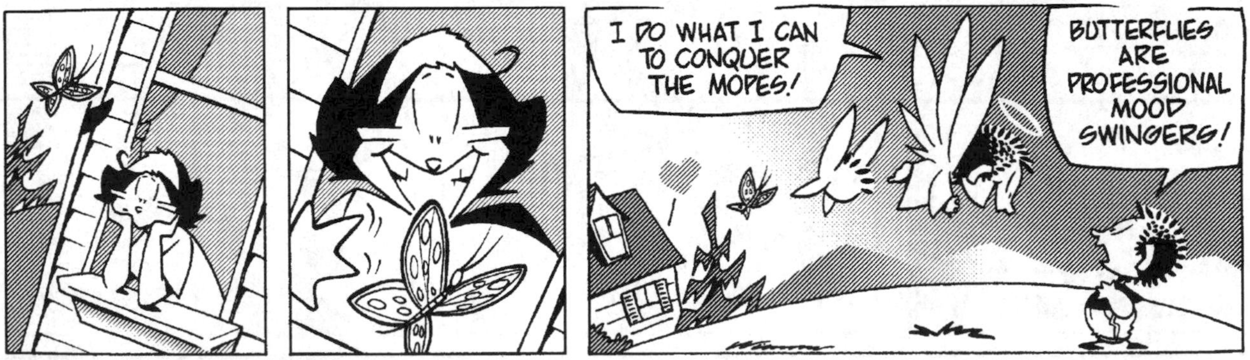
I DO WHAT I CAN TO CONQUER THE MOPES!
BUTTERFLIES ARE PROFESSIONAL MOOD SWINGERS!

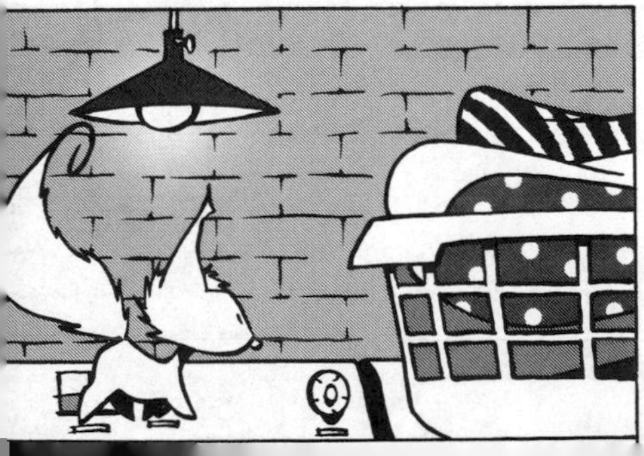

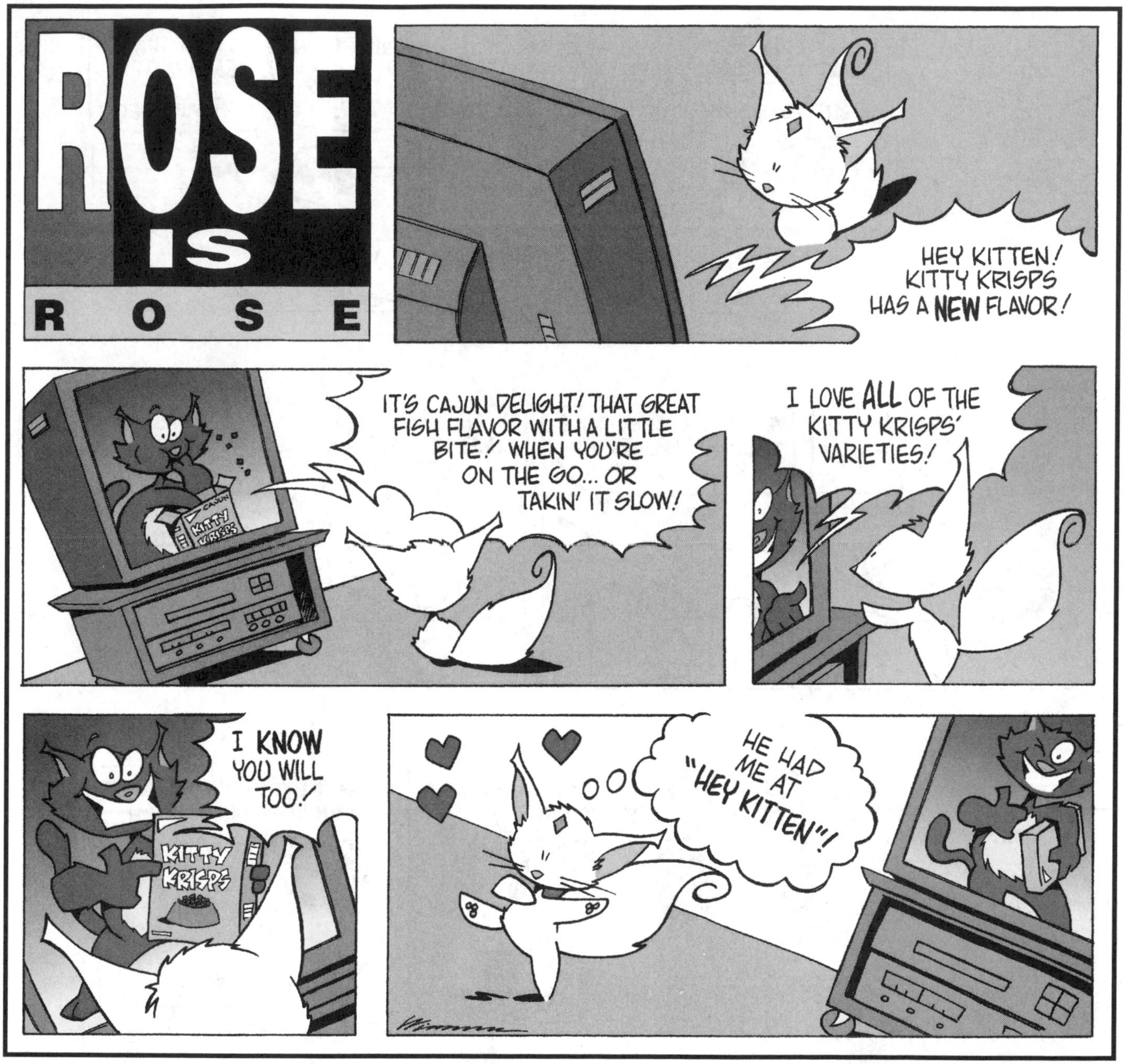
ROSE IS ROSE
HEY KITTEN! KITTY KRISPS HAS A NEW FLAVOR!
IT'S CAJUN DELIGHT! THAT GREAT FISH FLAVOR WITH A LITTLE BITE! WHEN YOU'RE ON THE GO... OR TAKIN' IT SLOW!
CAJUN KITTY KRISPS
I LOVE ALL OF THE KITTY KRISPS' VARIETIES!
I KNOW YOU WILL TOO!
KITTY KRISPS
HE HAD ME AT "HEY KITTEN"!

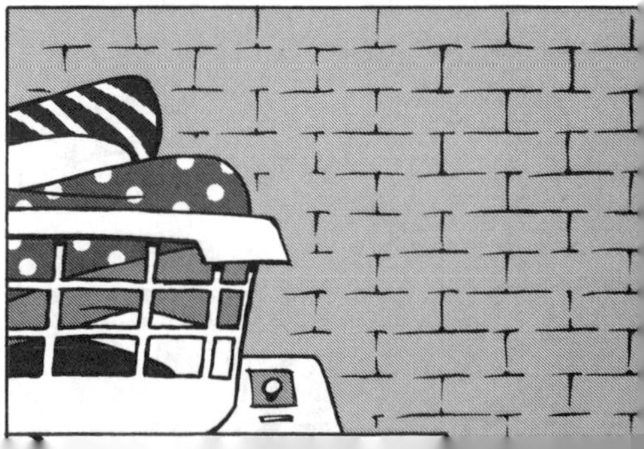

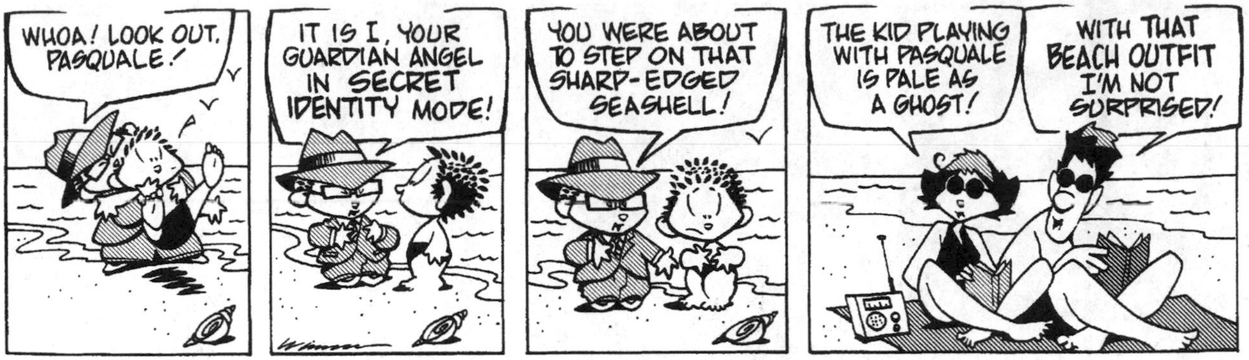
WHOA! LOOK OUT, PASQUALE!
IT IS I, YOUR GUARDIAN ANGEL IN SECRET IDENTITY MODE!
YOU WERE ABOUT TO STEP ON THAT SHARP-EDGED SEASHELL!
THE KID PLAYING WITH PASQUALE IS PALE AS A GHOST!
WITH THAT BEACH OUTFIT I'M NOT SURPRISED!

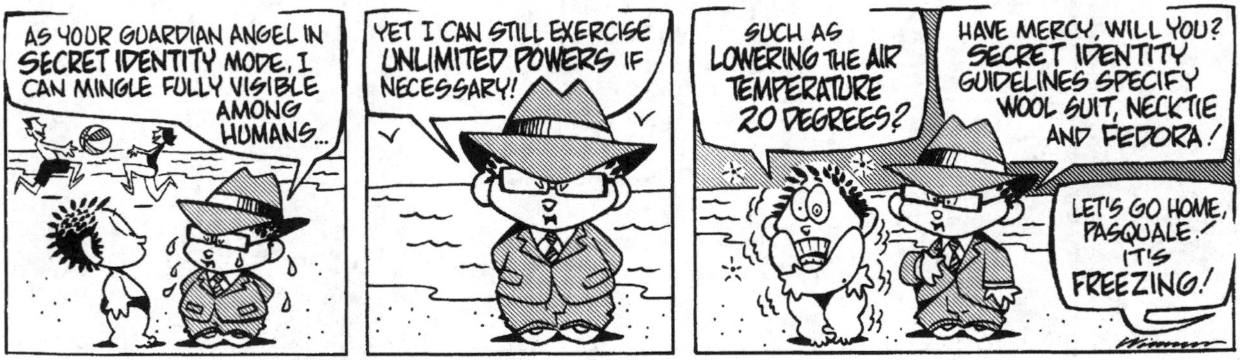
AS YOUR GUARDIAN ANGEL IN SECRET IDENTITY MODE, I CAN MINGLE FULLY VISIBLE AMONG HUMANS...
YET I CAN STILL EXERCISE UNLIMITED POWERS IF NECESSARY!
SUCH AS LOWERING THE AIR TEMPERATURE 20 DEGREES?
HAVE MERCY, WILL YOU? SECRET IDENTITY GUIDELINES SPECIFY WOOL SUIT, NECKTIE AND FEDORA!
LET'S GO HOME, PASQUALE! IT'S FREEZING!

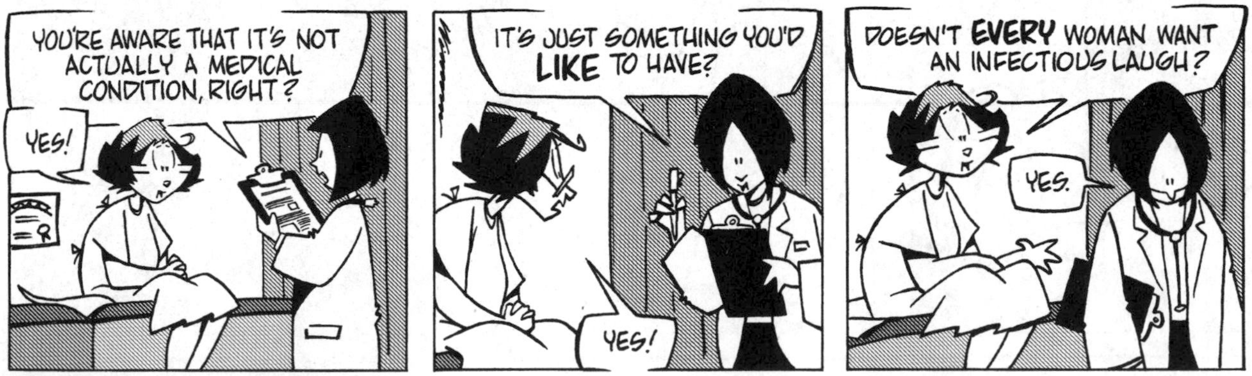
YOU'RE AWARE THAT IT'S NOT ACTUALLY A MEDICAL CONDITION, RIGHT?
YES!
IT'S JUST SOMETHING YOU'D LIKE TO HAVE?
YES!
DOESN'T EVERY WOMAN WANT AN INFECTIOUS LAUGH?
YES.

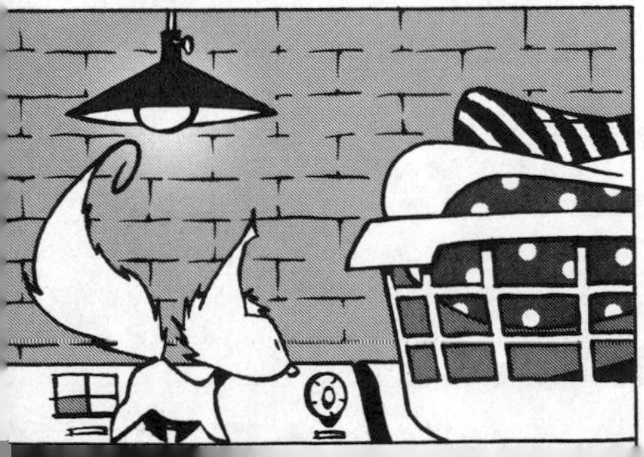

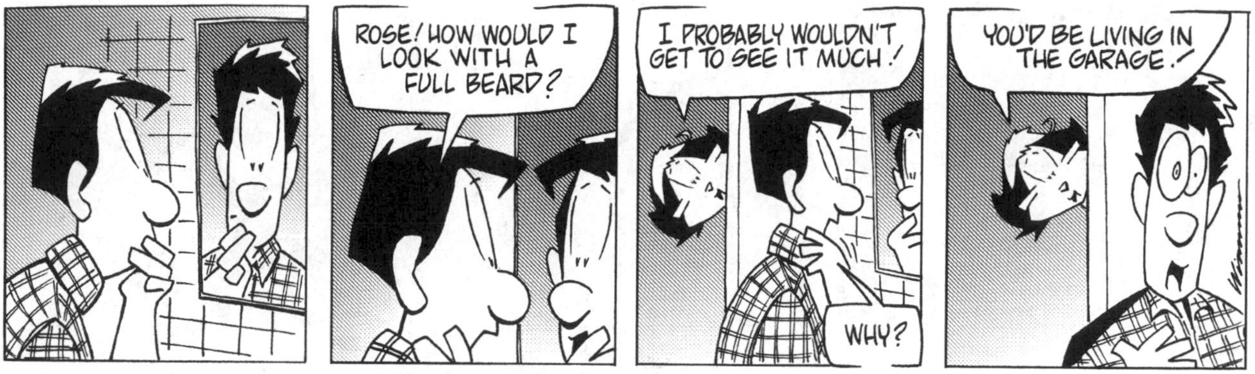
ROSE! HOW WOULD I LOOK WITH A FULL BEARD?
I PROBABLY WOULDN'T GET TO SEE IT MUCH!
WHY?
YOU'D BE LIVING IN THE GARAGE!

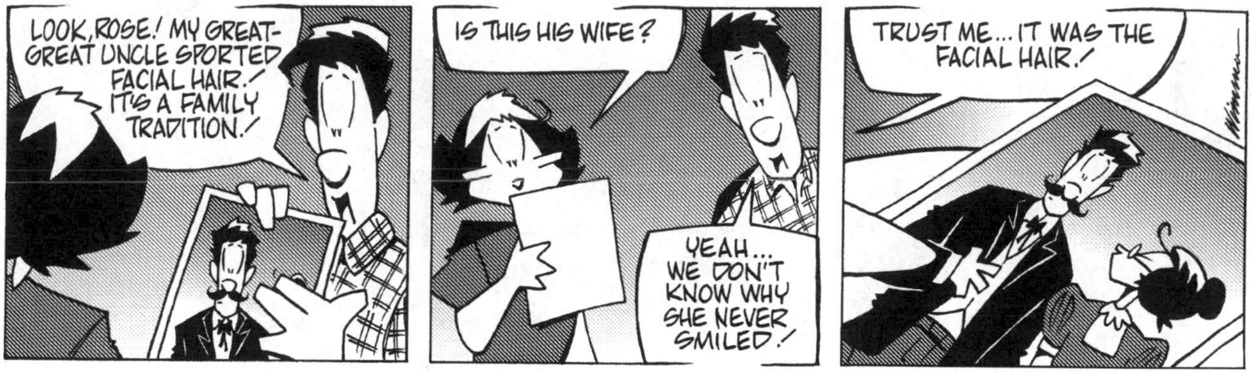
LOOK, ROSE! MY GREAT-GREAT UNCLE SPORTED FACIAL HAIR! IT'S A FAMILY TRADITION!
IS THIS HIS WIFE?
YEAH... WE DON'T KNOW WHY SHE NEVER SMILED!
TRUST ME... IT WAS THE FACIAL HAIR!

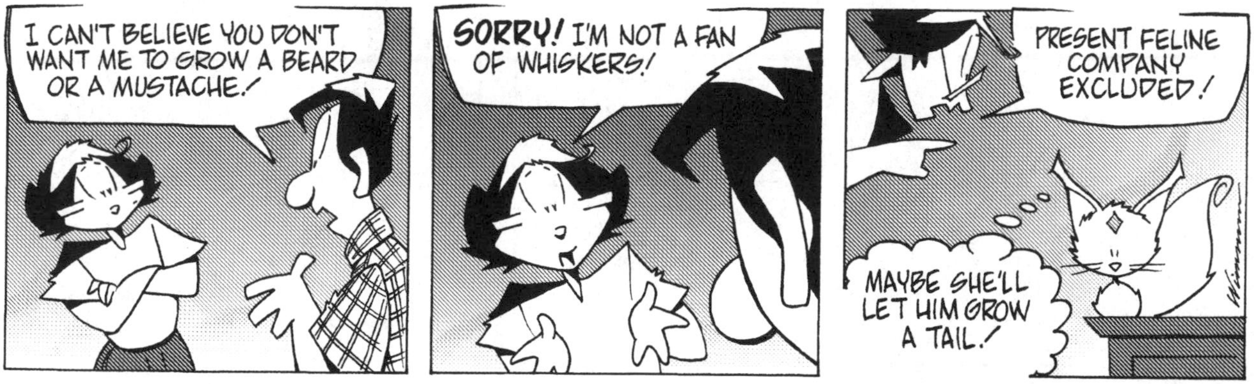
I CAN'T BELIEVE YOU DON'T WANT ME TO GROW A BEARD OR A MUSTACHE!
SORRY! I'M NOT A FAN OF WHISKERS!
PRESENT FELINE COMPANY EXCLUDED!
MAYBE SHE'LL LET HIM GROW A TAIL!

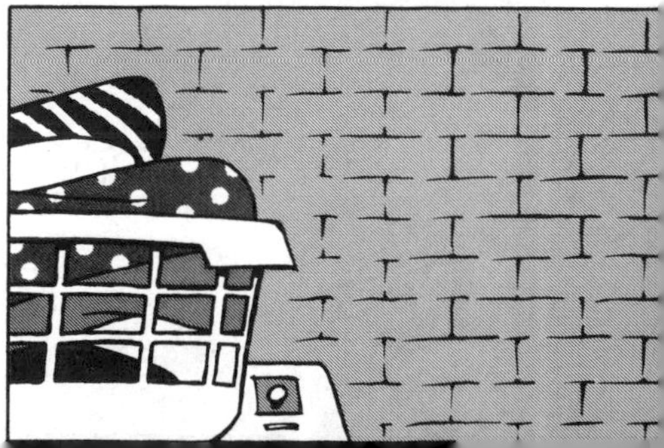

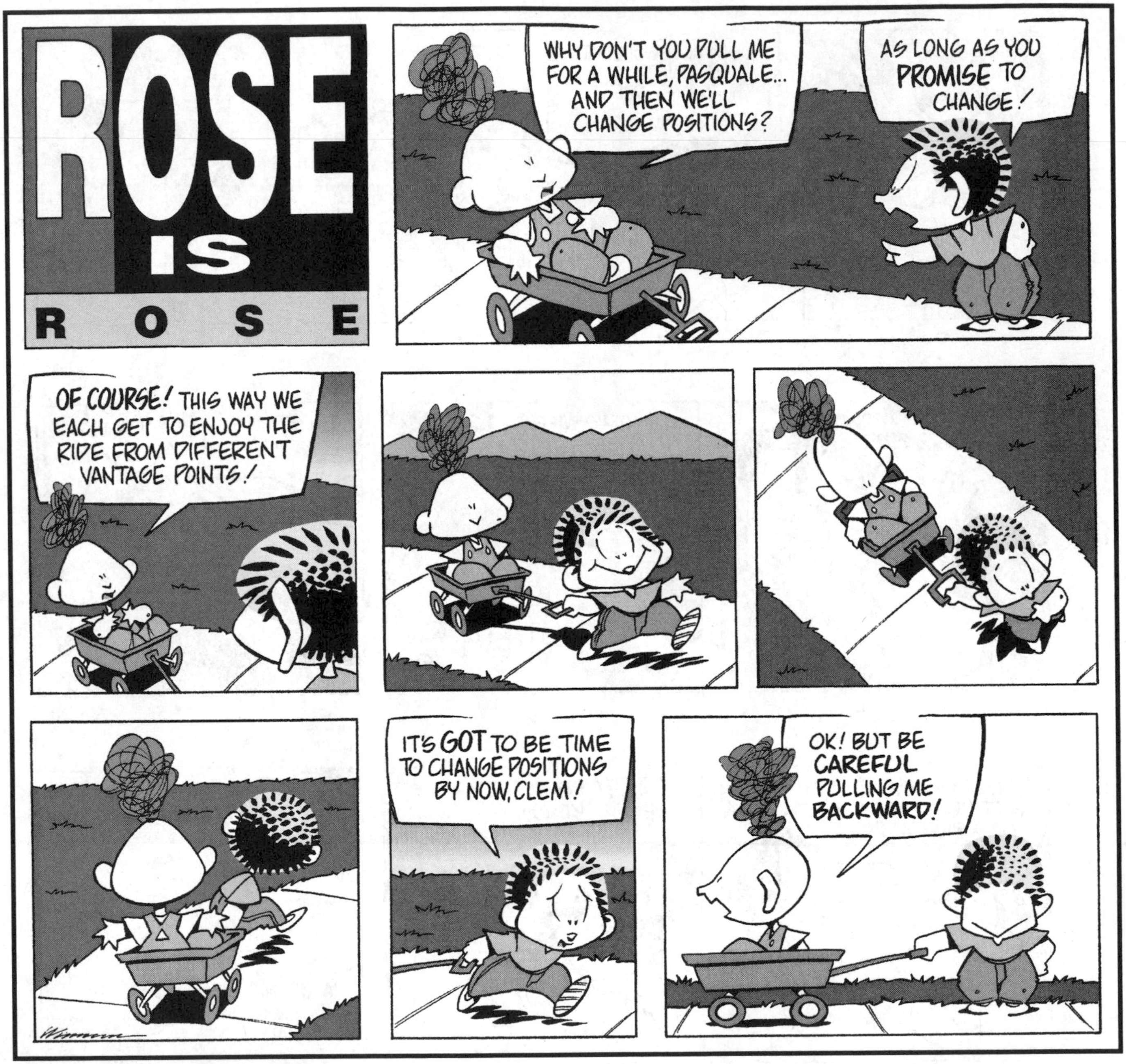
ROSE IS ROSE
WHY DON'T YOU PULL ME FOR A WHILE, PASQUALE... AND THEN WE'LL CHANGE POSITIONS?
AS LONG AS YOU PROMISE TO CHANGE!
OF COURSE! THIS WAY WE EACH GET TO ENJOY THE RIDE FROM DIFFERENT VANTAGE POINTS!
IT'S GOT TO BE TIME TO CHANGE POSITIONS BY NOW, CLEM!
OK! BUT BE CAREFUL PULLING ME BACKWARD!

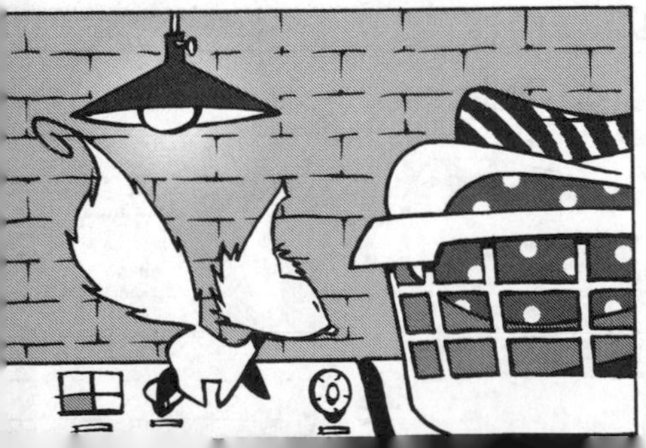

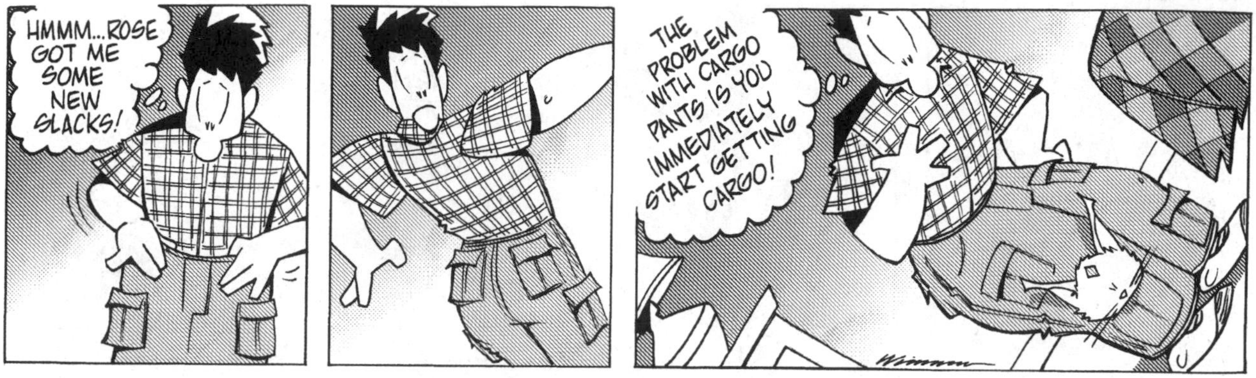
HMMM...ROSE GOT ME SOME NEW SLACKS!
THE PROBLEM WITH CARGO PANTS IS YOU IMMEDIATELY START GETTING CARGO!

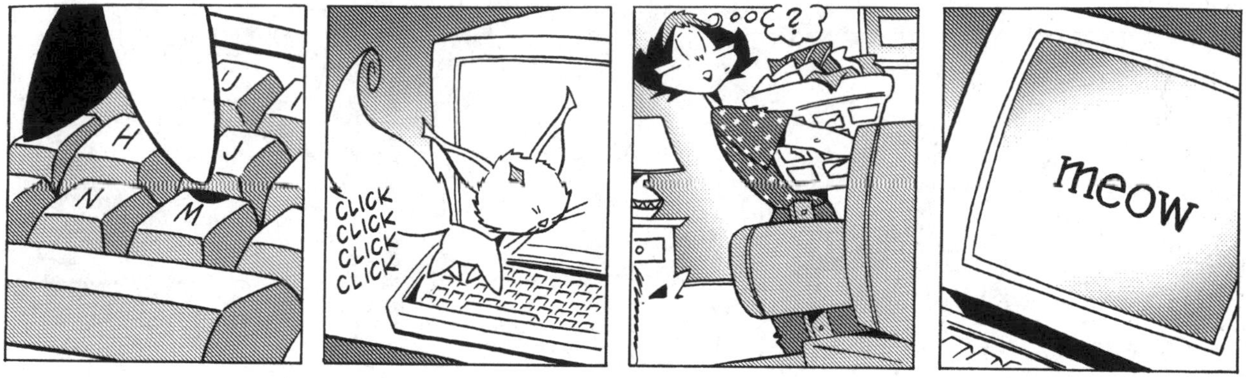
CLICK CLICK CLICK CLICK
?
meow

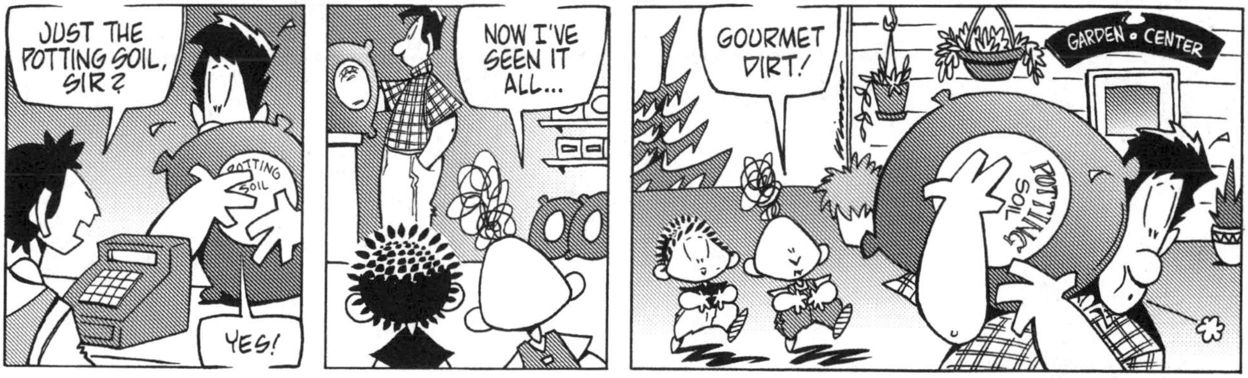
JUST THE POTTING SOIL, SIR?
POTTING SOIL
YES!
NOW I'VE SEEN IT ALL...
GOURMET DIRT!
GARDEN • CENTER
POTTING SOIL

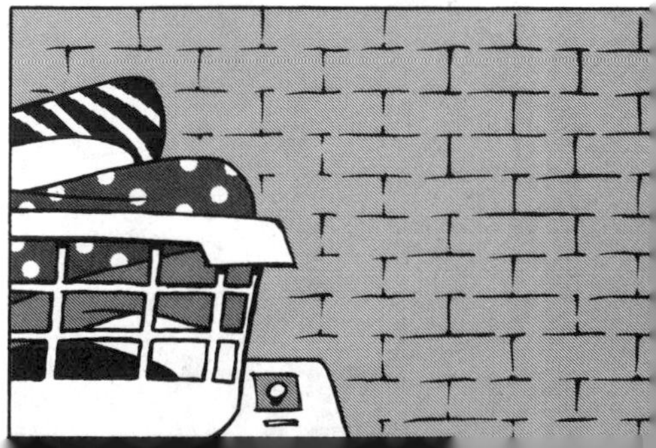

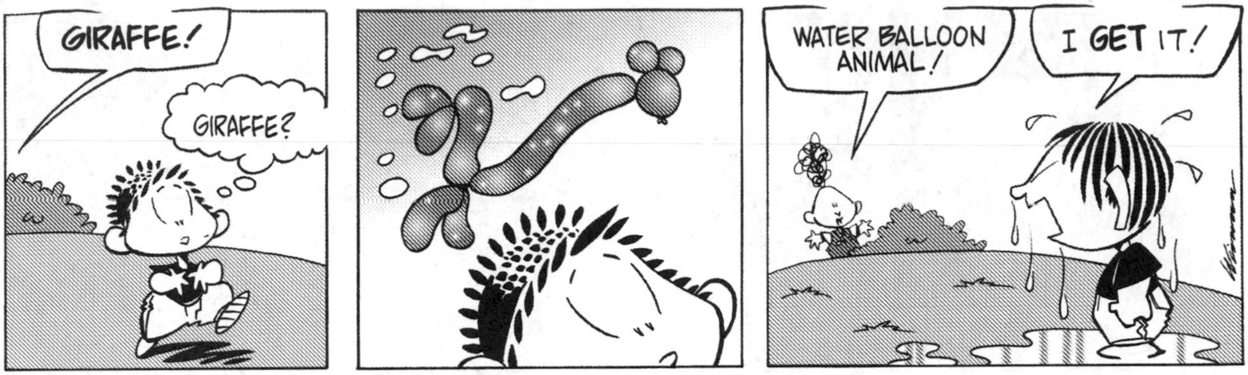
GIRAFFE!
GIRAFFE?
WATER BALLOON ANIMAL!
I GET IT!

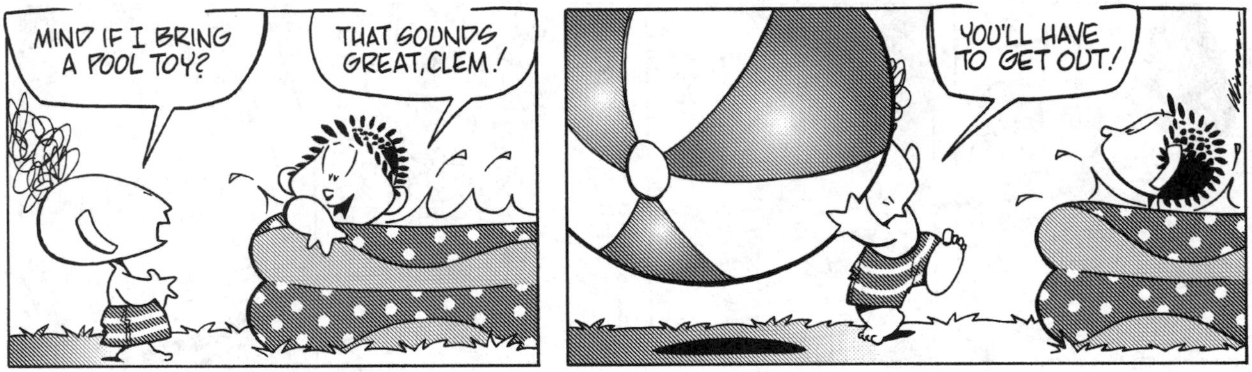
MIND IF I BRING A POOL TOY?
THAT SOUNDS GREAT, CLEM!
YOU'LL HAVE TO GET OUT!

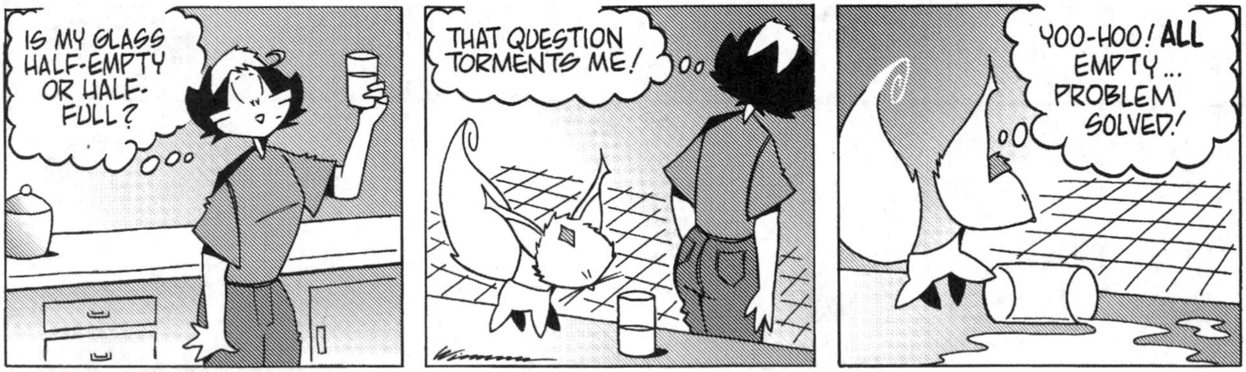
IS MY GLASS HALF-EMPTY OR HALF-FULL?
THAT QUESTION TORMENTS ME!
YOO-HOO! ALL EMPTY... PROBLEM SOLVED!

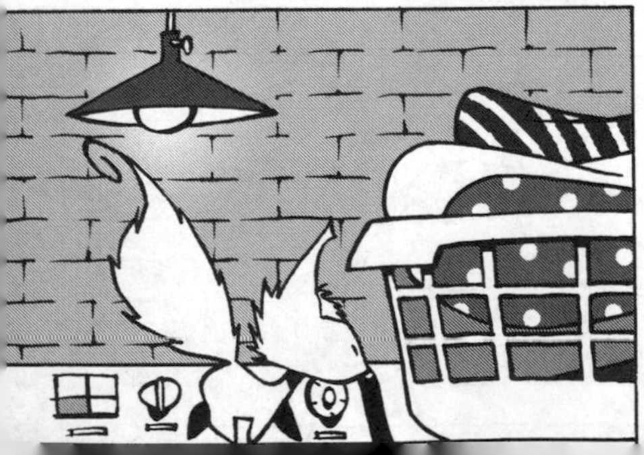

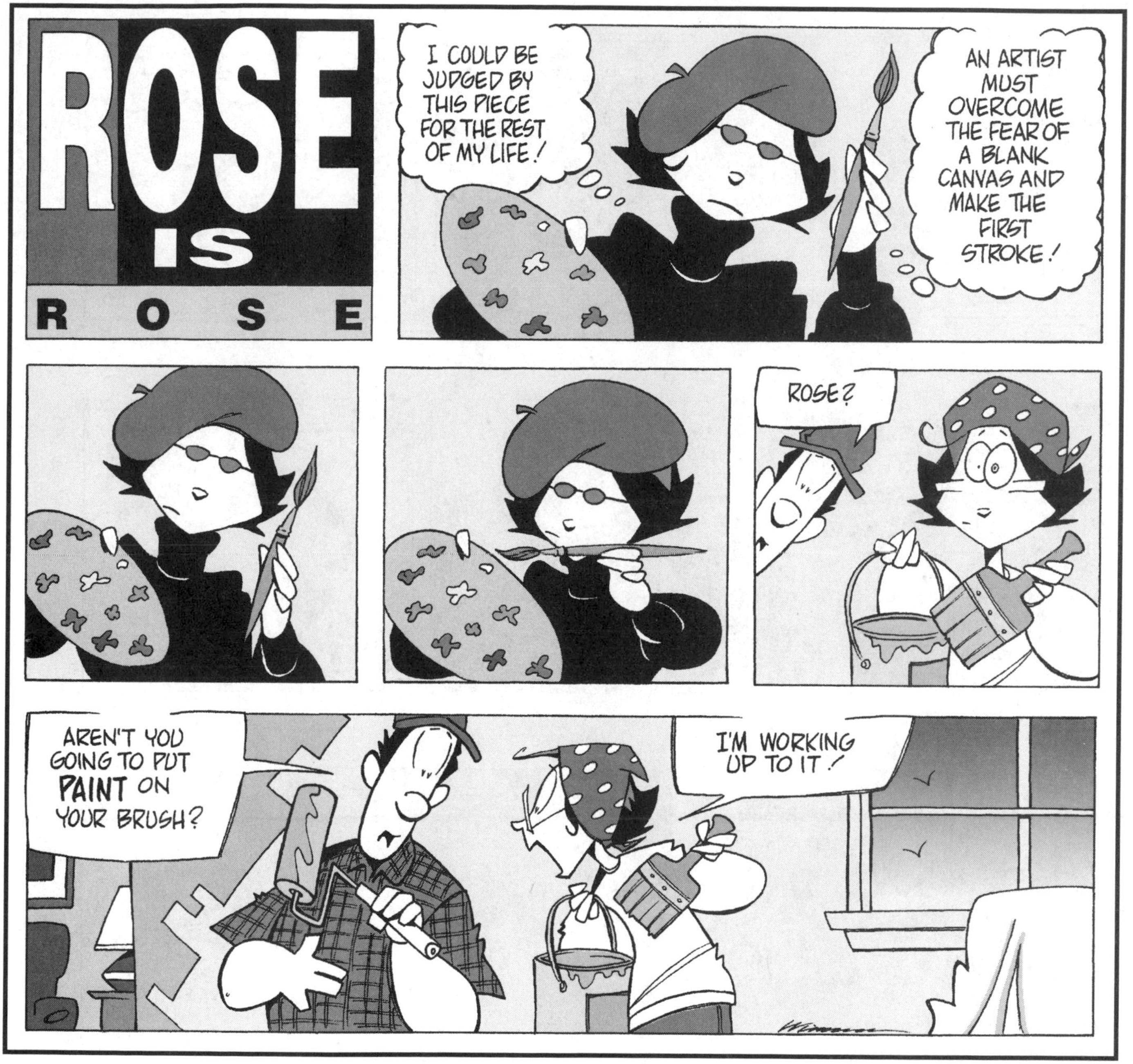
ROSE IS ROSE
I COULD BE JUDGED BY THIS PIECE FOR THE REST OF MY LIFE!
AN ARTIST MUST OVERCOME THE FEAR OF A BLANK CANVAS AND MAKE THE FIRST STROKE!
ROSE?
AREN'T YOU GOING TO PUT PAINT ON YOUR BRUSH?
I'M WORKING UP TO IT!

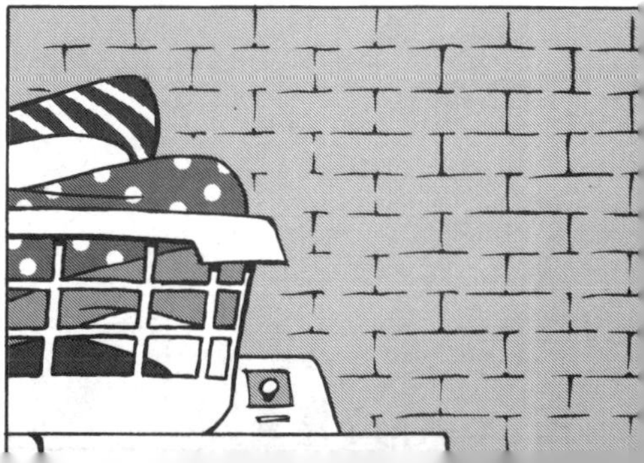

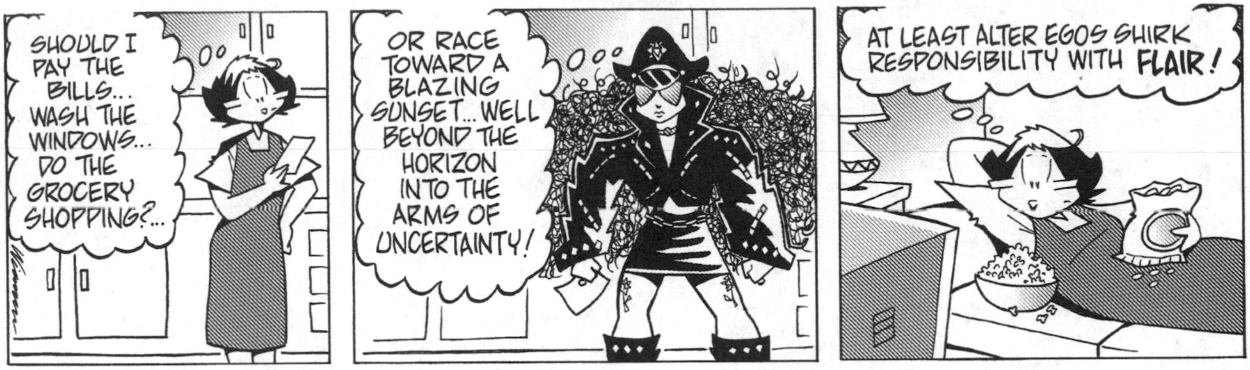
SHOULD I PAY THE BILLS... WASH THE WINDOWS... DO THE GROCERY SHOPPING?...
OR RACE TOWARD A BLAZING SUNSET... WELL BEYOND THE HORIZON INTO THE ARMS OF UNCERTAINTY!
AT LEAST ALTER EGOS SHIRK RESPONSIBILITY WITH FLAIR!

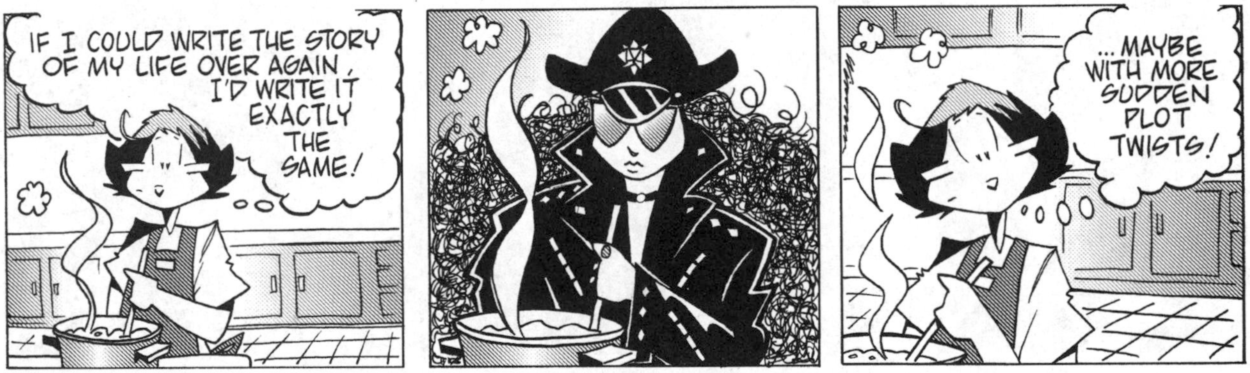
IF I COULD WRITE THE STORY OF MY LIFE OVER AGAIN, I'D WRITE IT EXACTLY THE SAME!
... MAYBE WITH MORE SUDDEN PLOT TWISTS!

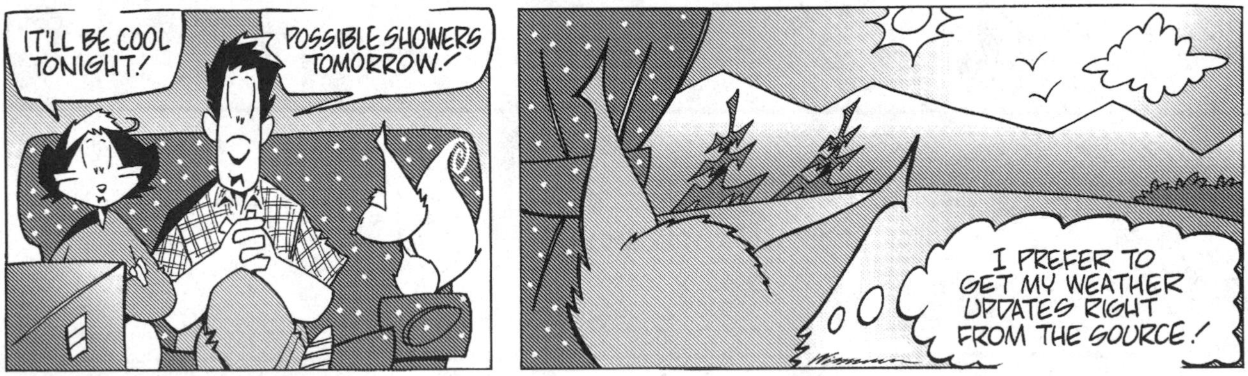
IT'LL BE COOL TONIGHT!
POSSIBLE SHOWERS TOMORROW!
I PREFER TO GET MY WEATHER UPDATES RIGHT FROM THE SOURCE!

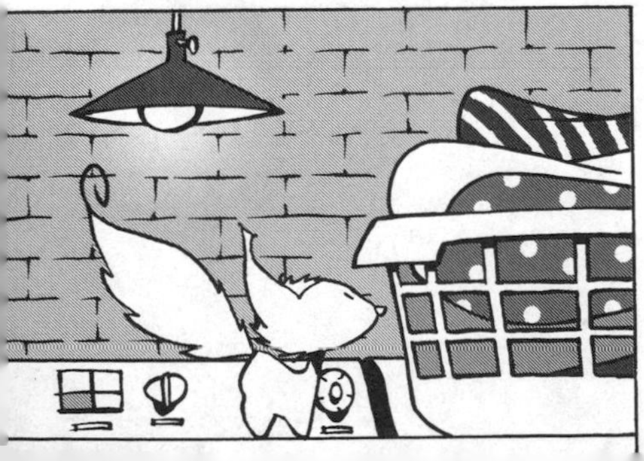

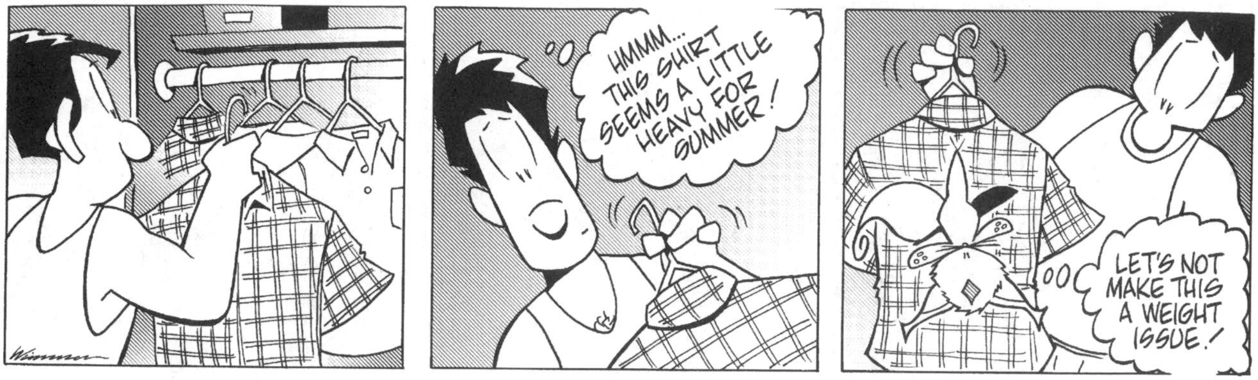
HMMM... THIS SHIRT SEEMS A LITTLE HEAVY FOR SUMMER!
LET'S NOT MAKE THIS A WEIGHT ISSUE!

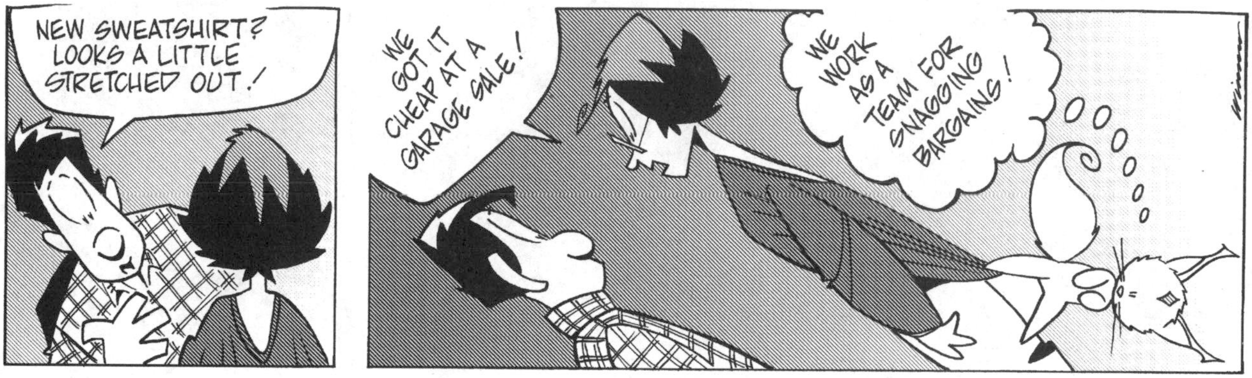
NEW SWEATSHIRT? LOOKS A LITTLE STRETCHED OUT!
WE GOT IT CHEAP AT A GARAGE SALE!
WE WORK AS A TEAM FOR SNAGGING BARGAINS!

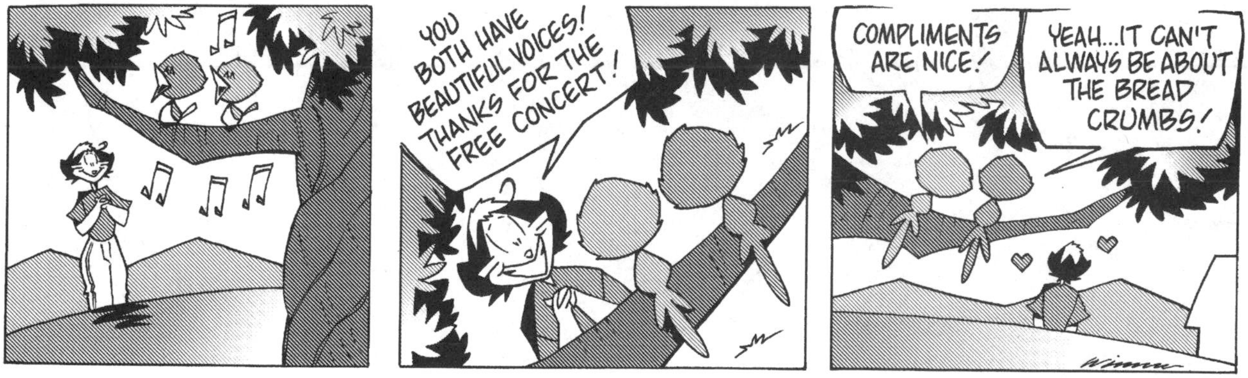
YOU BOTH HAVE BEAUTIFUL VOICES! THANKS FOR THE FREE CONCERT!
COMPLIMENTS ARE NICE!
YEAH...IT CAN'T ALWAYS BE ABOUT THE BREAD CRUMBS!

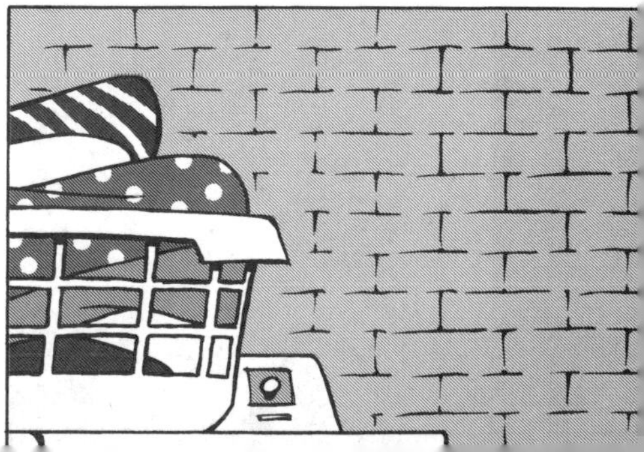

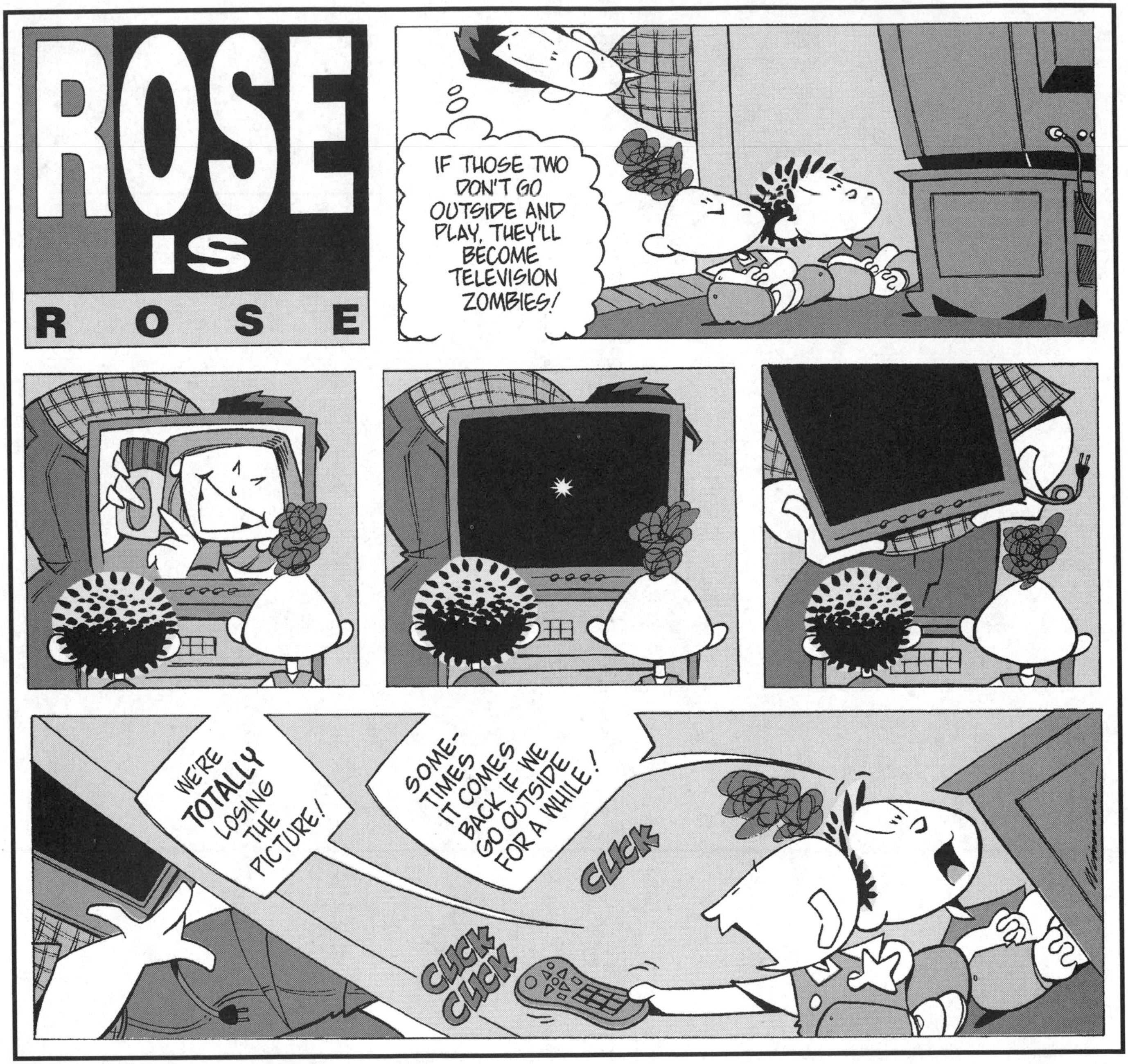

ROSE IS ROSE
IF THOSE TWO DON'T GO OUTSIDE AND PLAY, THEY'LL BECOME TELEVISION ZOMBIES!
WE'RE TOTALLY LOSING THE PICTURE!
SOME-TIMES IT COMES BACK IF WE GO OUTSIDE FOR A WHILE!
CLICK
CLICK CLICK

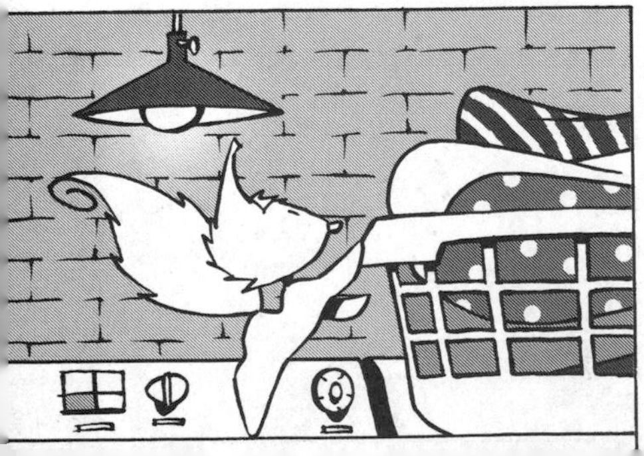

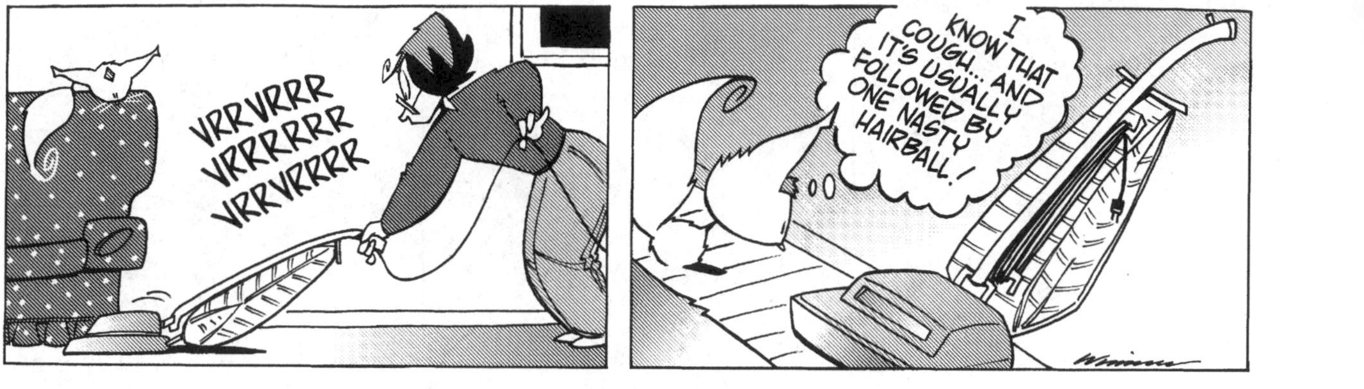
VRRVRRR
VRRRRRR
VRRVRRR
I KNOW THAT COUGH... AND IT'S USUALLY FOLLOWED BY ONE NASTY HAIRBALL!

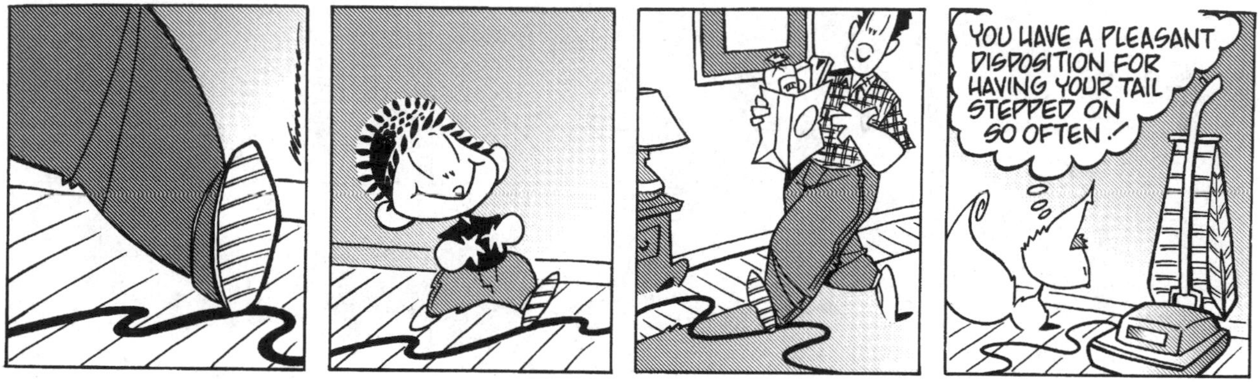
YOU HAVE A PLEASANT DISPOSITION FOR HAVING YOUR TAIL STEPPED ON SO OFTEN!

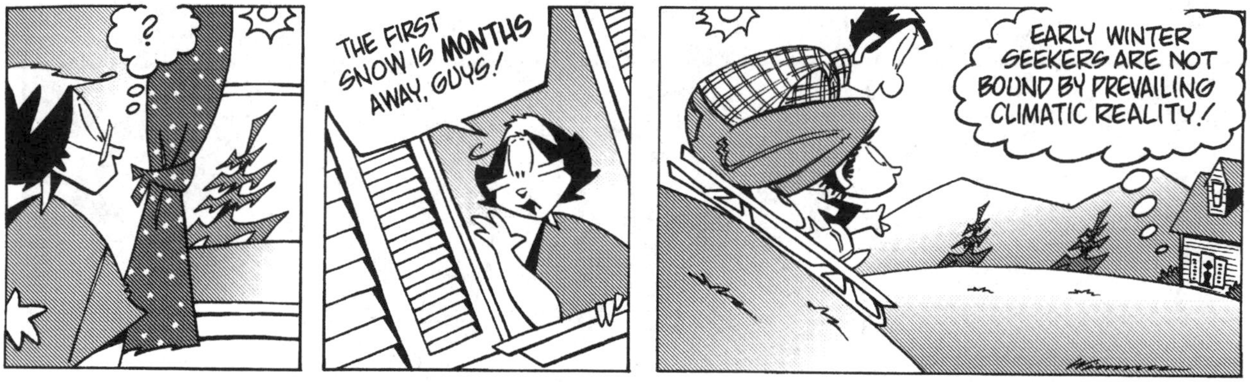
?
THE FIRST SNOW IS MONTHS AWAY, GUYS!
EARLY WINTER SEEKERS ARE NOT BOUND BY PREVAILING CLIMATIC REALITY!

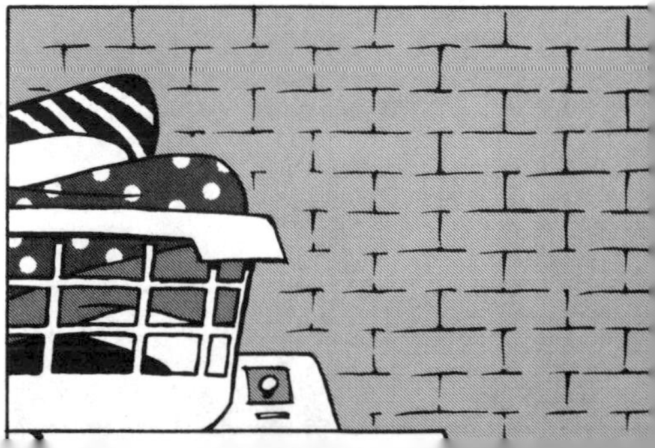

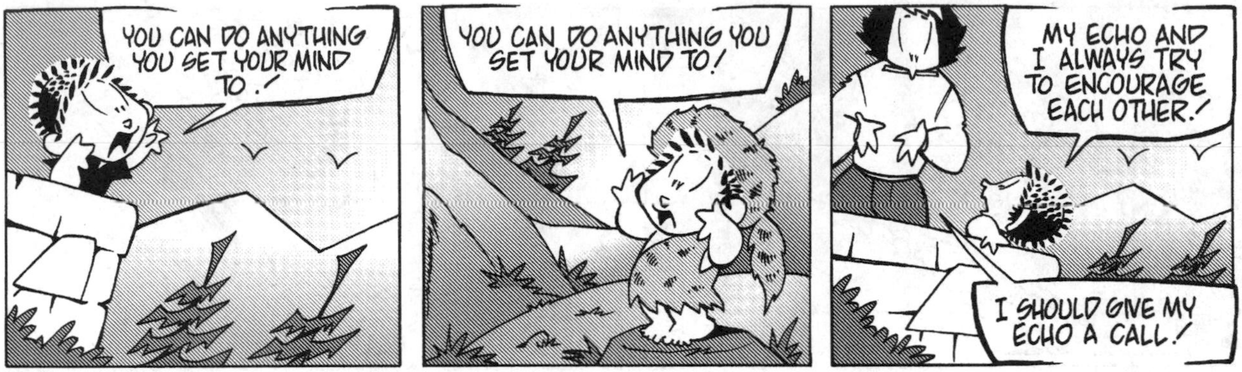
YOU CAN DO ANYTHING YOU SET YOUR MIND TO.!
YOU CAN DO ANYTHING YOU SET YOUR MIND TO!
MY ECHO AND I ALWAYS TRY TO ENCOURAGE EACH OTHER.!
I SHOULD GIVE MY ECHO A CALL.!

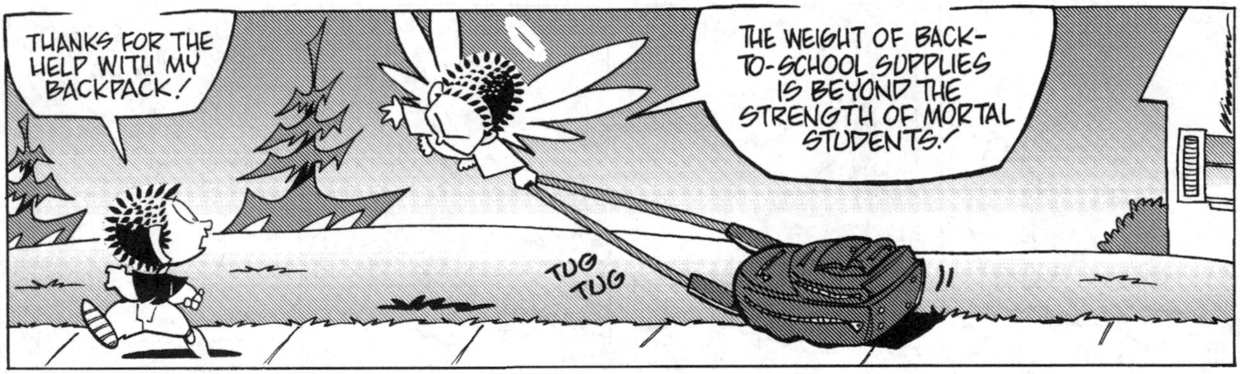
THANKS FOR THE HELP WITH MY BACKPACK.!
THE WEIGHT OF BACK-TO-SCHOOL SUPPLIES IS BEYOND THE STRENGTH OF MORTAL STUDENTS.!
TUG TUG

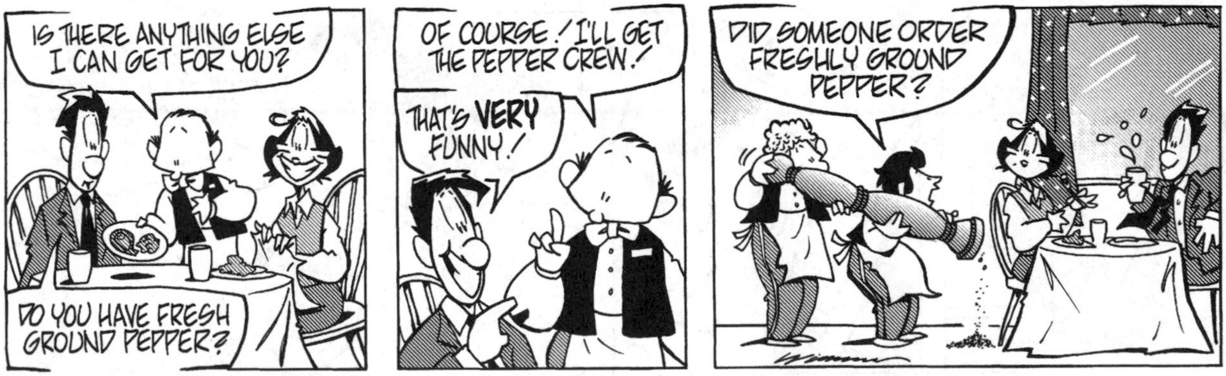
IS THERE ANYTHING ELSE I CAN GET FOR YOU?
DO YOU HAVE FRESH GROUND PEPPER?
OF COURSE.! I'LL GET THE PEPPER CREW.!
THAT'S **VERY** FUNNY.!
DID SOMEONE ORDER FRESHLY GROUND PEPPER?

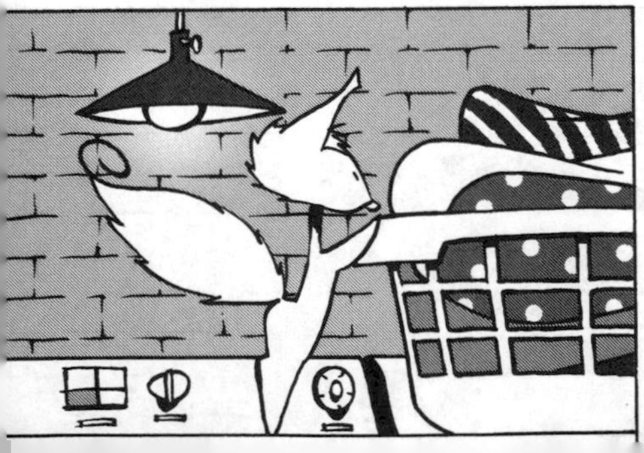

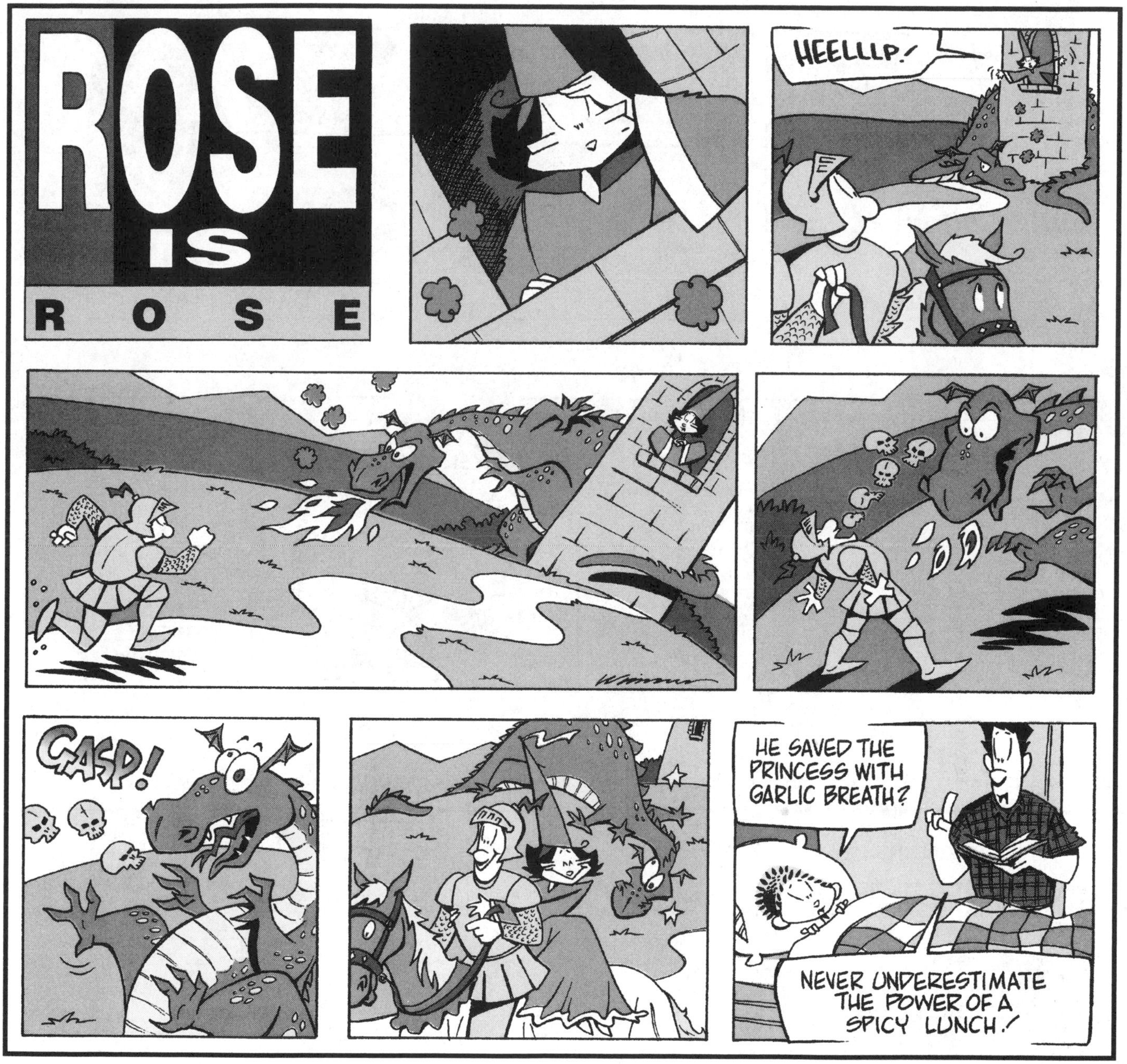
ROSE IS ROSE
HEELLLP!
GASP!
HE SAVED THE PRINCESS WITH GARLIC BREATH?
NEVER UNDERESTIMATE THE POWER OF A SPICY LUNCH!

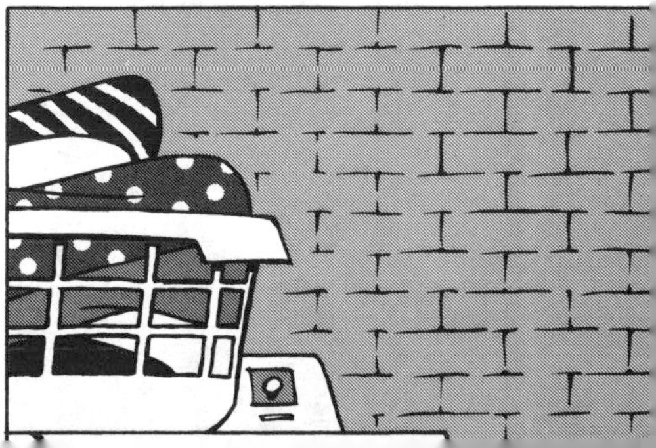

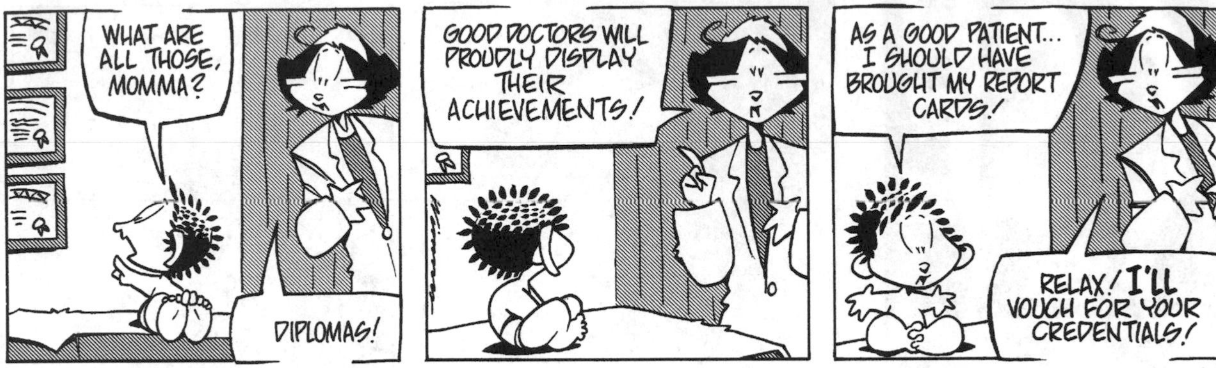
WHAT ARE ALL THOSE, MOMMA?
DIPLOMAS!
GOOD DOCTORS WILL PROUDLY DISPLAY THEIR ACHIEVEMENTS!
AS A GOOD PATIENT... I SHOULD HAVE BROUGHT MY REPORT CARDS!
RELAX! I'LL VOUCH FOR YOUR CREDENTIALS!

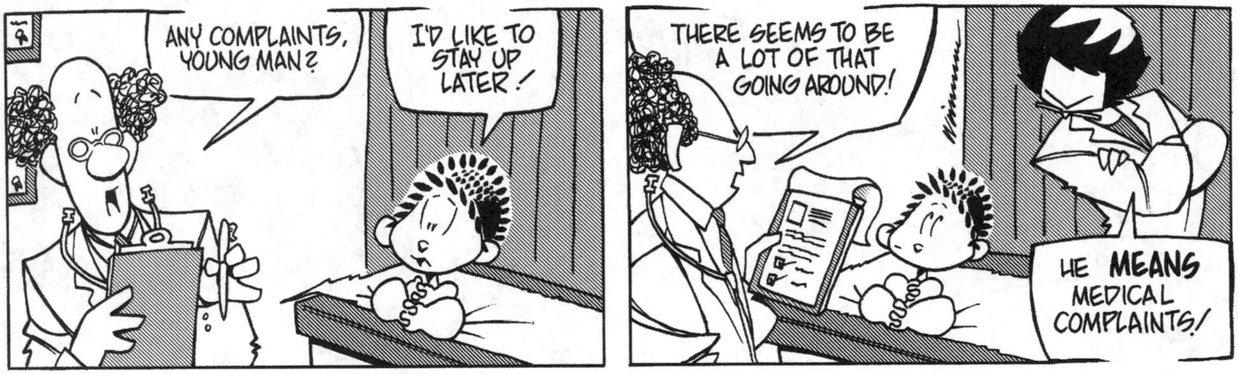
ANY COMPLAINTS, YOUNG MAN?
I'D LIKE TO STAY UP LATER!
THERE SEEMS TO BE A LOT OF THAT GOING AROUND!
HE MEANS MEDICAL COMPLAINTS!

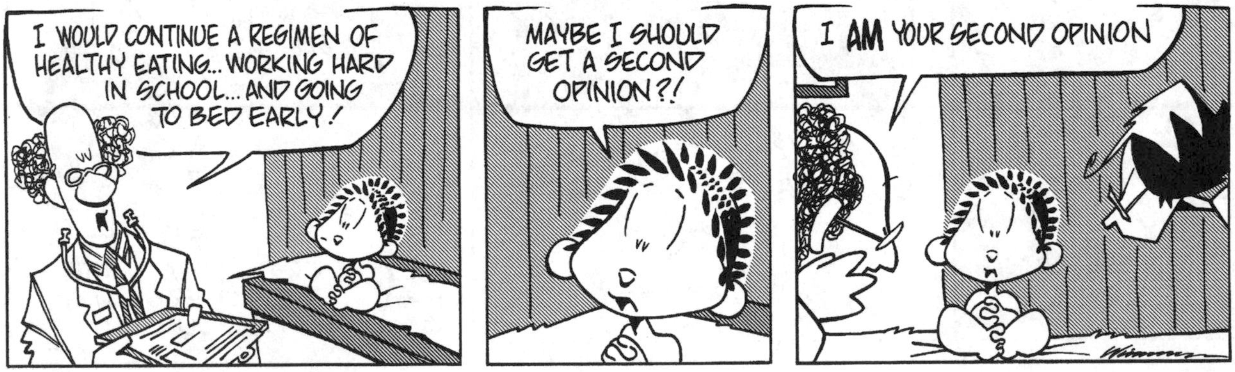
I WOULD CONTINUE A REGIMEN OF HEALTHY EATING... WORKING HARD IN SCHOOL... AND GOING TO BED EARLY!
MAYBE I SHOULD GET A SECOND OPINION?!
I AM YOUR SECOND OPINION

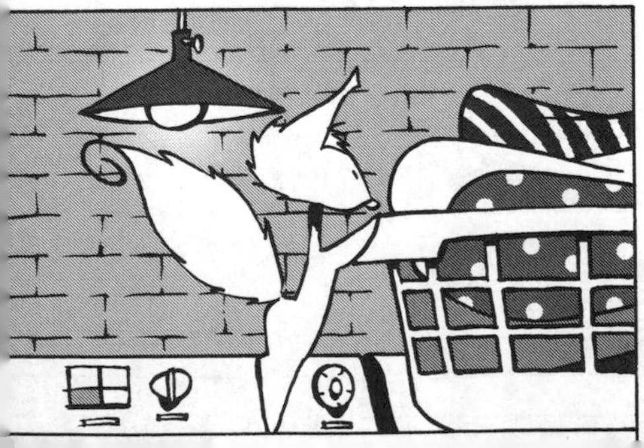

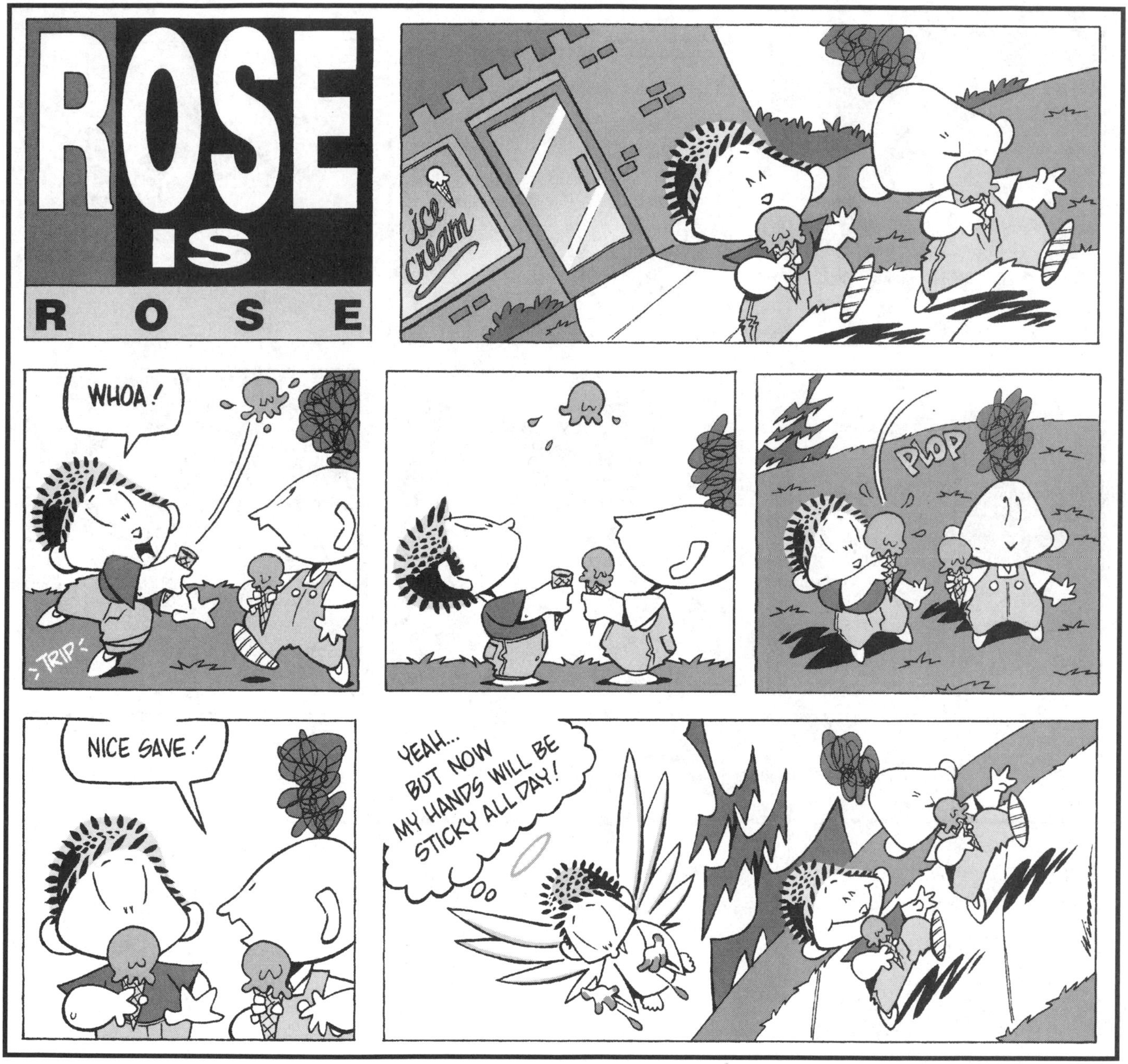
ROSE IS ROSE
ice cream
WHOA!
TRIP
PLOP
NICE SAVE!
YEAH... BUT NOW MY HANDS WILL BE STICKY ALL DAY!

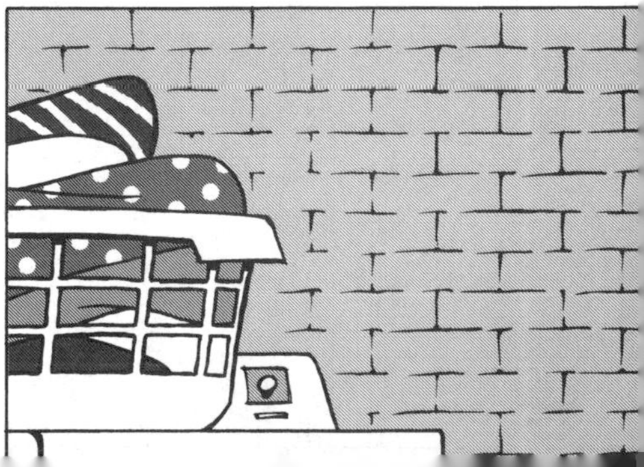

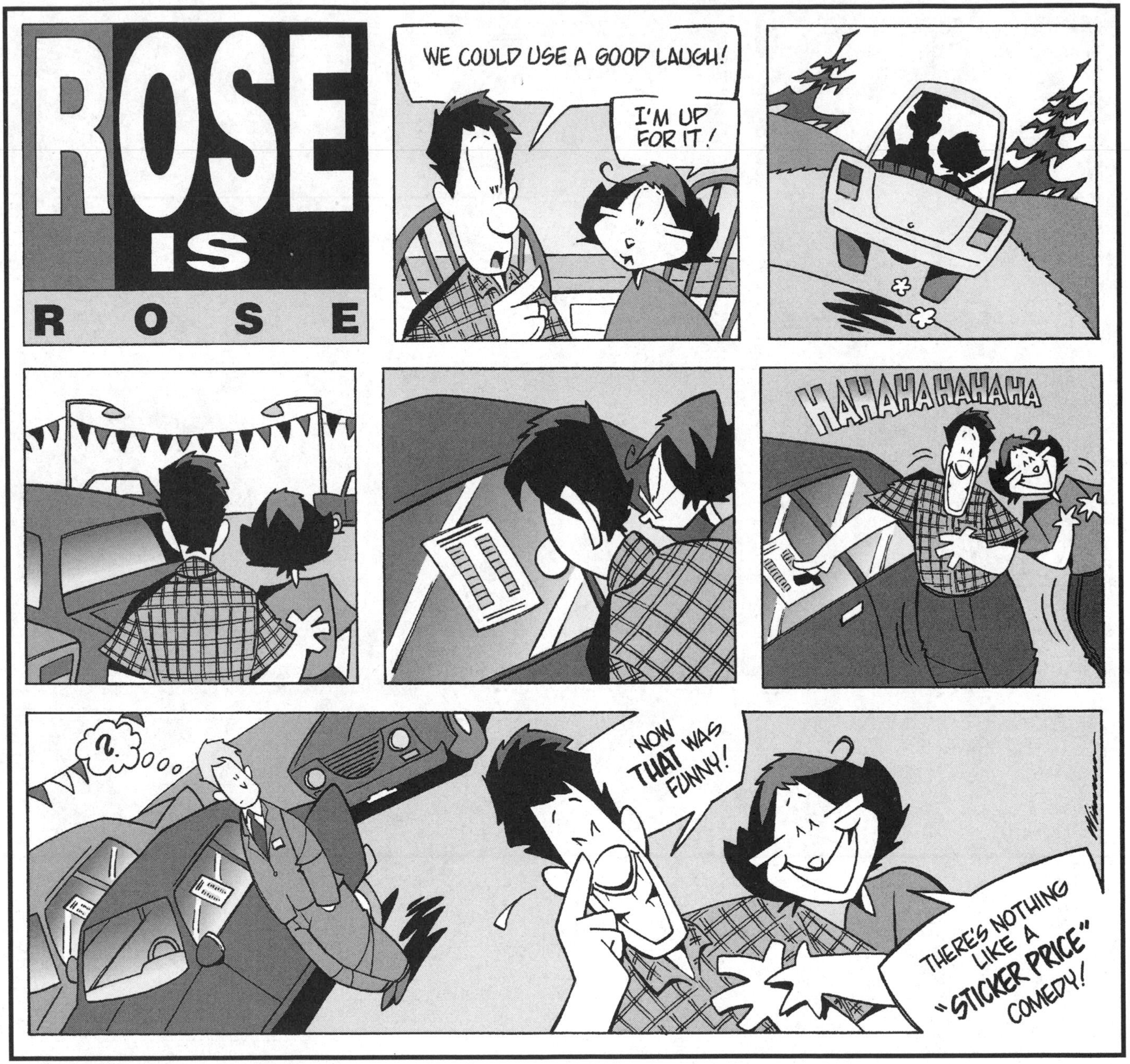
ROSE IS ROSE
WE COULD USE A GOOD LAUGH!
I'M UP FOR IT!
HAHAHAHAHAHA
?
NOW THAT WAS FUNNY!
THERE'S NOTHING LIKE A "STICKER PRICE" COMEDY!

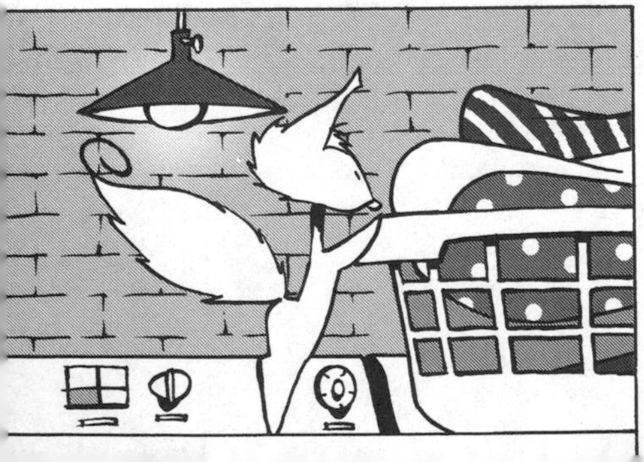

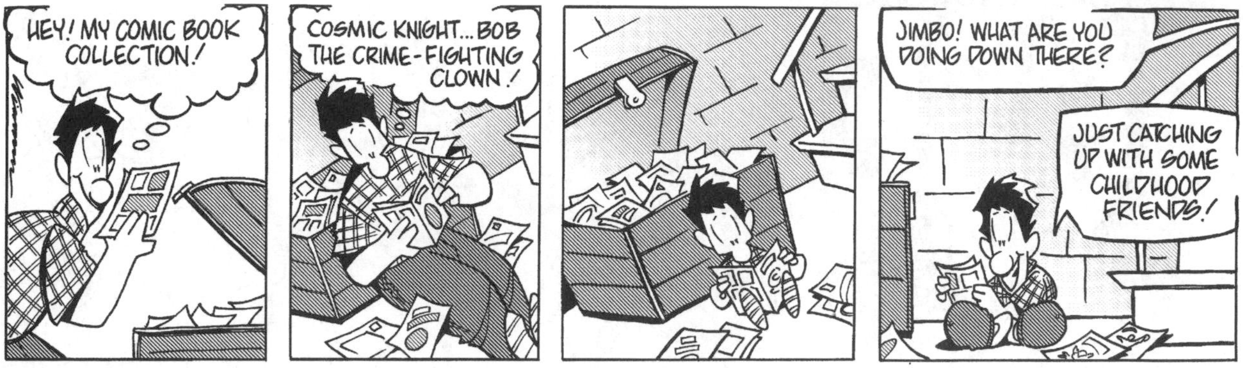
HEY! MY COMIC BOOK COLLECTION!
COSMIC KNIGHT... BOB THE CRIME-FIGHTING CLOWN!
JIMBO! WHAT ARE YOU DOING DOWN THERE?
JUST CATCHING UP WITH SOME CHILDHOOD FRIENDS!

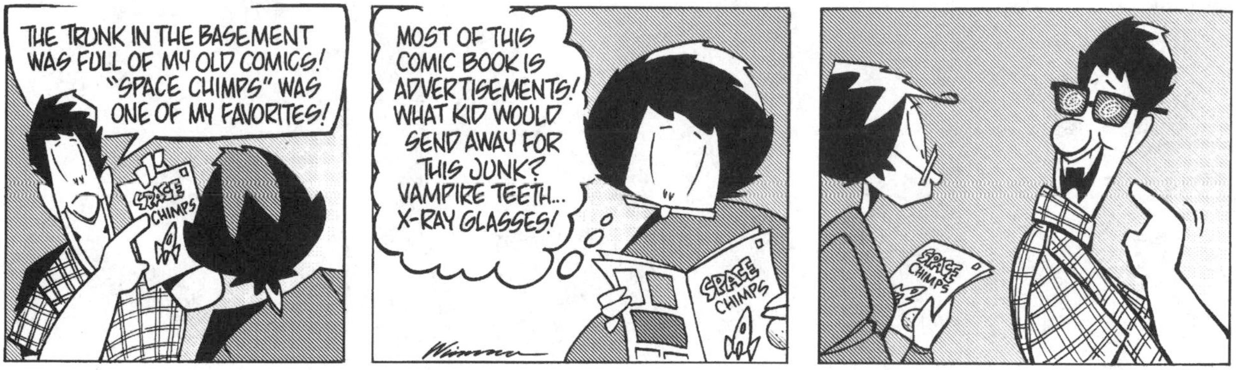
THE TRUNK IN THE BASEMENT WAS FULL OF MY OLD COMICS! "SPACE CHIMPS" WAS ONE OF MY FAVORITES!
SPACE CHIMPS
MOST OF THIS COMIC BOOK IS ADVERTISEMENTS! WHAT KID WOULD SEND AWAY FOR THIS JUNK? VAMPIRE TEETH... X-RAY GLASSES!
SPACE CHIMPS
SPACE CHIMPS

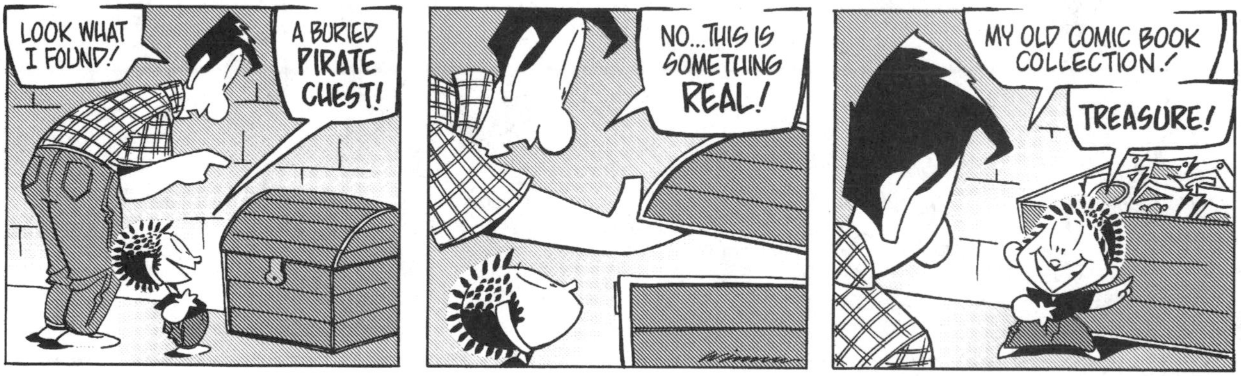
LOOK WHAT I FOUND!
A BURIED PIRATE CHEST!
NO... THIS IS SOMETHING REAL!
MY OLD COMIC BOOK COLLECTION!
TREASURE!

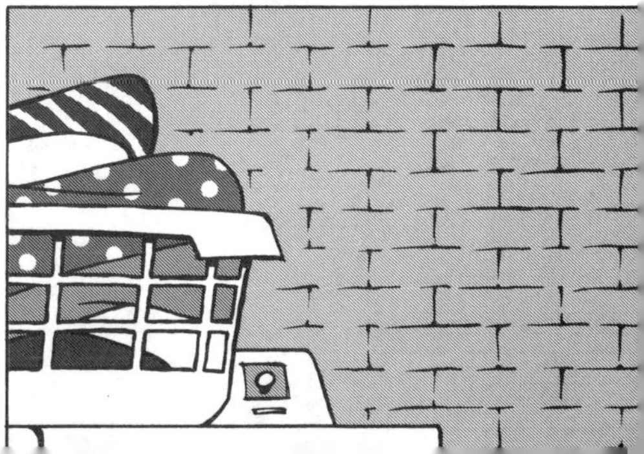

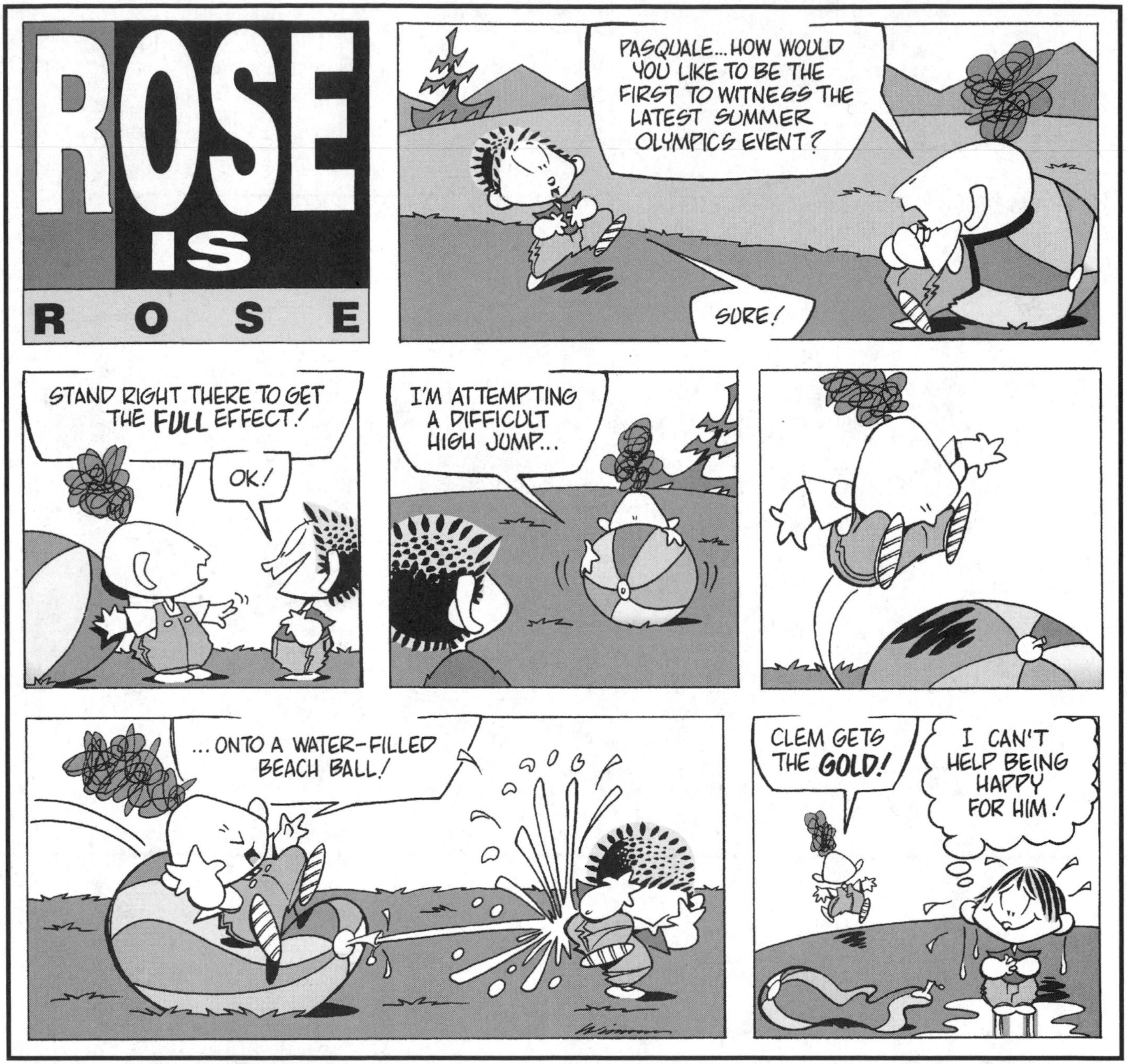
ROSE IS ROSE
PASQUALE...HOW WOULD YOU LIKE TO BE THE FIRST TO WITNESS THE LATEST SUMMER OLYMPICS EVENT?
SURE!
STAND RIGHT THERE TO GET THE FULL EFFECT!
OK!
I'M ATTEMPTING A DIFFICULT HIGH JUMP...
...ONTO A WATER-FILLED BEACH BALL!
CLEM GETS THE GOLD!
I CAN'T HELP BEING HAPPY FOR HIM!

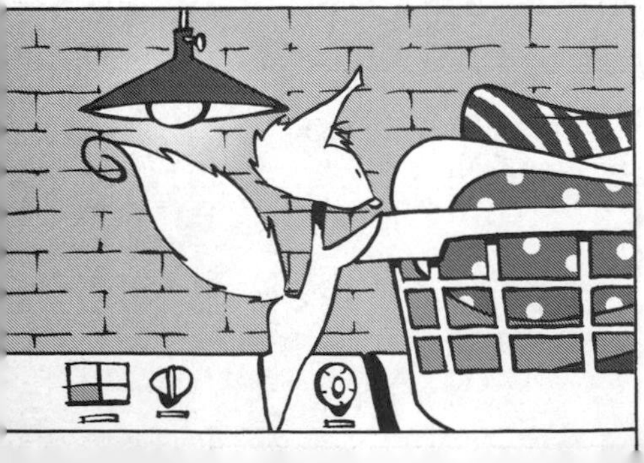

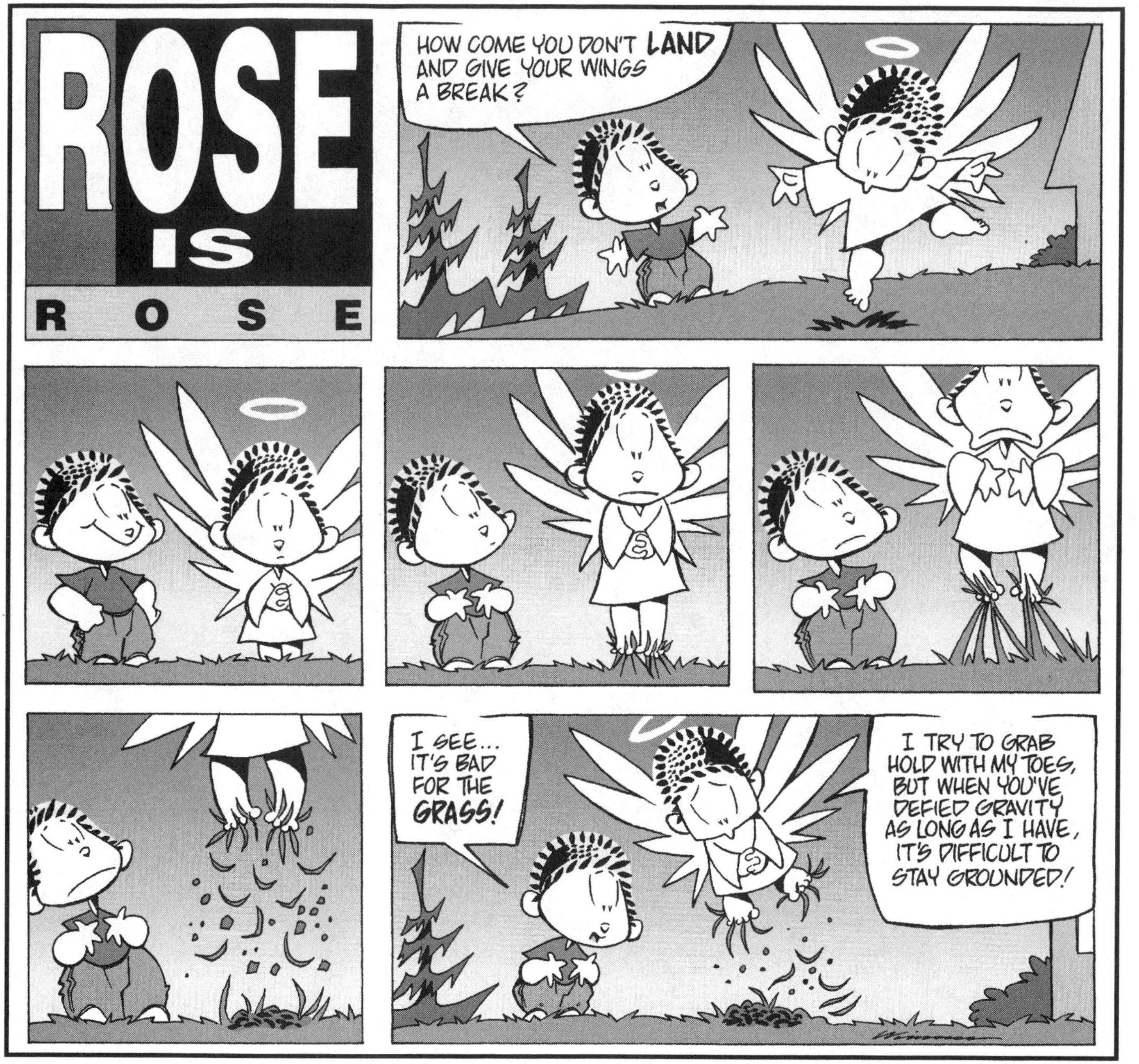
ROSE IS ROSE
HOW COME YOU DON'T **LAND** AND GIVE YOUR WINGS A BREAK?
I SEE... IT'S BAD FOR THE **GRASS!**
I TRY TO GRAB HOLD WITH MY TOES, BUT WHEN YOU'VE DEFIED GRAVITY AS LONG AS I HAVE, IT'S DIFFICULT TO STAY GROUNDED!

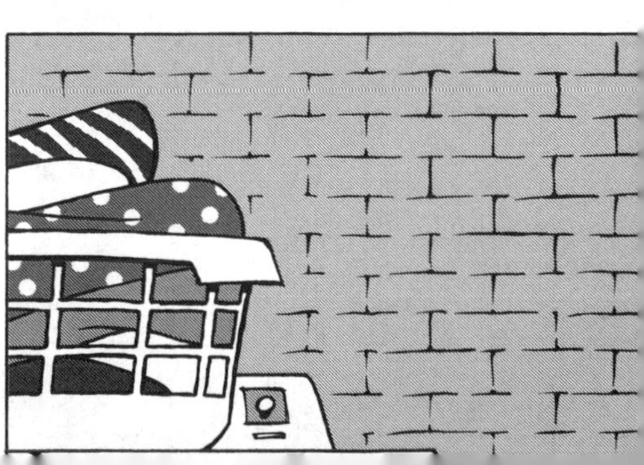

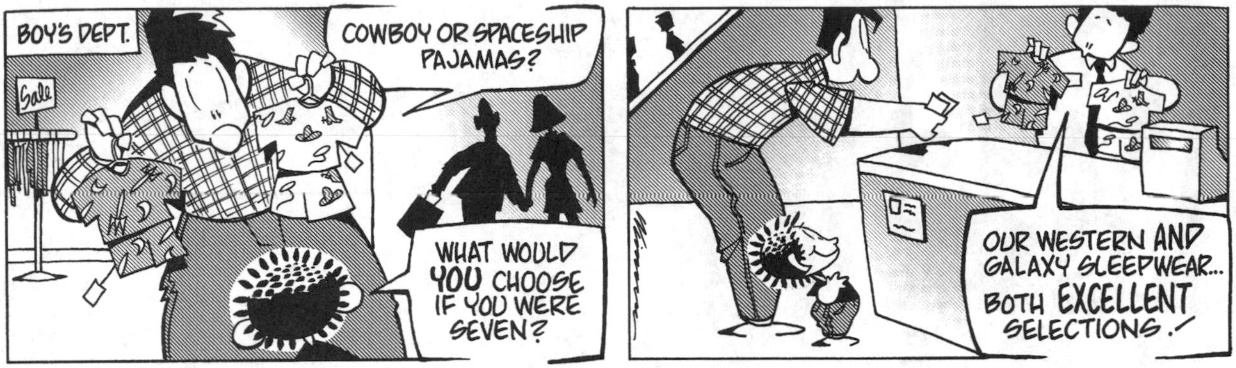
BOY'S DEPT.
Sale
COWBOY OR SPACESHIP PAJAMAS?
WHAT WOULD YOU CHOOSE IF YOU WERE SEVEN?
OUR WESTERN AND GALAXY SLEEPWEAR... BOTH EXCELLENT SELECTIONS!

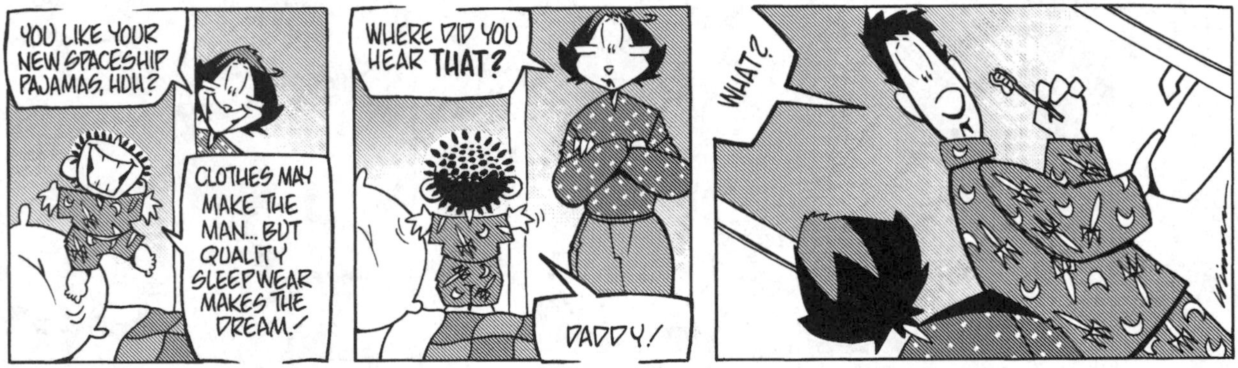
YOU LIKE YOUR NEW SPACESHIP PAJAMAS, HUH?
CLOTHES MAY MAKE THE MAN... BUT QUALITY SLEEPWEAR MAKES THE DREAM!
WHERE DID YOU HEAR THAT?
DADDY!
WHAT?

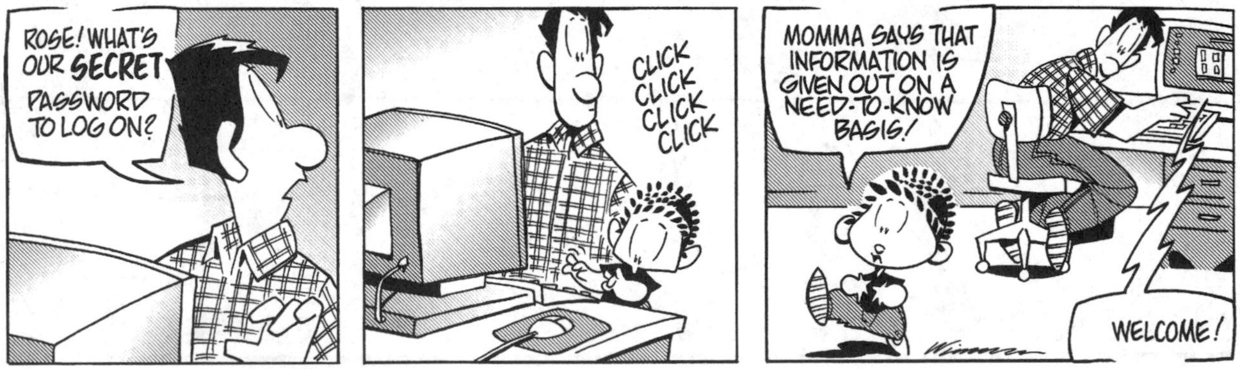
ROSE! WHAT'S OUR SECRET PASSWORD TO LOG ON?
CLICK CLICK CLICK CLICK
MOMMA SAYS THAT INFORMATION IS GIVEN OUT ON A NEED-TO-KNOW BASIS!
WELCOME!

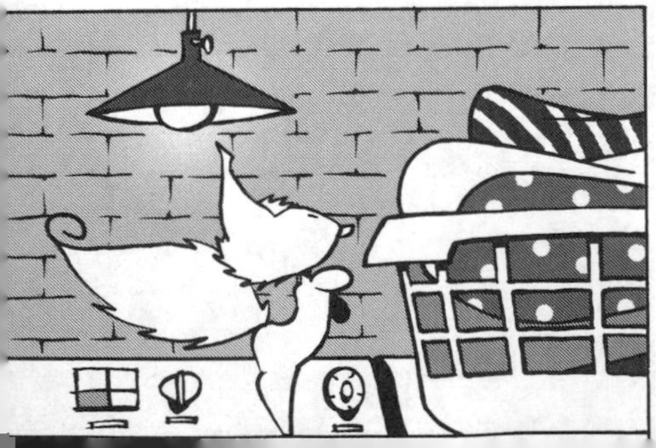

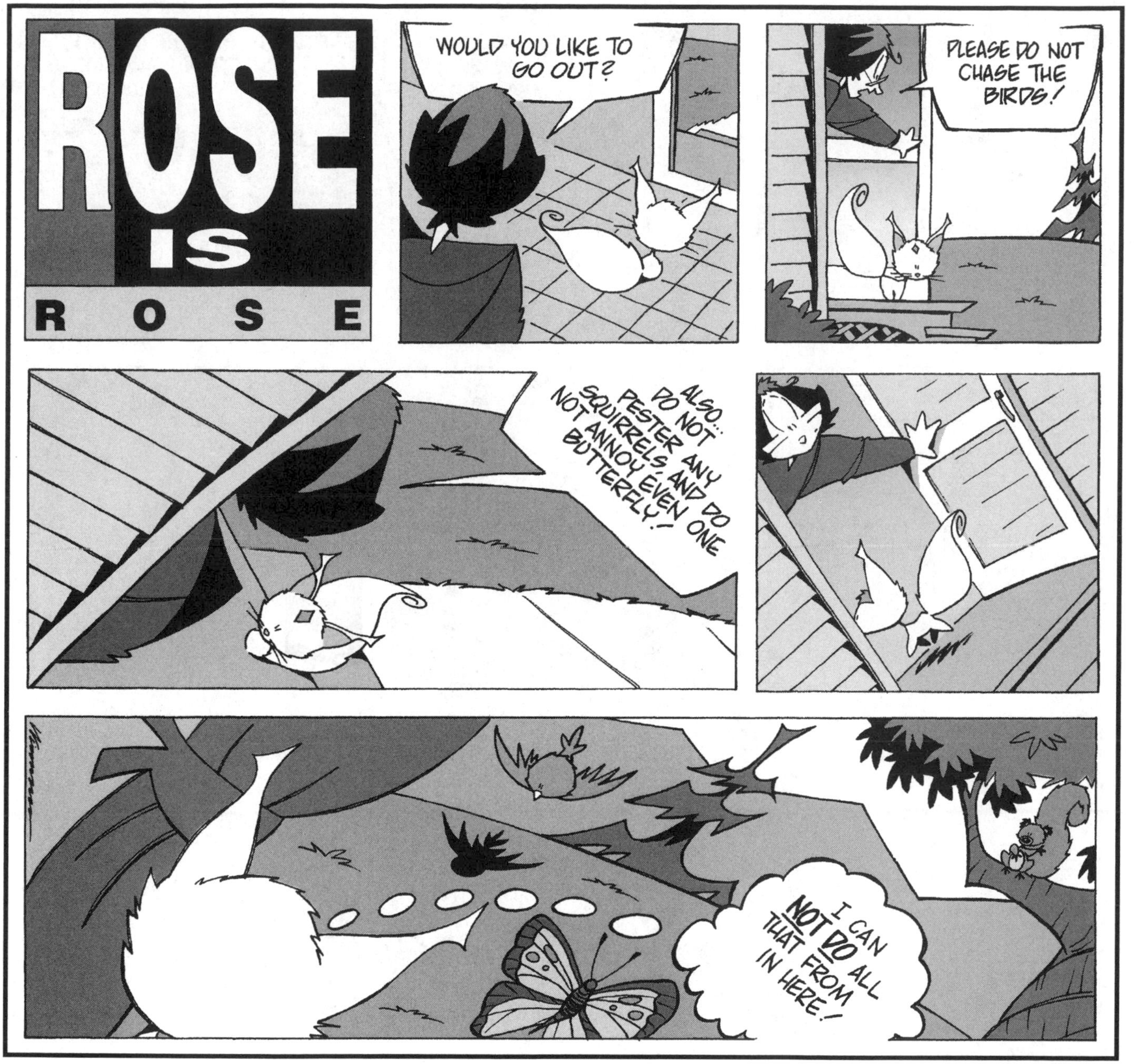
ROSE IS ROSE
WOULD YOU LIKE TO GO OUT?
PLEASE DO NOT CHASE THE BIRDS!
ALSO... DO NOT PESTER ANY SQUIRRELS, AND DO NOT ANNOY EVEN ONE BUTTERFLY!
I CAN NOT DO ALL THAT FROM IN HERE!

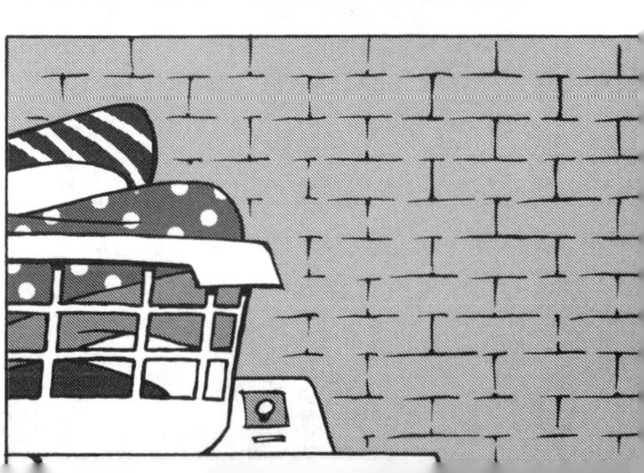

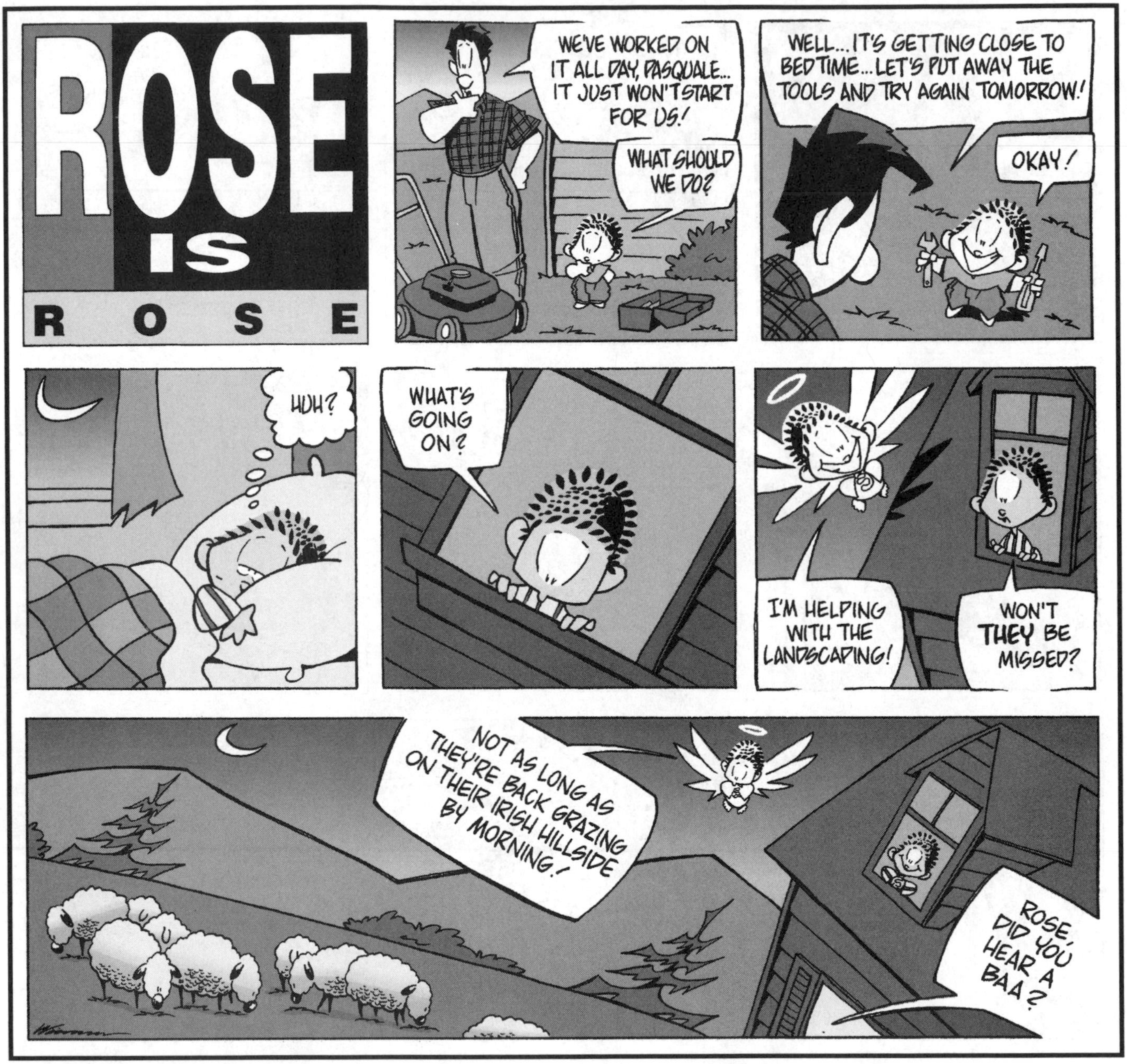
ROSE IS ROSE
WE'VE WORKED ON IT ALL DAY, PASQUALE... IT JUST WON'T START FOR US!
WHAT SHOULD WE DO?
WELL... IT'S GETTING CLOSE TO BEDTIME... LET'S PUT AWAY THE TOOLS AND TRY AGAIN TOMORROW!
OKAY!
HUH?
WHAT'S GOING ON?
I'M HELPING WITH THE LANDSCAPING!
WON'T THEY BE MISSED?
NOT AS LONG AS THEY'RE BACK GRAZING ON THEIR IRISH HILLSIDE BY MORNING!
ROSE, DID YOU HEAR A BAA?

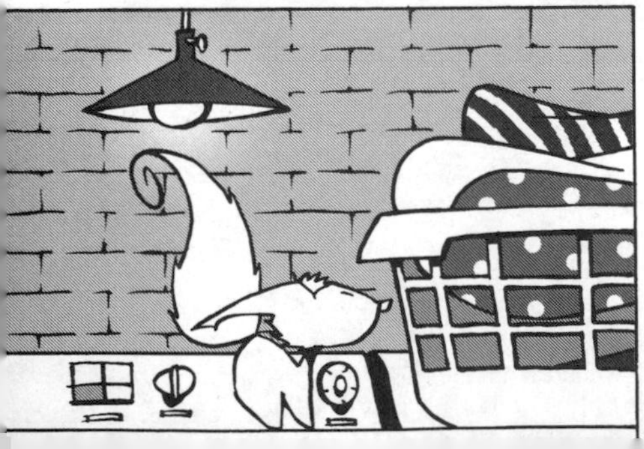

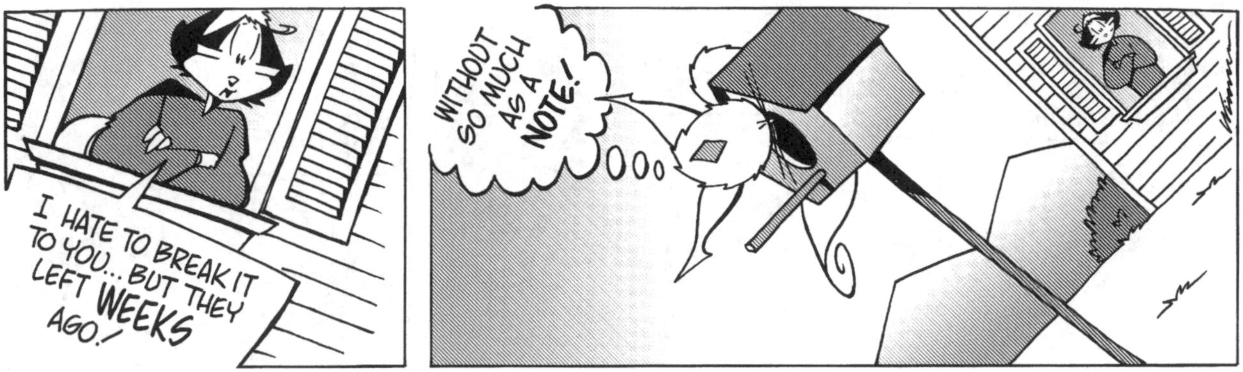
I HATE TO BREAK IT TO YOU... BUT THEY LEFT WEEKS AGO.!
WITHOUT SO MUCH AS A NOTE!

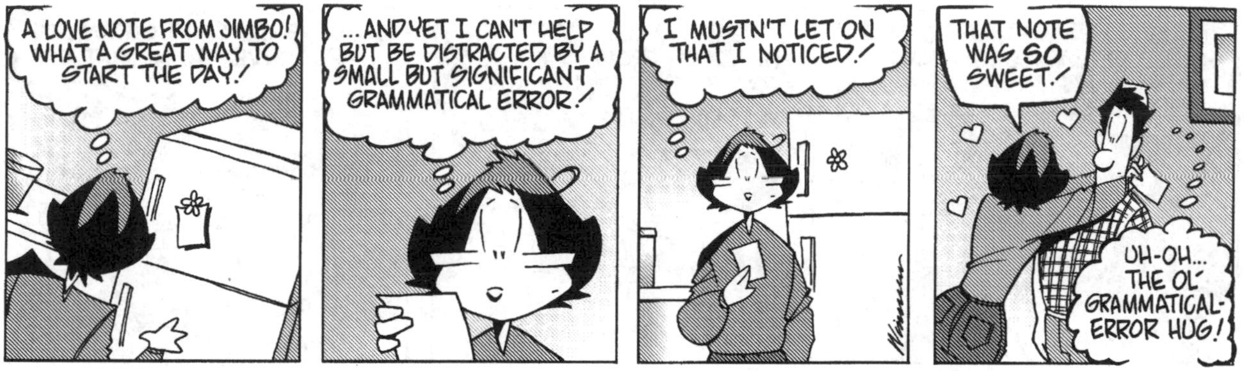
A LOVE NOTE FROM JIMBO! WHAT A GREAT WAY TO START THE DAY.!
...AND YET I CAN'T HELP BUT BE DISTRACTED BY A SMALL BUT SIGNIFICANT GRAMMATICAL ERROR.!
I MUSTN'T LET ON THAT I NOTICED.!
THAT NOTE WAS SO SWEET.!
UH-OH... THE OL' GRAMMATICAL-ERROR HUG!

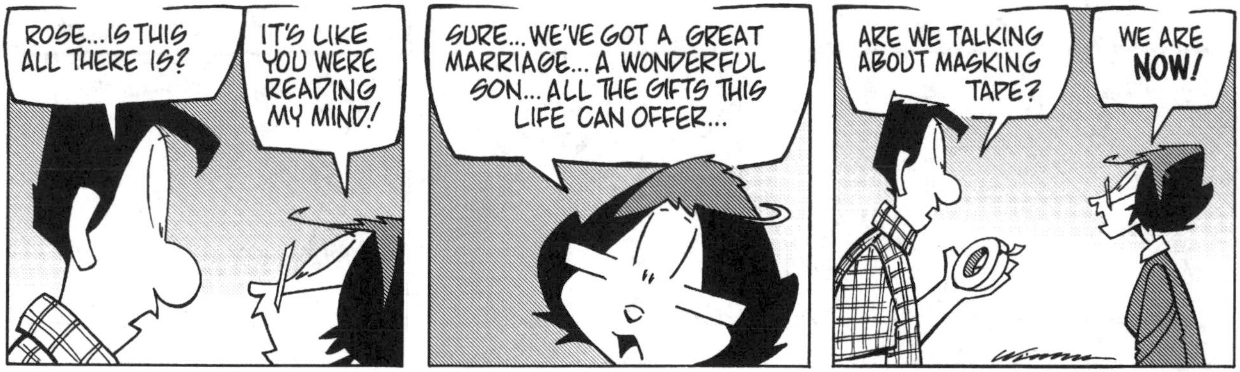
ROSE...IS THIS ALL THERE IS?
IT'S LIKE YOU WERE READING MY MIND!
SURE... WE'VE GOT A GREAT MARRIAGE... A WONDERFUL SON... ALL THE GIFTS THIS LIFE CAN OFFER...
ARE WE TALKING ABOUT MASKING TAPE?
WE ARE NOW!

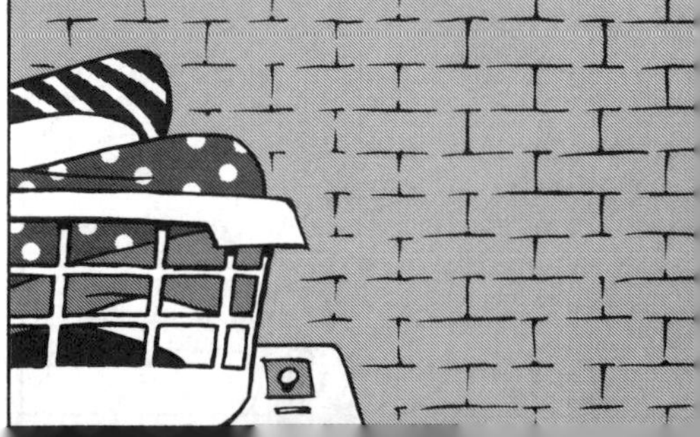

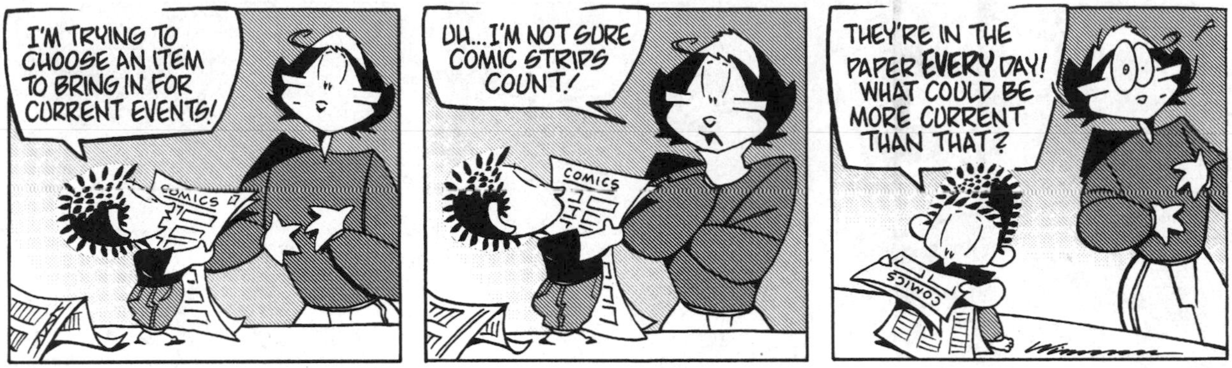
I'M TRYING TO CHOOSE AN ITEM TO BRING IN FOR CURRENT EVENTS!
COMICS
UH... I'M NOT SURE COMIC STRIPS COUNT!
COMICS
THEY'RE IN THE PAPER EVERY DAY! WHAT COULD BE MORE CURRENT THAN THAT?
COMICS

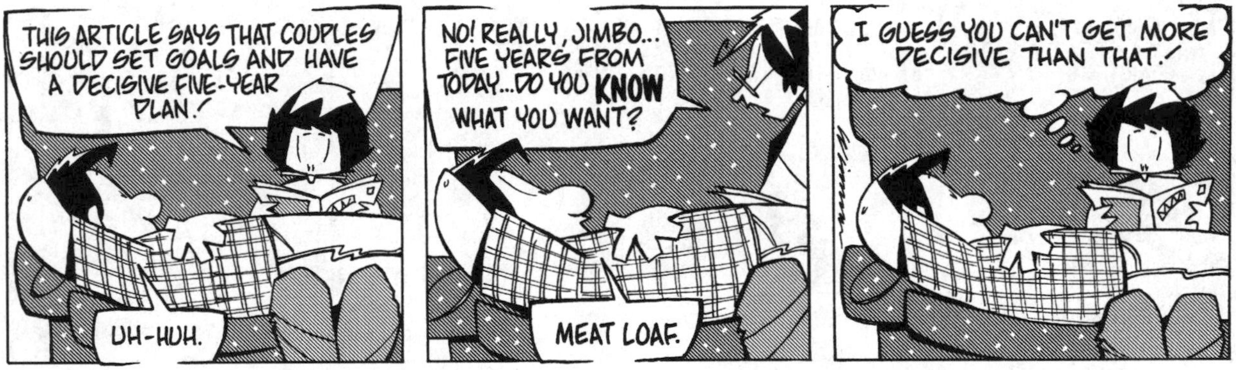
THIS ARTICLE SAYS THAT COUPLES SHOULD SET GOALS AND HAVE A DECISIVE FIVE-YEAR PLAN!
UH-HUH.
NO! REALLY, JIMBO... FIVE YEARS FROM TODAY...DO YOU KNOW WHAT YOU WANT?
MEAT LOAF.
I GUESS YOU CAN'T GET MORE DECISIVE THAN THAT!

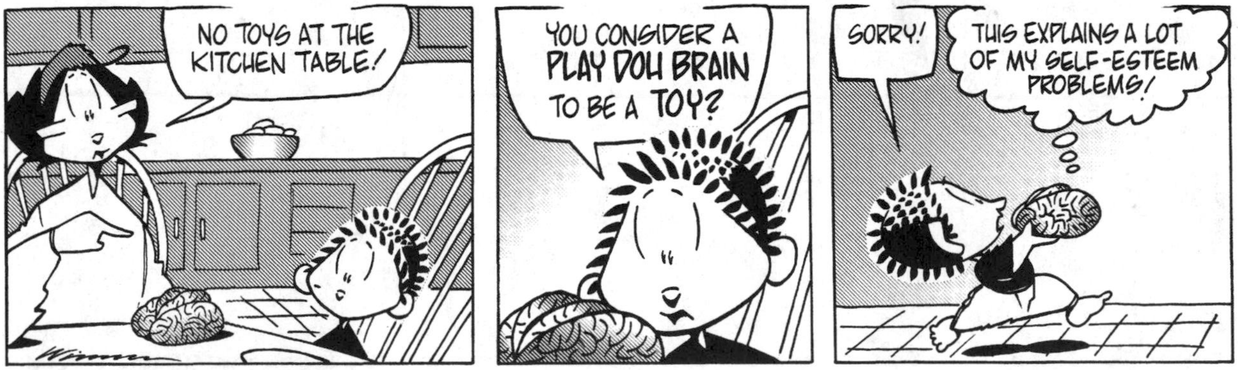
NO TOYS AT THE KITCHEN TABLE!
YOU CONSIDER A PLAY DOH BRAIN TO BE A TOY?
SORRY!
THIS EXPLAINS A LOT OF MY SELF-ESTEEM PROBLEMS!

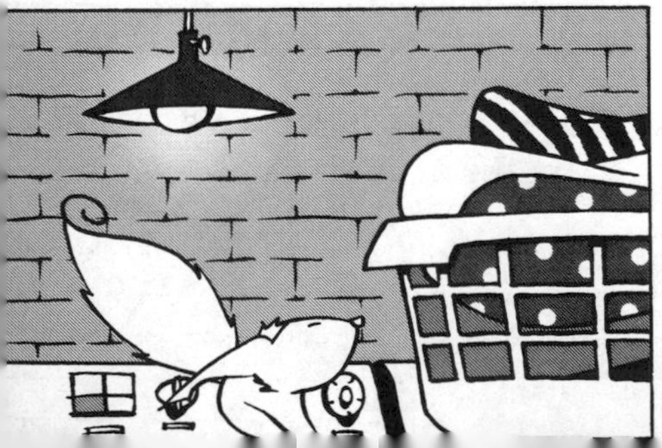

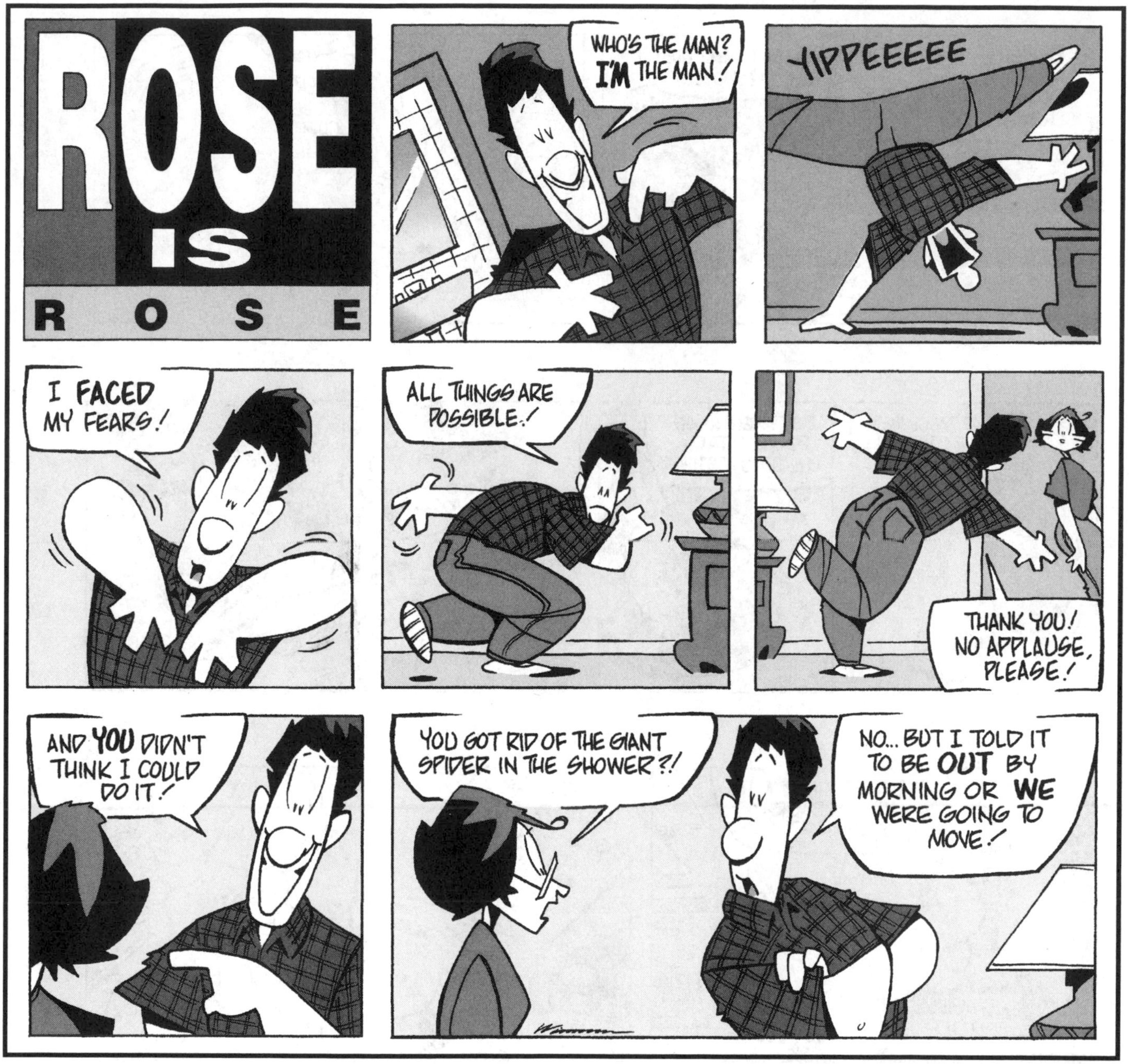
ROSE IS ROSE
WHO'S THE MAN? I'M THE MAN!
YIPPEEEEE
I FACED MY FEARS!
ALL THINGS ARE POSSIBLE!
THANK YOU! NO APPLAUSE, PLEASE!
AND YOU DIDN'T THINK I COULD DO IT!
YOU GOT RID OF THE GIANT SPIDER IN THE SHOWER?!
NO... BUT I TOLD IT TO BE OUT BY MORNING OR WE WERE GOING TO MOVE!

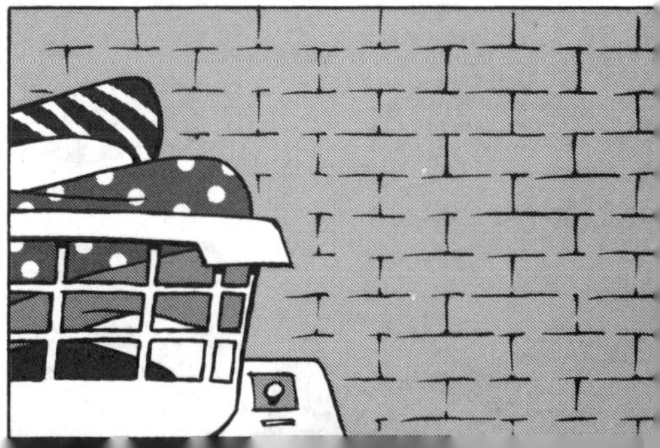

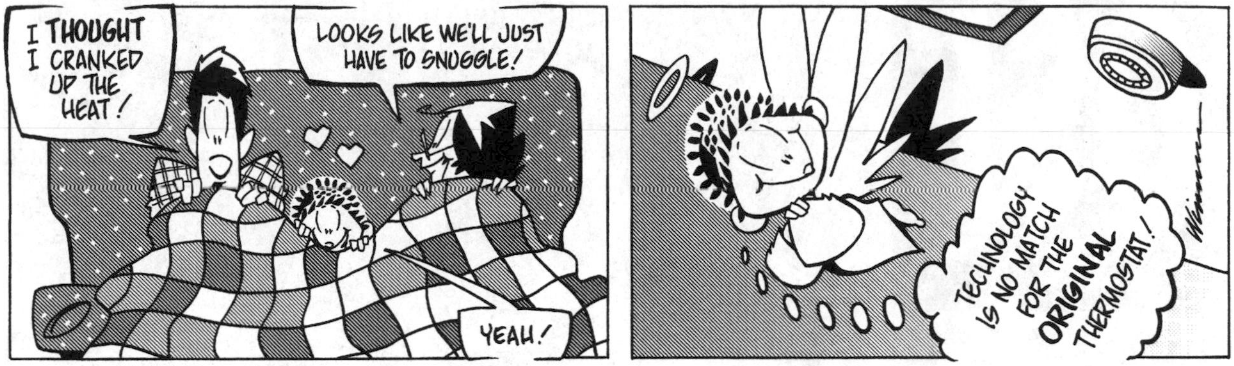
I THOUGHT I CRANKED UP THE HEAT!
LOOKS LIKE WE'LL JUST HAVE TO SNUGGLE!
YEAH!
TECHNOLOGY IS NO MATCH FOR THE ORIGINAL THERMOSTAT!

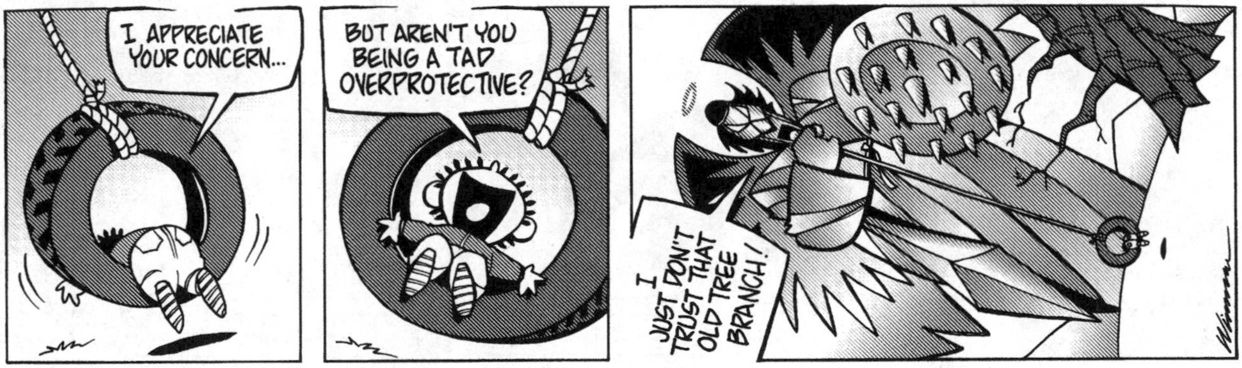
I APPRECIATE YOUR CONCERN...
BUT AREN'T YOU BEING A TAD OVERPROTECTIVE?
I JUST DON'T TRUST THAT OLD TREE BRANCH!

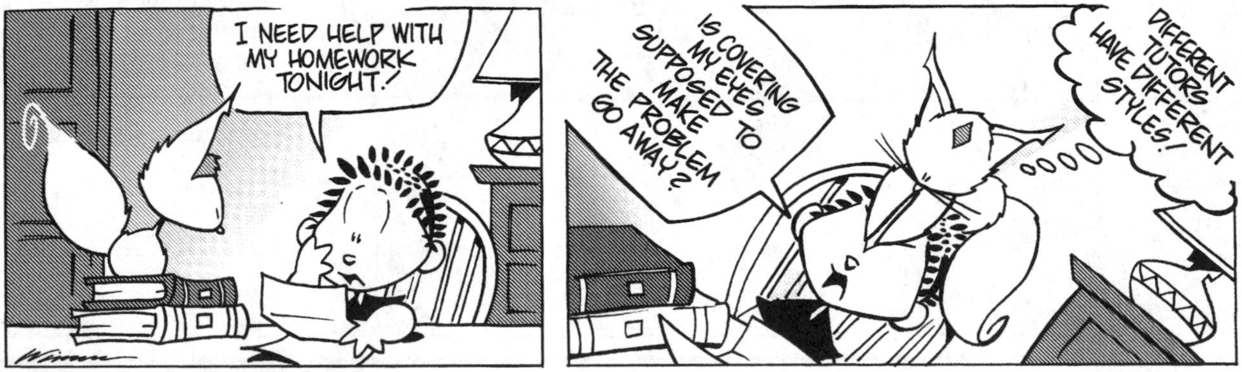
I NEED HELP WITH MY HOMEWORK TONIGHT!
IS COVERING MY EYES SUPPOSED TO MAKE THE PROBLEM GO AWAY?
DIFFERENT TUTORS HAVE DIFFERENT STYLES!

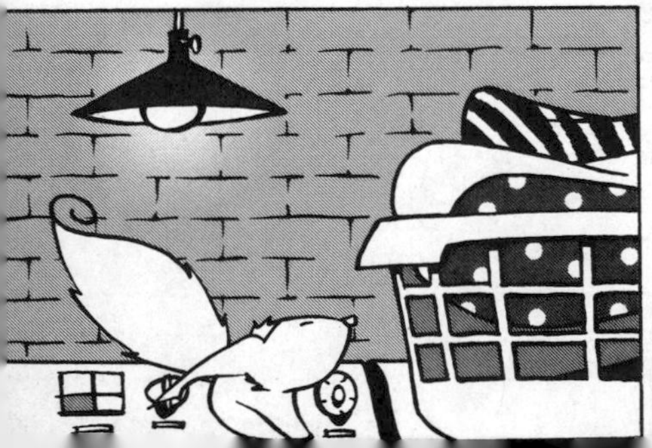

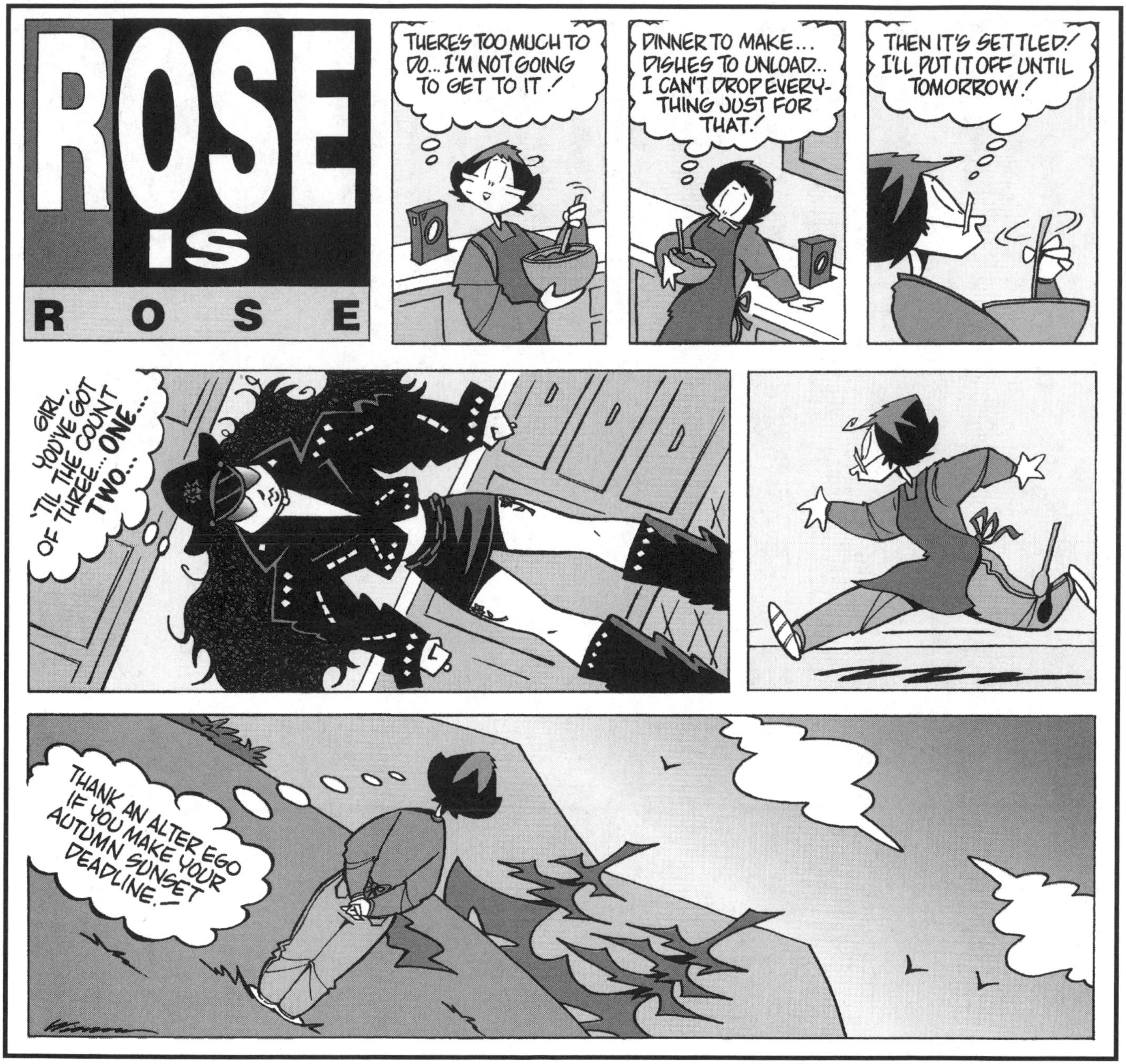
ROSE IS ROSE
THERE'S TOO MUCH TO DO... I'M NOT GOING TO GET TO IT!
DINNER TO MAKE... DISHES TO UNLOAD... I CAN'T DROP EVERYTHING JUST FOR THAT!
THEN IT'S SETTLED! I'LL PUT IT OFF UNTIL TOMORROW!
GIRL, YOU'VE GOT 'TIL THE COUNT OF THREE... ONE... TWO...
THANK AN ALTER EGO IF YOU MAKE YOUR AUTUMN SUNSET DEADLINE!

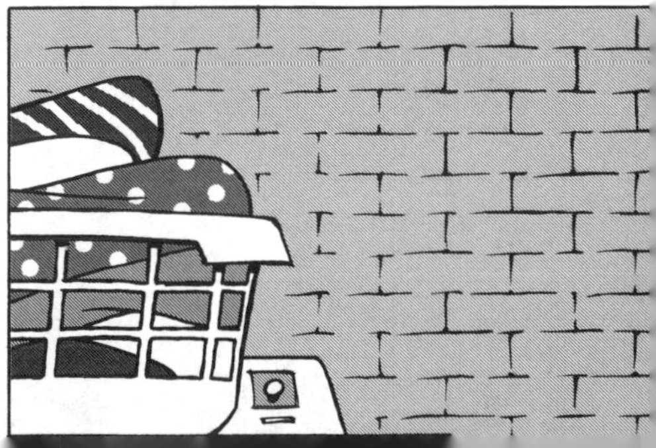

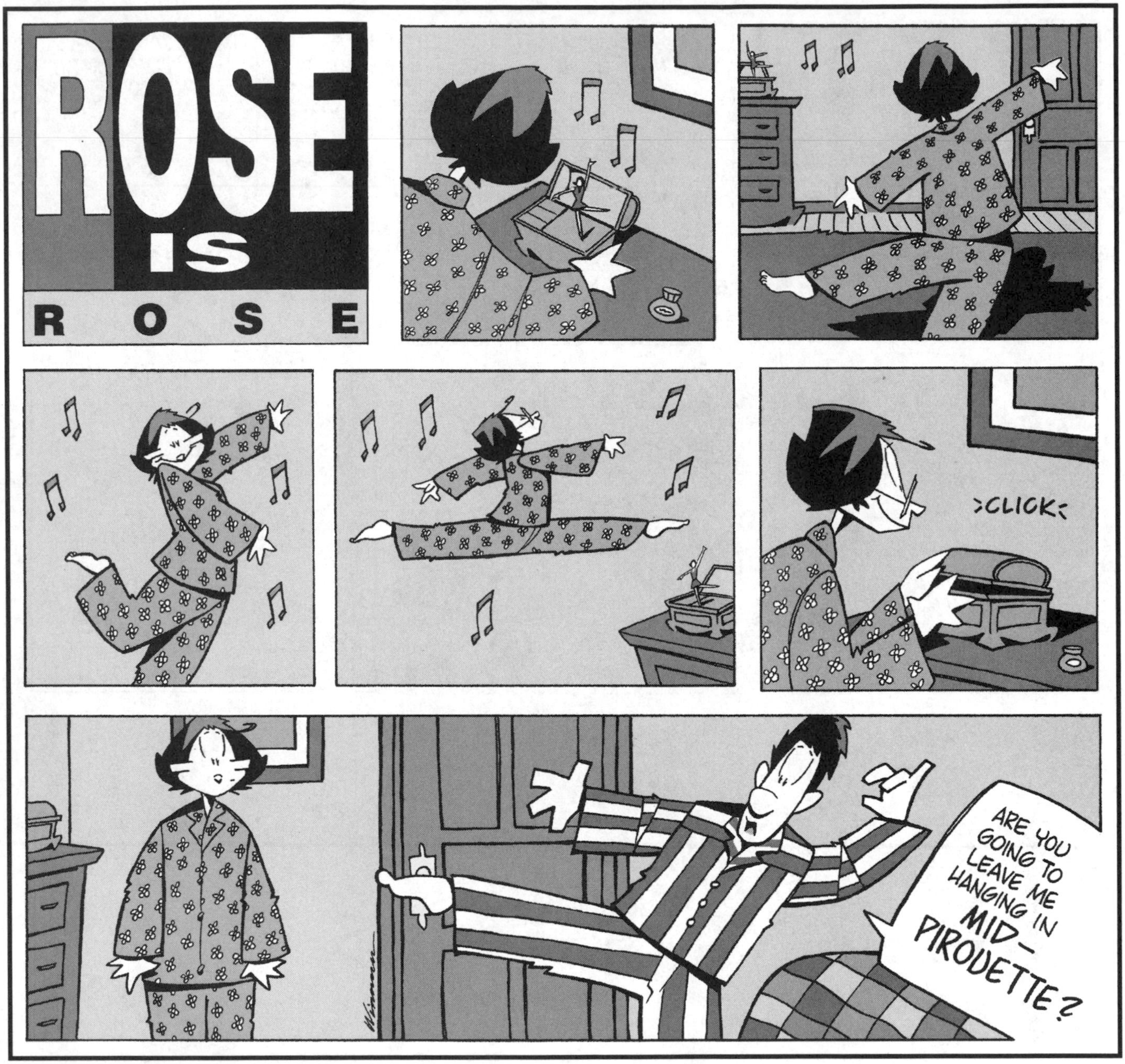
ROSE IS ROSE
>CLICK<
ARE YOU GOING TO LEAVE ME HANGING IN MID-PIROUETTE?

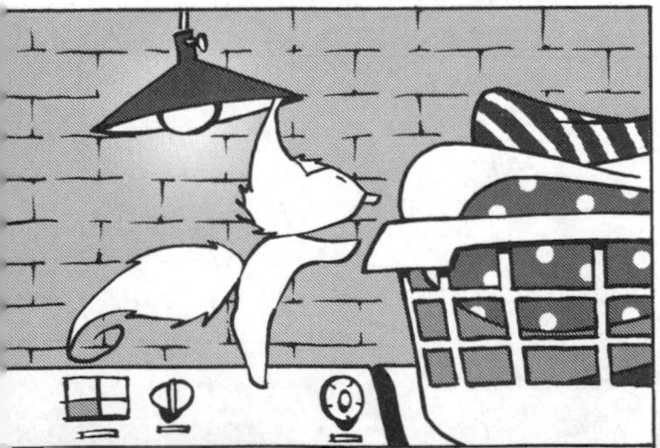

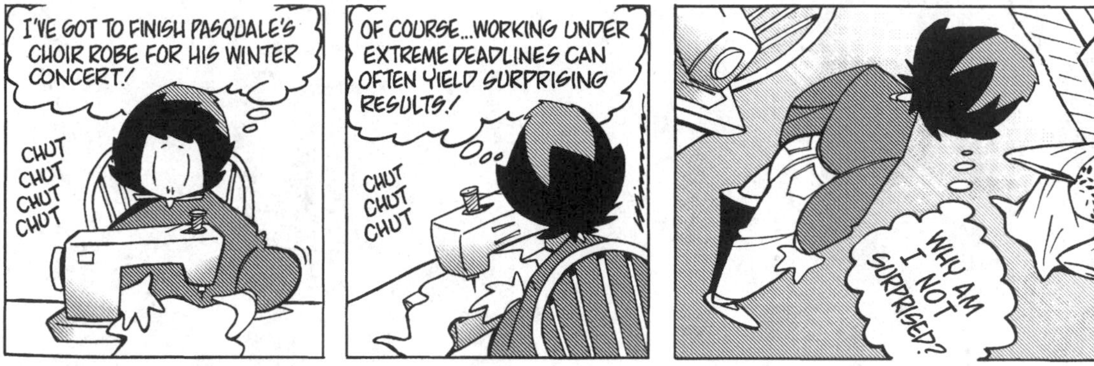
I'VE GOT TO FINISH PASQUALE'S CHOIR ROBE FOR HIS WINTER CONCERT!
CHUT CHUT CHUT CHUT
OF COURSE...WORKING UNDER EXTREME DEADLINES CAN OFTEN YIELD SURPRISING RESULTS!
CHUT CHUT CHUT
MOMMA? MOMMA ARE YOU OUT THERE?
WHY AM I NOT SURPRISED?

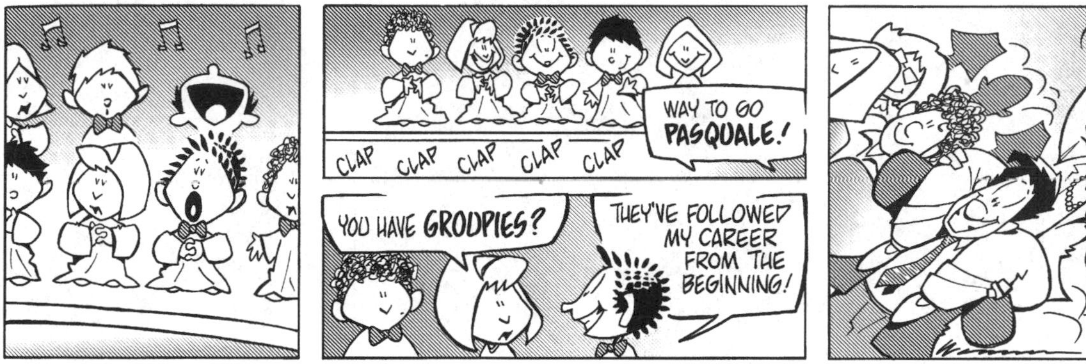
CLAP CLAP CLAP CLAP CLAP
WAY TO GO PASQUALE!
YOU HAVE GROUPIES?
THEY'VE FOLLOWED MY CAREER FROM THE BEGINNING!

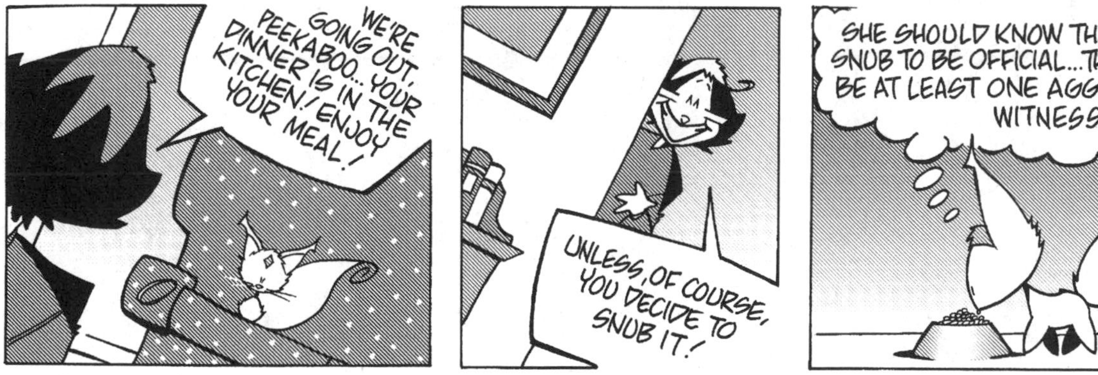
WE'RE GOING OUT, PEEKABOO... YOUR DINNER IS IN THE KITCHEN! ENJOY YOUR MEAL!
UNLESS, OF COURSE, YOU DECIDE TO SNUB IT!
SHE SHOULD KNOW THAT FOR A SNUB TO BE OFFICIAL...THERE MUST BE AT LEAST ONE AGGRAVATED WITNESS!

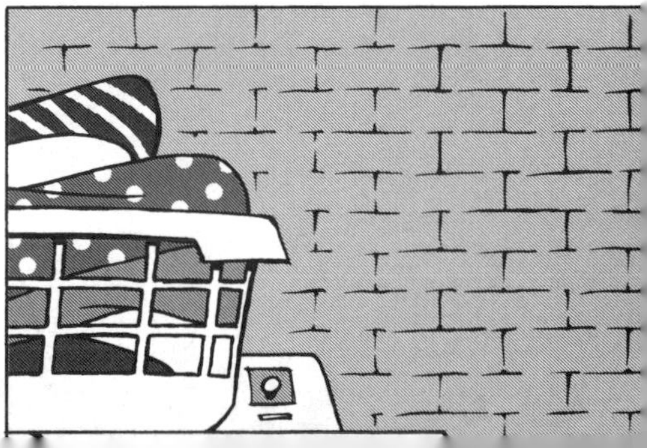

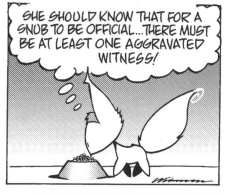

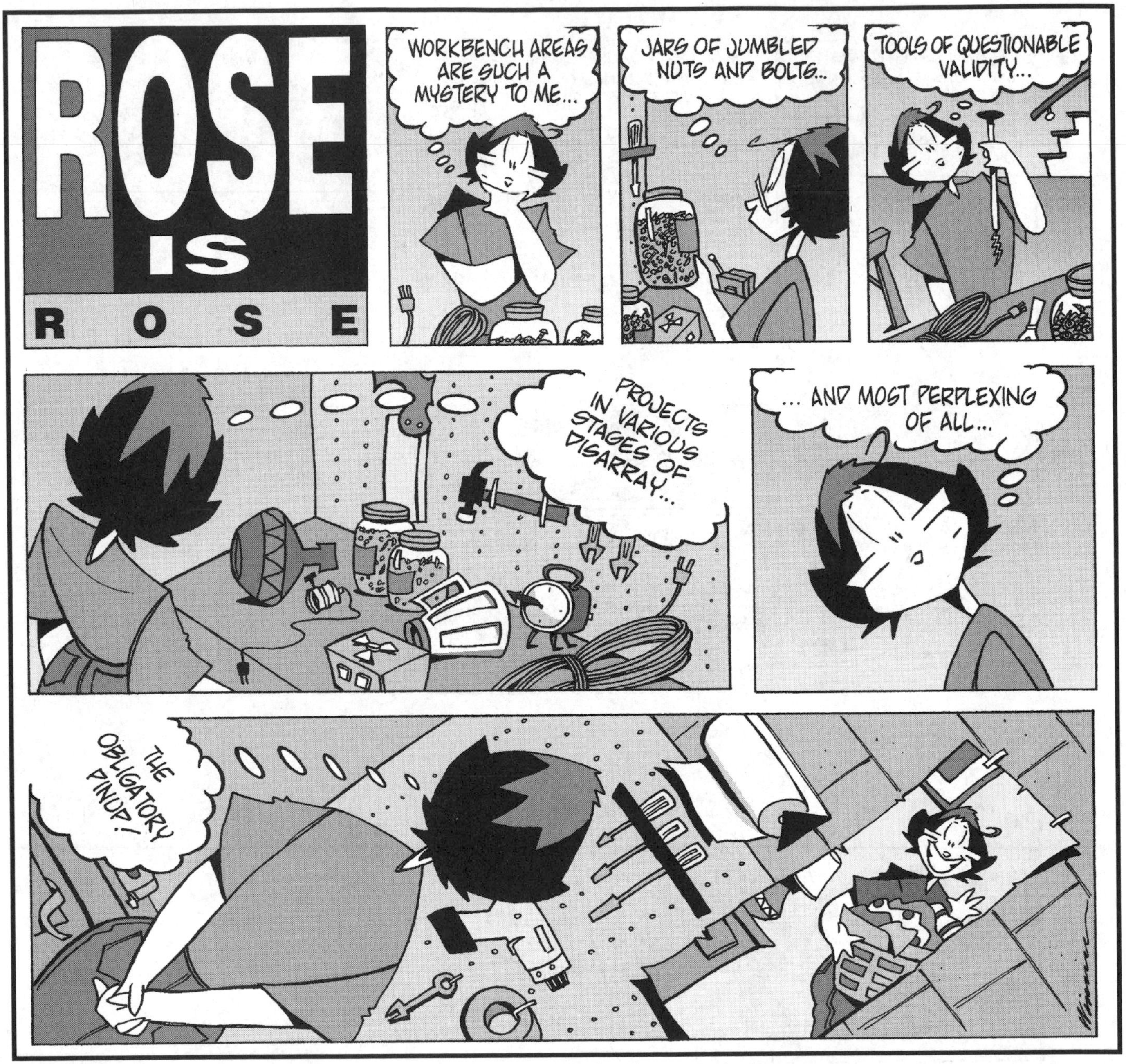
ROSE IS ROSE
WORKBENCH AREAS ARE SUCH A MYSTERY TO ME...
JARS OF JUMBLED NUTS AND BOLTS...
TOOLS OF QUESTIONABLE VALIDITY...
PROJECTS IN VARIOUS STAGES OF DISARRAY...
... AND MOST PERPLEXING OF ALL...
THE OBLIGATORY PINUP!

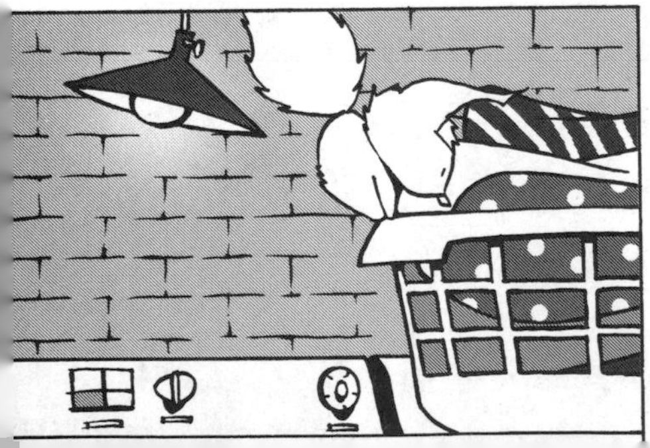

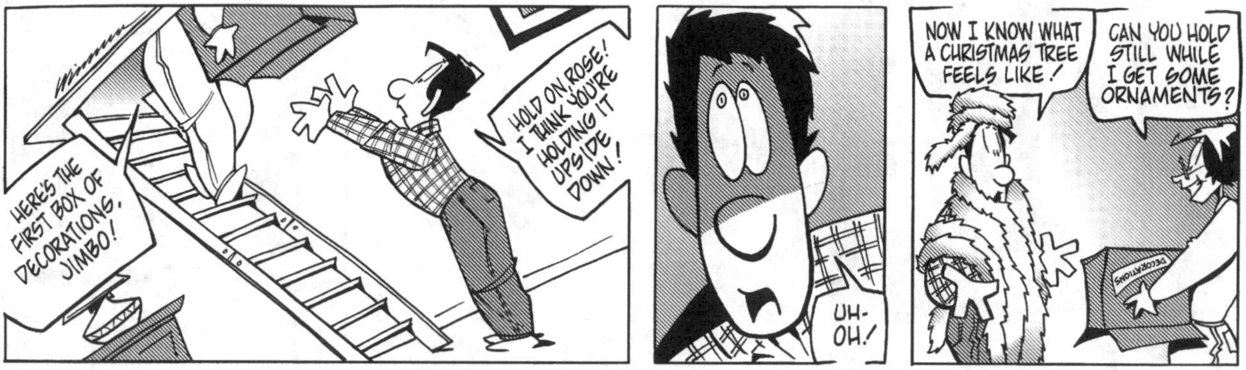
HERE'S THE FIRST BOX OF DECORATIONS, JIMBO!
HOLD ON ROSE! I THINK YOU'RE HOLDING IT UPSIDE DOWN!
UH-OH!
NOW I KNOW WHAT A CHRISTMAS TREE FEELS LIKE!
CAN YOU HOLD STILL WHILE I GET SOME ORNAMENTS?
DECORATIONS

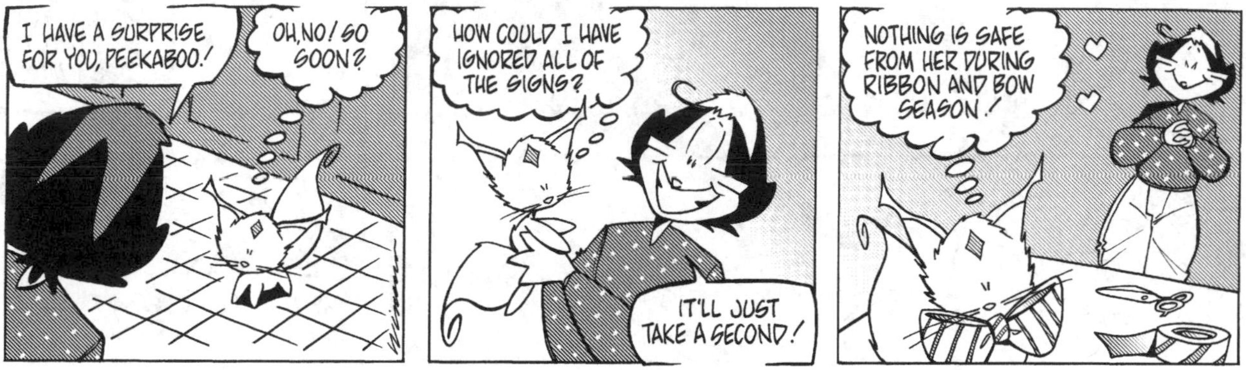
I HAVE A SURPRISE FOR YOU, PEEKABOO!
OH, NO! SO SOON?
HOW COULD I HAVE IGNORED ALL OF THE SIGNS?
IT'LL JUST TAKE A SECOND!
NOTHING IS SAFE FROM HER DURING RIBBON AND BOW SEASON!

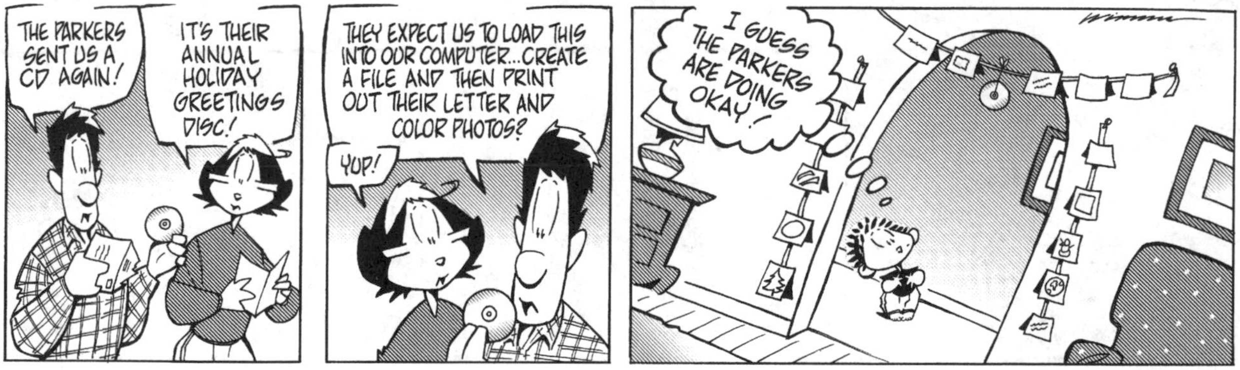
THE PARKERS SENT US A CD AGAIN!
IT'S THEIR ANNUAL HOLIDAY GREETINGS DISC!
THEY EXPECT US TO LOAD THIS INTO OUR COMPUTER...CREATE A FILE AND THEN PRINT OUT THEIR LETTER AND COLOR PHOTOS?
YUP!
I GUESS THE PARKERS ARE DOING OKAY!

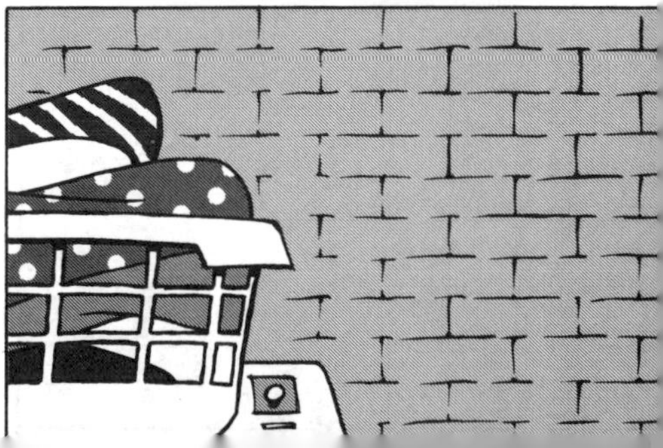

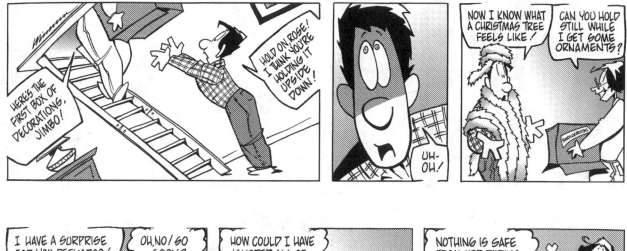

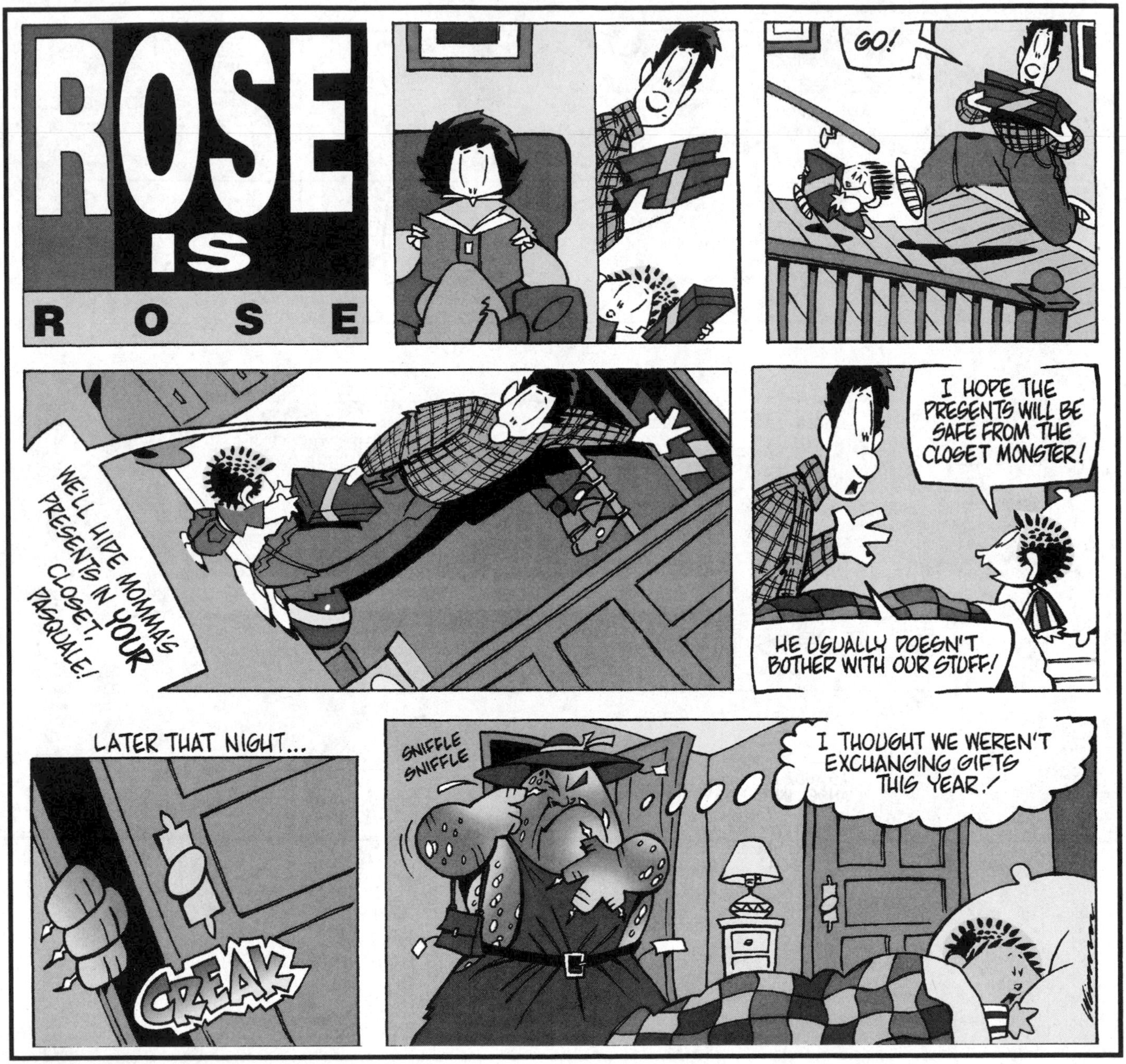
ROSE IS ROSE
GO!
WE'LL HIDE MOMMA'S PRESENTS IN YOUR CLOSET, PASQUALE!
I HOPE THE PRESENTS WILL BE SAFE FROM THE CLOSET MONSTER!
HE USUALLY DOESN'T BOTHER WITH OUR STUFF!
LATER THAT NIGHT...
CREAK
SNIFFLE SNIFFLE
I THOUGHT WE WEREN'T EXCHANGING GIFTS THIS YEAR.!

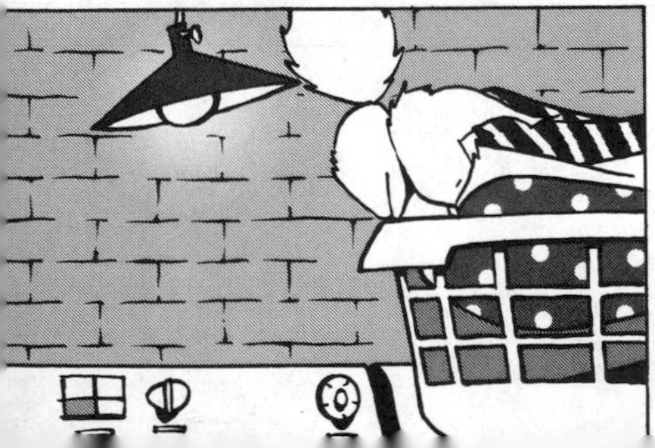

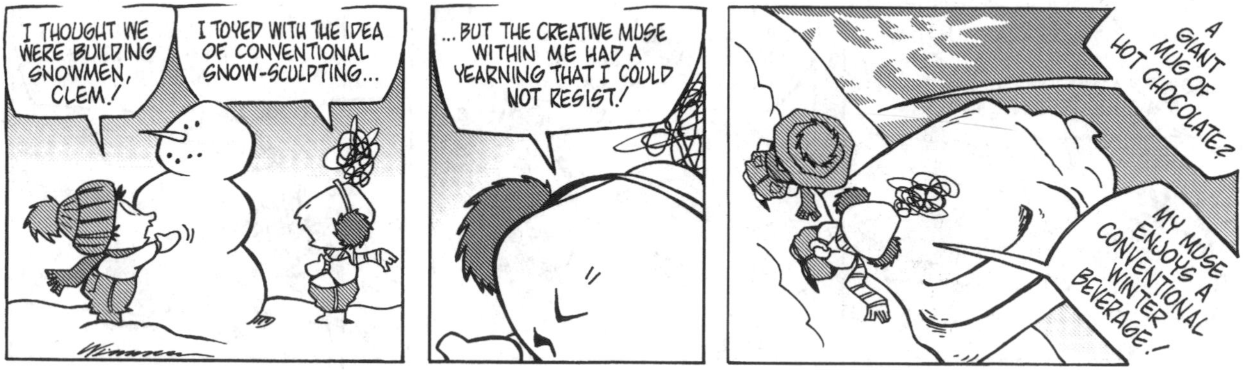
I THOUGHT WE WERE BUILDING SNOWMEN, CLEM!
I TOYED WITH THE IDEA OF CONVENTIONAL SNOW-SCULPTING...
...BUT THE CREATIVE MUSE WITHIN ME HAD A YEARNING THAT I COULD NOT RESIST!
A GIANT MUG OF HOT CHOCOLATE?
MY MUSE ENJOYS A CONVENTIONAL WINTER BEVERAGE!

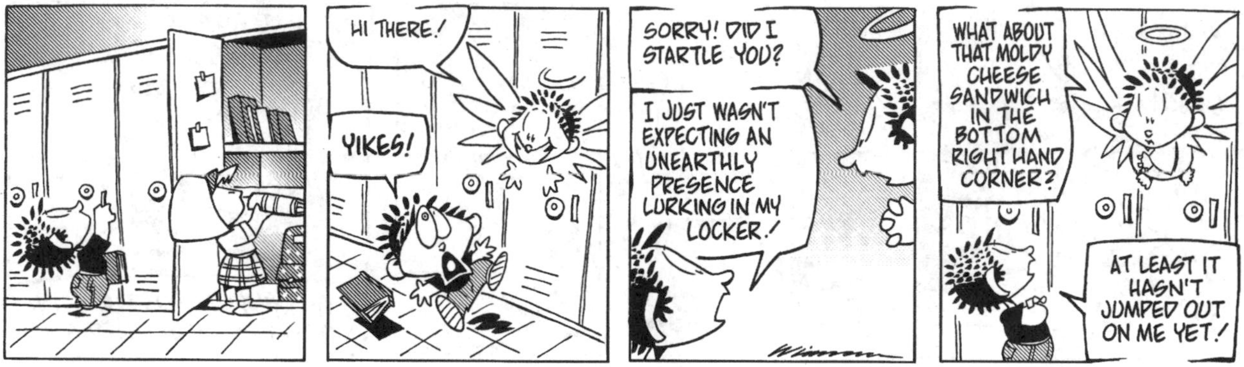
HI THERE!
YIKES!
SORRY! DID I STARTLE YOU?
I JUST WASN'T EXPECTING AN UNEARTHLY PRESENCE LURKING IN MY LOCKER!
WHAT ABOUT THAT MOLDY CHEESE SANDWICH IN THE BOTTOM RIGHT HAND CORNER?
AT LEAST IT HASN'T JUMPED OUT ON ME YET!

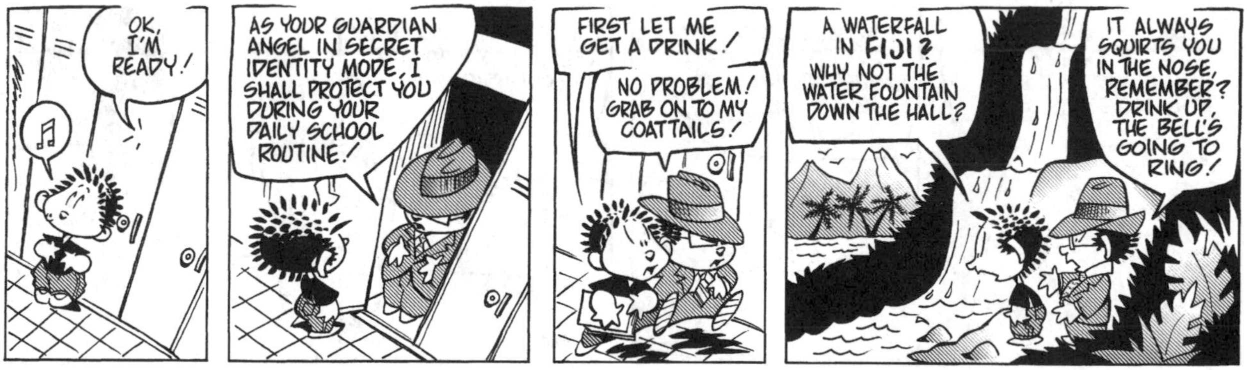
OK, I'M READY!
AS YOUR GUARDIAN ANGEL IN SECRET IDENTITY MODE, I SHALL PROTECT YOU DURING YOUR DAILY SCHOOL ROUTINE!
FIRST LET ME GET A DRINK!
NO PROBLEM! GRAB ON TO MY COATTAILS!
A WATERFALL IN FIJI? WHY NOT THE WATER FOUNTAIN DOWN THE HALL?
IT ALWAYS SQUIRTS YOU IN THE NOSE, REMEMBER? DRINK UP, THE BELL'S GOING TO RING!

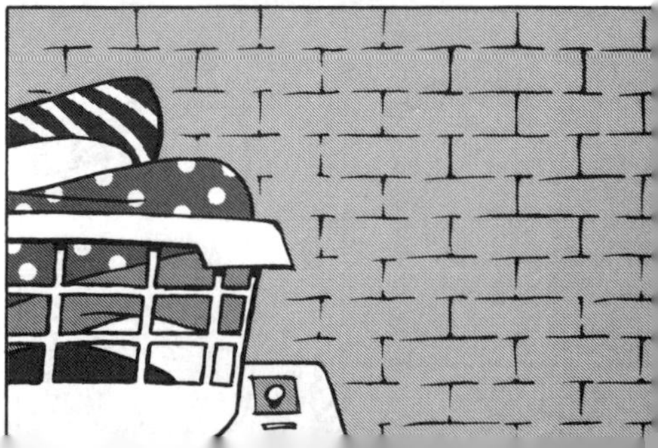

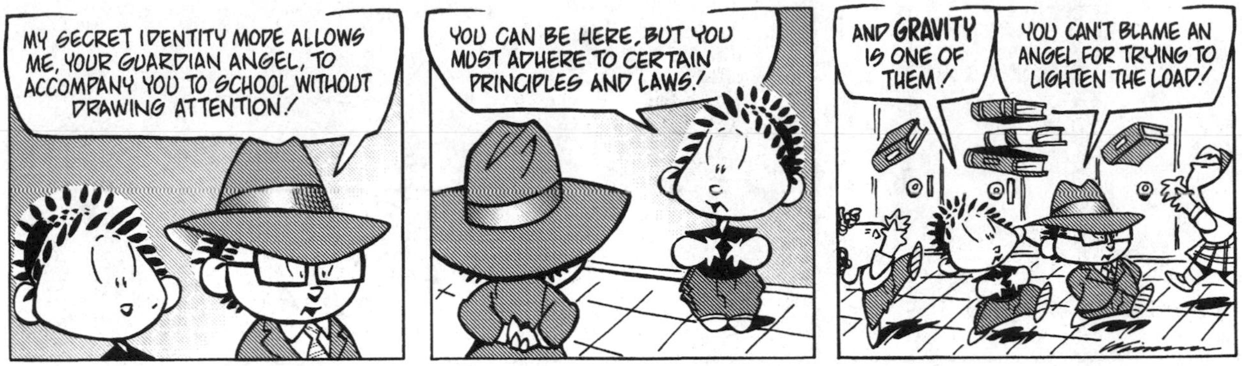
MY SECRET IDENTITY MODE ALLOWS ME, YOUR GUARDIAN ANGEL, TO ACCOMPANY YOU TO SCHOOL WITHOUT DRAWING ATTENTION!
YOU CAN BE HERE, BUT YOU MUST ADHERE TO CERTAIN PRINCIPLES AND LAWS!
AND GRAVITY IS ONE OF THEM!
YOU CAN'T BLAME AN ANGEL FOR TRYING TO LIGHTEN THE LOAD!

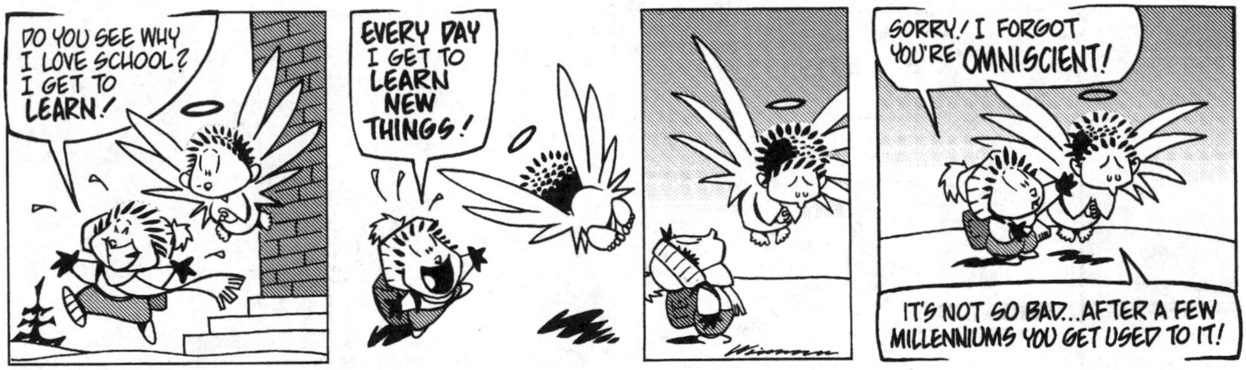
DO YOU SEE WHY I LOVE SCHOOL? I GET TO LEARN!
EVERY DAY I GET TO LEARN NEW THINGS!
SORRY! I FORGOT YOU'RE OMNISCIENT!
IT'S NOT SO BAD...AFTER A FEW MILLENNIUMS YOU GET USED TO IT!

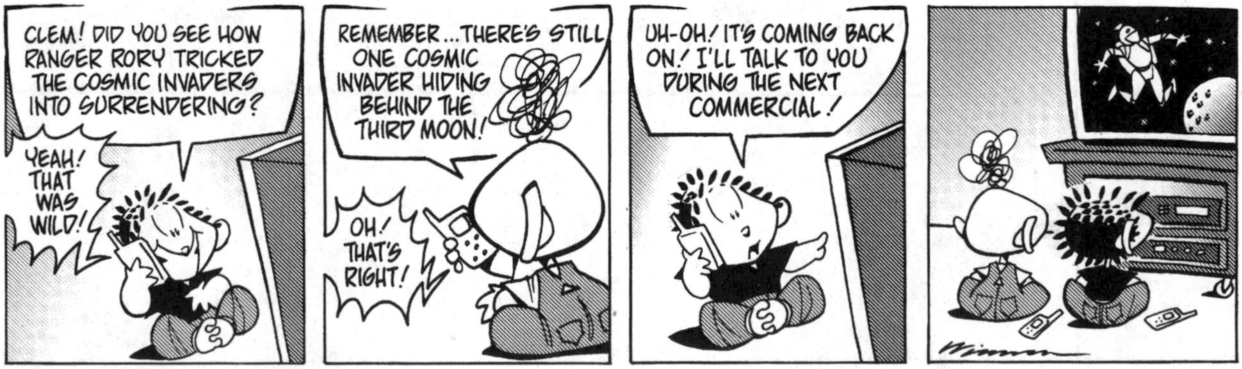
CLEM! DID YOU SEE HOW RANGER RORY TRICKED THE COSMIC INVADERS INTO SURRENDERING?
YEAH! THAT WAS WILD!
REMEMBER...THERE'S STILL ONE COSMIC INVADER HIDING BEHIND THE THIRD MOON!
OH! THAT'S RIGHT!
UH-OH! IT'S COMING BACK ON! I'LL TALK TO YOU DURING THE NEXT COMMERCIAL!

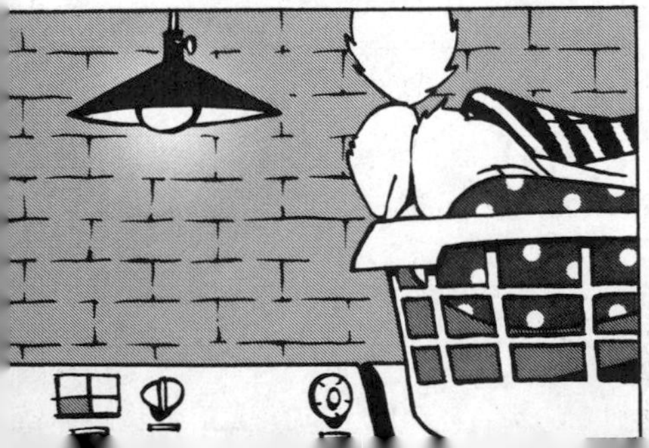

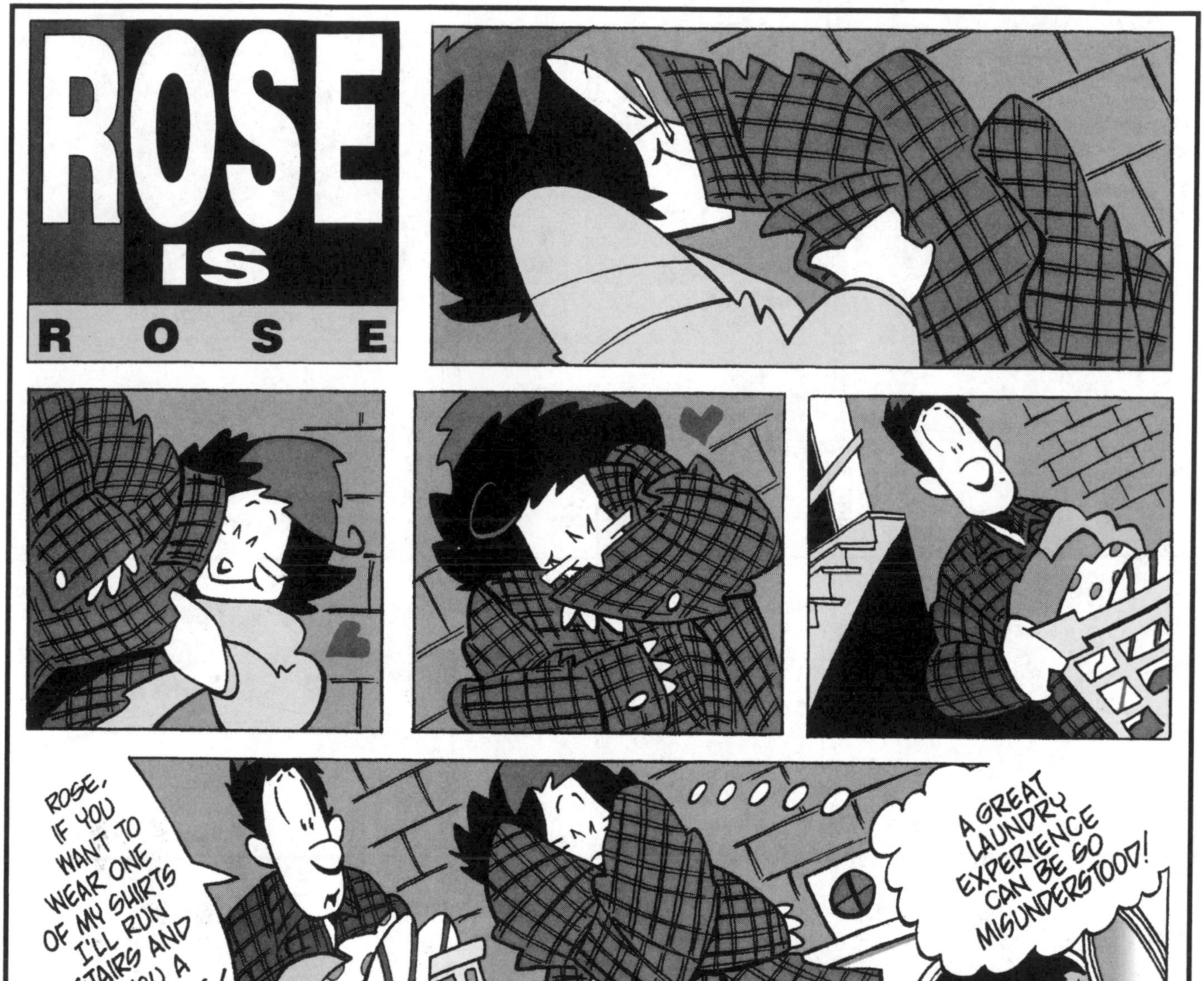
ROSE IS ROSE
ROSE, IF YOU WANT TO WEAR ONE OF MY SHIRTS I'LL RUN UPSTAIRS AND GET YOU A CLEAN ONE!
A GREAT LAUNDRY EXPERIENCE CAN BE SO MISUNDERSTOOD!

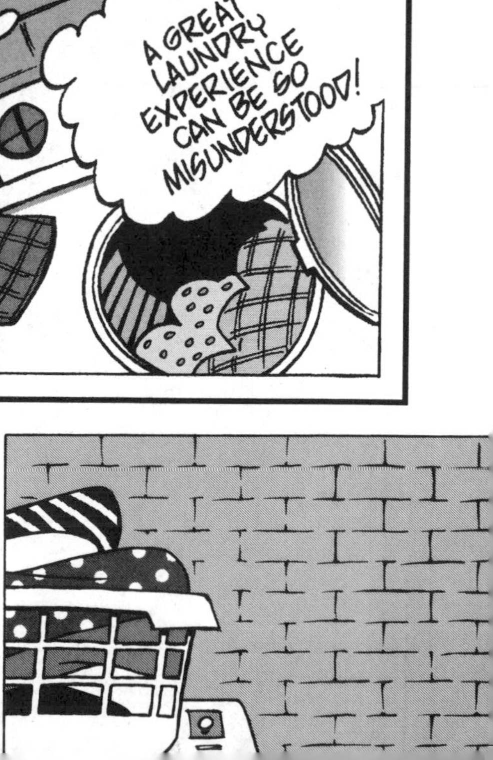

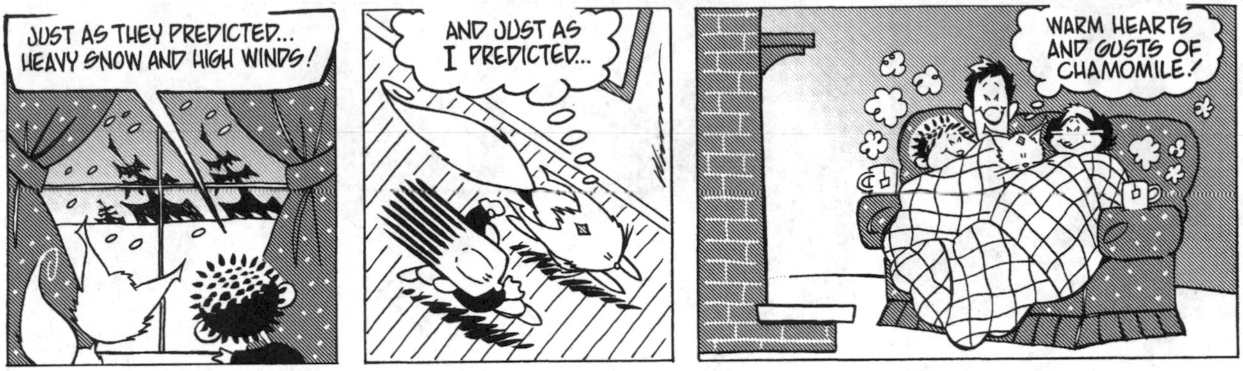
JUST AS THEY PREDICTED... HEAVY SNOW AND HIGH WINDS!
AND JUST AS I PREDICTED...
WARM HEARTS AND GUSTS OF CHAMOMILE!

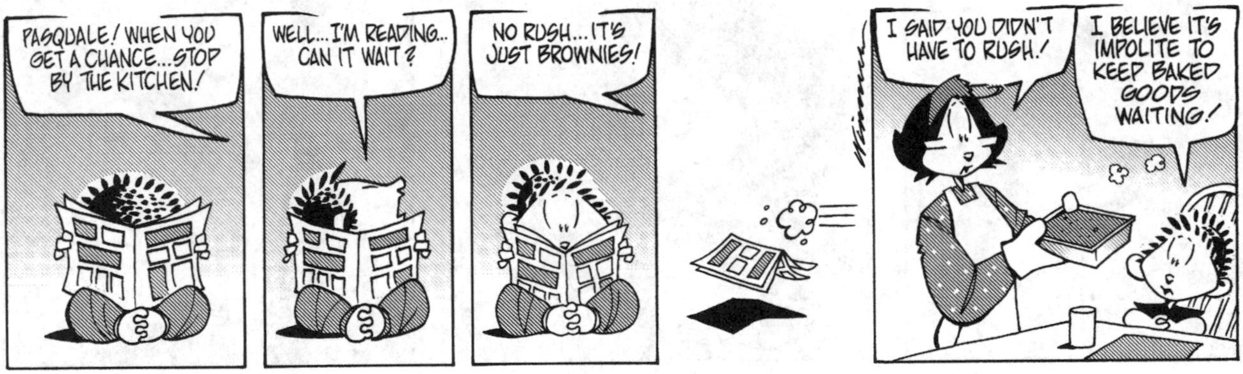
PASQUALE! WHEN YOU GET A CHANCE...STOP BY THE KITCHEN!
WELL... I'M READING... CAN IT WAIT?
NO RUSH... IT'S JUST BROWNIES!
I SAID YOU DIDN'T HAVE TO RUSH!
I BELIEVE IT'S IMPOLITE TO KEEP BAKED GOODS WAITING!

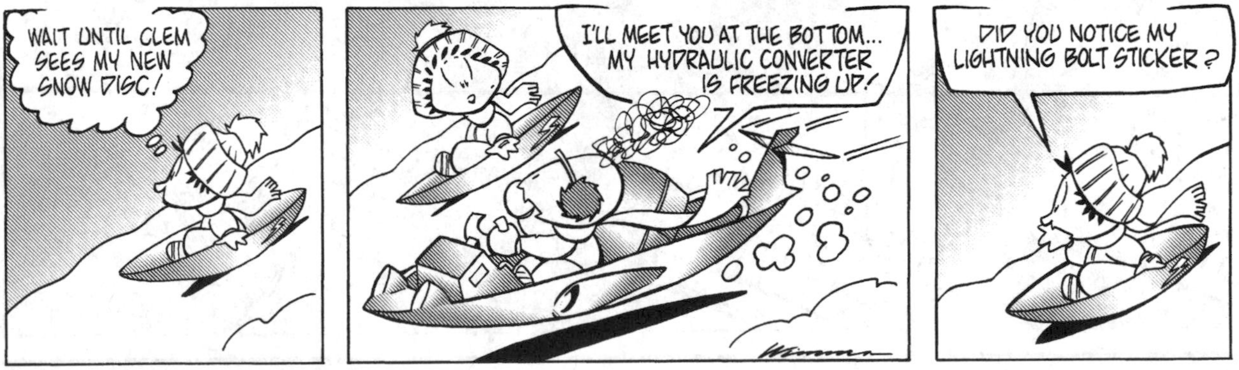
WAIT UNTIL CLEM SEES MY NEW SNOW DISC!
I'LL MEET YOU AT THE BOTTOM... MY HYDRAULIC CONVERTER IS FREEZING UP!
DID YOU NOTICE MY LIGHTNING BOLT STICKER?

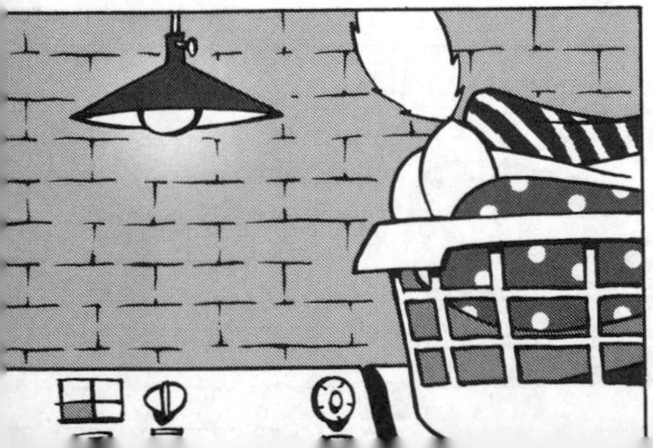

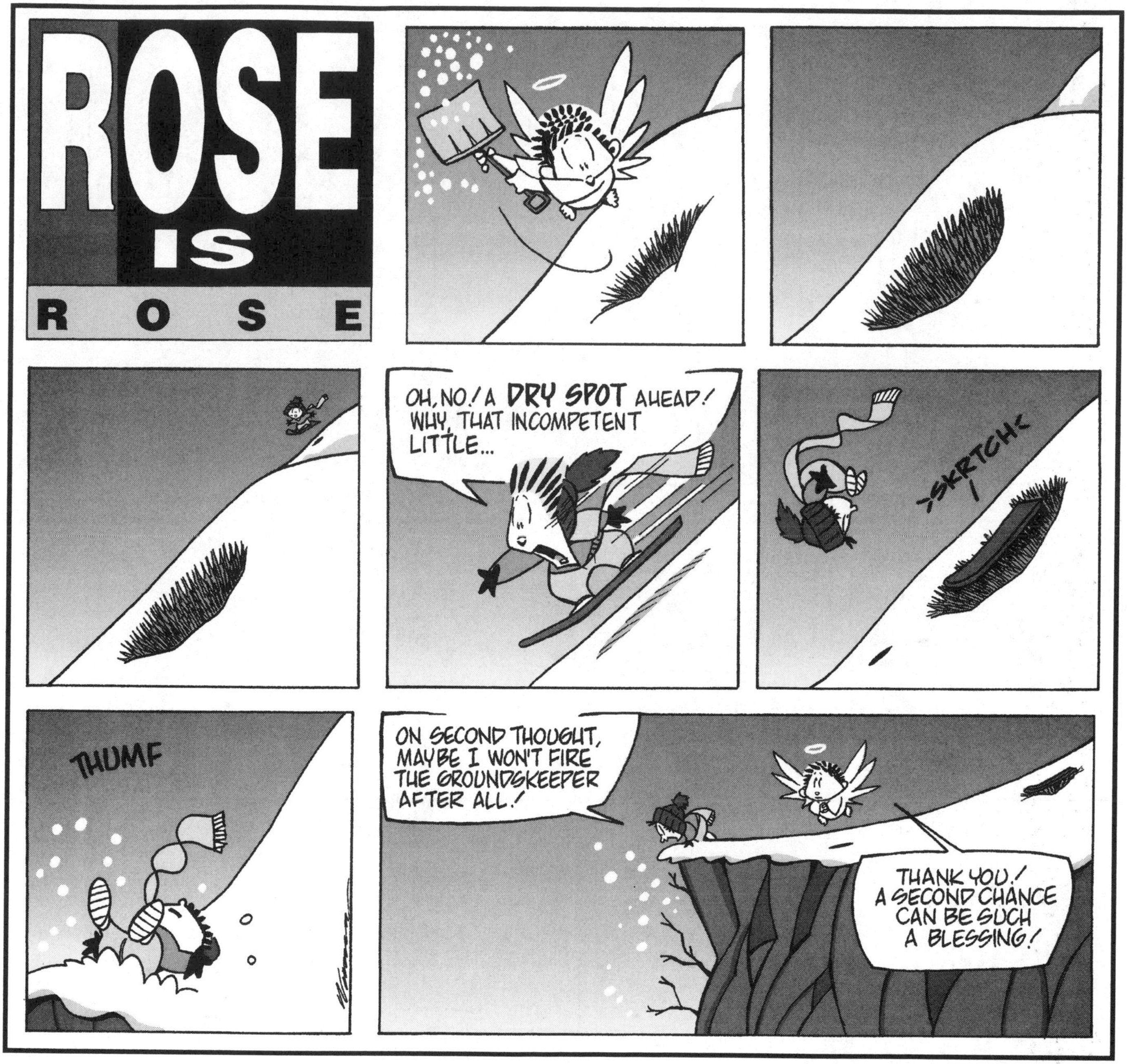
ROSE IS ROSE
OH, NO! A DRY SPOT AHEAD! WHY, THAT INCOMPETENT LITTLE...
SKRTCH
THUMF
ON SECOND THOUGHT, MAYBE I WON'T FIRE THE GROUNDSKEEPER AFTER ALL!
THANK YOU! A SECOND CHANCE CAN BE SUCH A BLESSING!

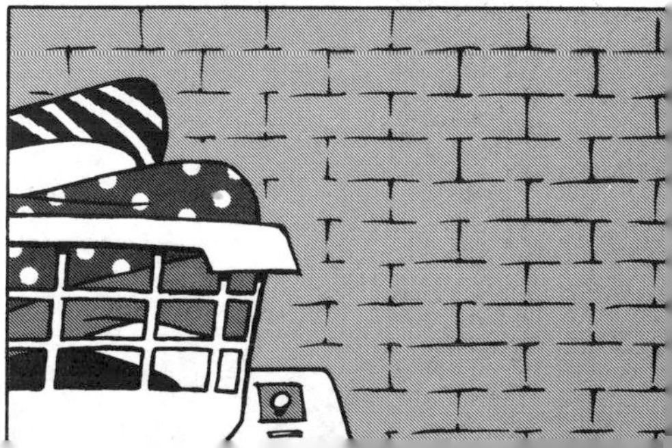

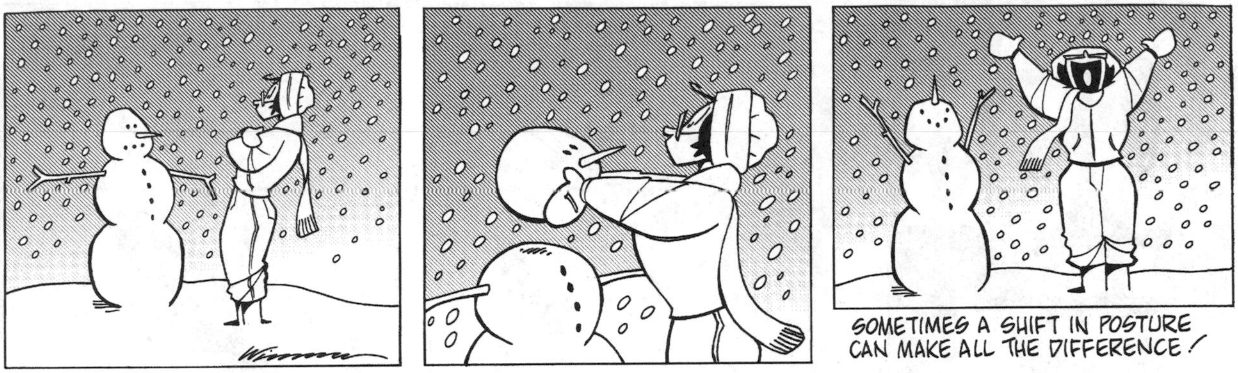
SOMETIMES A SHIFT IN POSTURE CAN MAKE ALL THE DIFFERENCE!

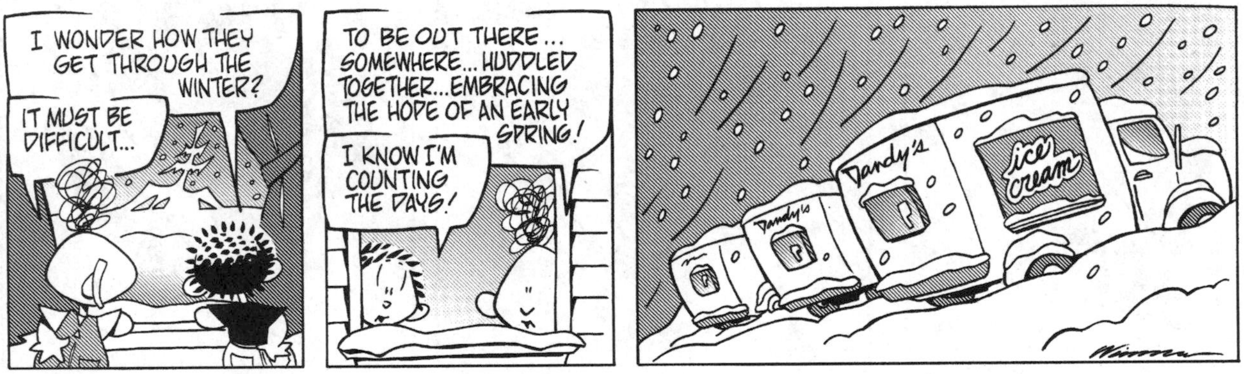
I WONDER HOW THEY GET THROUGH THE WINTER?
IT MUST BE DIFFICULT...
TO BE OUT THERE... SOMEWHERE... HUDDLED TOGETHER...EMBRACING THE HOPE OF AN EARLY SPRING!
I KNOW I'M COUNTING THE DAYS!
Dandy's
ice cream
Dandy's

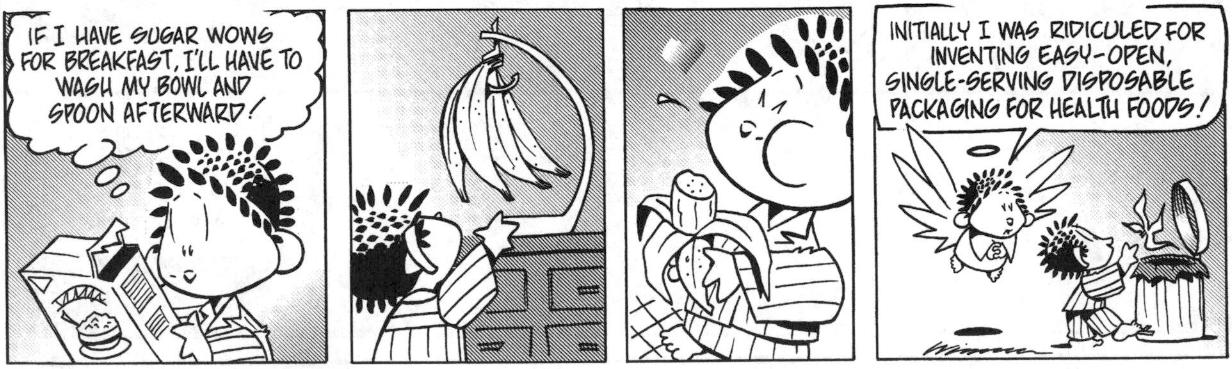
IF I HAVE SUGAR WOWS FOR BREAKFAST, I'LL HAVE TO WASH MY BOWL AND SPOON AFTERWARD!
INITIALLY I WAS RIDICULED FOR INVENTING EASY-OPEN, SINGLE-SERVING DISPOSABLE PACKAGING FOR HEALTH FOODS!

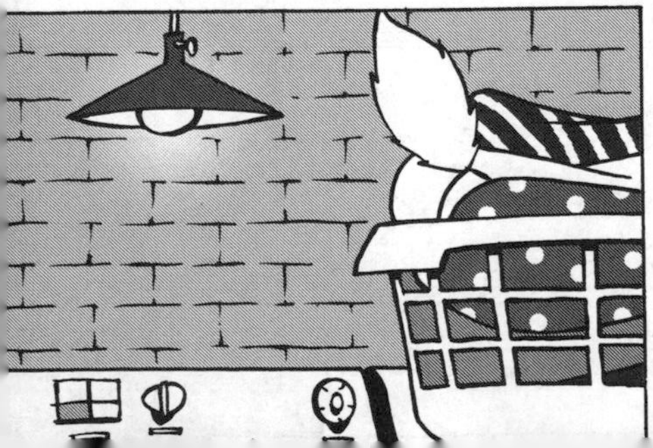

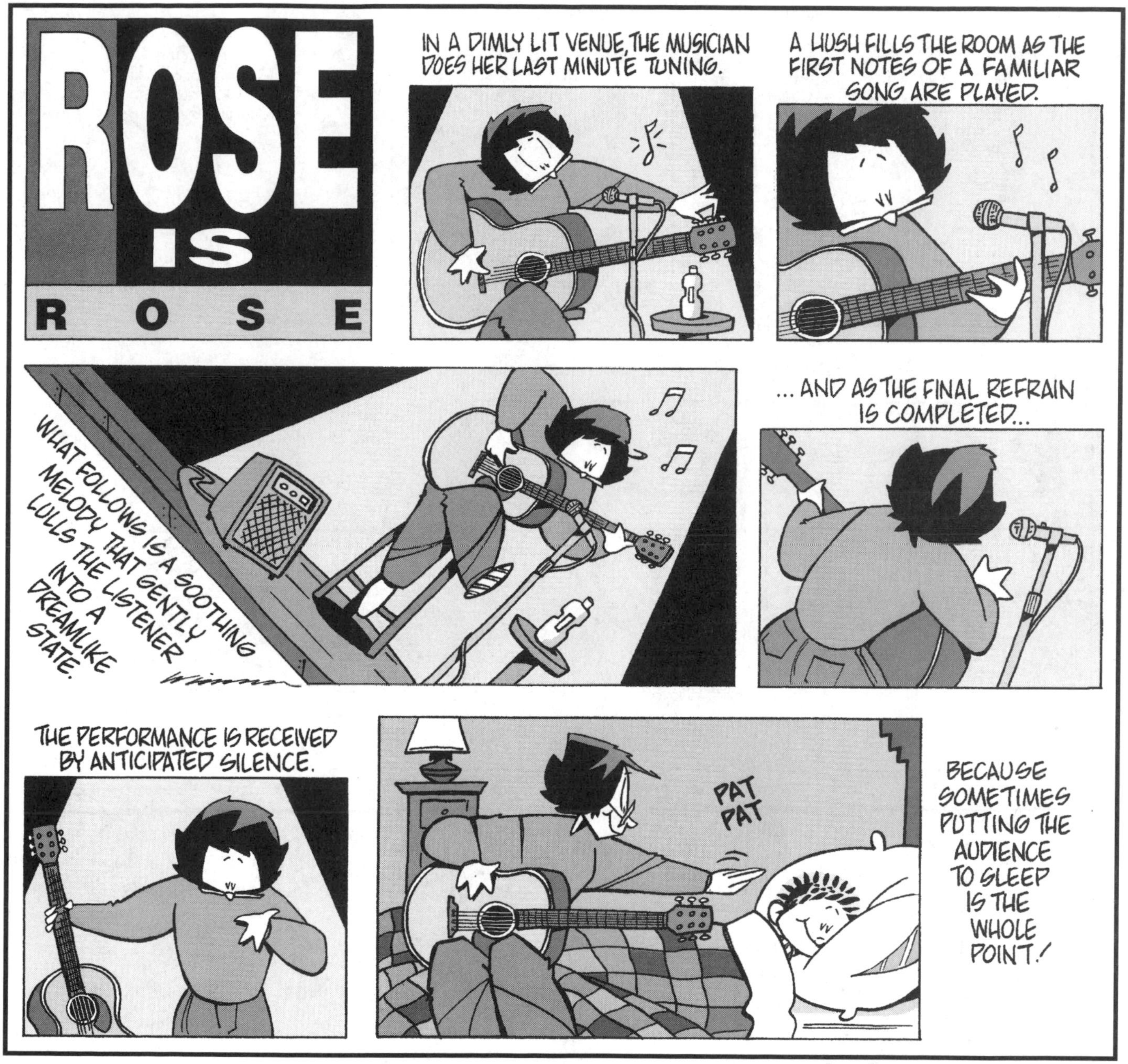
ROSE IS ROSE
IN A DIMLY LIT VENUE, THE MUSICIAN DOES HER LAST MINUTE TUNING.
A HUSH FILLS THE ROOM AS THE FIRST NOTES OF A FAMILIAR SONG ARE PLAYED.
WHAT FOLLOWS IS A SOOTHING MELODY THAT GENTLY LULLS THE LISTENER INTO A DREAMLIKE STATE.
... AND AS THE FINAL REFRAIN IS COMPLETED...
THE PERFORMANCE IS RECEIVED BY ANTICIPATED SILENCE.
PAT PAT
BECAUSE SOMETIMES PUTTING THE AUDIENCE TO SLEEP IS THE WHOLE POINT.!

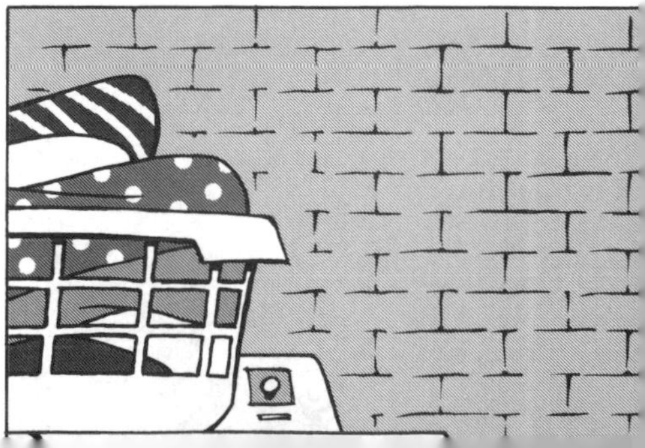

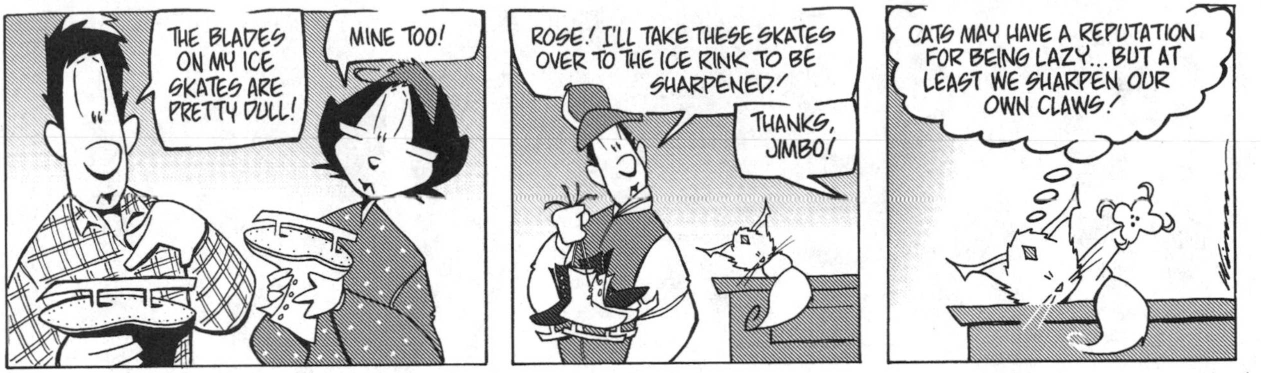
THE BLADES ON MY ICE SKATES ARE PRETTY DULL!
MINE TOO!
ROSE! I'LL TAKE THESE SKATES OVER TO THE ICE RINK TO BE SHARPENED!
THANKS, JIMBO!
CATS MAY HAVE A REPUTATION FOR BEING LAZY... BUT AT LEAST WE SHARPEN OUR OWN CLAWS!

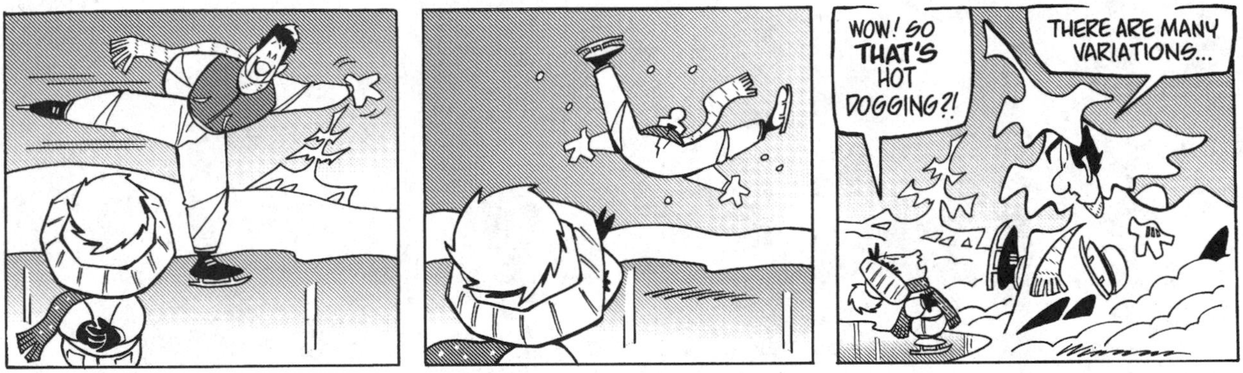
WOW! SO **THAT'S** HOT DOGGING?!
THERE ARE MANY VARIATIONS...

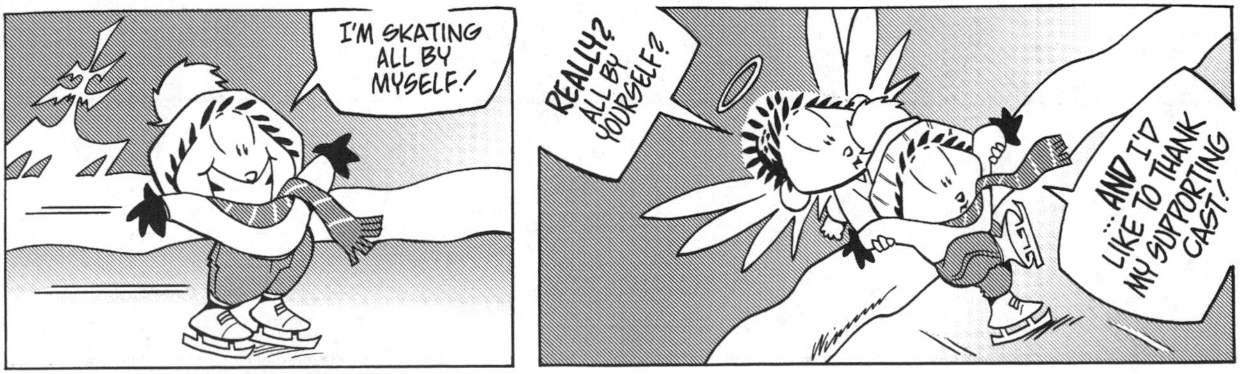
I'M SKATING ALL BY MYSELF!
REALLY? ALL BY YOURSELF?
...**AND** I'D LIKE TO THANK MY SUPPORTING CAST!

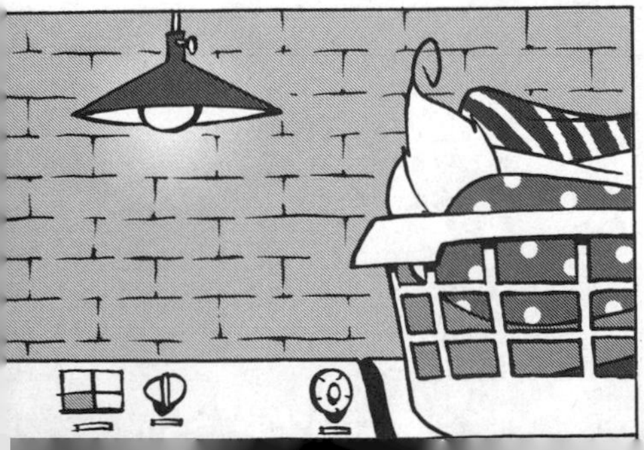

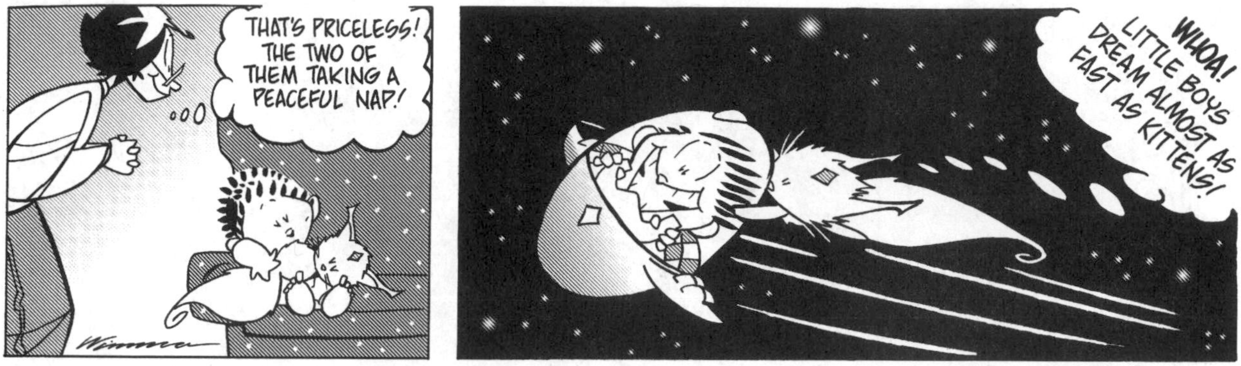
THAT'S PRICELESS! THE TWO OF THEM TAKING A PEACEFUL NAP!
WHOA! LITTLE BOYS DREAM ALMOST AS FAST AS KITTENS!

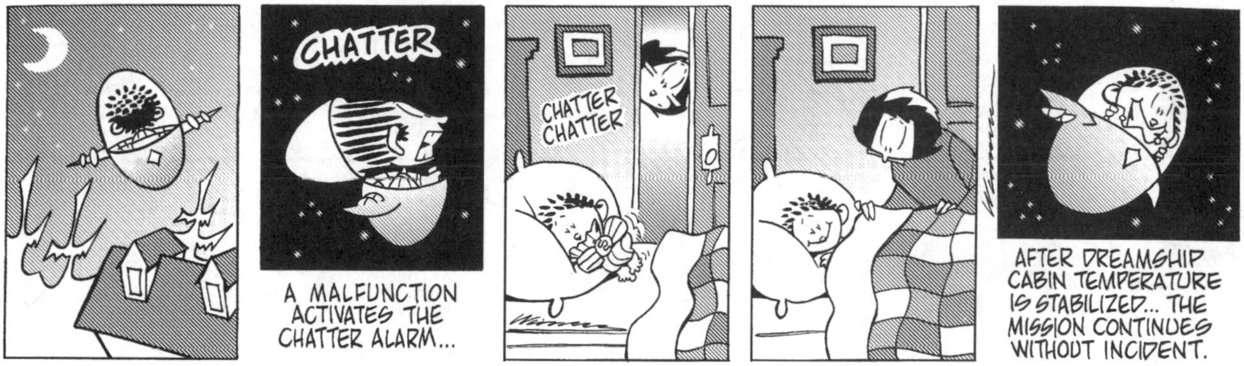
CHATTER
A MALFUNCTION ACTIVATES THE CHATTER ALARM...
CHATTER CHATTER
AFTER DREAMSHIP CABIN TEMPERATURE IS STABILIZED... THE MISSION CONTINUES WITHOUT INCIDENT.

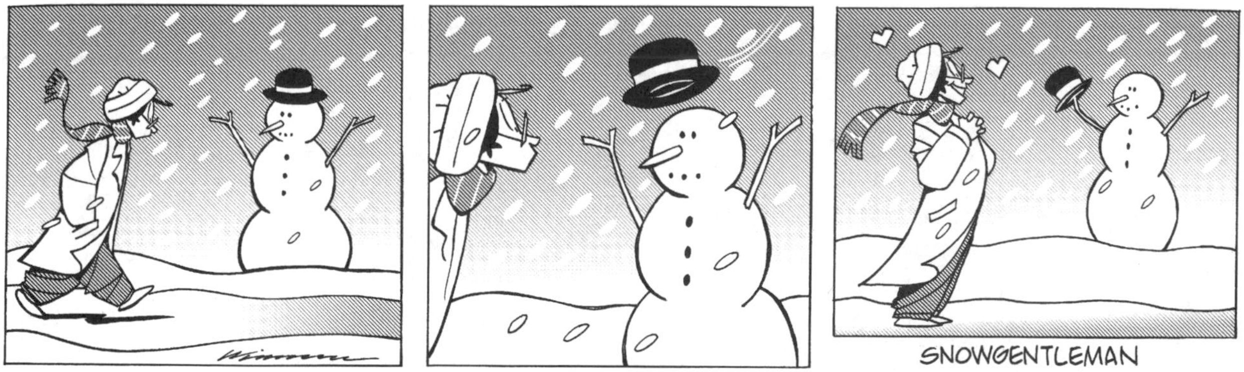
SNOWGENTLEMAN

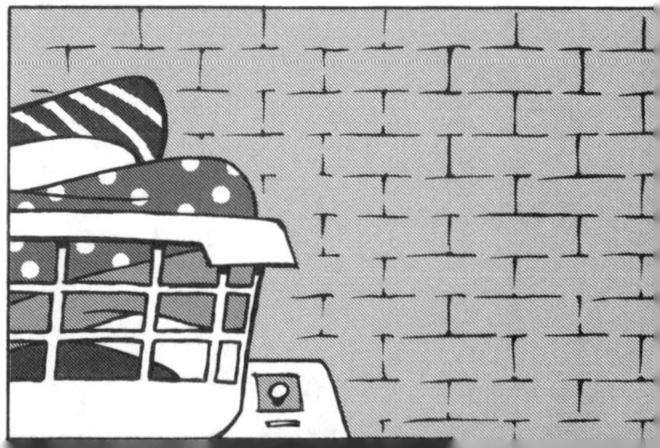

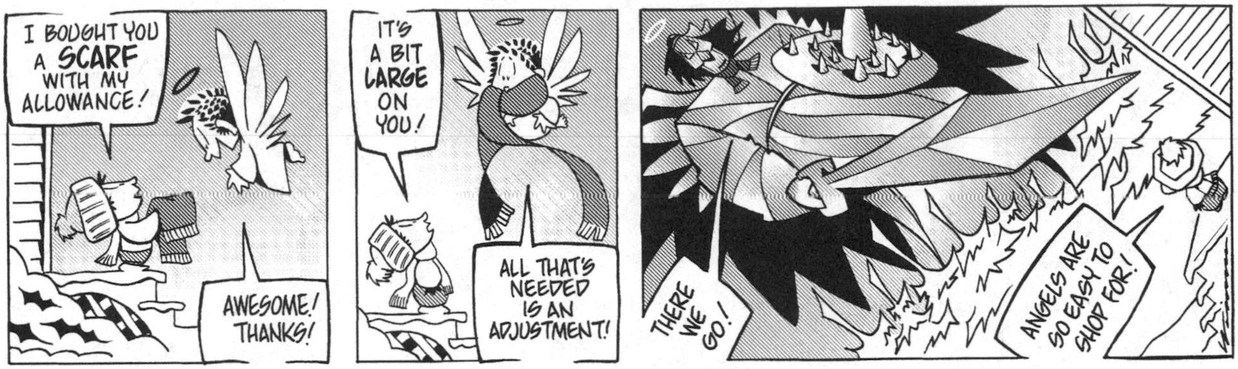
I BOUGHT YOU A SCARF WITH MY ALLOWANCE!
AWESOME! THANKS!
IT'S A BIT LARGE ON YOU!
ALL THAT'S NEEDED IS AN ADJUSTMENT!
THERE WE GO!
ANGELS ARE SO EASY TO SHOP FOR!

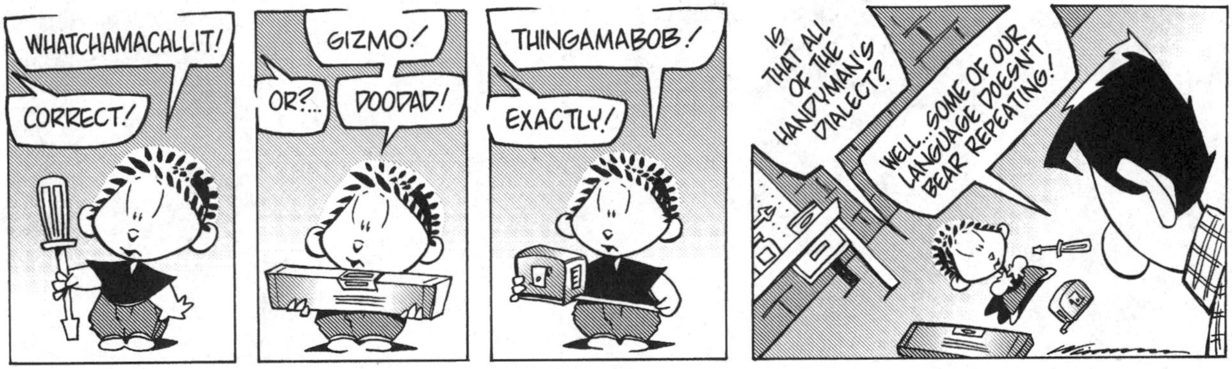
WHATCHAMACALLIT!
CORRECT!
GIZMO!
OR?...
DOODAD!
THINGAMABOB!
EXACTLY!
IS THAT ALL OF THE HANDYMAN'S DIALECT?
WELL... SOME OF OUR LANGUAGE DOESN'T BEAR REPEATING!

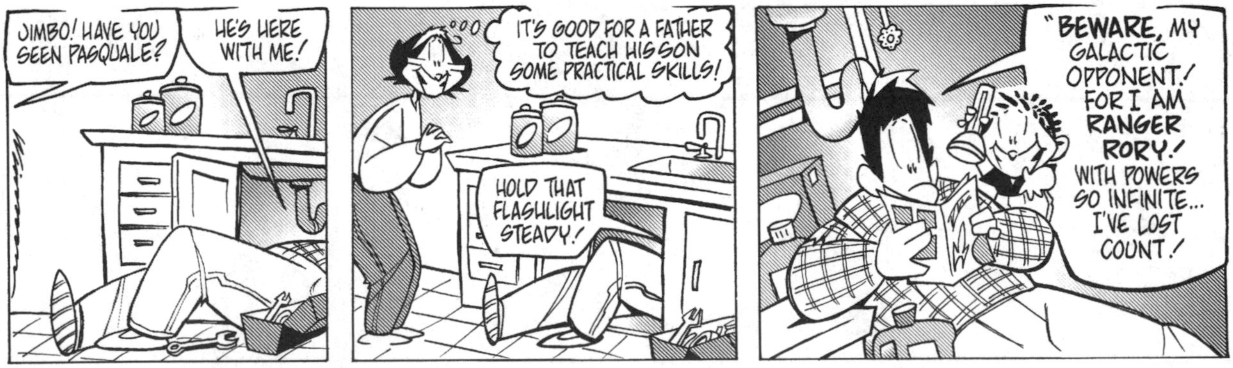
JIMBO! HAVE YOU SEEN PASQUALE?
HE'S HERE WITH ME!
IT'S GOOD FOR A FATHER TO TEACH HIS SON SOME PRACTICAL SKILLS!
HOLD THAT FLASHLIGHT STEADY!
"BEWARE, MY GALACTIC OPPONENT! FOR I AM RANGER RORY! WITH POWERS SO INFINITE... I'VE LOST COUNT!

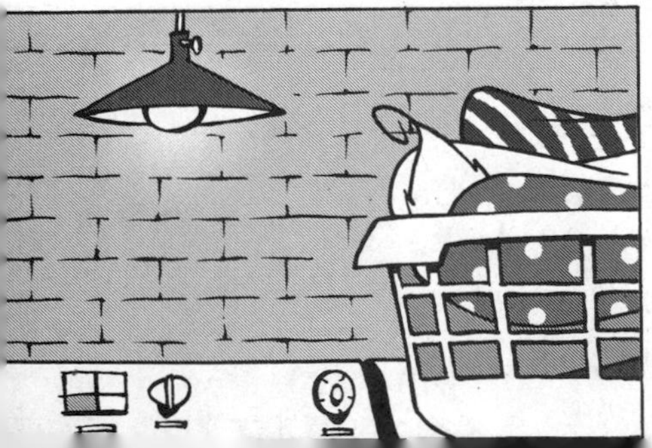

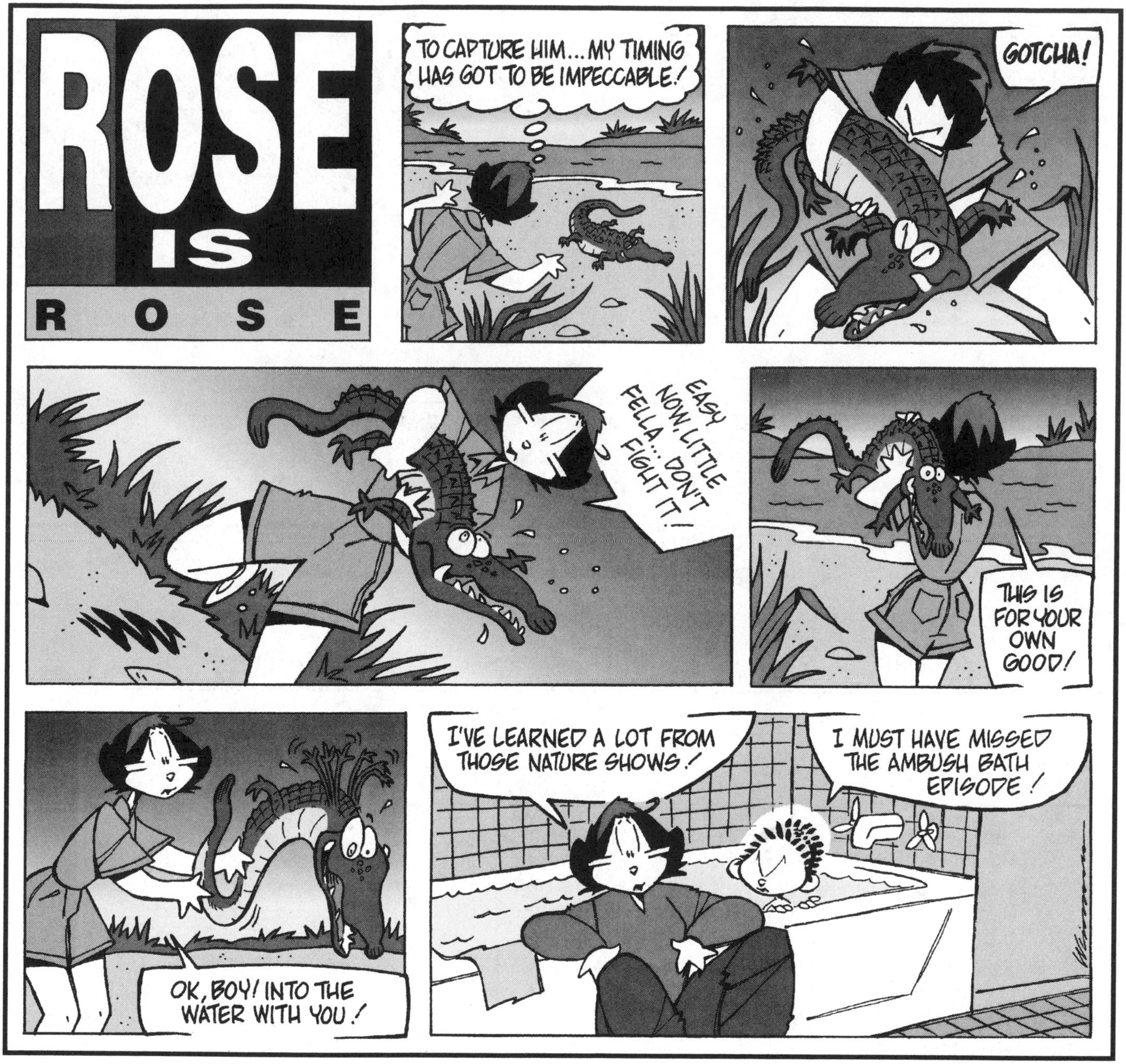
ROSE IS ROSE
TO CAPTURE HIM... MY TIMING HAS GOT TO BE IMPECCABLE!
GOTCHA!
EASY NOW, LITTLE FELLA... DON'T FIGHT IT!
THIS IS FOR YOUR OWN GOOD!
OK, BOY! INTO THE WATER WITH YOU!
I'VE LEARNED A LOT FROM THOSE NATURE SHOWS!
I MUST HAVE MISSED THE AMBUSH BATH EPISODE!

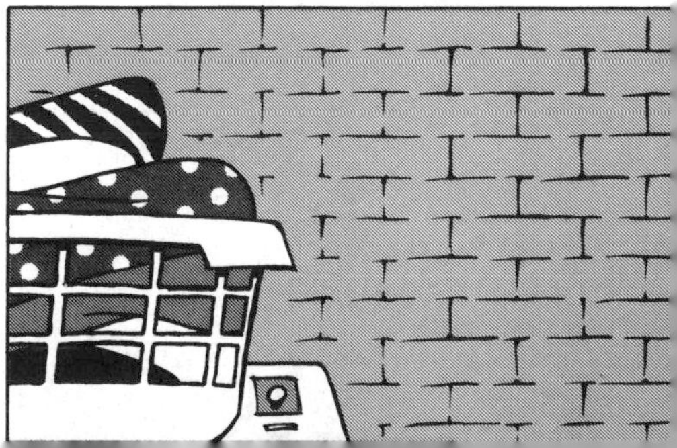

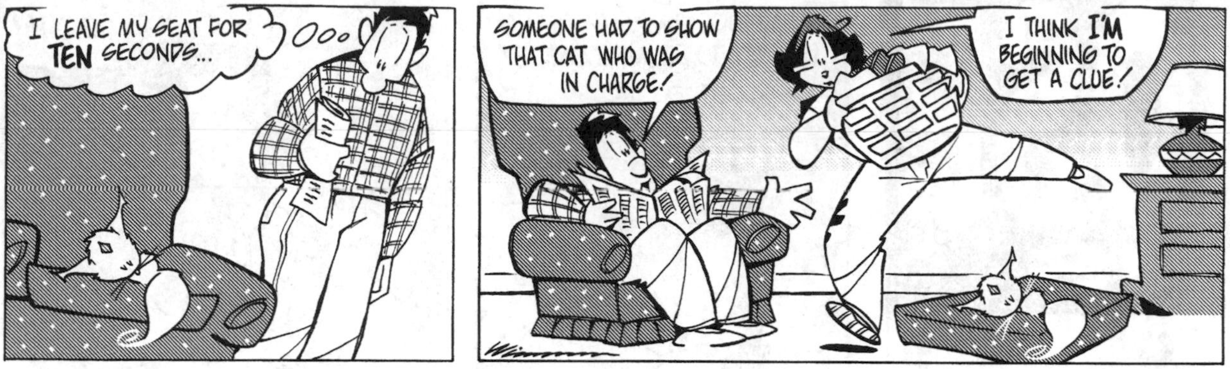
I LEAVE MY SEAT FOR TEN SECONDS...
SOMEONE HAD TO SHOW THAT CAT WHO WAS IN CHARGE!
I THINK I'M BEGINNING TO GET A CLUE!

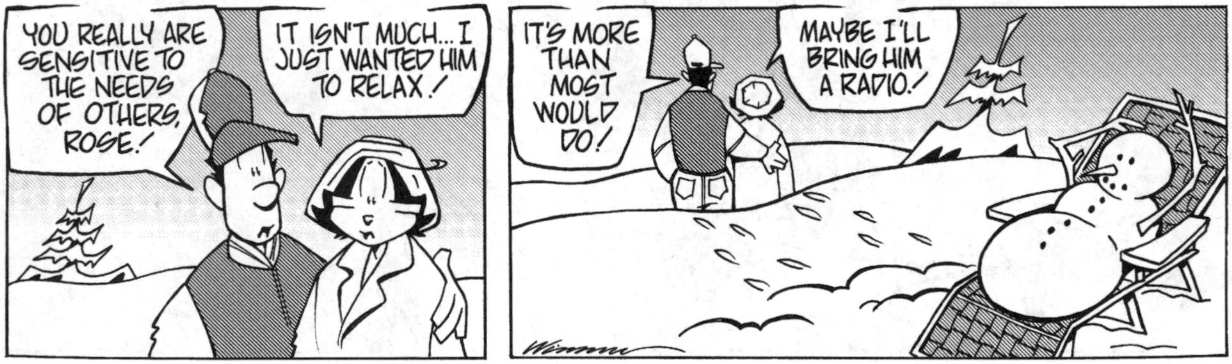
YOU REALLY ARE SENSITIVE TO THE NEEDS OF OTHERS, ROSE!
IT ISN'T MUCH... I JUST WANTED HIM TO RELAX!
IT'S MORE THAN MOST WOULD DO!
MAYBE I'LL BRING HIM A RADIO!

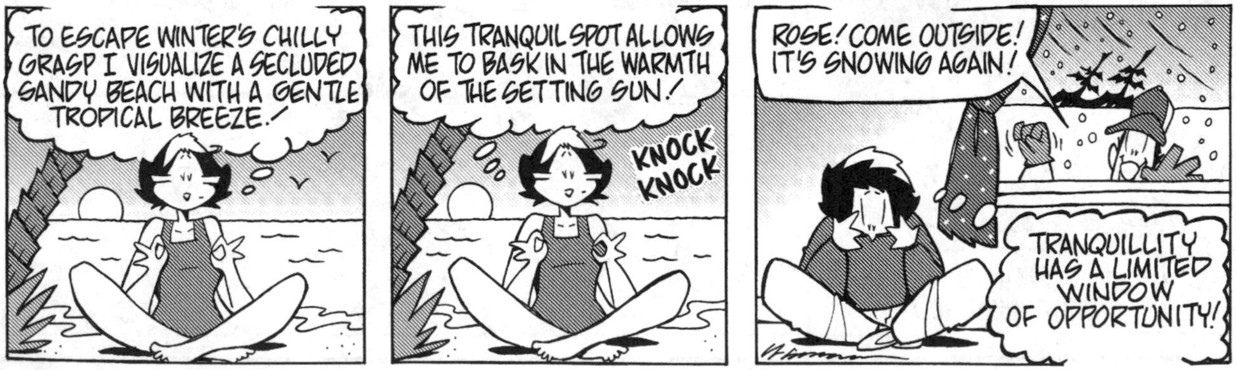
TO ESCAPE WINTER'S CHILLY GRASP I VISUALIZE A SECLUDED SANDY BEACH WITH A GENTLE TROPICAL BREEZE!
THIS TRANQUIL SPOT ALLOWS ME TO BASK IN THE WARMTH OF THE SETTING SUN!
KNOCK KNOCK
ROSE! COME OUTSIDE! IT'S SNOWING AGAIN!
TRANQUILLITY HAS A LIMITED WINDOW OF OPPORTUNITY!

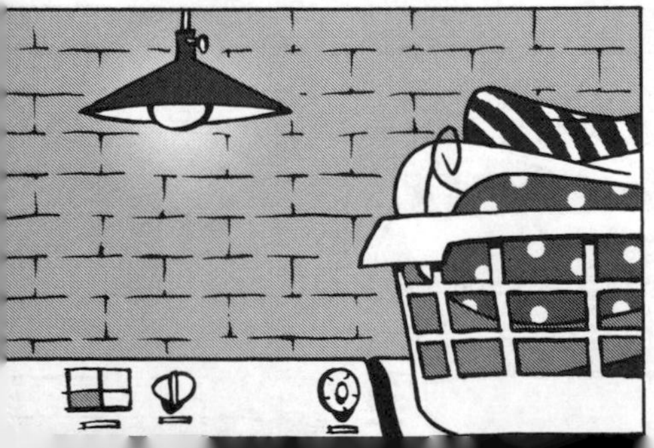

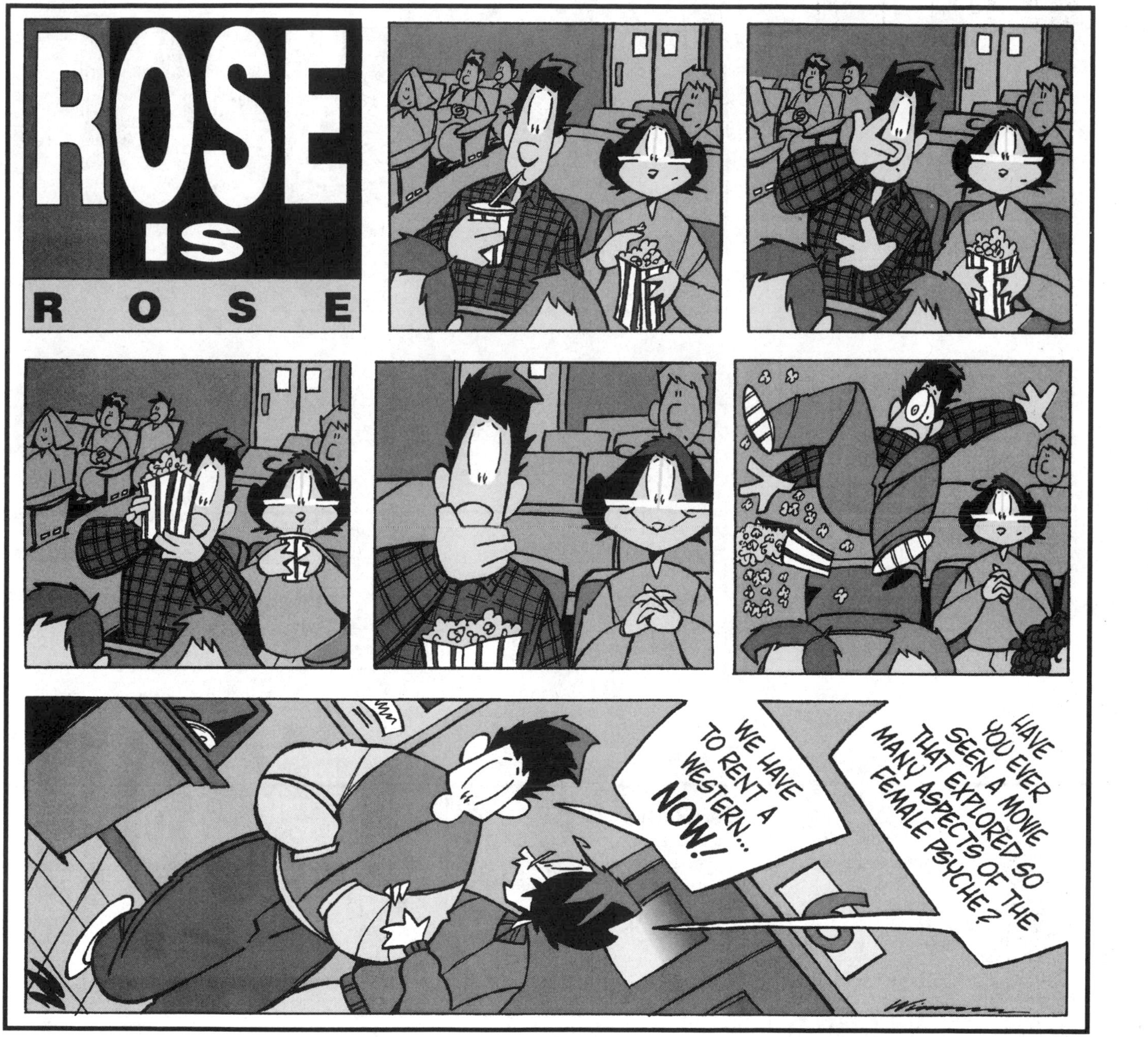
ROSE IS ROSE
HAVE YOU EVER SEEN A MOVIE THAT EXPLORED SO MANY ASPECTS OF THE FEMALE PSYCHE?
WE HAVE TO RENT A WESTERN... NOW!

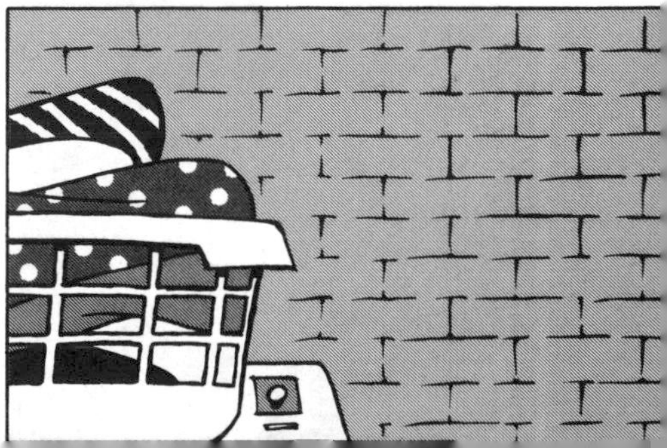

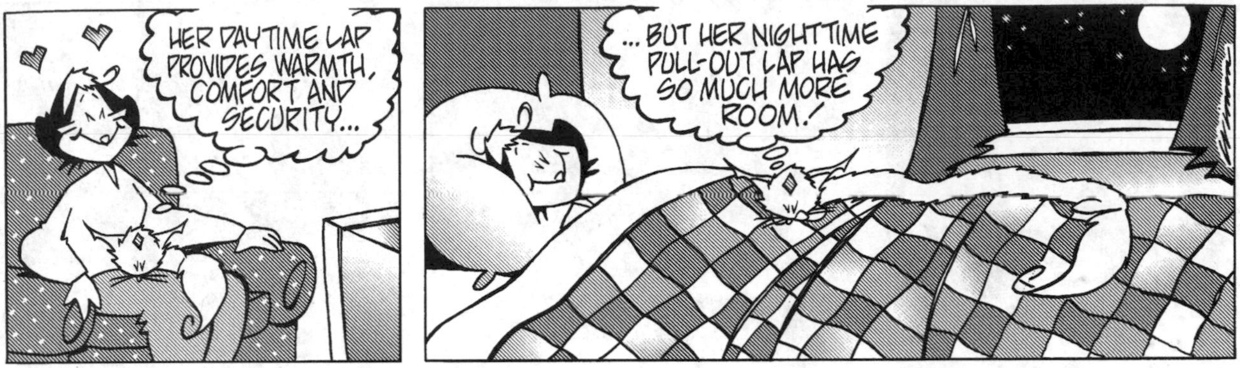
HER DAYTIME LAP PROVIDES WARMTH, COMFORT AND SECURITY...
... BUT HER NIGHTTIME PULL-OUT LAP HAS SO MUCH MORE ROOM!

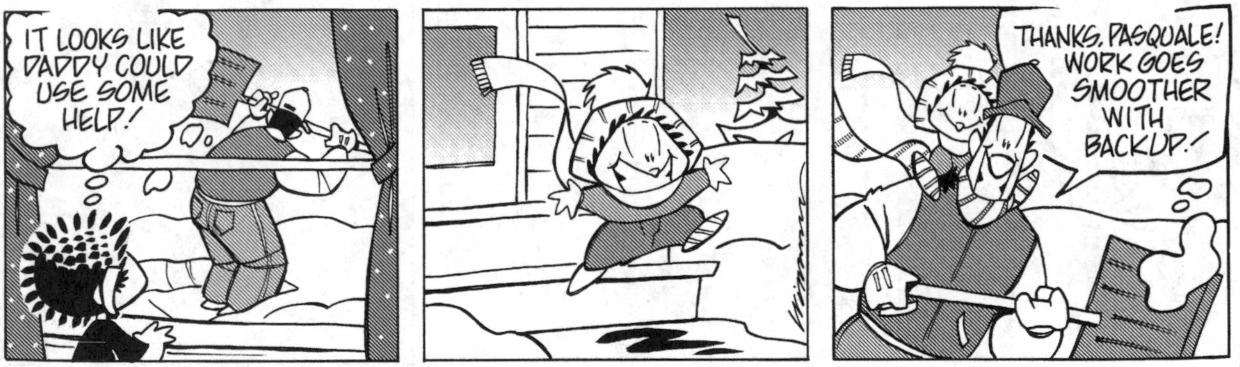
IT LOOKS LIKE DADDY COULD USE SOME HELP!
THANKS, PASQUALE! WORK GOES SMOOTHER WITH BACKUP!

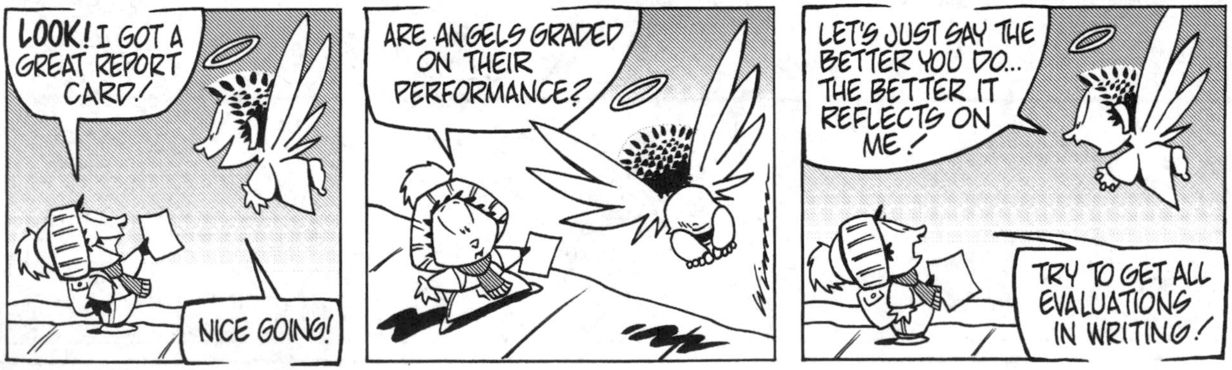
LOOK! I GOT A GREAT REPORT CARD!
NICE GOING!
ARE ANGELS GRADED ON THEIR PERFORMANCE?
LET'S JUST SAY THE BETTER YOU DO... THE BETTER IT REFLECTS ON ME!
TRY TO GET ALL EVALUATIONS IN WRITING!

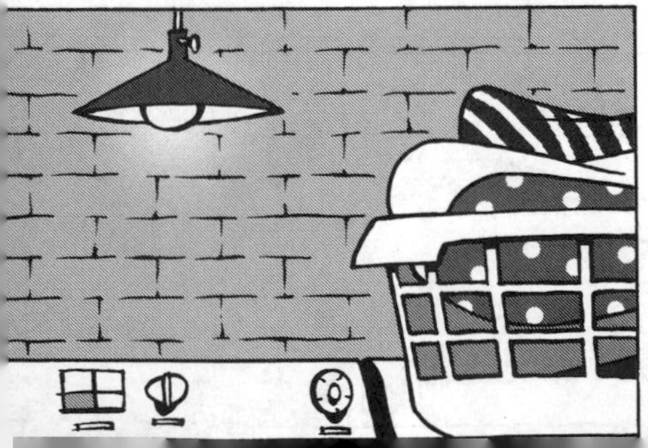

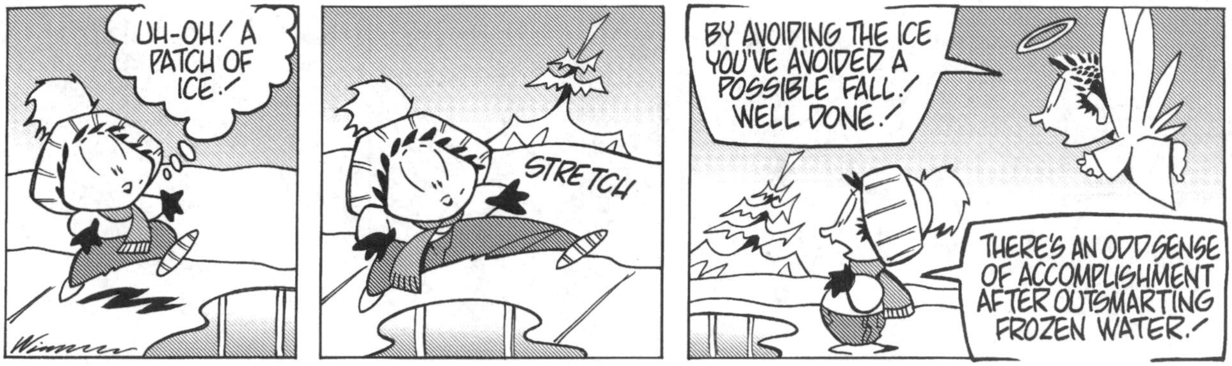
UH-OH! A PATCH OF ICE.!
STRETCH
BY AVOIDING THE ICE YOU'VE AVOIDED A POSSIBLE FALL! WELL DONE.!
THERE'S AN ODD SENSE OF ACCOMPLISHMENT AFTER OUTSMARTING FROZEN WATER.!

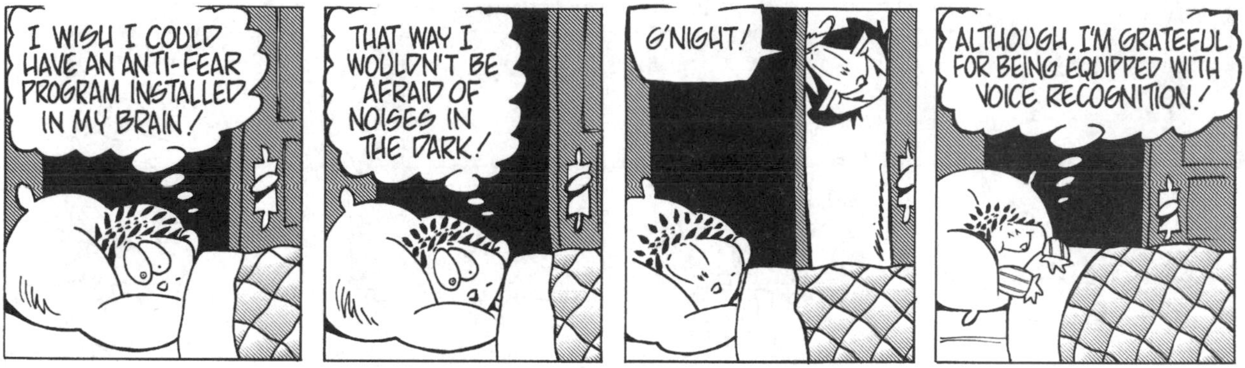
I WISH I COULD HAVE AN ANTI-FEAR PROGRAM INSTALLED IN MY BRAIN!
THAT WAY I WOULDN'T BE AFRAID OF NOISES IN THE DARK!
G'NIGHT!
ALTHOUGH, I'M GRATEFUL FOR BEING EQUIPPED WITH VOICE RECOGNITION!

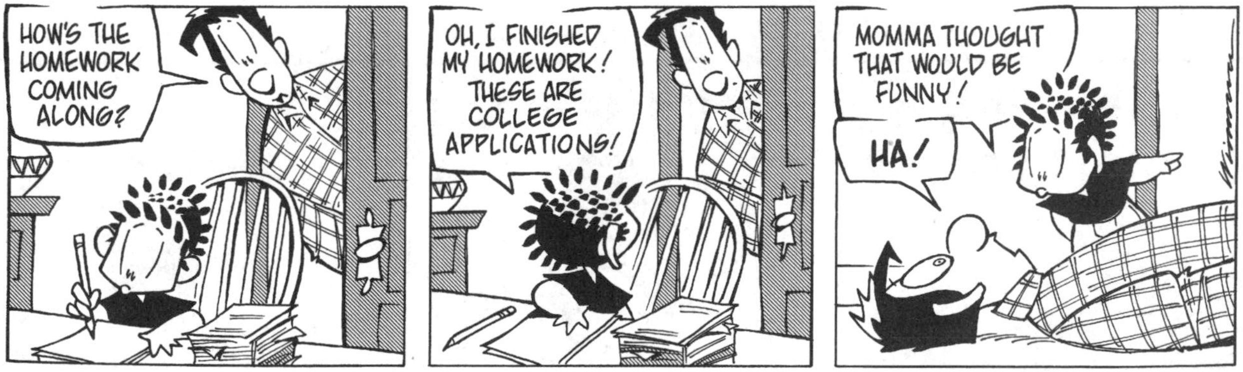
HOW'S THE HOMEWORK COMING ALONG?
OH, I FINISHED MY HOMEWORK! THESE ARE COLLEGE APPLICATIONS!
MOMMA THOUGHT THAT WOULD BE FUNNY!
HA!

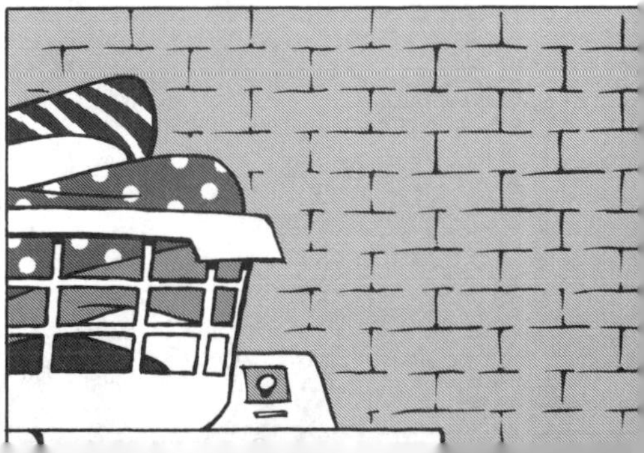

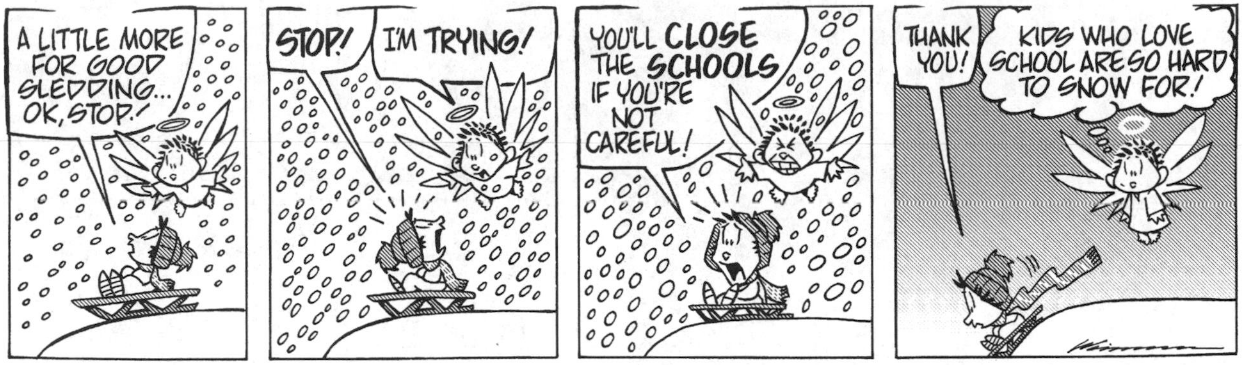
A LITTLE MORE FOR GOOD SLEDDING... OK, STOP!
STOP!
I'M TRYING!
YOU'LL CLOSE THE SCHOOLS IF YOU'RE NOT CAREFUL!
THANK YOU!
KIDS WHO LOVE SCHOOL ARE SO HARD TO SNOW FOR!

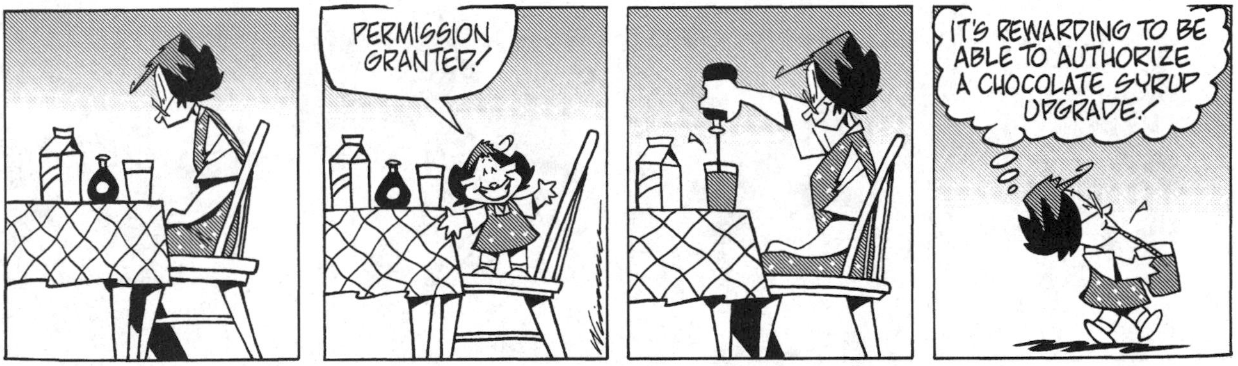
PERMISSION GRANTED!
IT'S REWARDING TO BE ABLE TO AUTHORIZE A CHOCOLATE SYRUP UPGRADE!

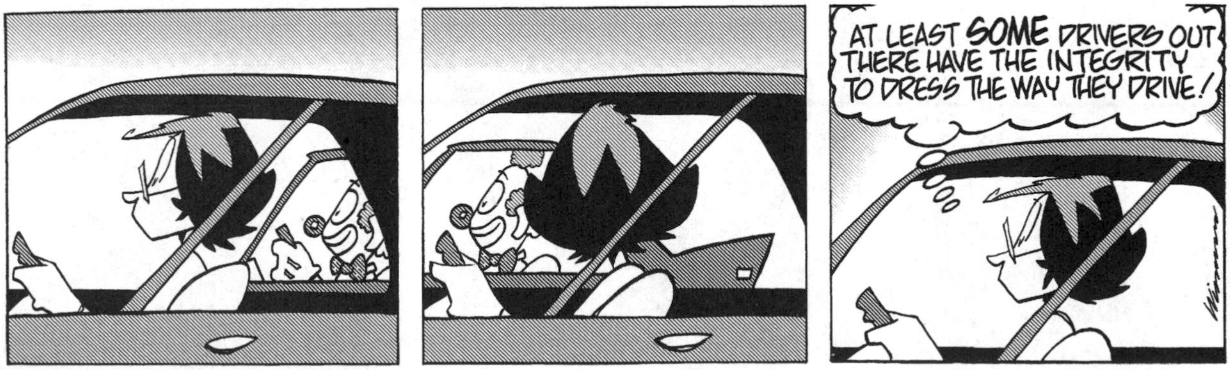
AT LEAST SOME DRIVERS OUT THERE HAVE THE INTEGRITY TO DRESS THE WAY THEY DRIVE!

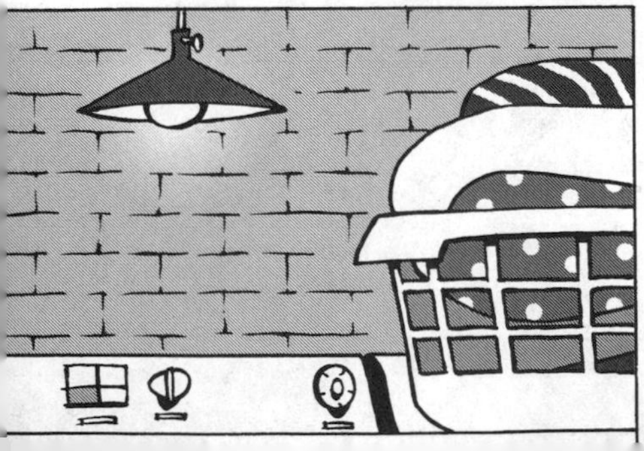

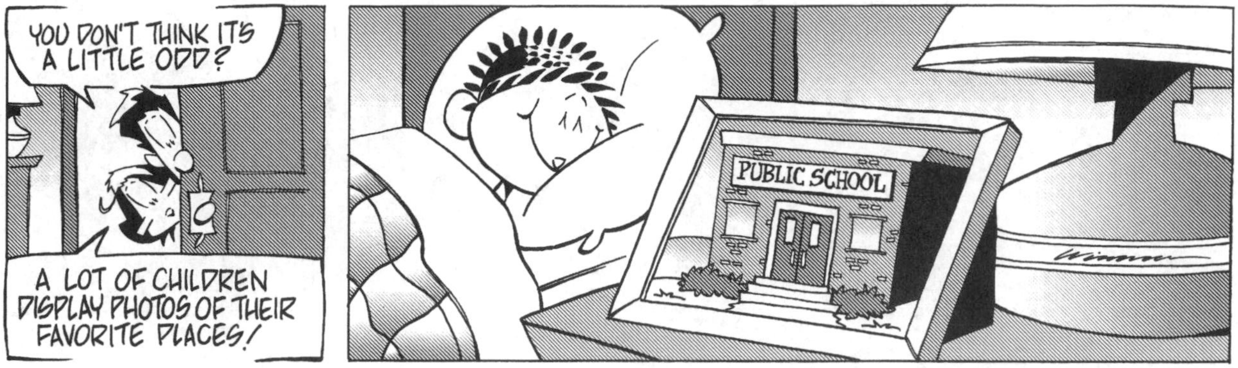
YOU DON'T THINK IT'S A LITTLE ODD?
A LOT OF CHILDREN DISPLAY PHOTOS OF THEIR FAVORITE PLACES!
PUBLIC SCHOOL

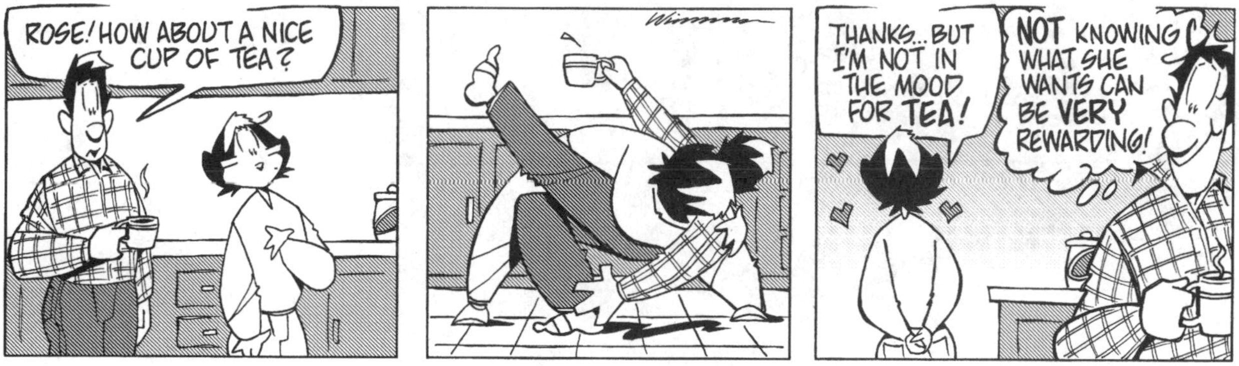
ROSE! HOW ABOUT A NICE CUP OF TEA?
THANKS... BUT I'M NOT IN THE MOOD FOR TEA!
NOT KNOWING WHAT SHE WANTS CAN BE VERY REWARDING!

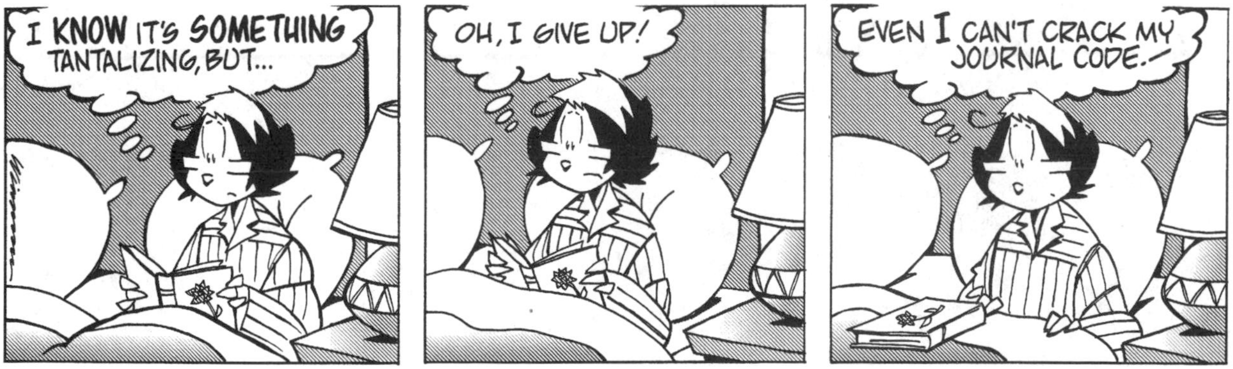
I KNOW IT'S SOMETHING TANTALIZING, BUT...
OH, I GIVE UP!
EVEN I CAN'T CRACK MY JOURNAL CODE.

FLIP THE PAGE CORNERS FROM FRONT TO BACK AND WATCH BOTH SIDES TOGETHER!

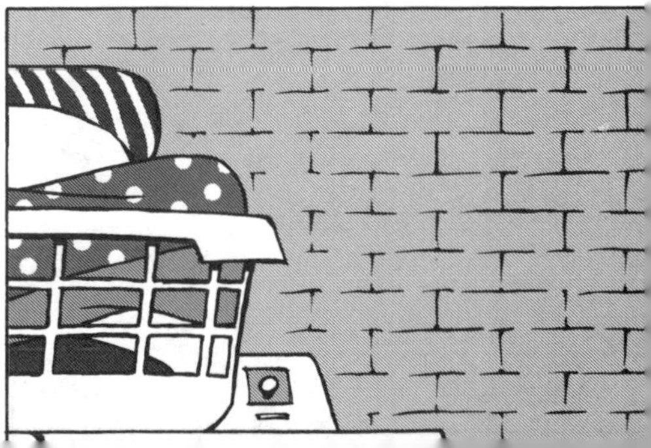

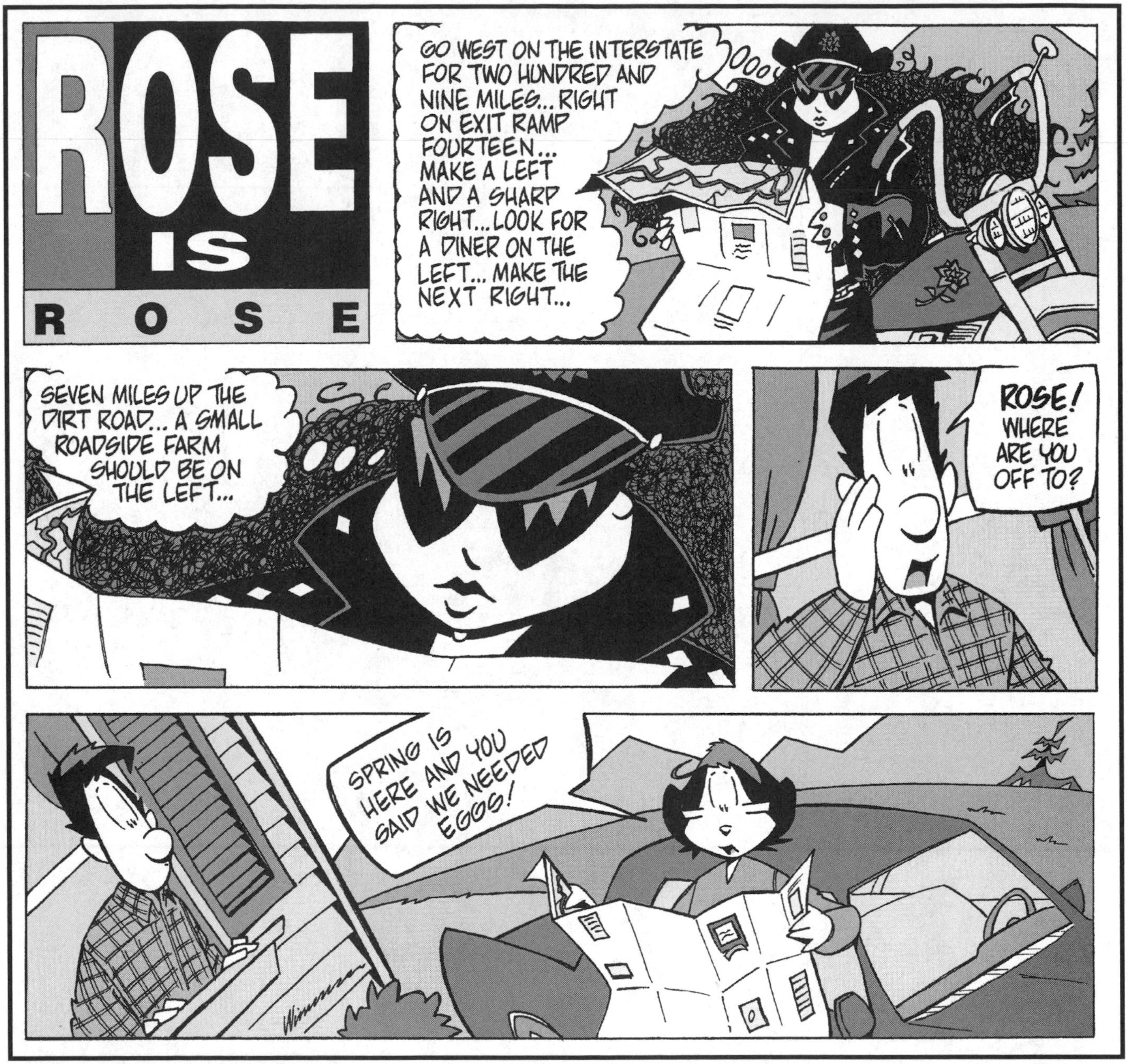
ROSE IS ROSE
GO WEST ON THE INTERSTATE FOR TWO HUNDRED AND NINE MILES... RIGHT ON EXIT RAMP FOURTEEN... MAKE A LEFT AND A SHARP RIGHT... LOOK FOR A DINER ON THE LEFT... MAKE THE NEXT RIGHT...
SEVEN MILES UP THE DIRT ROAD... A SMALL ROADSIDE FARM SHOULD BE ON THE LEFT...
ROSE! WHERE ARE YOU OFF TO?
SPRING IS HERE AND YOU SAID WE NEEDED EGGS!

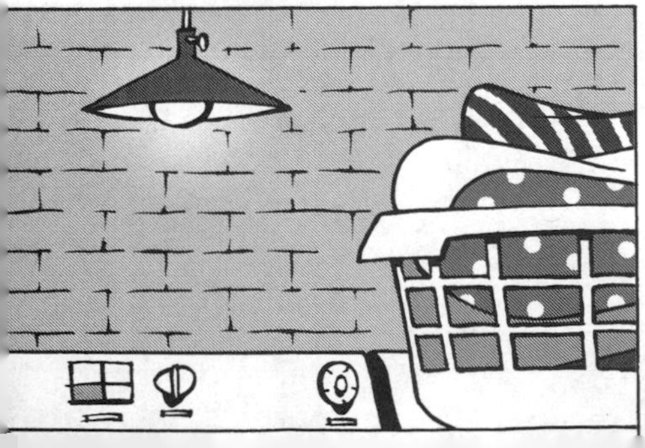

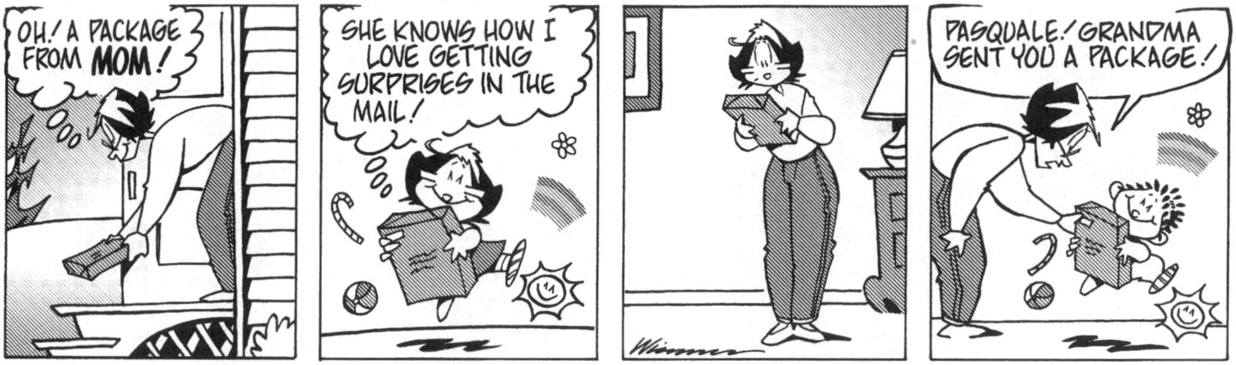
OH! A PACKAGE FROM MOM!
SHE KNOWS HOW I LOVE GETTING SURPRISES IN THE MAIL!
PASQUALE! GRANDMA SENT YOU A PACKAGE!

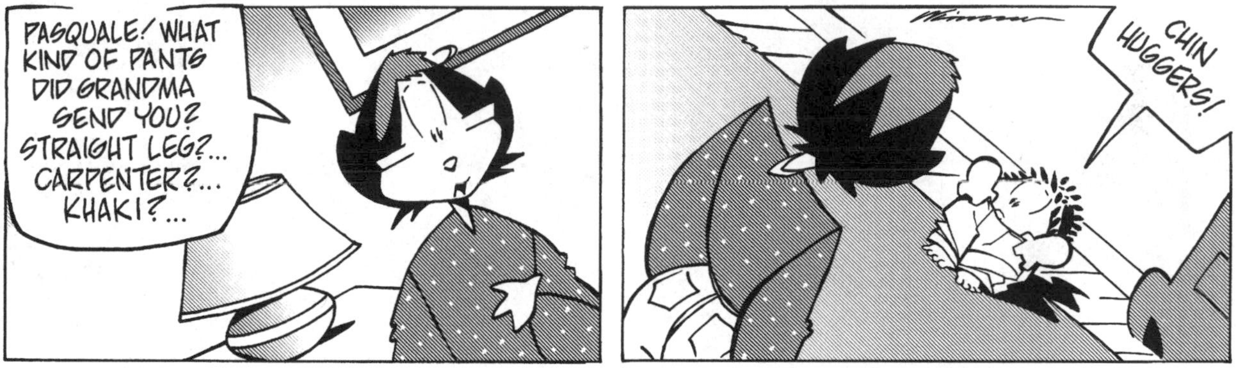
PASQUALE! WHAT KIND OF PANTS DID GRANDMA SEND YOU? STRAIGHT LEG?... CARPENTER?... KHAKI?...
CHIN HUGGERS!

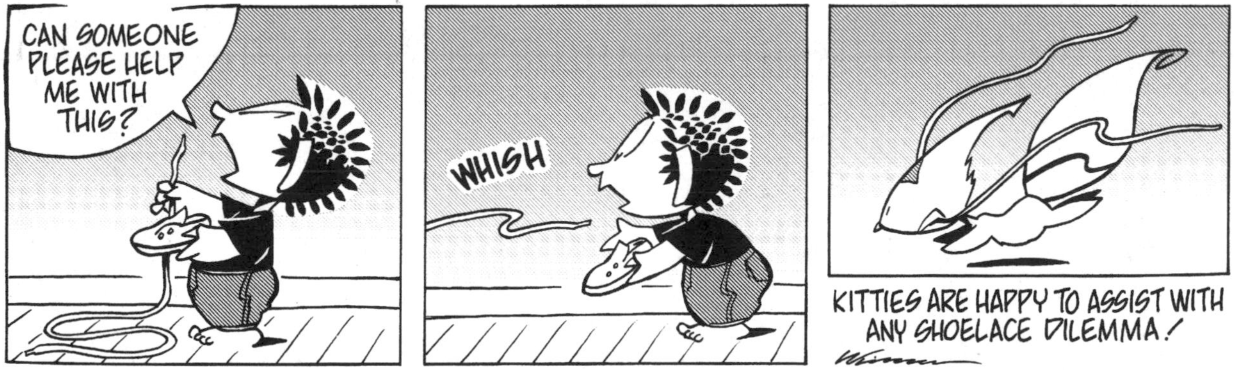
CAN SOMEONE PLEASE HELP ME WITH THIS?
WHISH
KITTIES ARE HAPPY TO ASSIST WITH ANY SHOELACE DILEMMA!

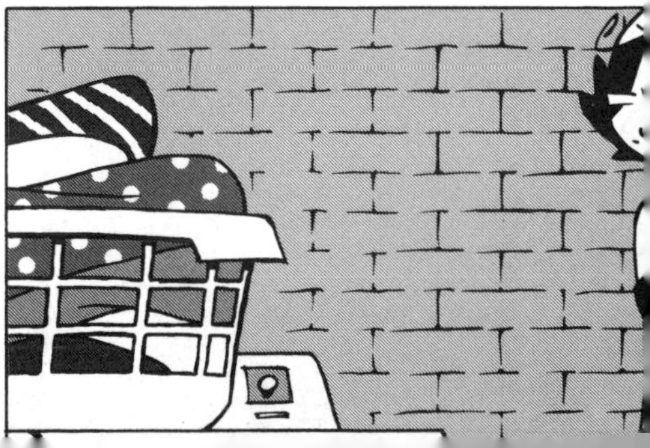

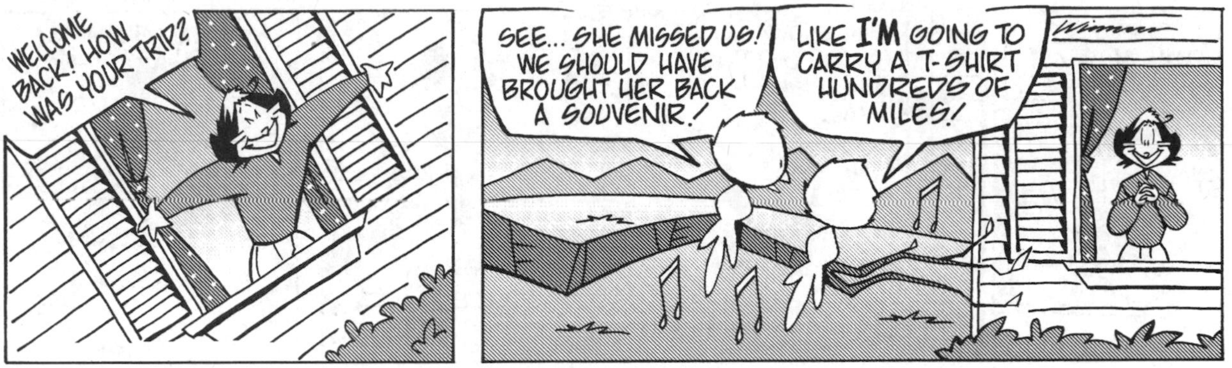
WELCOME BACK! HOW WAS YOUR TRIP?
SEE... SHE MISSED US! WE SHOULD HAVE BROUGHT HER BACK A SOUVENIR!
LIKE I'M GOING TO CARRY A T-SHIRT HUNDREDS OF MILES!

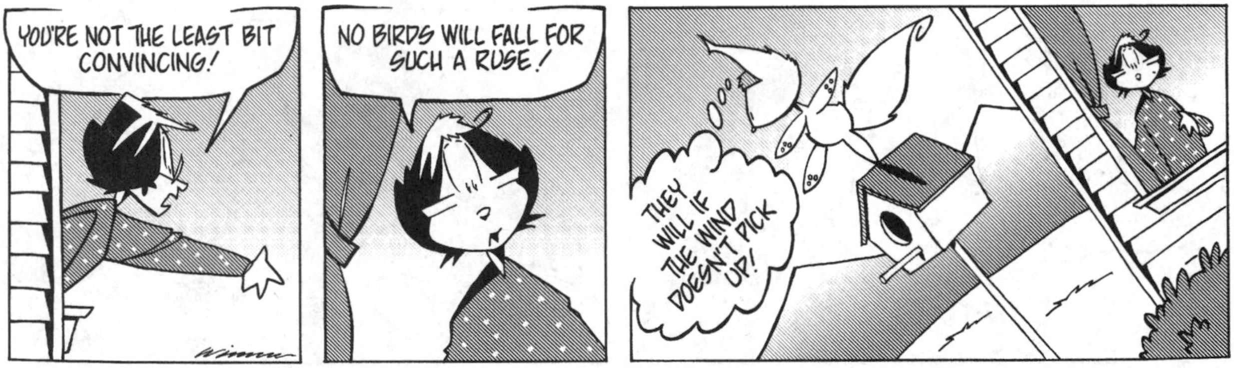
YOU'RE NOT THE LEAST BIT CONVINCING!
NO BIRDS WILL FALL FOR SUCH A RUSE!
THEY WILL IF THE WIND DOESN'T PICK UP!

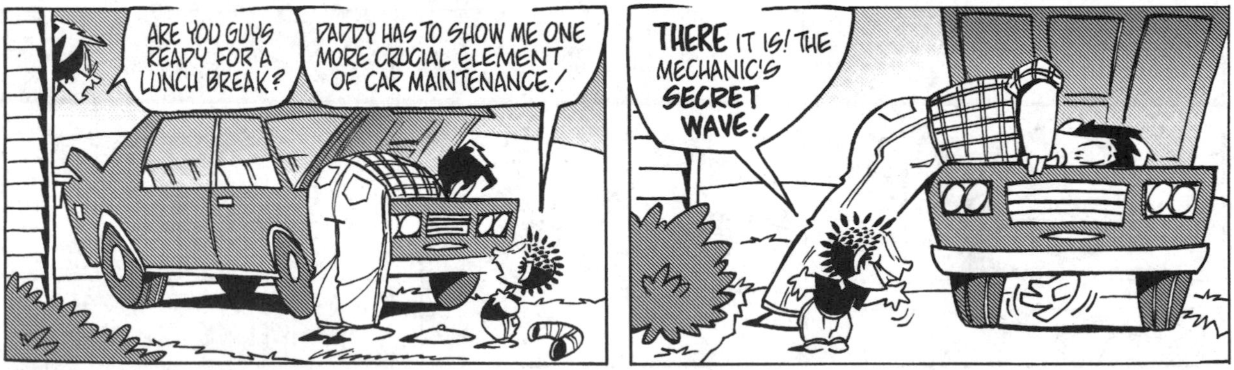
ARE YOU GUYS READY FOR A LUNCH BREAK?
DADDY HAS TO SHOW ME ONE MORE CRUCIAL ELEMENT OF CAR MAINTENANCE!
THERE IT IS! THE MECHANIC'S SECRET WAVE!

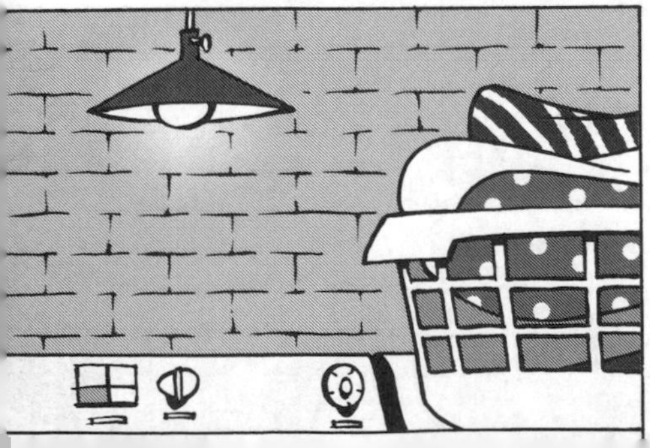

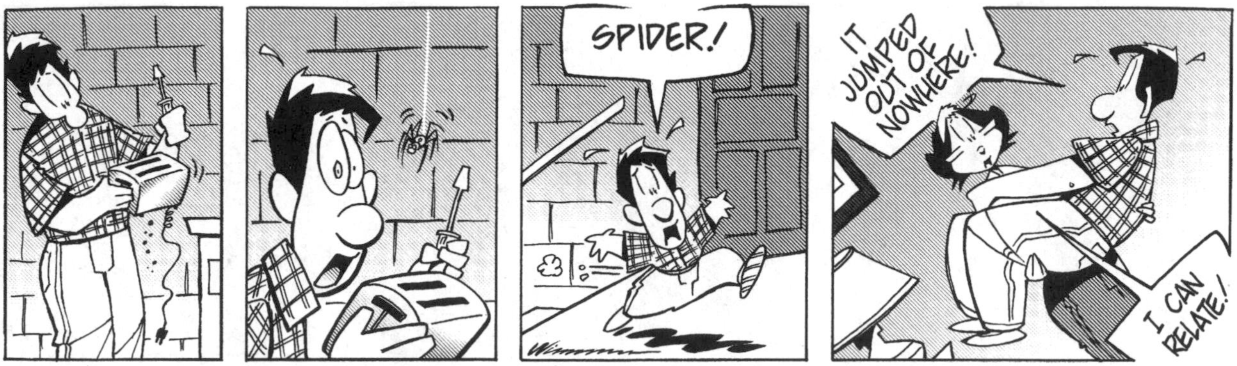
SPIDER!
IT JUMPED OUT OF NOWHERE!
I CAN RELATE!

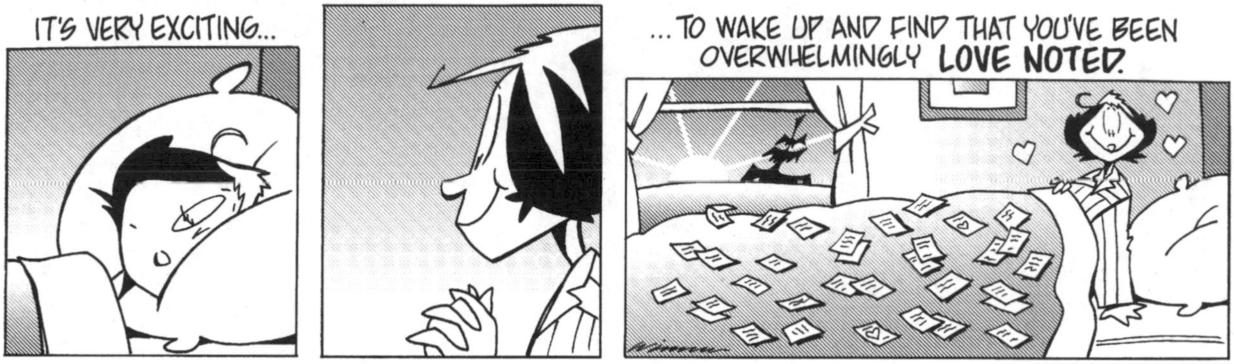
IT'S VERY EXCITING...
...TO WAKE UP AND FIND THAT YOU'VE BEEN OVERWHELMINGLY LOVE NOTED.

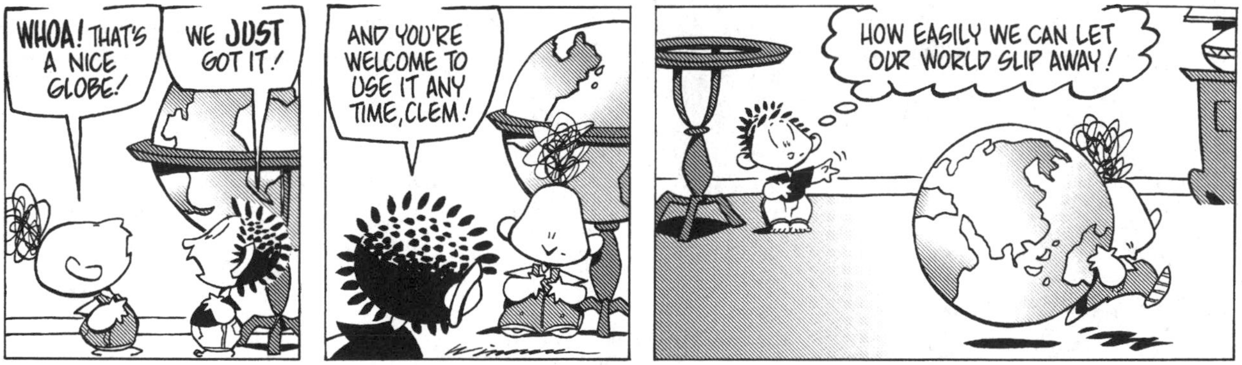
WHOA! THAT'S A NICE GLOBE!
WE JUST GOT IT!
AND YOU'RE WELCOME TO USE IT ANY TIME, CLEM!
HOW EASILY WE CAN LET OUR WORLD SLIP AWAY!

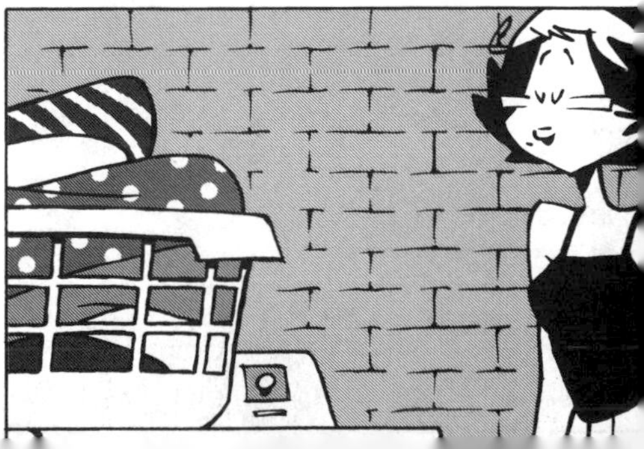

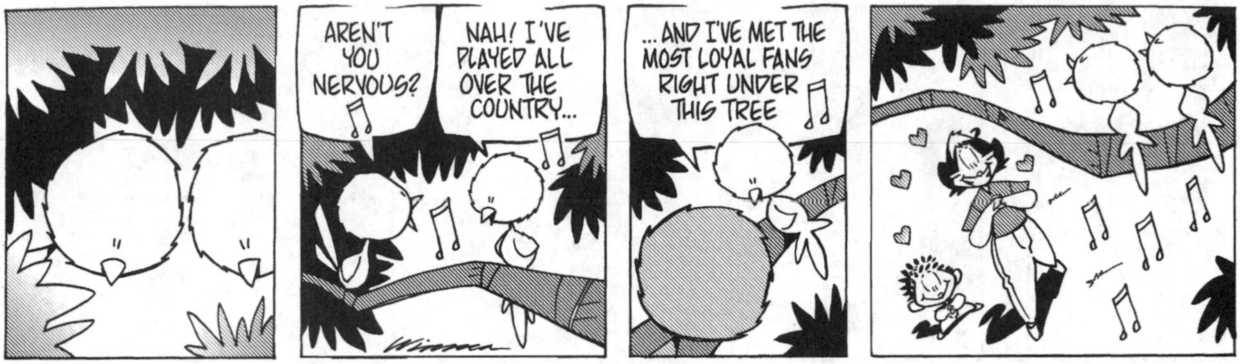
AREN'T YOU NERVOUS?
NAH! I'VE PLAYED ALL OVER THE COUNTRY...
...AND I'VE MET THE MOST LOYAL FANS RIGHT UNDER THIS TREE

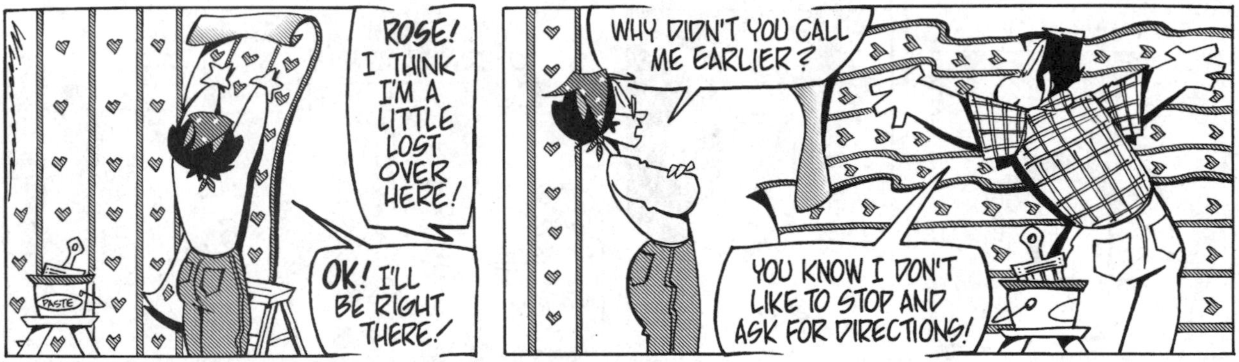
ROSE! I THINK I'M A LITTLE LOST OVER HERE!
OK! I'LL BE RIGHT THERE!
PASTE
WHY DIDN'T YOU CALL ME EARLIER?
YOU KNOW I DON'T LIKE TO STOP AND ASK FOR DIRECTIONS!

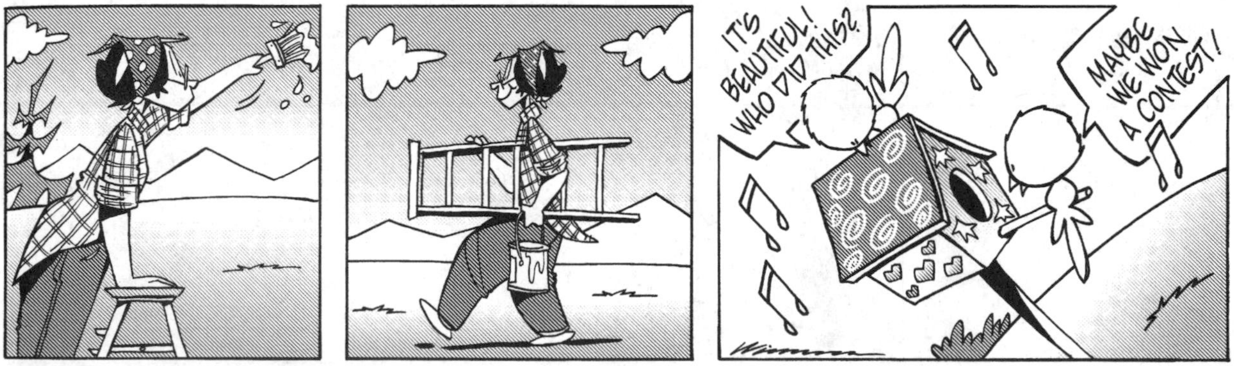
IT'S BEAUTIFUL! WHO DID THIS?
MAYBE WE WON A CONTEST!

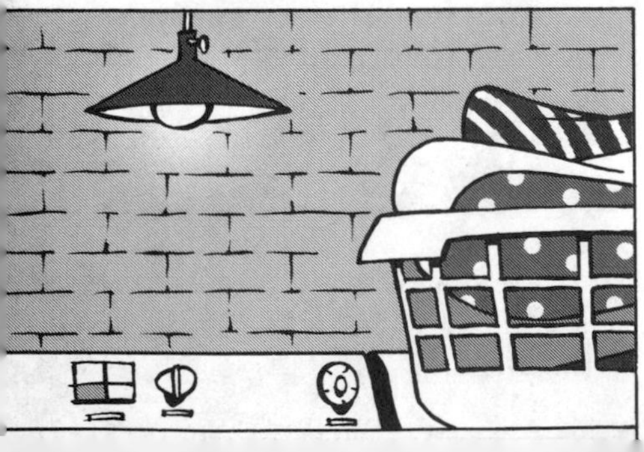

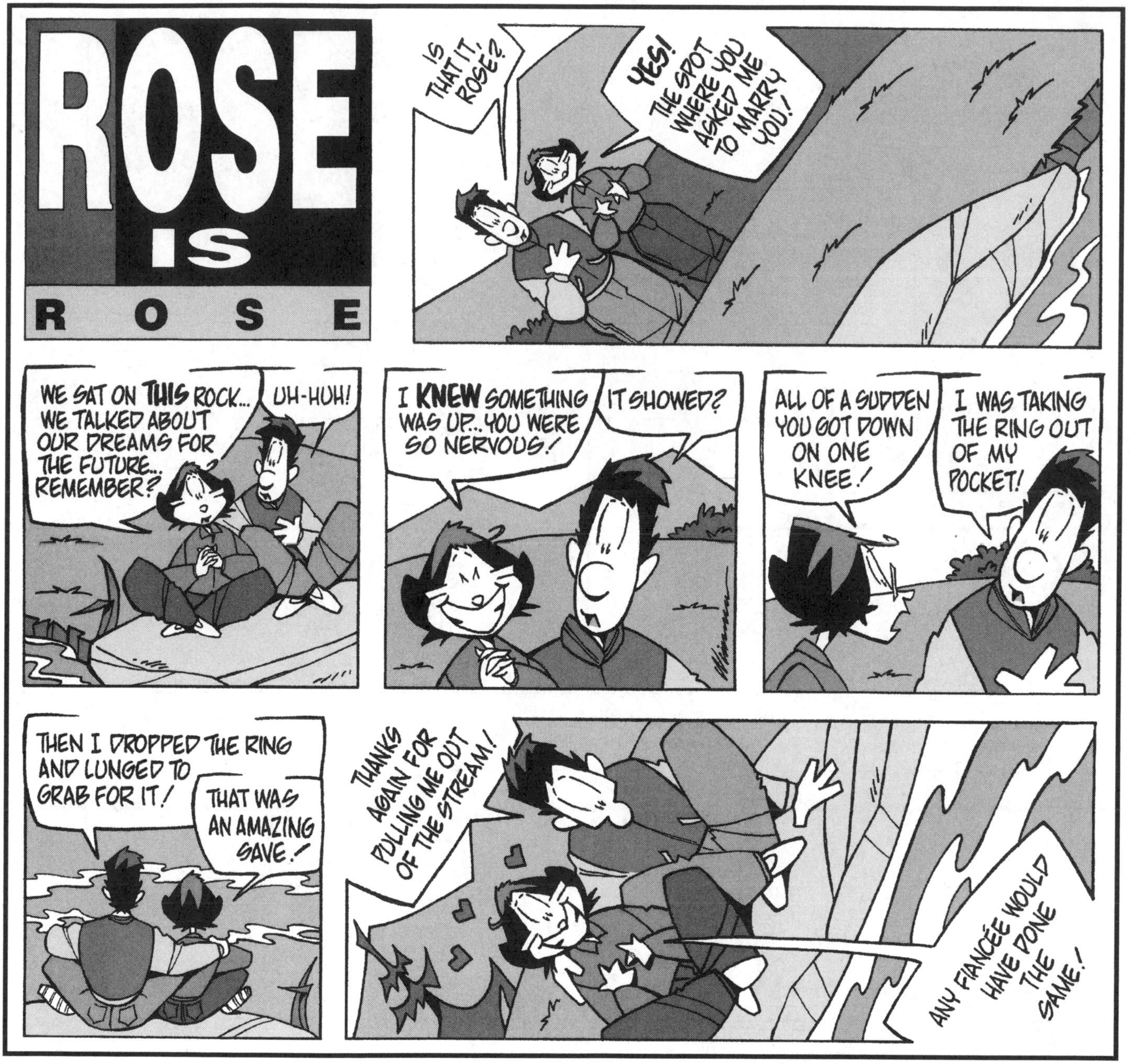
ROSE IS ROSE
IS THAT IT, ROSE?
YES! THE SPOT WHERE YOU ASKED ME TO MARRY YOU!
WE SAT ON THIS ROCK... WE TALKED ABOUT OUR DREAMS FOR THE FUTURE... REMEMBER?
UH-HUH!
I KNEW SOMETHING WAS UP... YOU WERE SO NERVOUS!
IT SHOWED?
ALL OF A SUDDEN YOU GOT DOWN ON ONE KNEE!
I WAS TAKING THE RING OUT OF MY POCKET!
THEN I DROPPED THE RING AND LUNGED TO GRAB FOR IT!
THAT WAS AN AMAZING SAVE!
THANKS AGAIN FOR PULLING ME OUT OF THE STREAM!
ANY FIANCÉE WOULD HAVE DONE THE SAME!

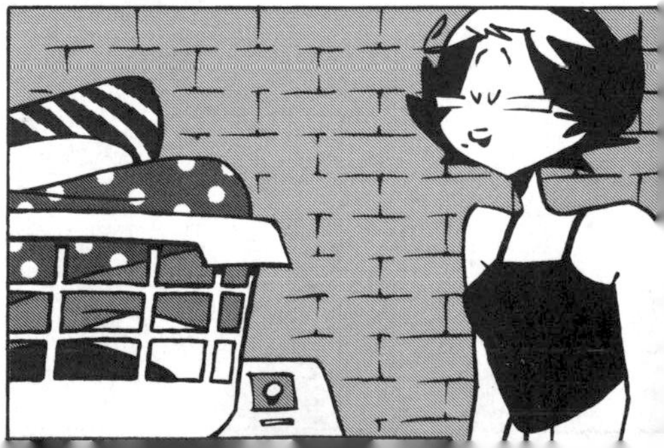

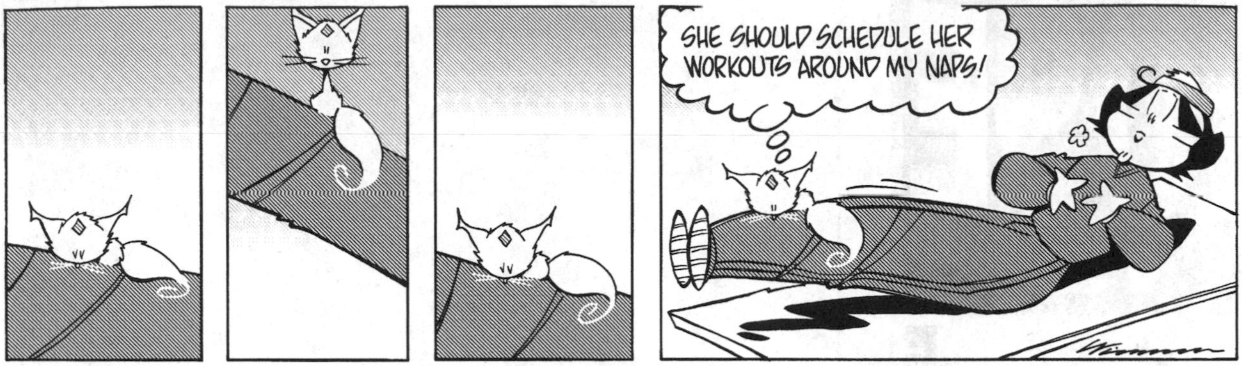
SHE SHOULD SCHEDULE HER WORKOUTS AROUND MY NAPS!

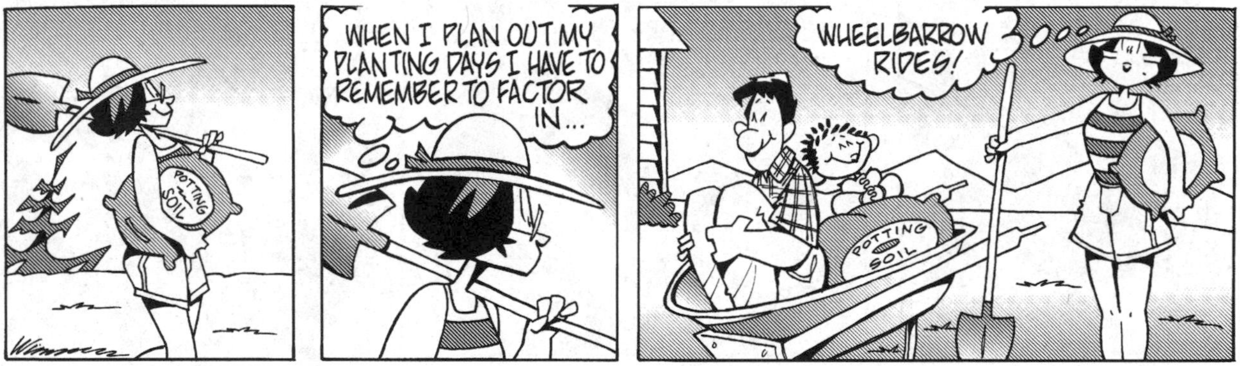
POTTING SOIL
WHEN I PLAN OUT MY PLANTING DAYS I HAVE TO REMEMBER TO FACTOR IN...
WHEELBARROW RIDES!
POTTING SOIL

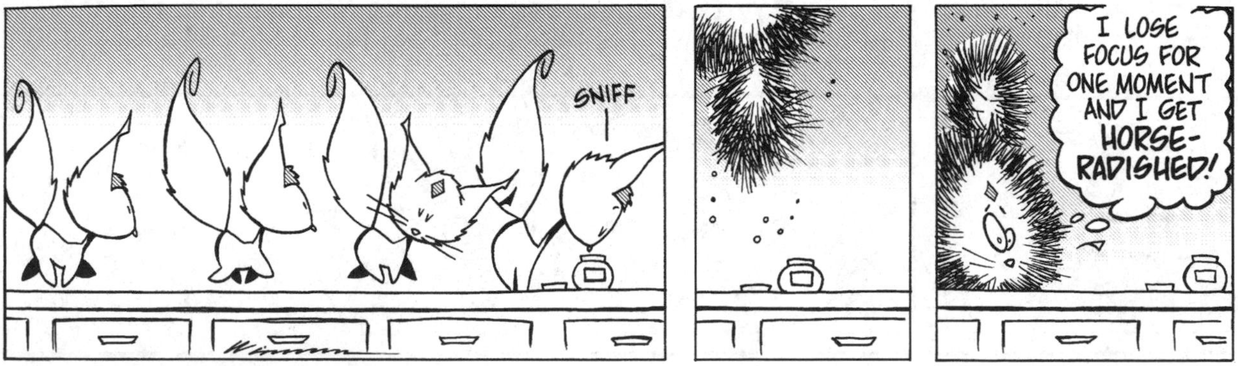
SNIFF
I LOSE FOCUS FOR ONE MOMENT AND I GET HORSE-RADISHED!

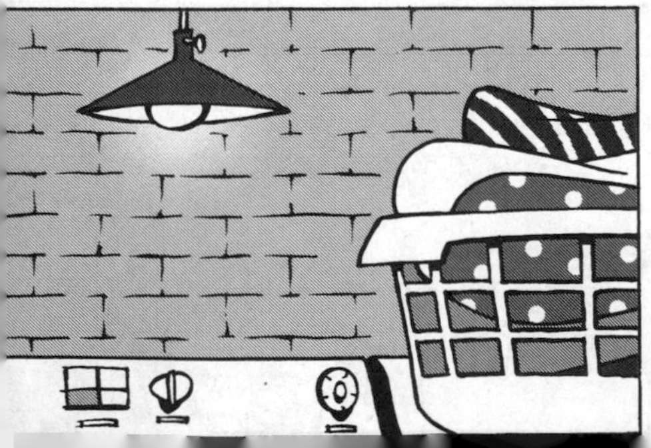

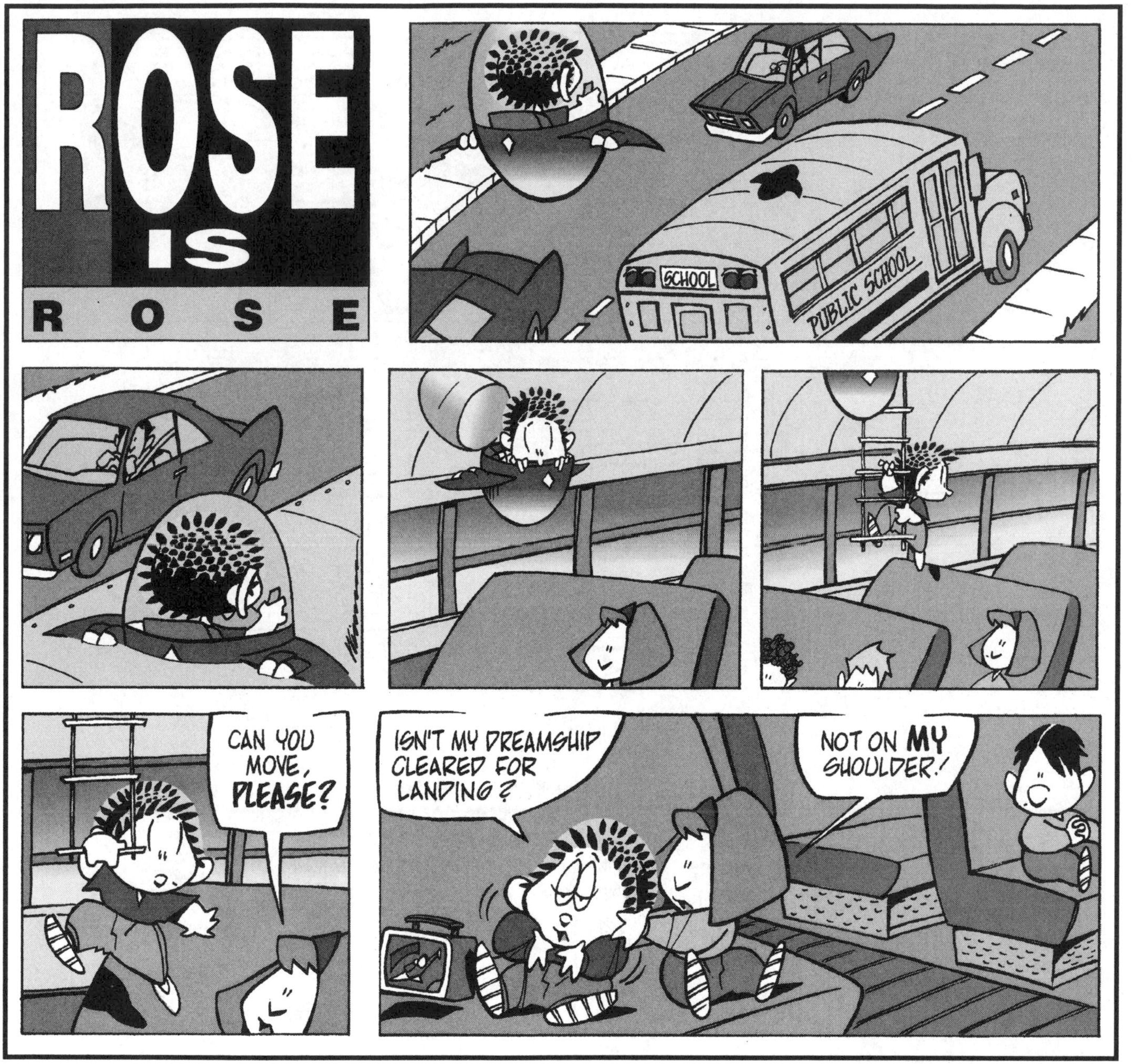
ROSE IS ROSE
SCHOOL
PUBLIC SCHOOL
CAN YOU MOVE, PLEASE?
ISN'T MY DREAMSHIP CLEARED FOR LANDING?
NOT ON MY SHOULDER!

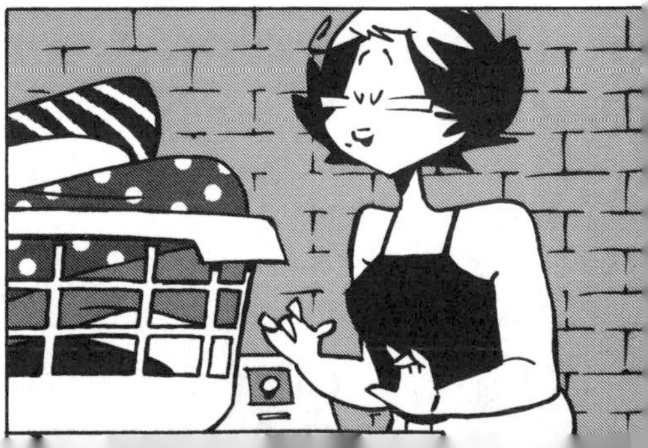

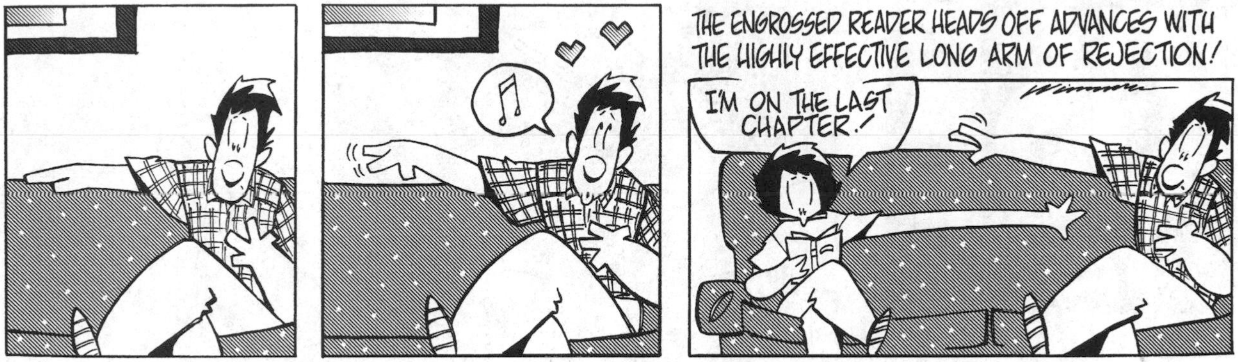
THE ENGROSSED READER HEADS OFF ADVANCES WITH THE HIGHLY EFFECTIVE LONG ARM OF REJECTION!
I'M ON THE LAST CHAPTER.!

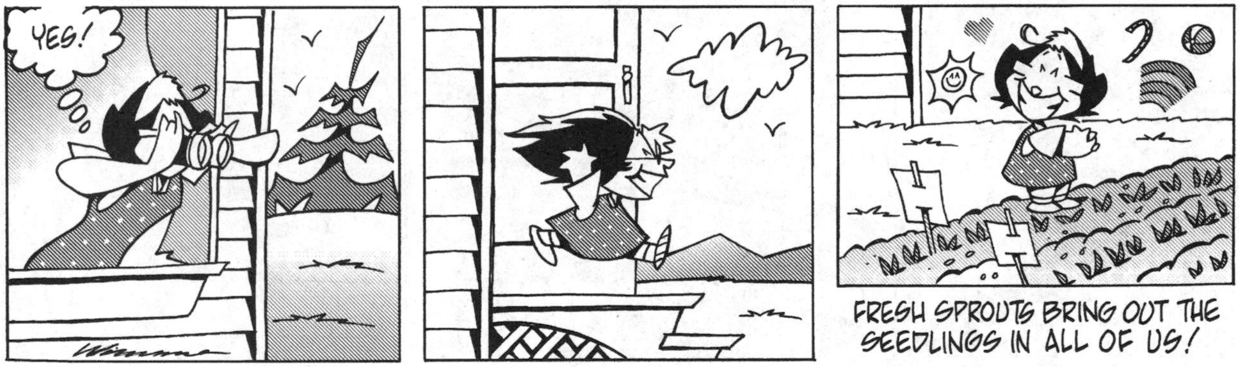
YES!
FRESH SPROUTS BRING OUT THE SEEDLINGS IN ALL OF US!

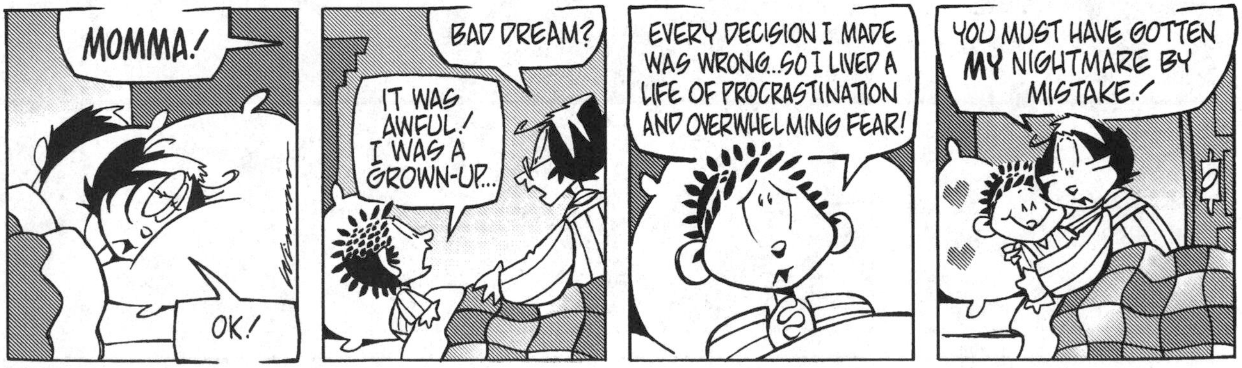
MOMMA!
OK!
BAD DREAM?
IT WAS AWFUL! I WAS A GROWN-UP...
EVERY DECISION I MADE WAS WRONG...SO I LIVED A LIFE OF PROCRASTINATION AND OVERWHELMING FEAR!
YOU MUST HAVE GOTTEN MY NIGHTMARE BY MISTAKE!

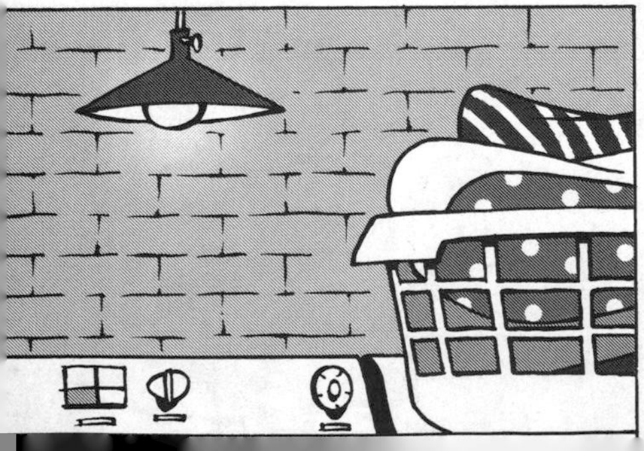

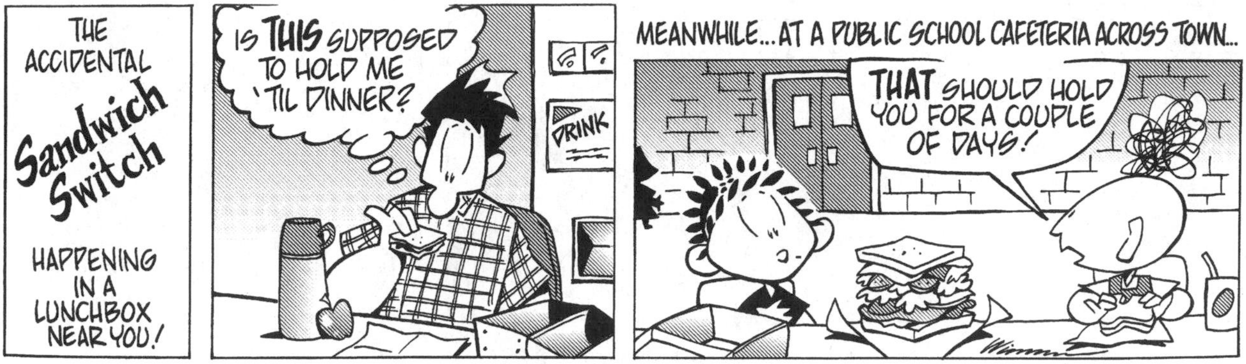
THE ACCIDENTAL
Sandwich Switch
HAPPENING IN A LUNCHBOX NEAR YOU!
IS THIS SUPPOSED TO HOLD ME 'TIL DINNER?
DRINK
MEANWHILE... AT A PUBLIC SCHOOL CAFETERIA ACROSS TOWN...
THAT SHOULD HOLD YOU FOR A COUPLE OF DAYS!

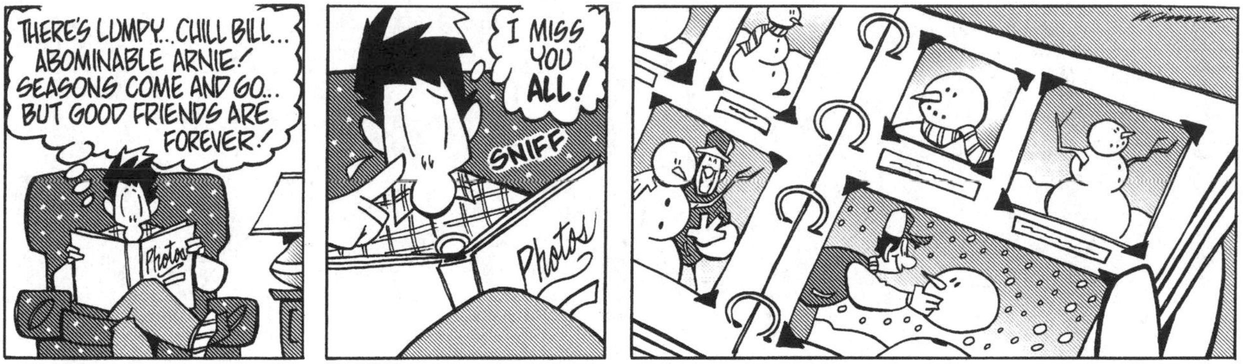
THERE'S LUMPY... CHILL BILL... ABOMINABLE ARNIE! SEASONS COME AND GO... BUT GOOD FRIENDS ARE FOREVER!
Photos
I MISS YOU ALL!
SNIFF
Photos

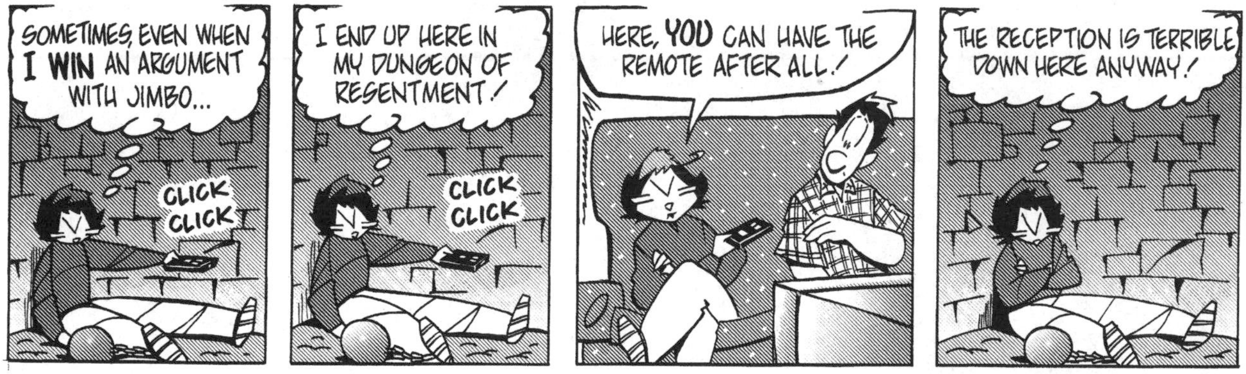
SOMETIMES, EVEN WHEN I WIN AN ARGUMENT WITH JIMBO...
CLICK CLICK
I END UP HERE IN MY DUNGEON OF RESENTMENT!
CLICK CLICK
HERE, YOU CAN HAVE THE REMOTE AFTER ALL!
THE RECEPTION IS TERRIBLE DOWN HERE ANYWAY!

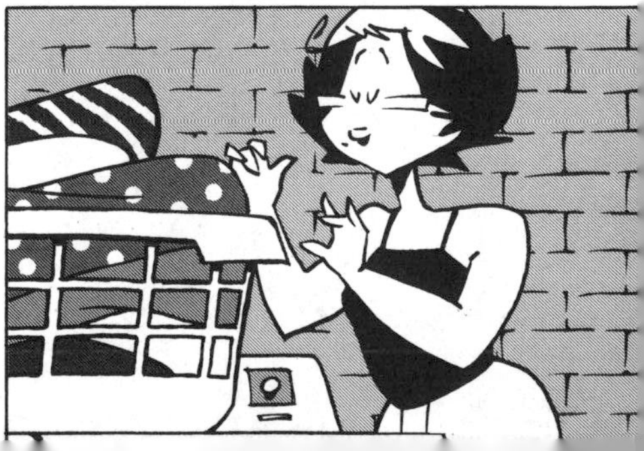

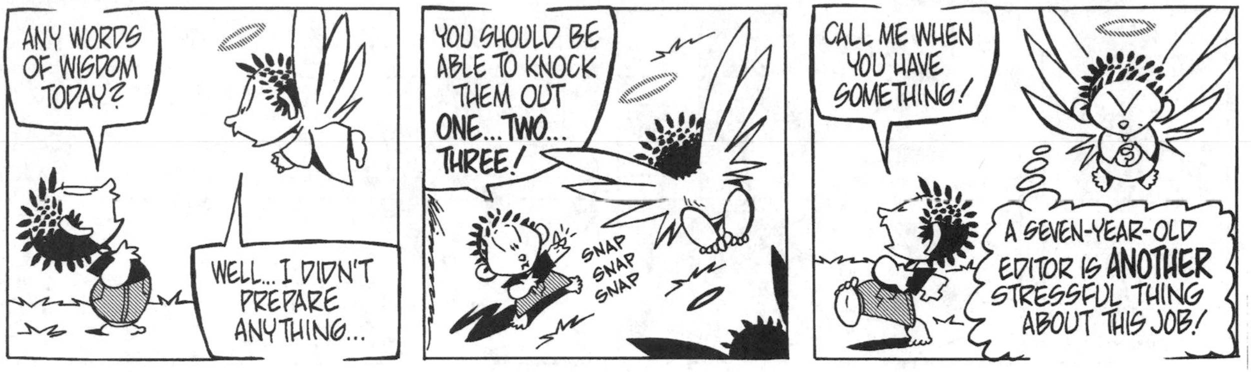
ANY WORDS OF WISDOM TODAY?
WELL... I DIDN'T PREPARE ANYTHING...
YOU SHOULD BE ABLE TO KNOCK THEM OUT ONE... TWO... THREE!
SNAP SNAP SNAP
CALL ME WHEN YOU HAVE SOMETHING!
A SEVEN-YEAR-OLD EDITOR IS ANOTHER STRESSFUL THING ABOUT THIS JOB!

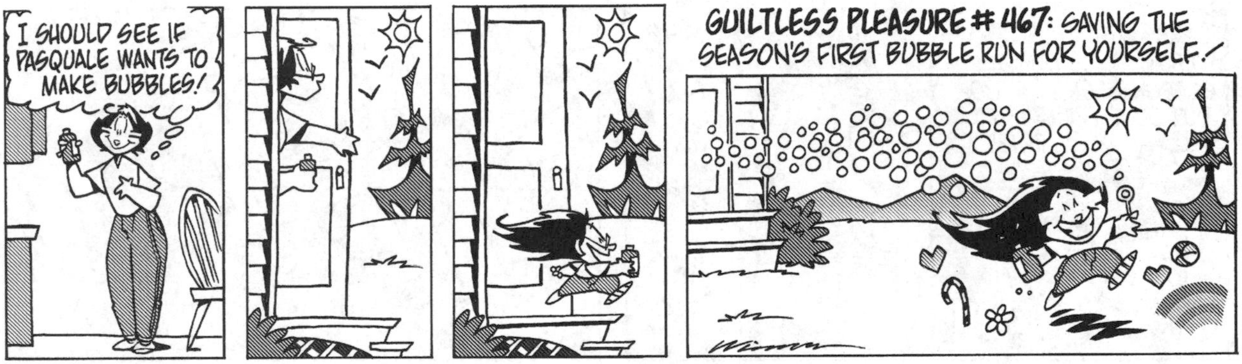
I SHOULD SEE IF PASQUALE WANTS TO MAKE BUBBLES!
GUILTLESS PLEASURE # 467: SAVING THE SEASON'S FIRST BUBBLE RUN FOR YOURSELF!

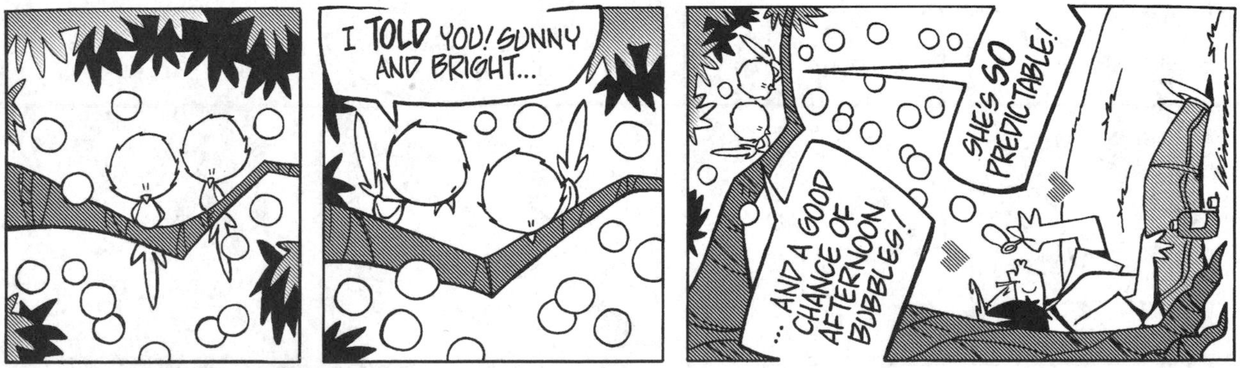
I TOLD YOU! SUNNY AND BRIGHT...
... AND A GOOD CHANCE OF AFTERNOON BUBBLES!
SHE'S SO PREDICTABLE!

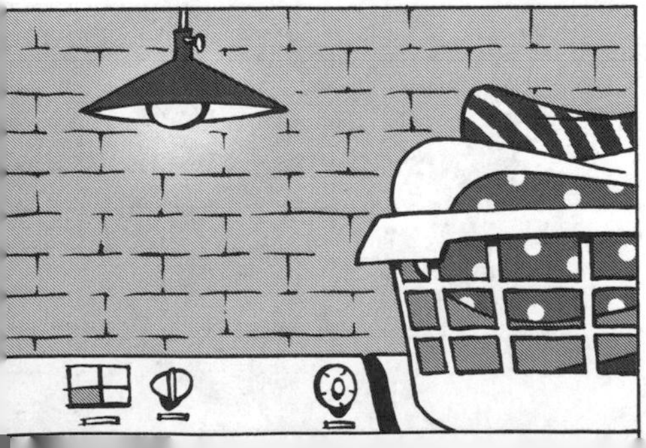

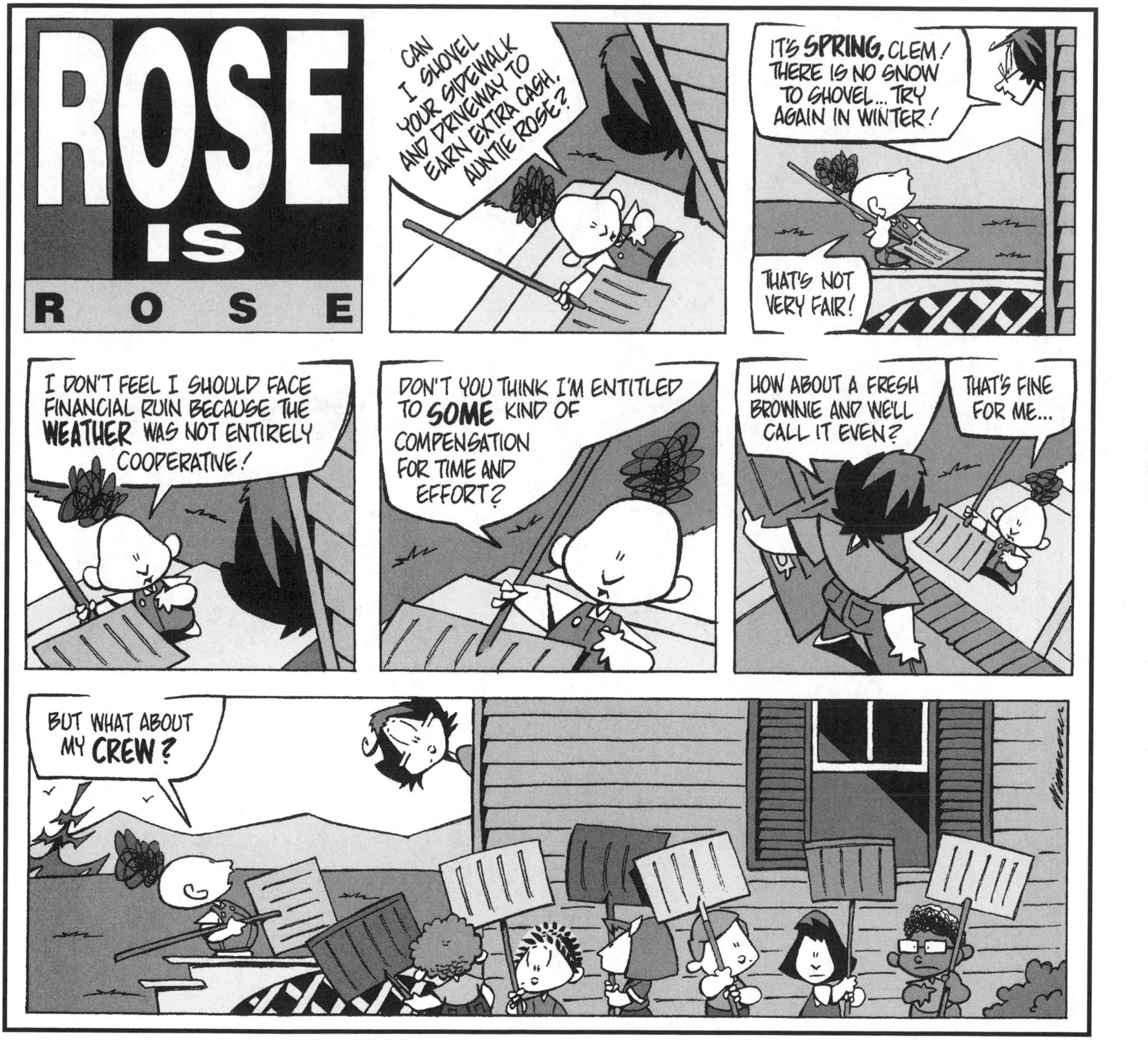
ROSE IS ROSE
CAN I SHOVEL YOUR SIDEWALK AND DRIVEWAY TO EARN EXTRA CASH, AUNTIE ROSE?
IT'S SPRING, CLEM! THERE IS NO SNOW TO SHOVEL... TRY AGAIN IN WINTER!
THAT'S NOT VERY FAIR!
I DON'T FEEL I SHOULD FACE FINANCIAL RUIN BECAUSE THE WEATHER WAS NOT ENTIRELY COOPERATIVE!
DON'T YOU THINK I'M ENTITLED TO SOME KIND OF COMPENSATION FOR TIME AND EFFORT?
HOW ABOUT A FRESH BROWNIE AND WE'LL CALL IT EVEN?
THAT'S FINE FOR ME...
BUT WHAT ABOUT MY CREW?

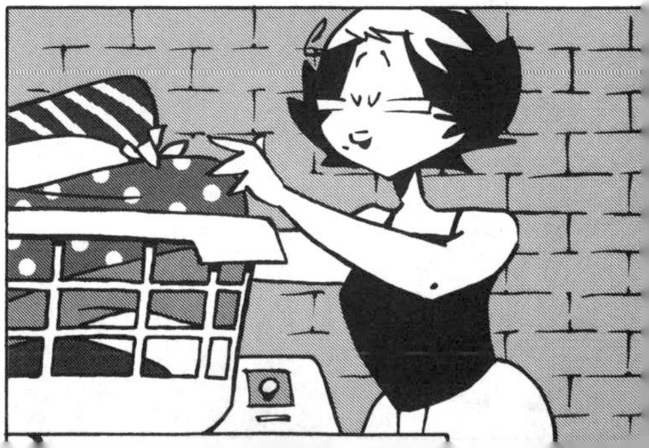

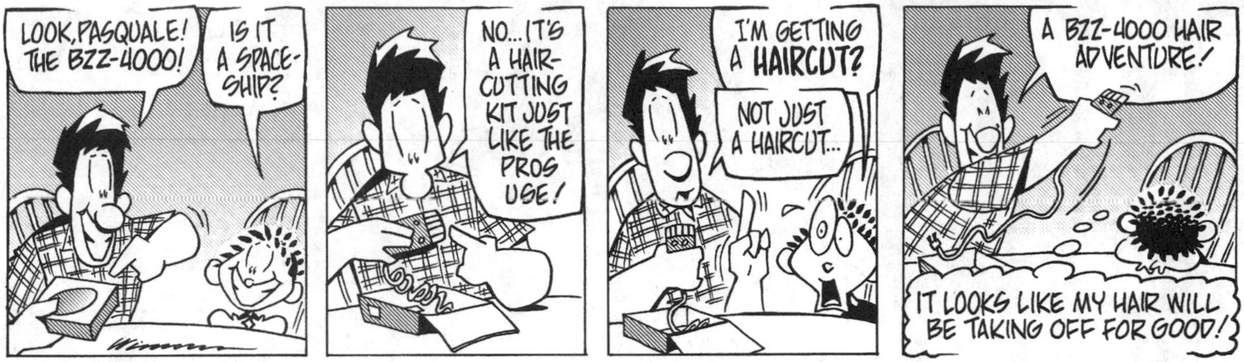
LOOK, PASQUALE! THE BZZ-4000!
IS IT A SPACE-SHIP?
NO... IT'S A HAIR-CUTTING KIT JUST LIKE THE PROS USE!
I'M GETTING A HAIRCUT?
NOT JUST A HAIRCUT...
A BZZ-4000 HAIR ADVENTURE!
IT LOOKS LIKE MY HAIR WILL BE TAKING OFF FOR GOOD!

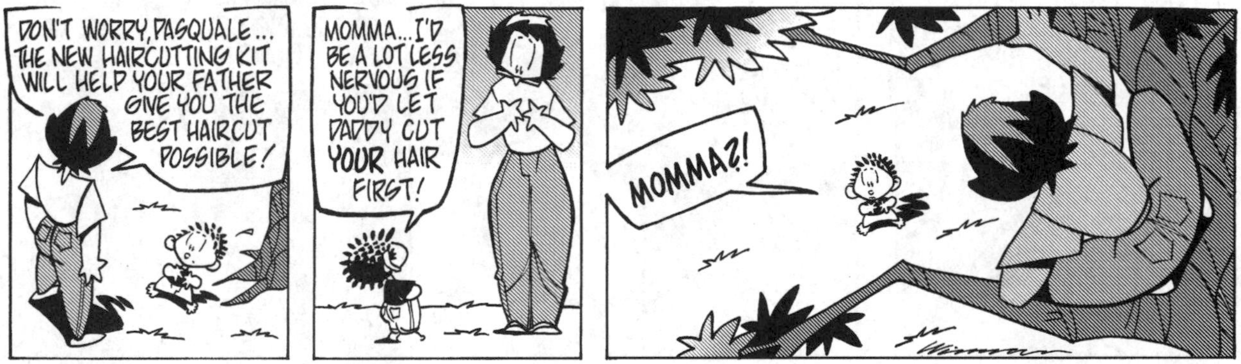
DON'T WORRY, PASQUALE... THE NEW HAIRCUTTING KIT WILL HELP YOUR FATHER GIVE YOU THE BEST HAIRCUT POSSIBLE!
MOMMA... I'D BE A LOT LESS NERVOUS IF YOU'D LET DADDY CUT YOUR HAIR FIRST!
MOMMA?!

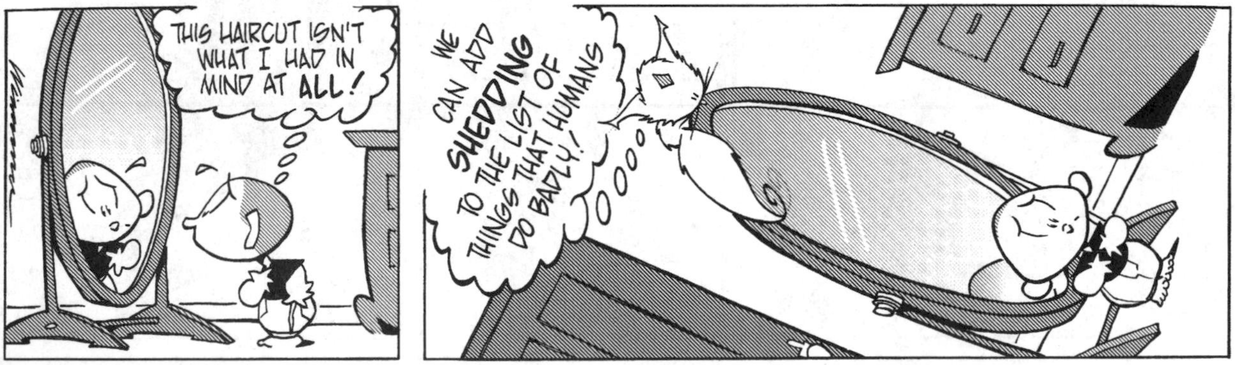
THIS HAIRCUT ISN'T WHAT I HAD IN MIND AT ALL!
WE CAN ADD SHEDDING TO THE LIST OF THINGS THAT HUMANS DO BADLY!

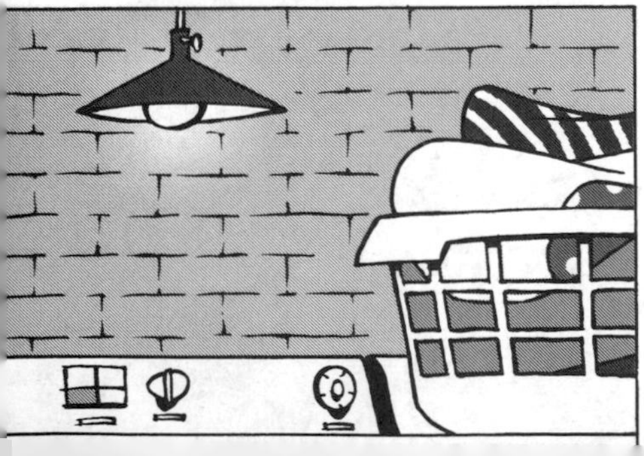

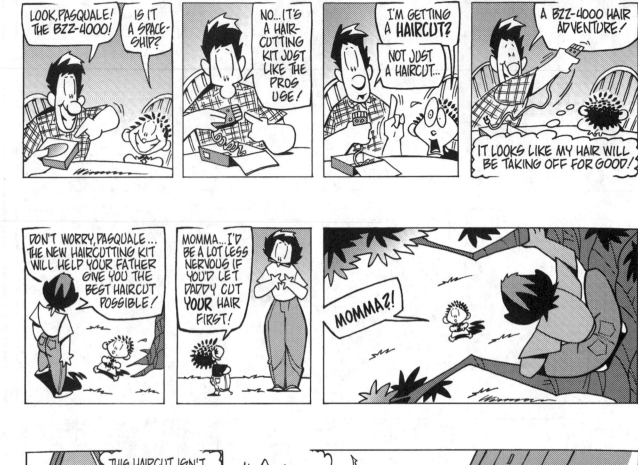

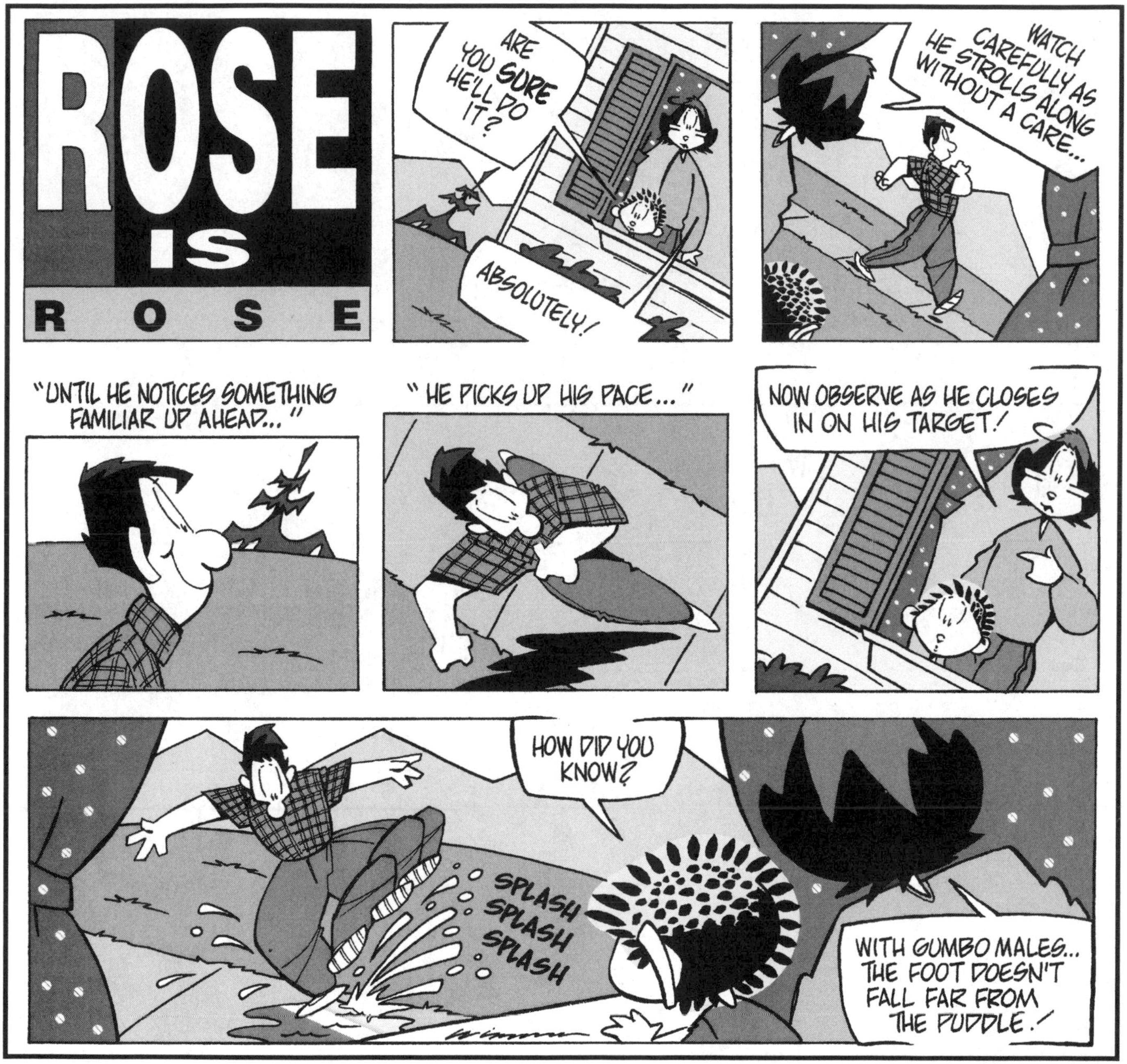
ROSE IS ROSE
ARE YOU SURE HE'LL DO IT?
ABSOLUTELY!
WATCH CAREFULLY AS HE STROLLS ALONG WITHOUT A CARE...
"UNTIL HE NOTICES SOMETHING FAMILIAR UP AHEAD..."
" HE PICKS UP HIS PACE..."
NOW OBSERVE AS HE CLOSES IN ON HIS TARGET!
HOW DID YOU KNOW?
SPLASH SPLASH SPLASH SPLASH
WITH GUMBO MALES... THE FOOT DOESN'T FALL FAR FROM THE PUDDLE!

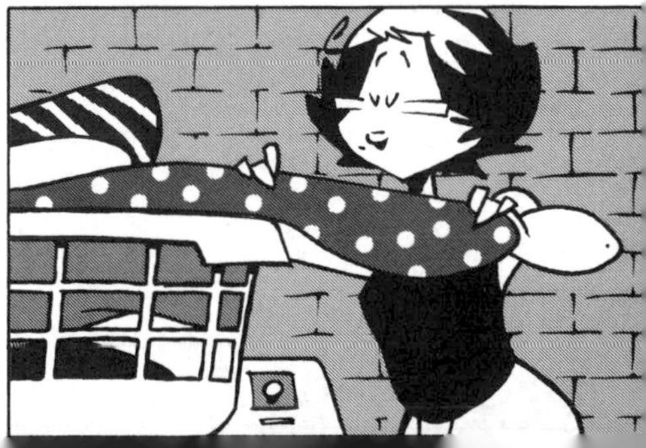

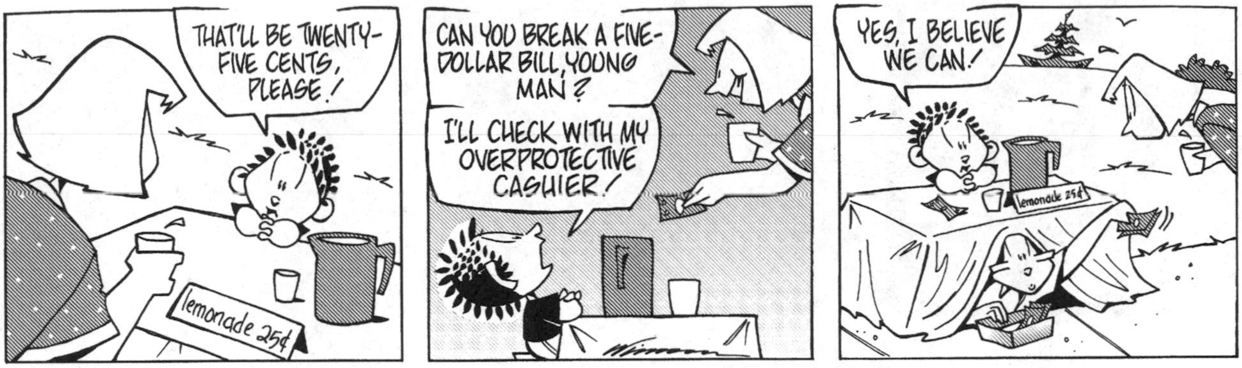
THAT'LL BE TWENTY-FIVE CENTS, PLEASE!
lemonade 25¢
CAN YOU BREAK A FIVE-DOLLAR BILL, YOUNG MAN?
I'LL CHECK WITH MY OVERPROTECTIVE CASHIER!
YES, I BELIEVE WE CAN!
lemonade 25¢

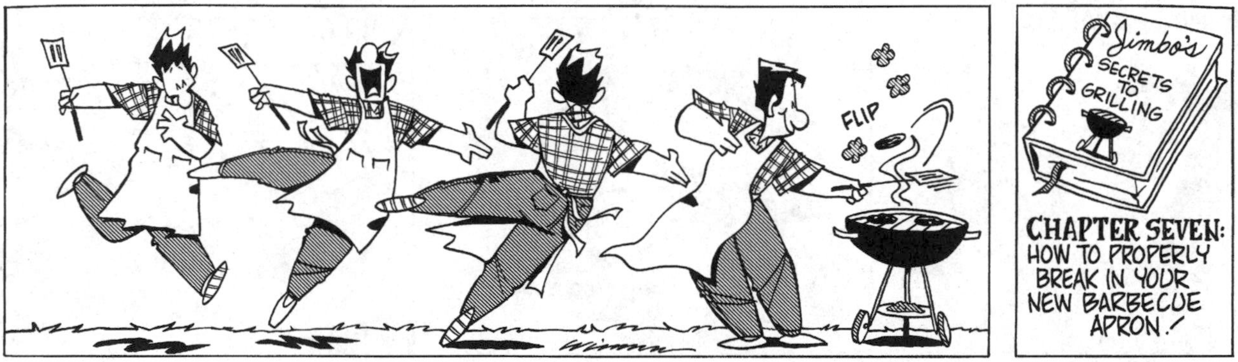
FLIP
Jimbo's SECRETS TO GRILLING
CHAPTER SEVEN: HOW TO PROPERLY BREAK IN YOUR NEW BARBECUE APRON!

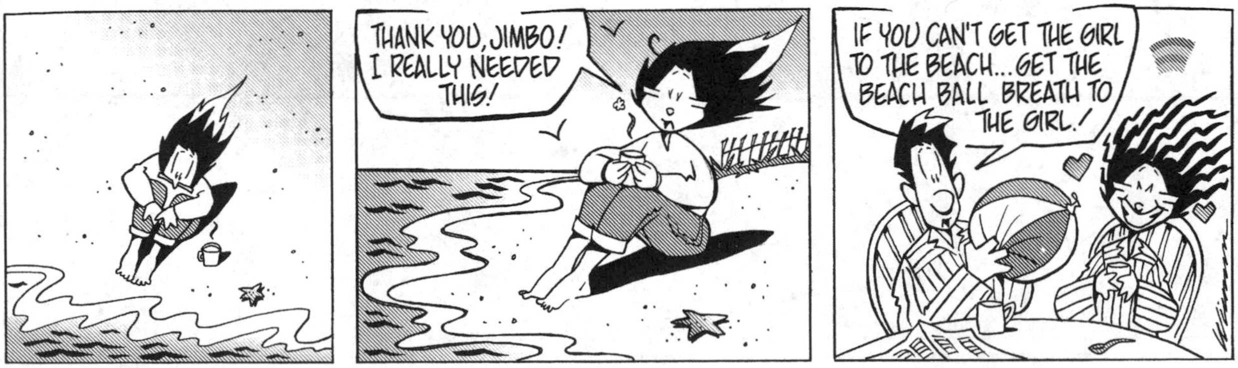
THANK YOU, JIMBO! I REALLY NEEDED THIS!
IF YOU CAN'T GET THE GIRL TO THE BEACH...GET THE BEACH BALL BREATH TO THE GIRL!

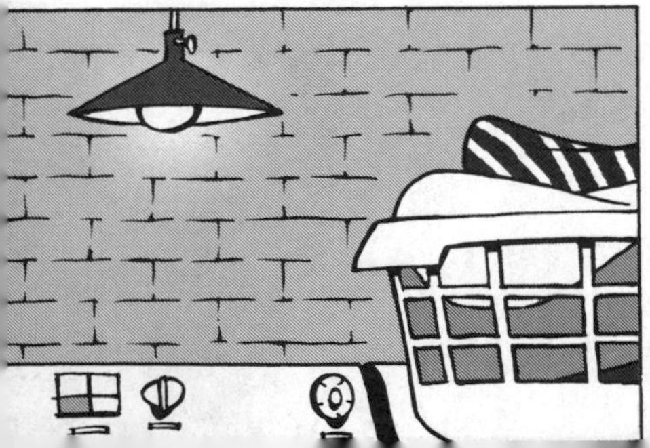

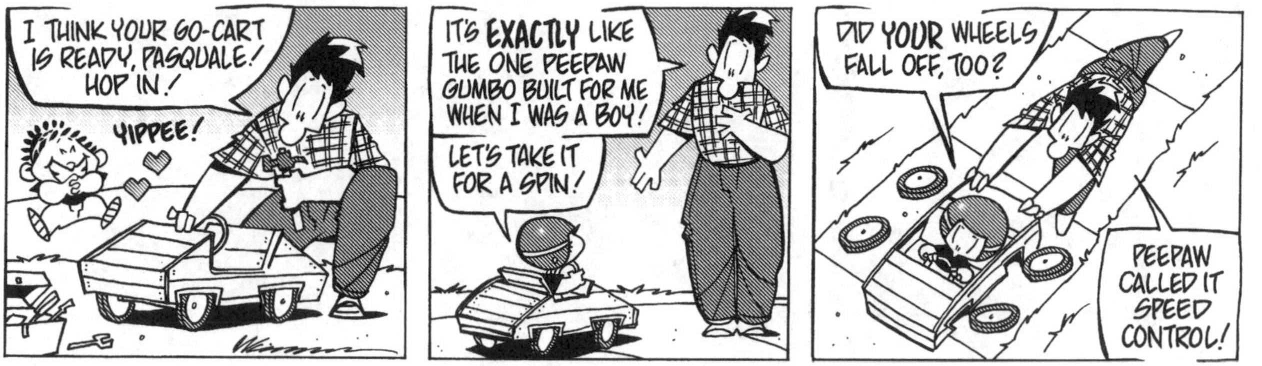
I THINK YOUR GO-CART IS READY, PASQUALE! HOP IN!
YIPPEE!
IT'S EXACTLY LIKE THE ONE PEEPAW GUMBO BUILT FOR ME WHEN I WAS A BOY!
LET'S TAKE IT FOR A SPIN!
DID YOUR WHEELS FALL OFF, TOO?
PEEPAW CALLED IT SPEED CONTROL!

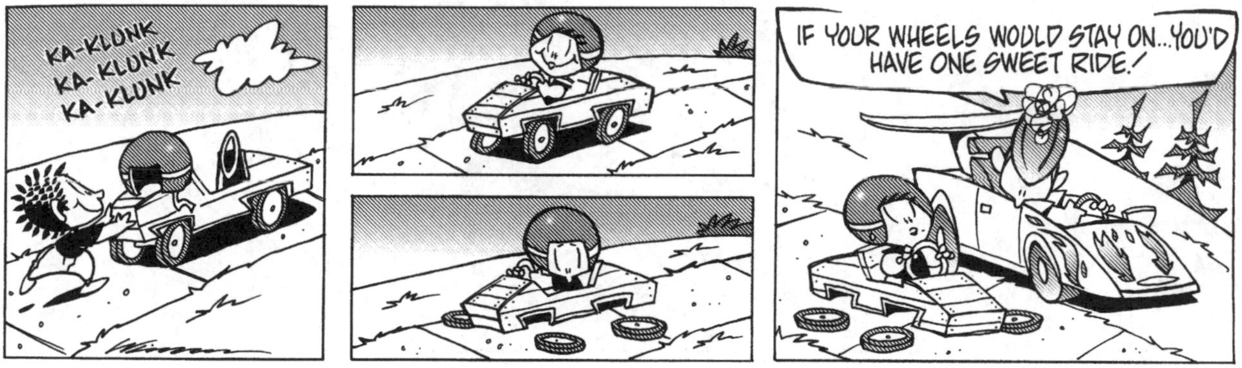
KA-KLUNK
KA-KLUNK
KA-KLUNK
IF YOUR WHEELS WOULD STAY ON...YOU'D HAVE ONE SWEET RIDE!

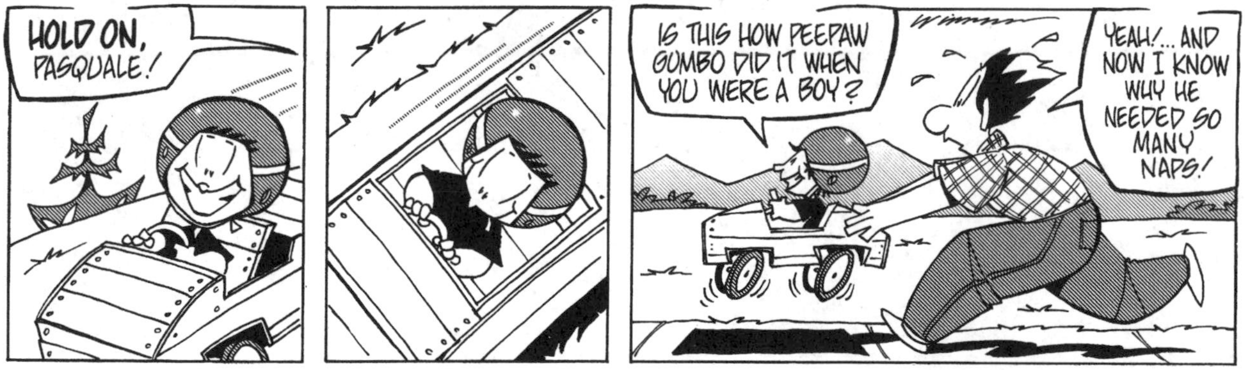
HOLD ON, PASQUALE!
IS THIS HOW PEEPAW GUMBO DID IT WHEN YOU WERE A BOY?
YEAH!... AND NOW I KNOW WHY HE NEEDED SO MANY NAPS!

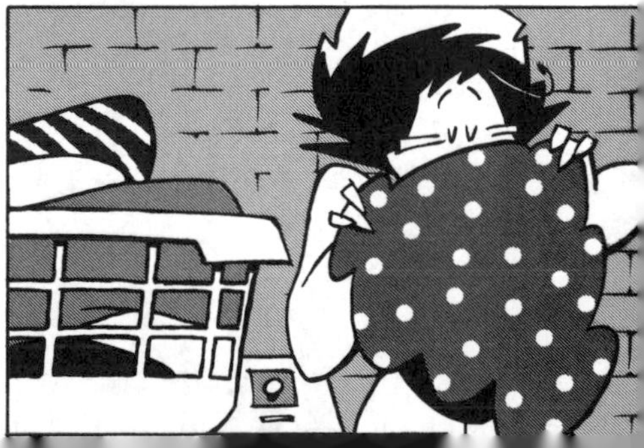

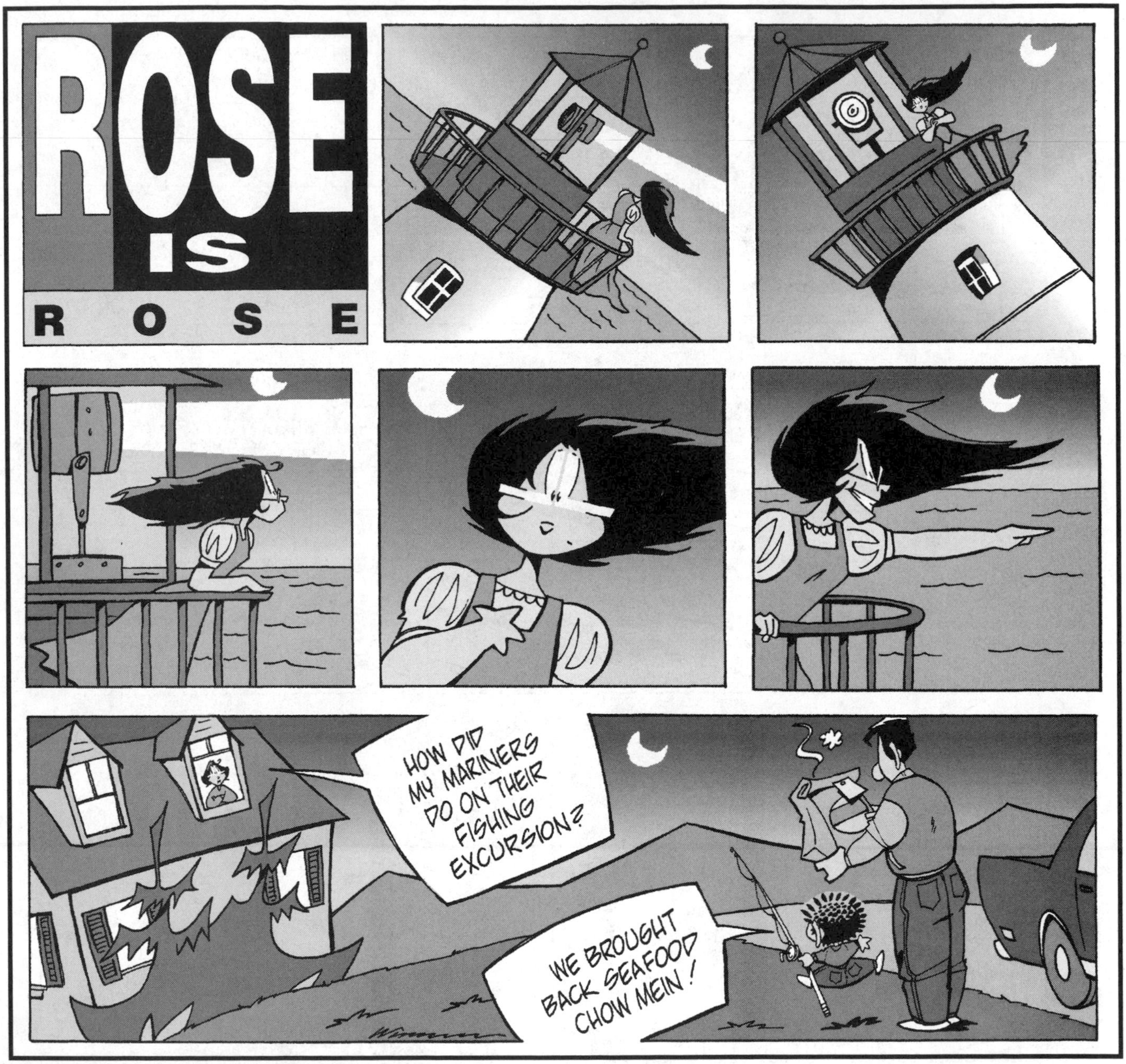
ROSE IS ROSE
HOW DID MY MARINERS DO ON THEIR FISHING EXCURSION?
WE BROUGHT BACK SEAFOOD CHOW MEIN!

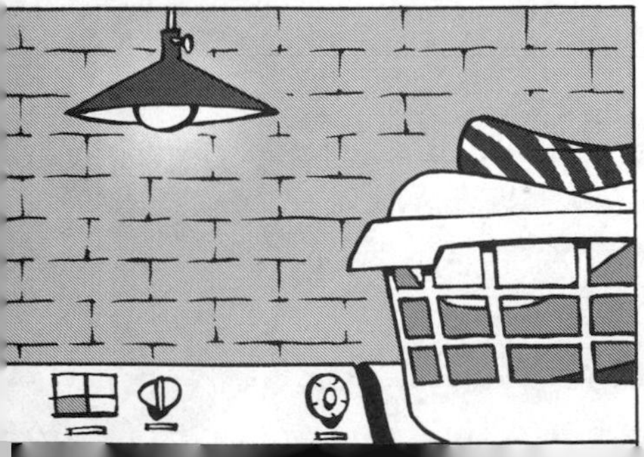

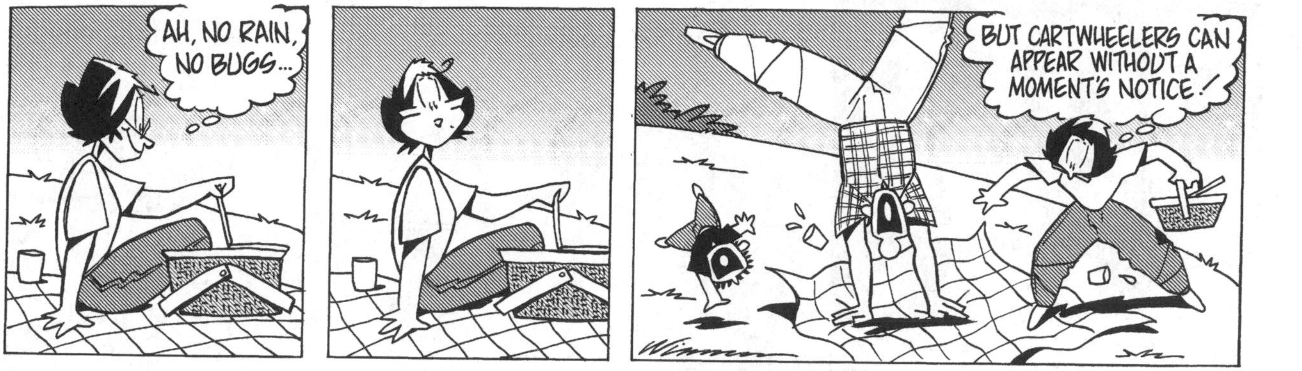
AH, NO RAIN, NO BUGS...
BUT CARTWHEELERS CAN APPEAR WITHOUT A MOMENT'S NOTICE!

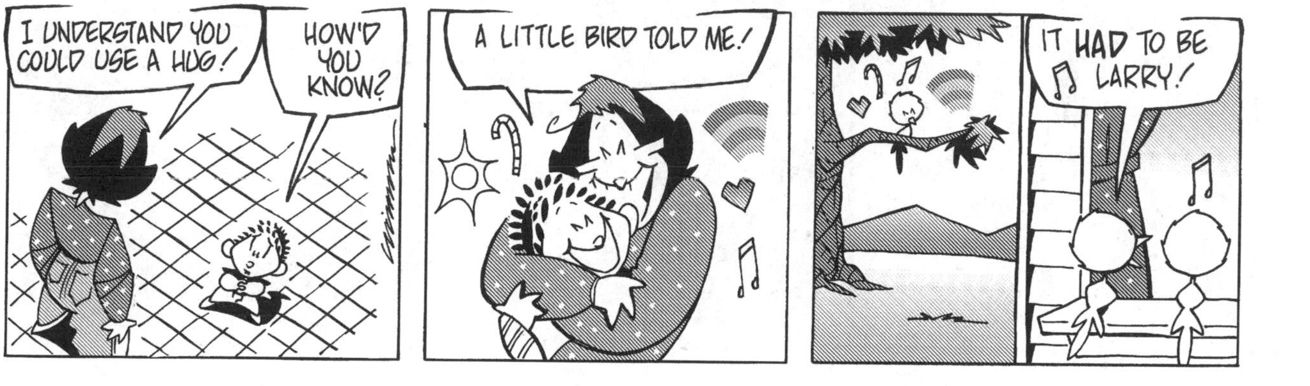
I UNDERSTAND YOU COULD USE A HUG!
HOW'D YOU KNOW?
A LITTLE BIRD TOLD ME!
IT HAD TO BE LARRY!

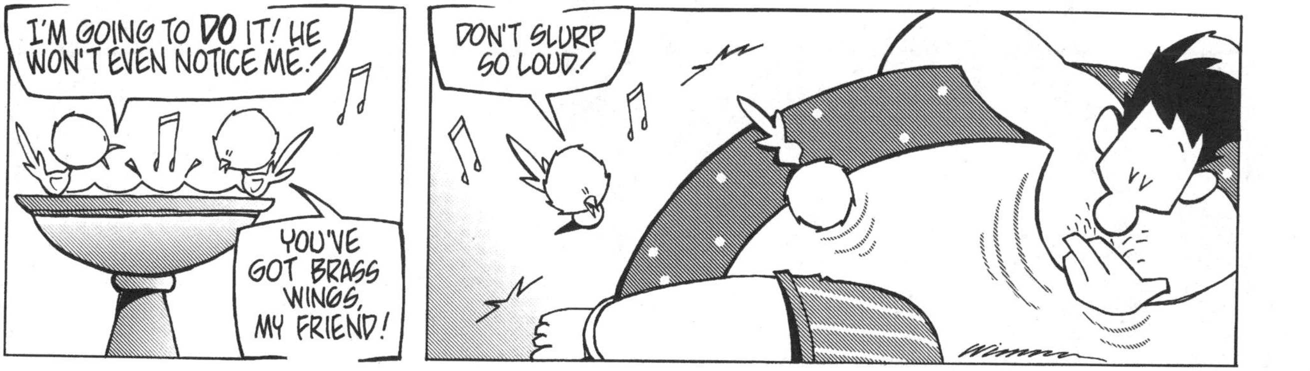
I'M GOING TO DO IT! HE WON'T EVEN NOTICE ME!
YOU'VE GOT BRASS WINGS, MY FRIEND!
DON'T SLURP SO LOUD!

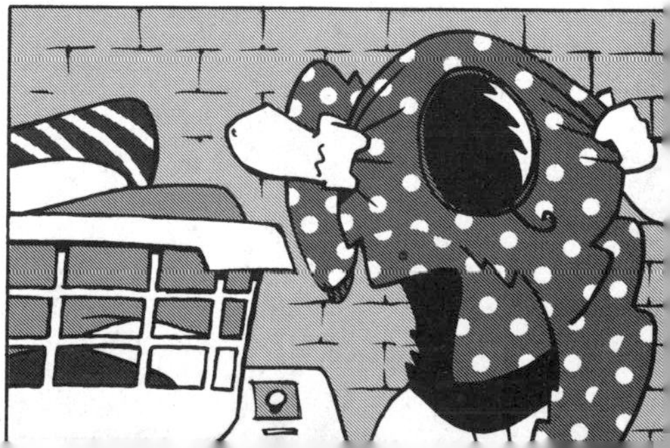

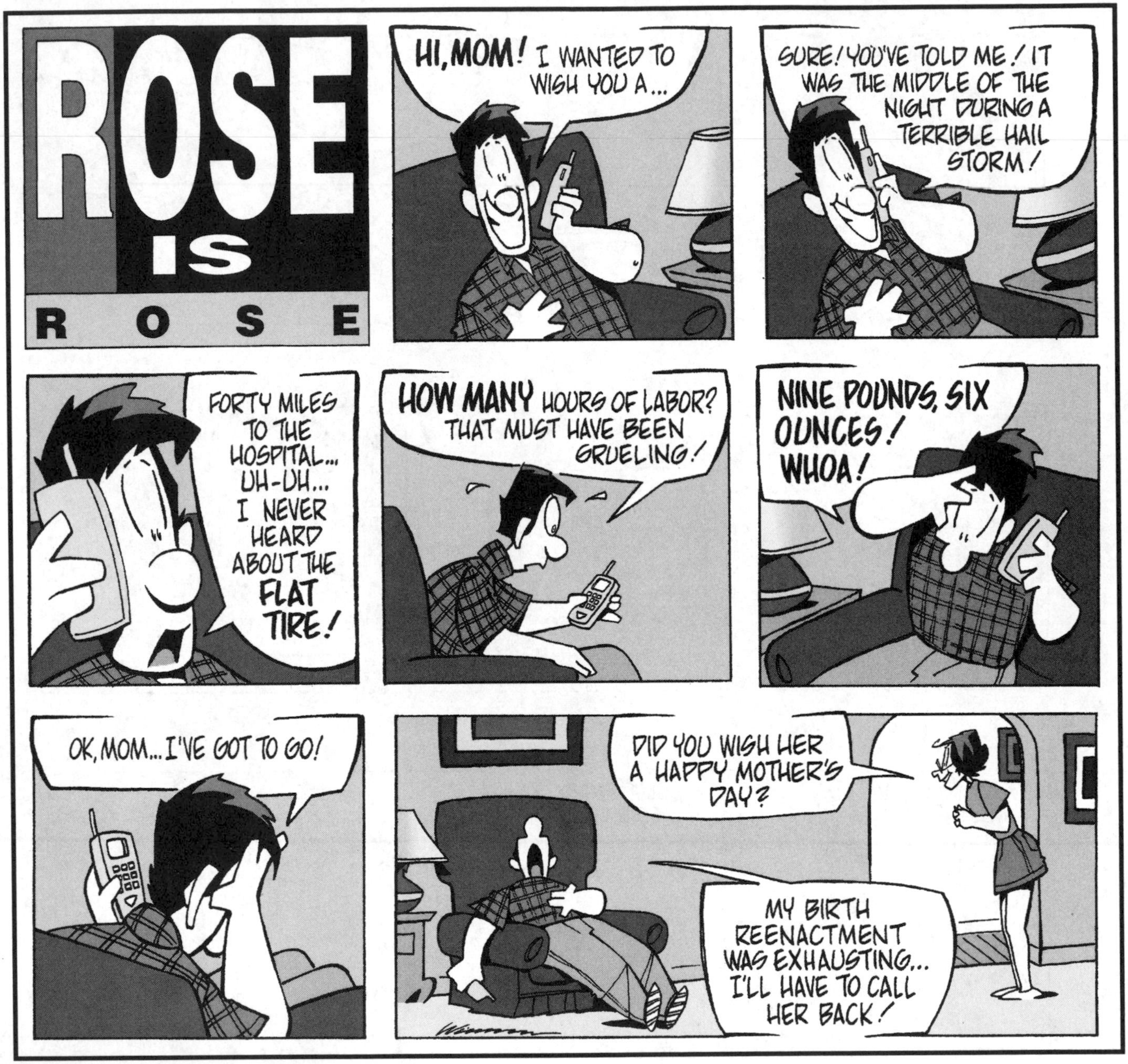
ROSE IS ROSE
HI, MOM! I WANTED TO WISH YOU A...
SURE! YOU'VE TOLD ME! IT WAS THE MIDDLE OF THE NIGHT DURING A TERRIBLE HAIL STORM!
FORTY MILES TO THE HOSPITAL... UH-UH... I NEVER HEARD ABOUT THE FLAT TIRE!
HOW MANY HOURS OF LABOR? THAT MUST HAVE BEEN GRUELING!
NINE POUNDS, SIX OUNCES! WHOA!
OK, MOM... I'VE GOT TO GO!
DID YOU WISH HER A HAPPY MOTHER'S DAY?
MY BIRTH REENACTMENT WAS EXHAUSTING... I'LL HAVE TO CALL HER BACK!

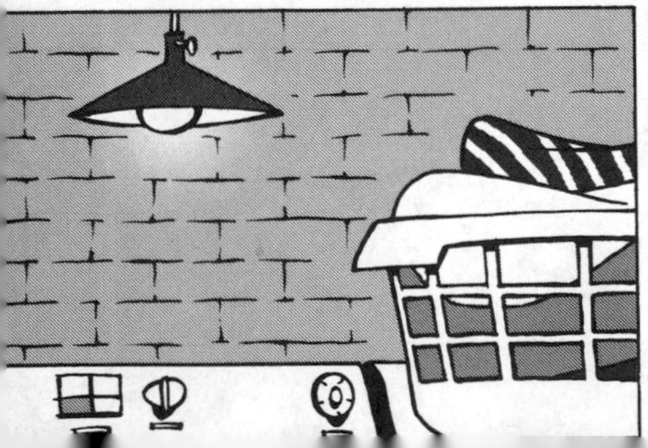

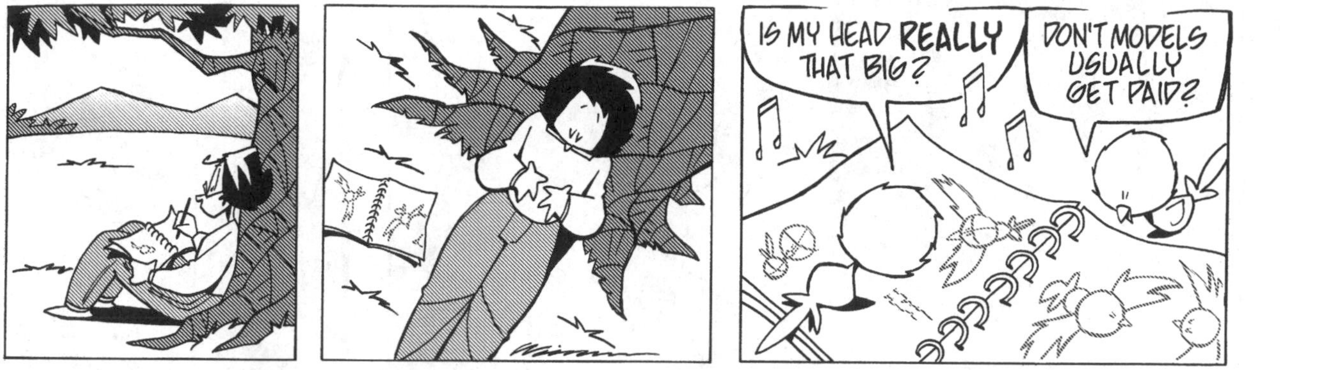
IS MY HEAD **REALLY** THAT BIG?
DON'T MODELS USUALLY GET PAID?

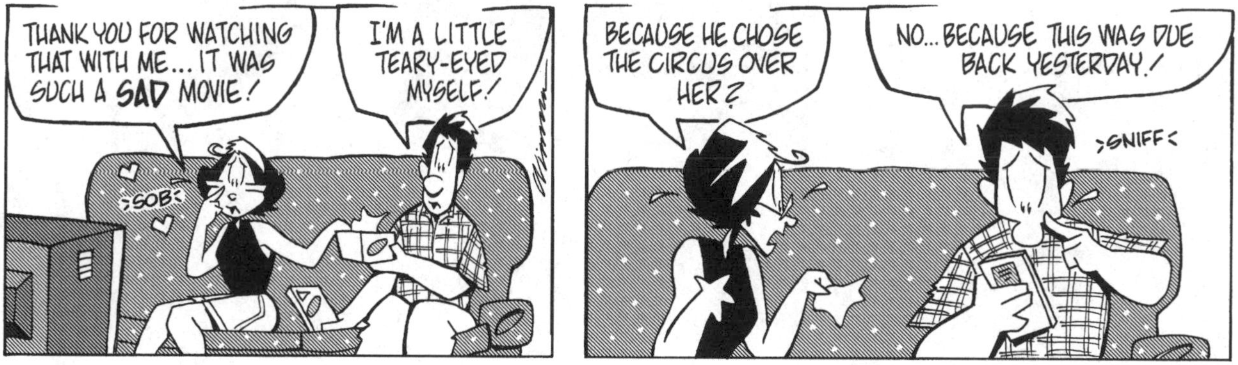
THANK YOU FOR WATCHING THAT WITH ME... IT WAS SUCH A **SAD** MOVIE!
I'M A LITTLE TEARY-EYED MYSELF!
>SOB<
BECAUSE HE CHOSE THE CIRCUS OVER HER?
NO... BECAUSE THIS WAS DUE BACK YESTERDAY!
>SNIFF<

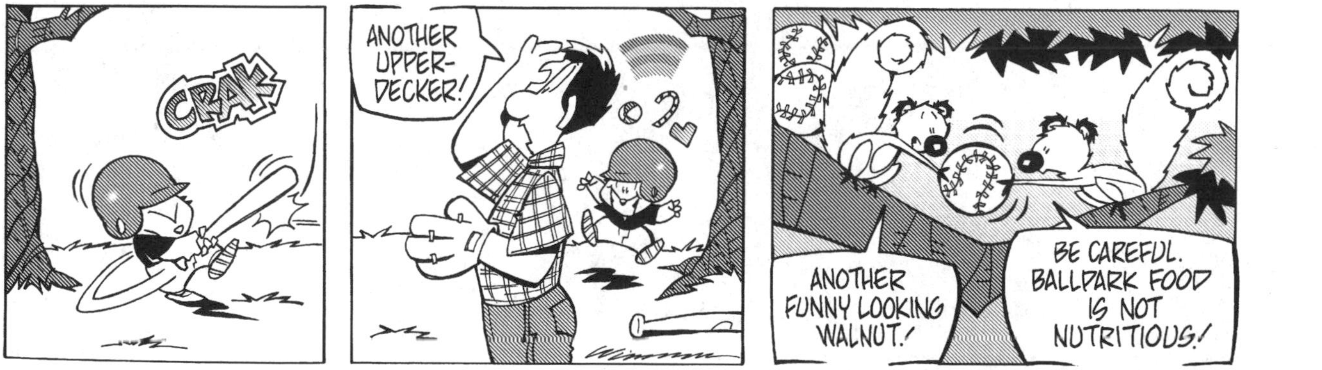
CRAK
ANOTHER UPPER-DECKER!
ANOTHER FUNNY LOOKING WALNUT!
BE CAREFUL. BALLPARK FOOD IS NOT NUTRITIOUS!

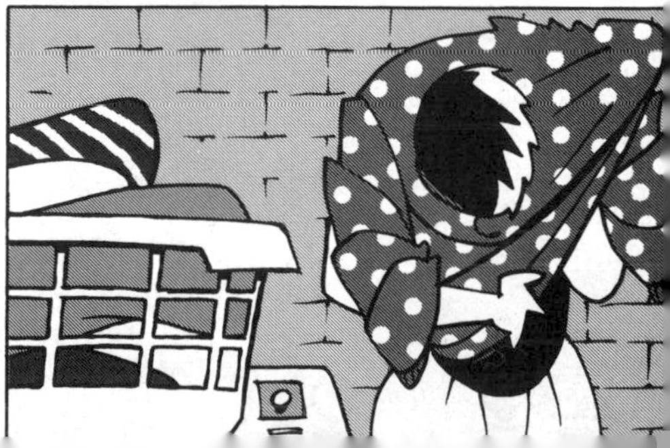

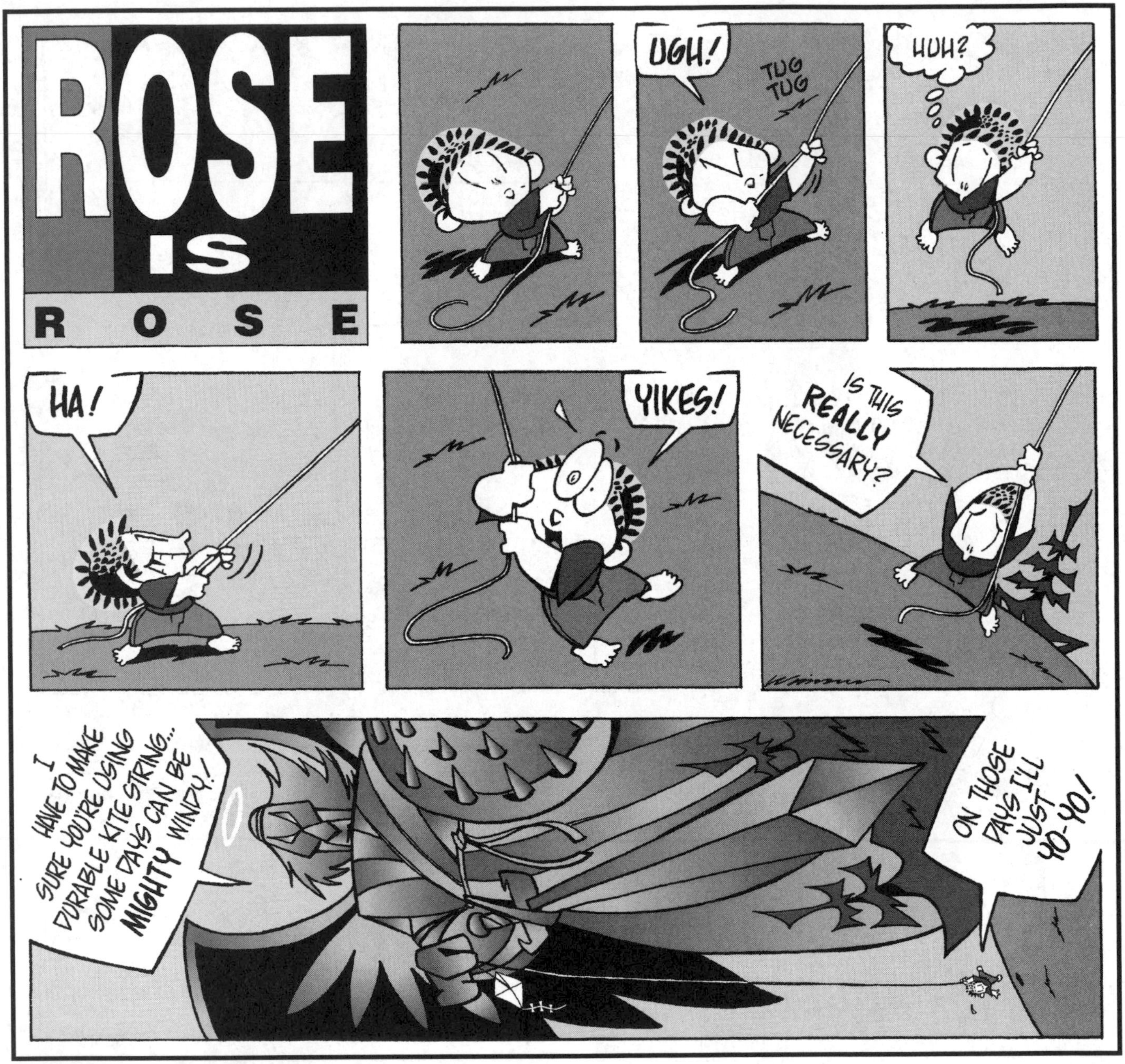
ROSE IS ROSE
UGH!
TUG TUG
HUH?
HA!
YIKES!
IS THIS REALLY NECESSARY?
I HAVE TO MAKE SURE YOU'RE USING DURABLE KITE STRING... SOME DAYS CAN BE MIGHTY WINDY!
ON THOSE DAYS I'LL JUST YO-YO!

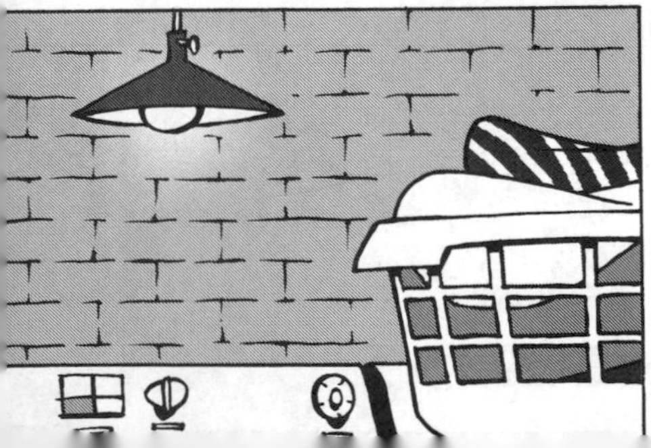

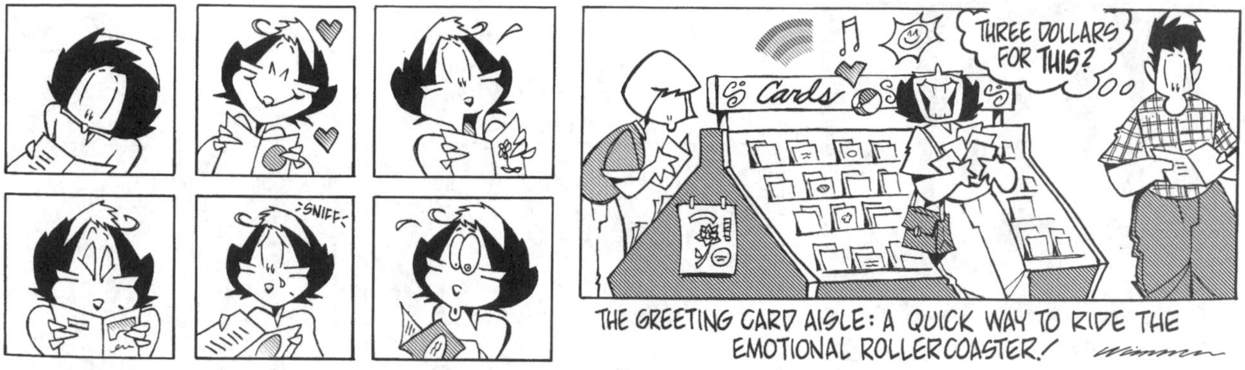
SNIFF
Cards
THREE DOLLARS FOR THIS?
THE GREETING CARD AISLE: A QUICK WAY TO RIDE THE EMOTIONAL ROLLERCOASTER!

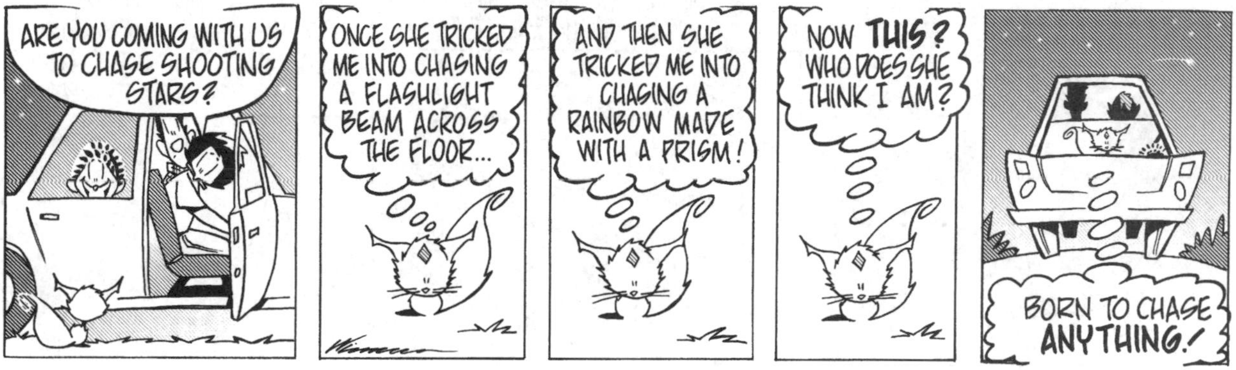
ARE YOU COMING WITH US TO CHASE SHOOTING STARS?
ONCE SHE TRICKED ME INTO CHASING A FLASHLIGHT BEAM ACROSS THE FLOOR...
AND THEN SHE TRICKED ME INTO CHASING A RAINBOW MADE WITH A PRISM!
NOW THIS? WHO DOES SHE THINK I AM?
BORN TO CHASE ANYTHING!

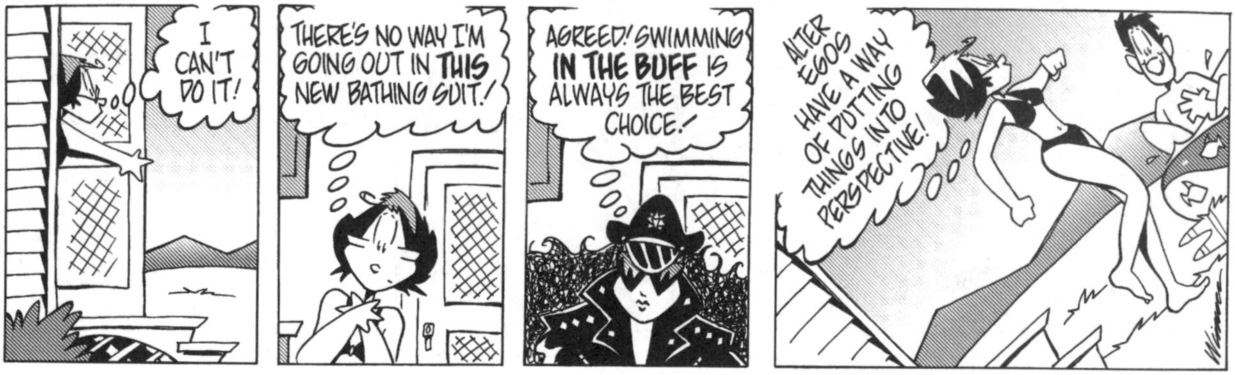
I CAN'T DO IT!
THERE'S NO WAY I'M GOING OUT IN THIS NEW BATHING SUIT!
AGREED! SWIMMING IN THE BUFF IS ALWAYS THE BEST CHOICE!
ALTER EGOS HAVE A WAY OF PUTTING THINGS INTO PERSPECTIVE!

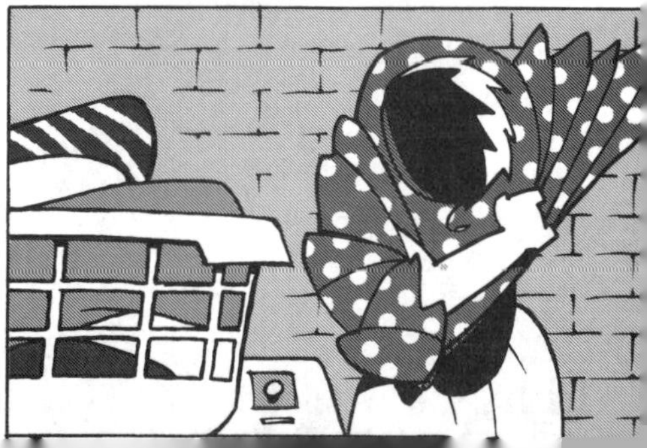

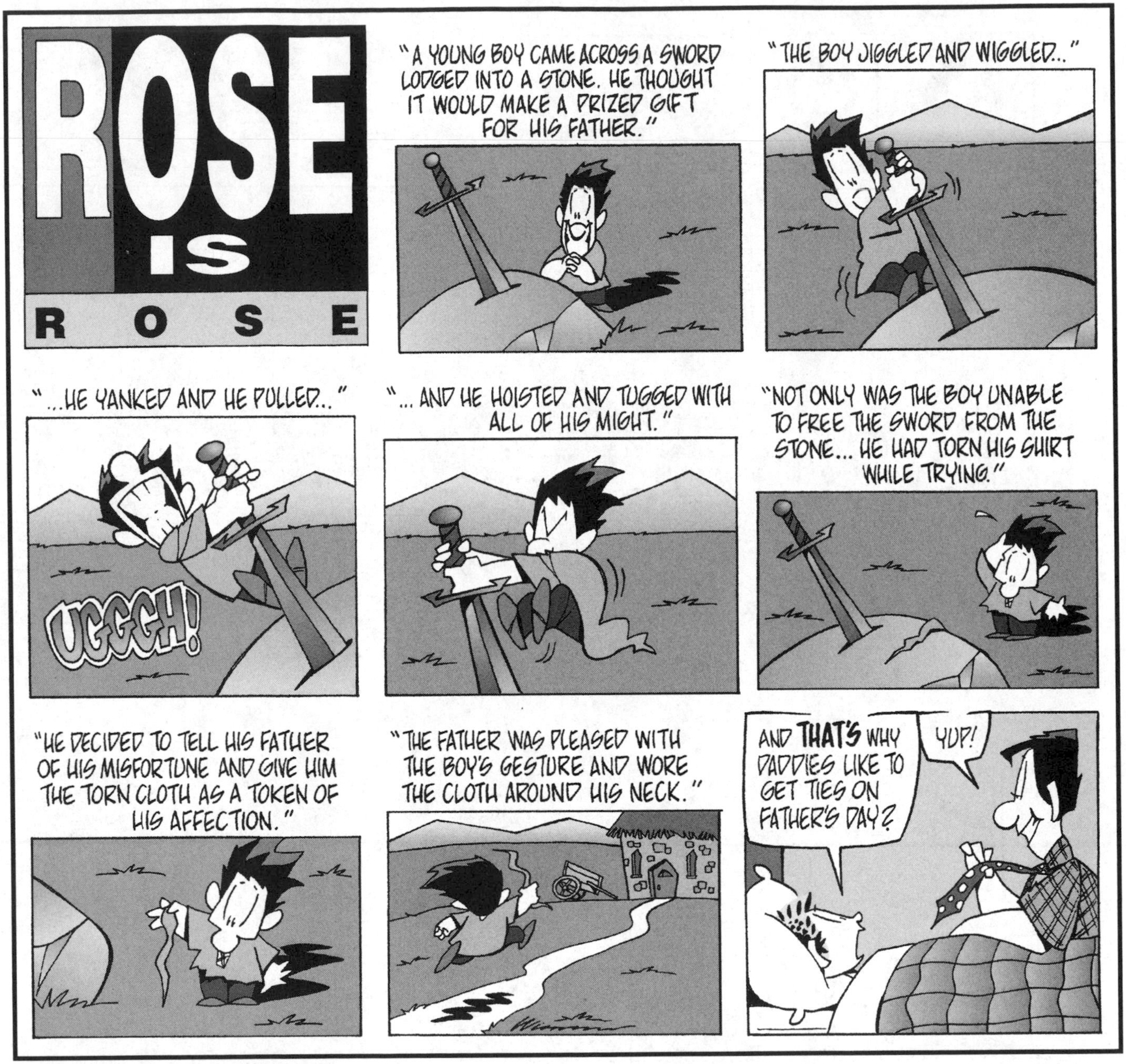
ROSE IS ROSE
"A YOUNG BOY CAME ACROSS A SWORD LODGED INTO A STONE. HE THOUGHT IT WOULD MAKE A PRIZED GIFT FOR HIS FATHER."
"THE BOY JIGGLED AND WIGGLED..."
"...HE YANKED AND HE PULLED..."
UGGGH!
"... AND HE HOISTED AND TUGGED WITH ALL OF HIS MIGHT."
"NOT ONLY WAS THE BOY UNABLE TO FREE THE SWORD FROM THE STONE... HE HAD TORN HIS SHIRT WHILE TRYING."
"HE DECIDED TO TELL HIS FATHER OF HIS MISFORTUNE AND GIVE HIM THE TORN CLOTH AS A TOKEN OF HIS AFFECTION."
"THE FATHER WAS PLEASED WITH THE BOY'S GESTURE AND WORE THE CLOTH AROUND HIS NECK."
AND THAT'S WHY DADDIES LIKE TO GET TIES ON FATHER'S DAY?
YUP!

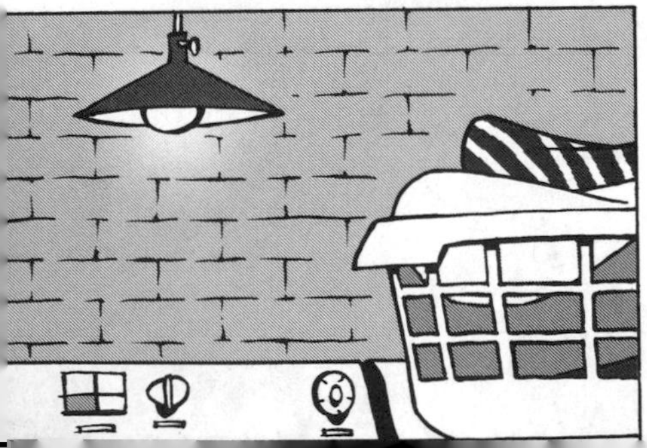

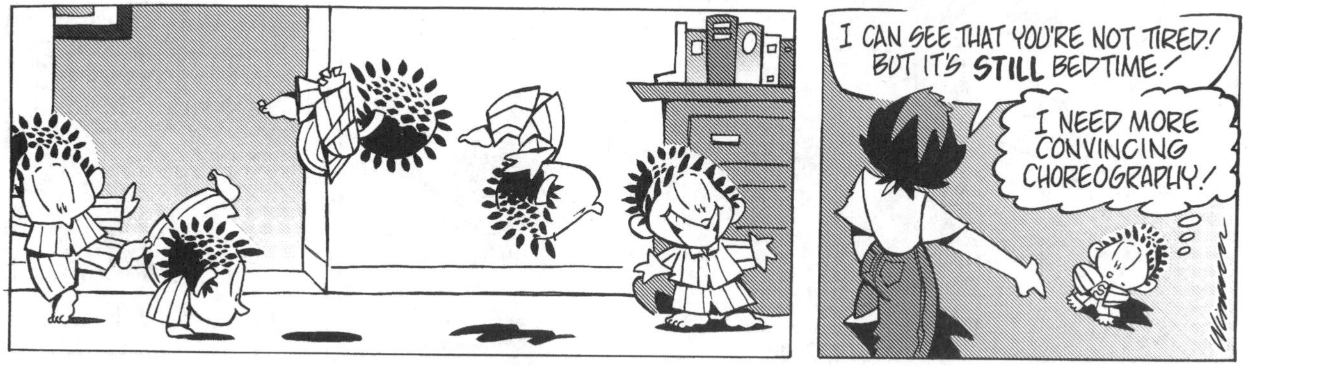
I CAN SEE THAT YOU'RE NOT TIRED! BUT IT'S **STILL** BEDTIME!
I NEED MORE CONVINCING CHOREOGRAPHY!

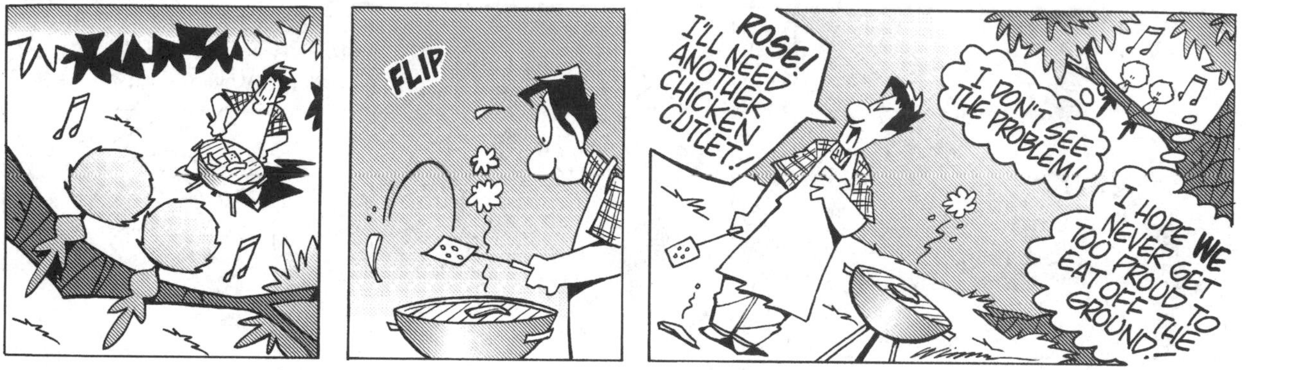
FLIP
ROSE! I'LL NEED ANOTHER CHICKEN CUTLET!
I DON'T SEE THE PROBLEM!
I HOPE **WE** NEVER GET TOO PROUD TO EAT OFF THE GROUND!

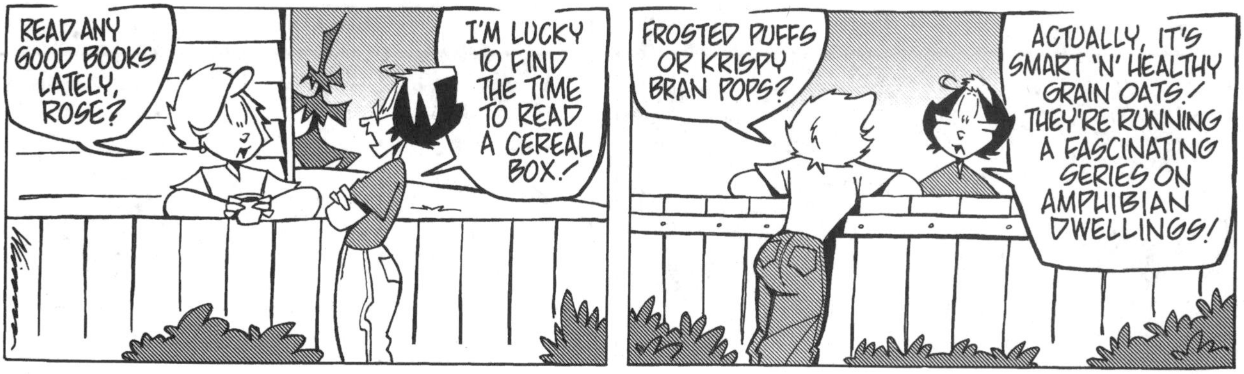
READ ANY GOOD BOOKS LATELY, ROSE?
I'M LUCKY TO FIND THE TIME TO READ A CEREAL BOX!
FROSTED PUFFS OR KRISPY BRAN POPS?
ACTUALLY, IT'S SMART 'N' HEALTHY GRAIN OATS! THEY'RE RUNNING A FASCINATING SERIES ON AMPHIBIAN DWELLINGS!

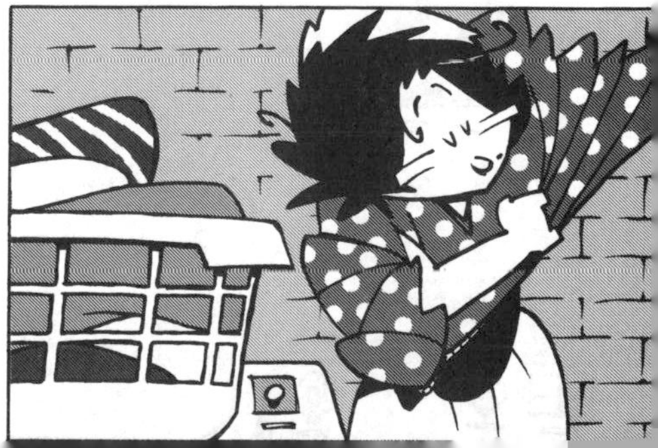

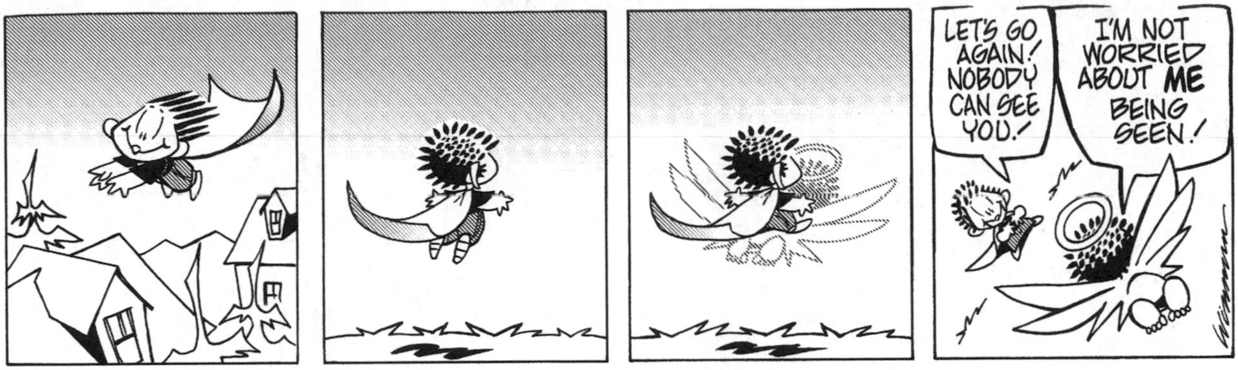
LET'S GO AGAIN! NOBODY CAN SEE YOU!
I'M NOT WORRIED ABOUT ME BEING SEEN!

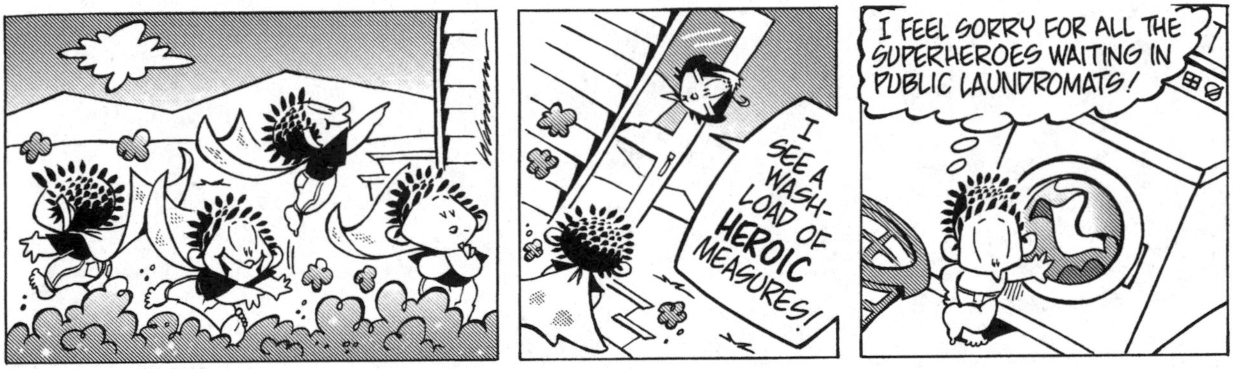
I SEE A WASH-LOAD OF HEROIC MEASURES!
I FEEL SORRY FOR ALL THE SUPERHEROES WAITING IN PUBLIC LAUNDROMATS!

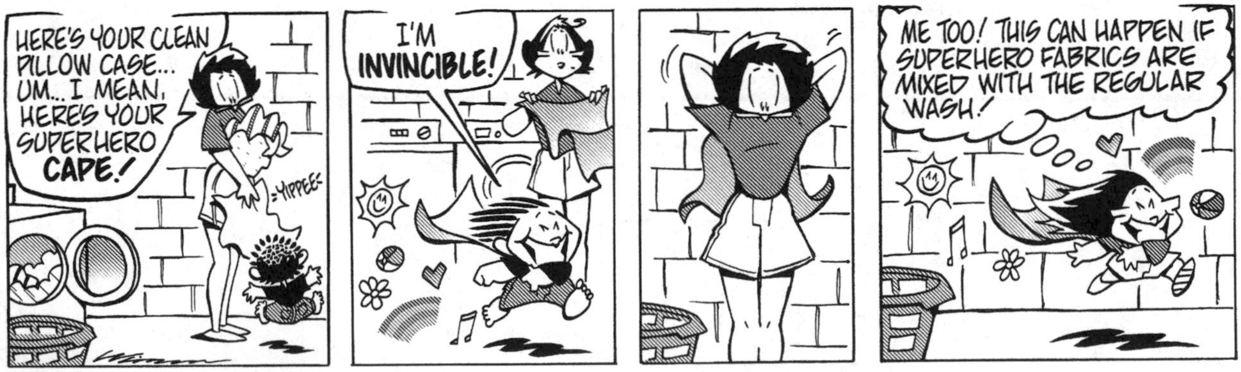
HERE'S YOUR CLEAN PILLOW CASE... UM... I MEAN, HERE'S YOUR SUPERHERO CAPE!
=YIPPEE=
I'M INVINCIBLE!
ME TOO! THIS CAN HAPPEN IF SUPERHERO FABRICS ARE MIXED WITH THE REGULAR WASH!

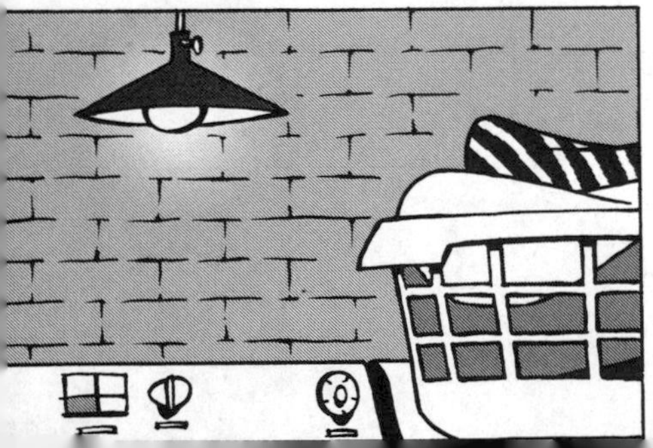

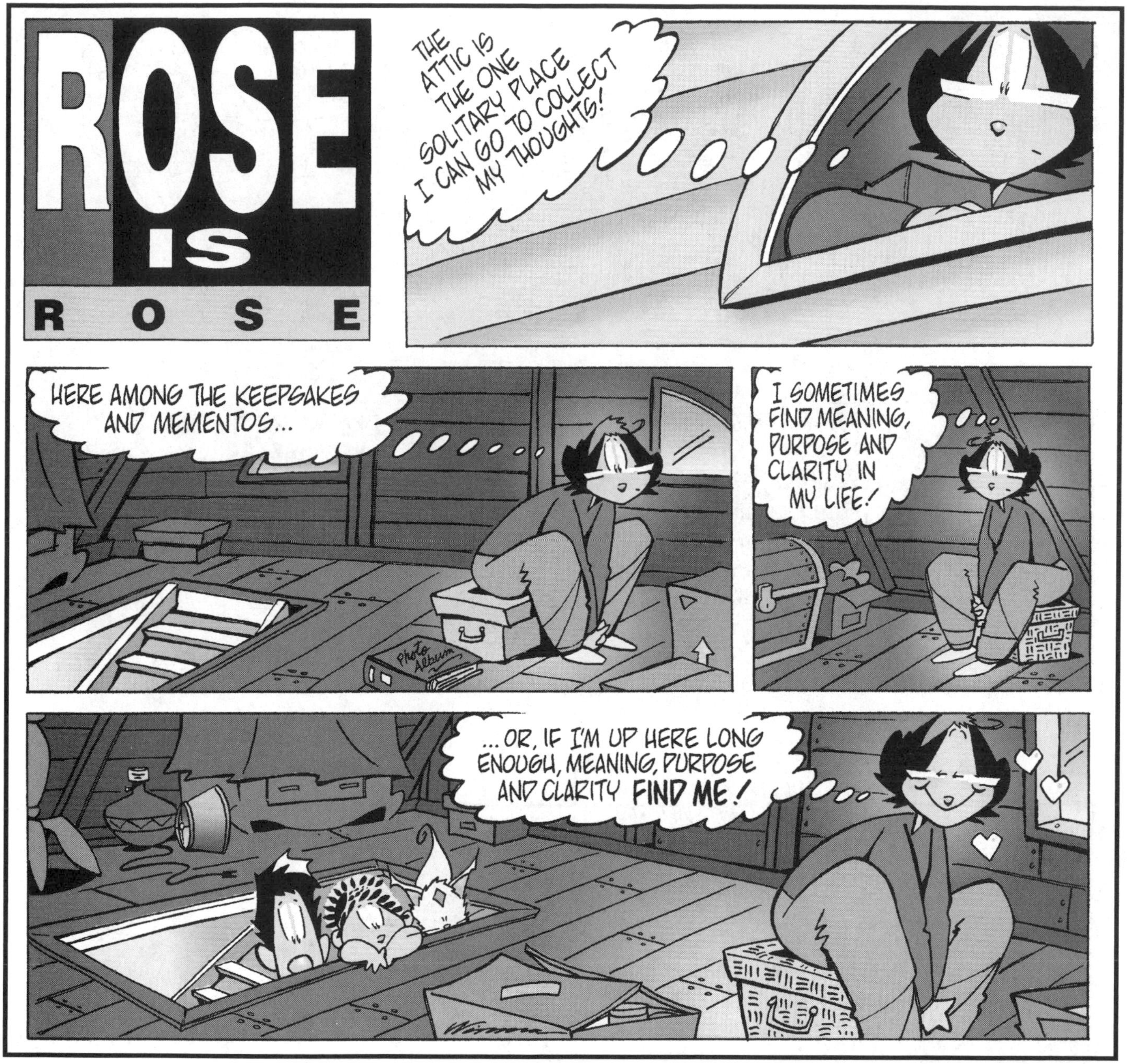
ROSE IS ROSE
THE ATTIC IS THE ONE SOLITARY PLACE I CAN GO TO COLLECT MY THOUGHTS!
HERE AMONG THE KEEPSAKES AND MEMENTOS...
Photo Album
I SOMETIMES FIND MEANING, PURPOSE AND CLARITY IN MY LIFE!
...OR, IF I'M UP HERE LONG ENOUGH, MEANING, PURPOSE AND CLARITY FIND ME!

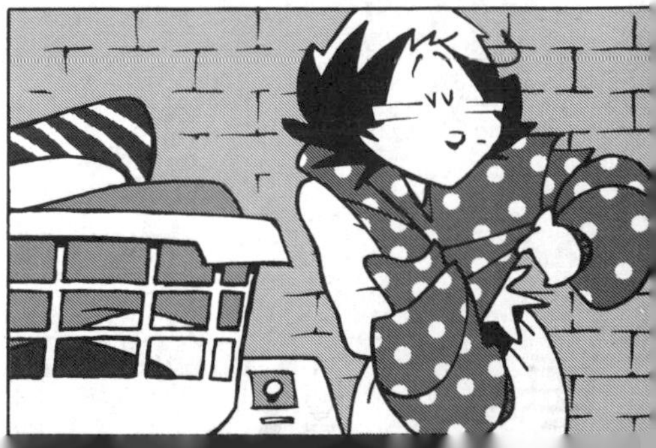

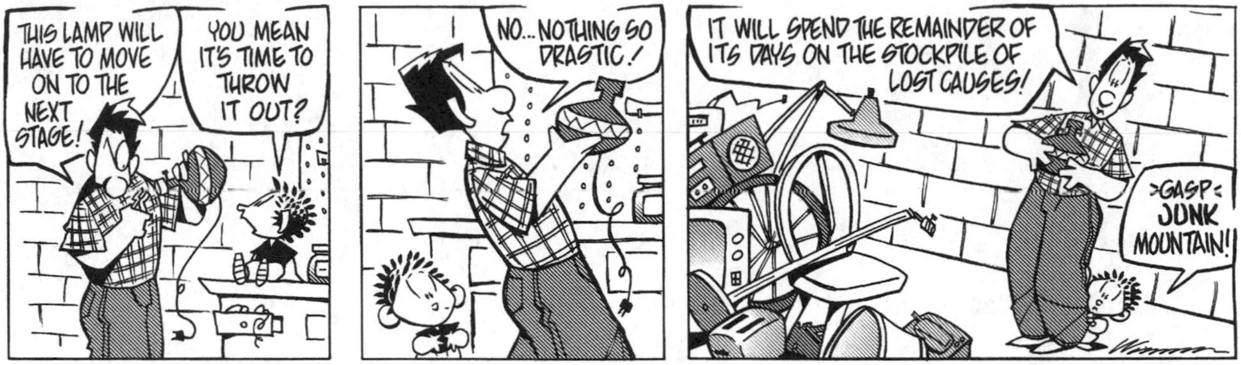
THIS LAMP WILL HAVE TO MOVE ON TO THE NEXT STAGE!
YOU MEAN IT'S TIME TO THROW IT OUT?
NO... NOTHING SO DRASTIC!
IT WILL SPEND THE REMAINDER OF ITS DAYS ON THE STOCKPILE OF LOST CAUSES!
>GASP< JUNK MOUNTAIN!

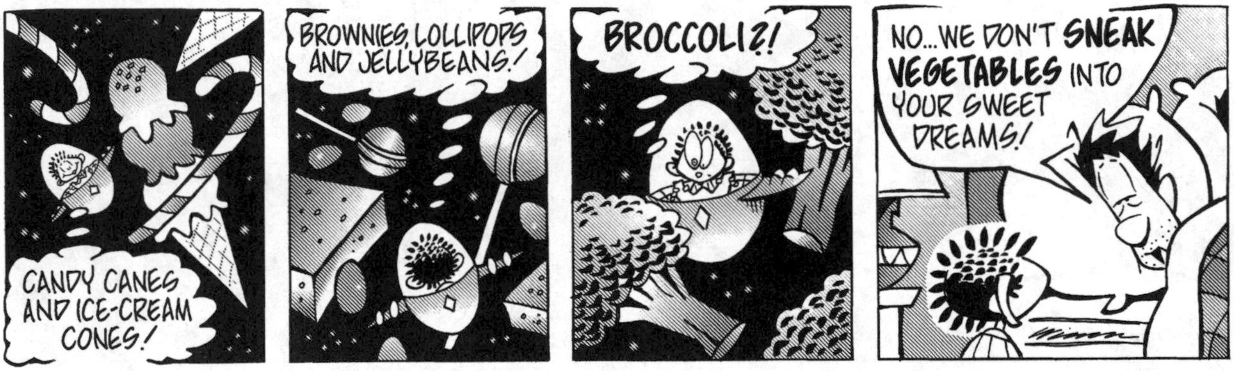
CANDY CANES AND ICE-CREAM CONES!
BROWNIES, LOLLIPOPS AND JELLYBEANS!
BROCCOLI?!
NO... WE DON'T SNEAK VEGETABLES INTO YOUR SWEET DREAMS!

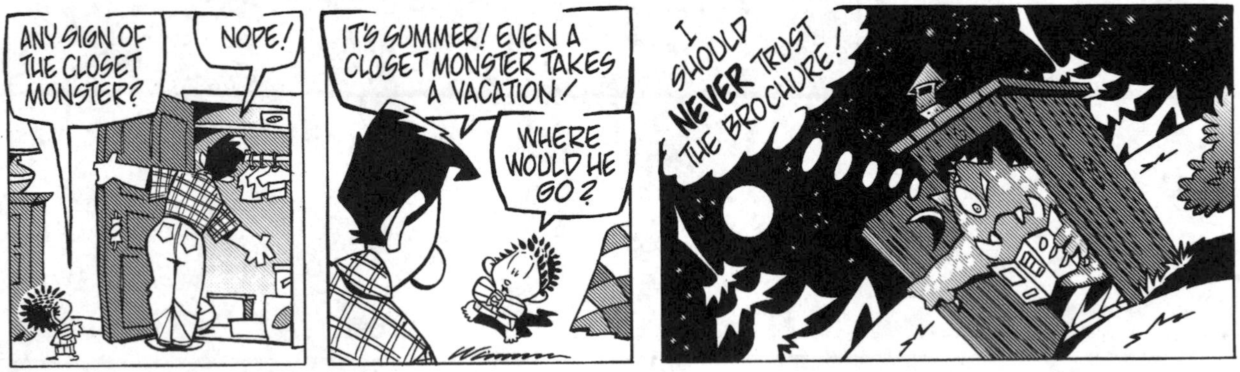
ANY SIGN OF THE CLOSET MONSTER?
NOPE!
IT'S SUMMER! EVEN A CLOSET MONSTER TAKES A VACATION!
WHERE WOULD HE GO?
I SHOULD NEVER TRUST THE BROCHURE!

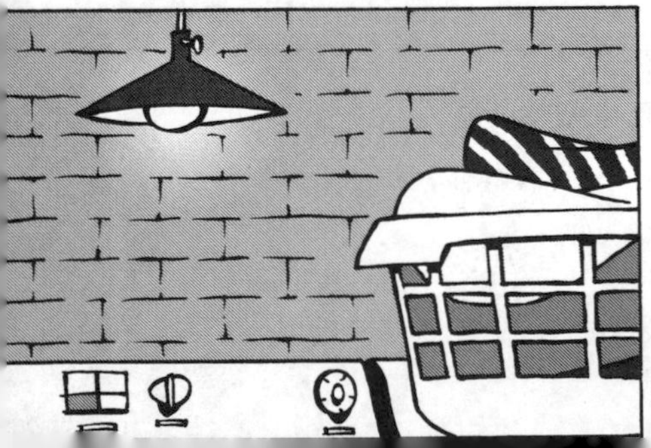

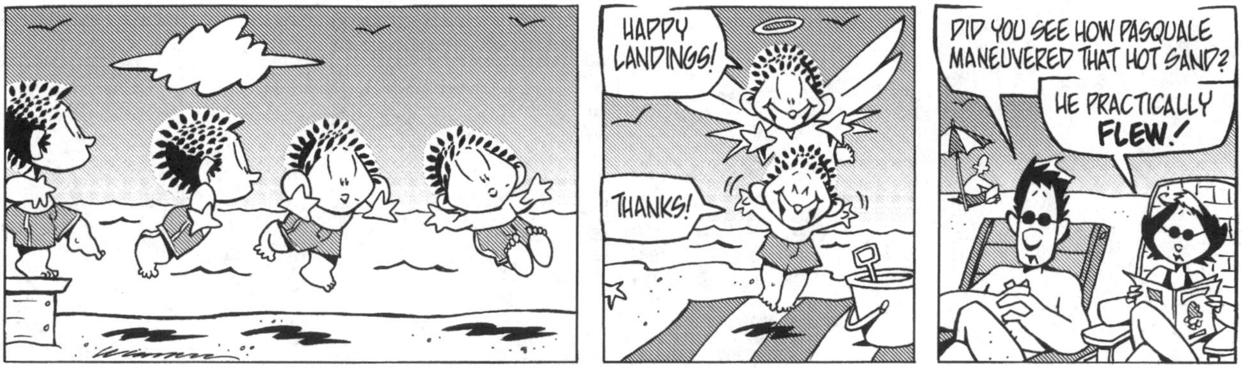
HAPPY LANDINGS!
THANKS!
DID YOU SEE HOW PASQUALE MANEUVERED THAT HOT SAND?
HE PRACTICALLY FLEW!

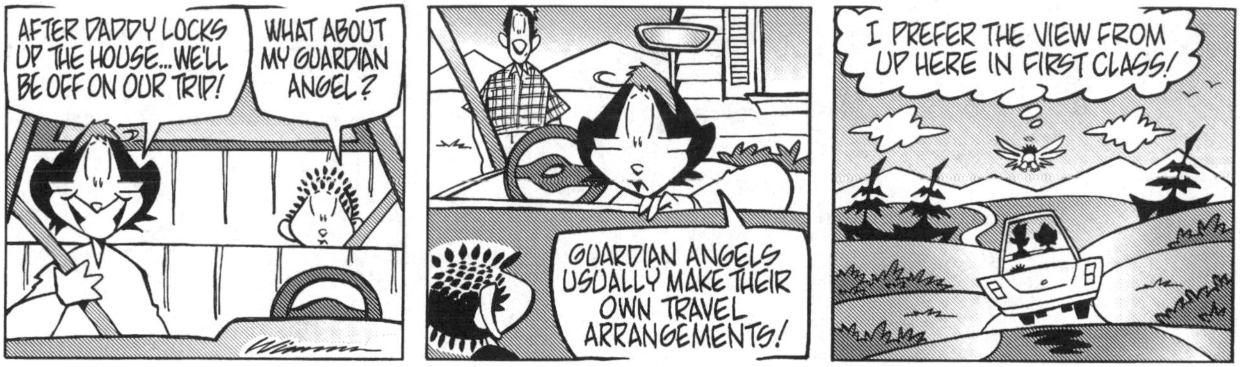
AFTER DADDY LOCKS UP THE HOUSE... WE'LL BE OFF ON OUR TRIP!
WHAT ABOUT MY GUARDIAN ANGEL?
GUARDIAN ANGELS USUALLY MAKE THEIR OWN TRAVEL ARRANGEMENTS!
I PREFER THE VIEW FROM UP HERE IN FIRST CLASS!

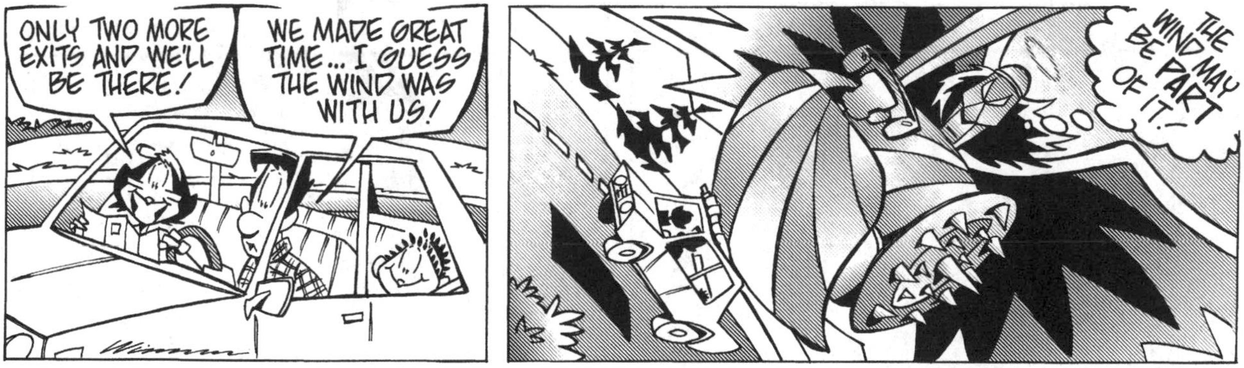
ONLY TWO MORE EXITS AND WE'LL BE THERE!
WE MADE GREAT TIME... I GUESS THE WIND WAS WITH US!
THE WIND MAY BE PART OF IT!

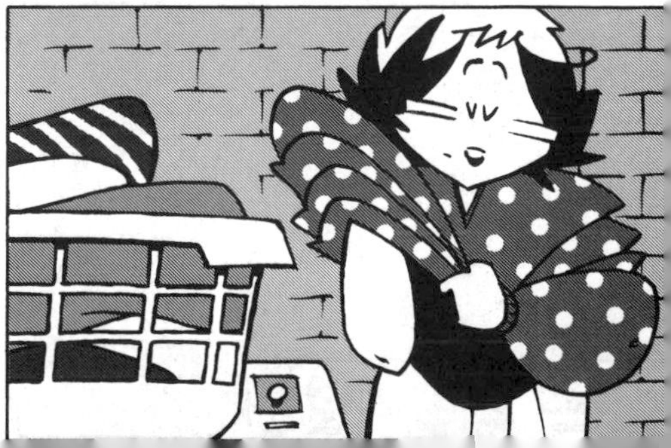

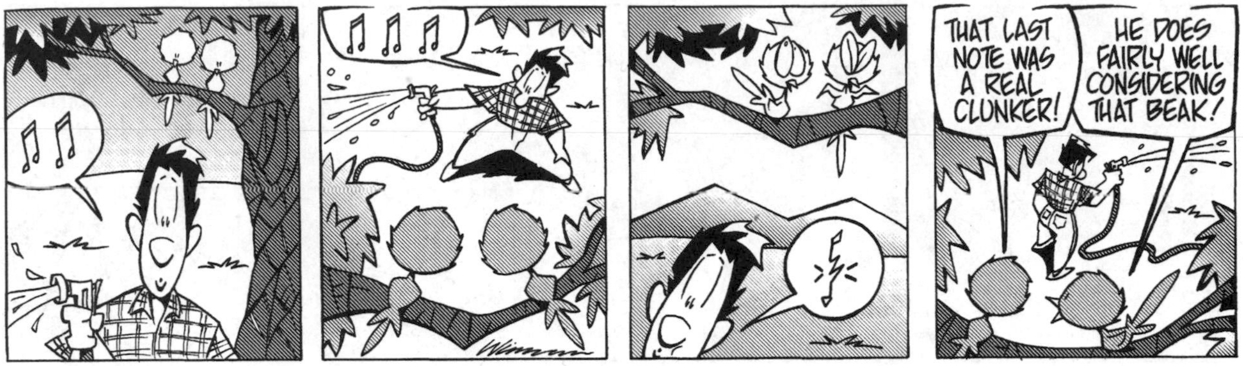
THAT LAST NOTE WAS A REAL CLUNKER!
HE DOES FAIRLY WELL CONSIDERING THAT BEAK!

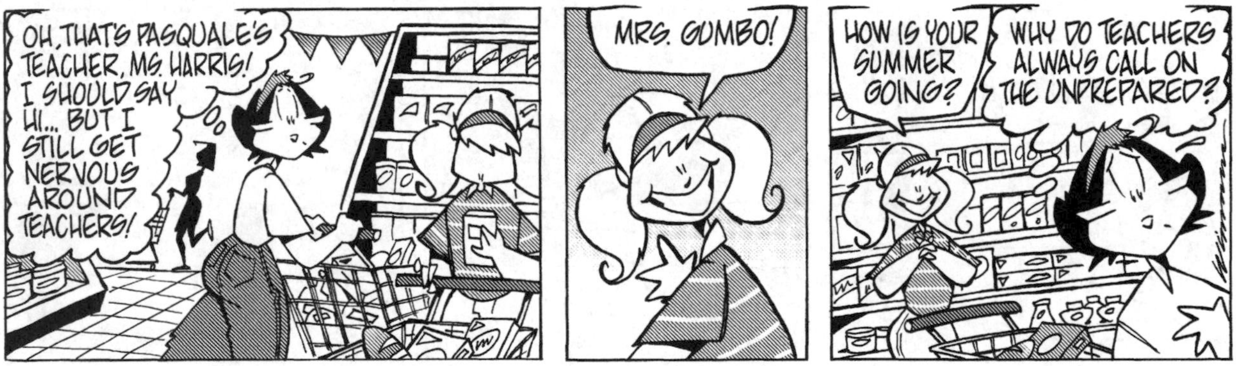
OH, THAT'S PASQUALE'S TEACHER, MS. HARRIS! I SHOULD SAY HI... BUT I STILL GET NERVOUS AROUND TEACHERS!
MRS. GUMBO!
HOW IS YOUR SUMMER GOING?
WHY DO TEACHERS ALWAYS CALL ON THE UNPREPARED?

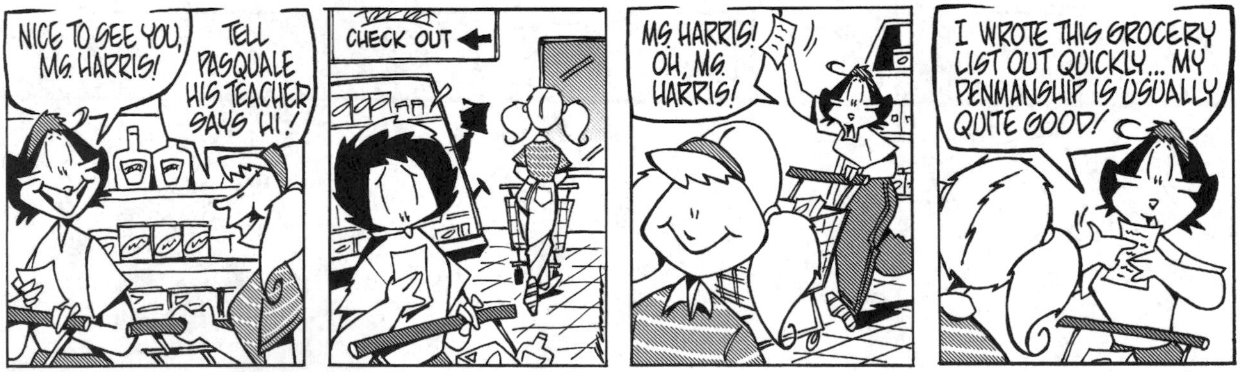
NICE TO SEE YOU, MS. HARRIS!
TELL PASQUALE HIS TEACHER SAYS HI!
CHECK OUT
MS. HARRIS! OH, MS. HARRIS!
I WROTE THIS GROCERY LIST OUT QUICKLY... MY PENMANSHIP IS USUALLY QUITE GOOD!

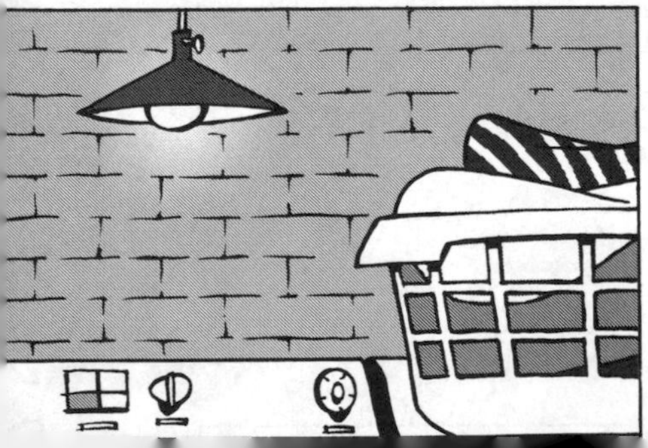

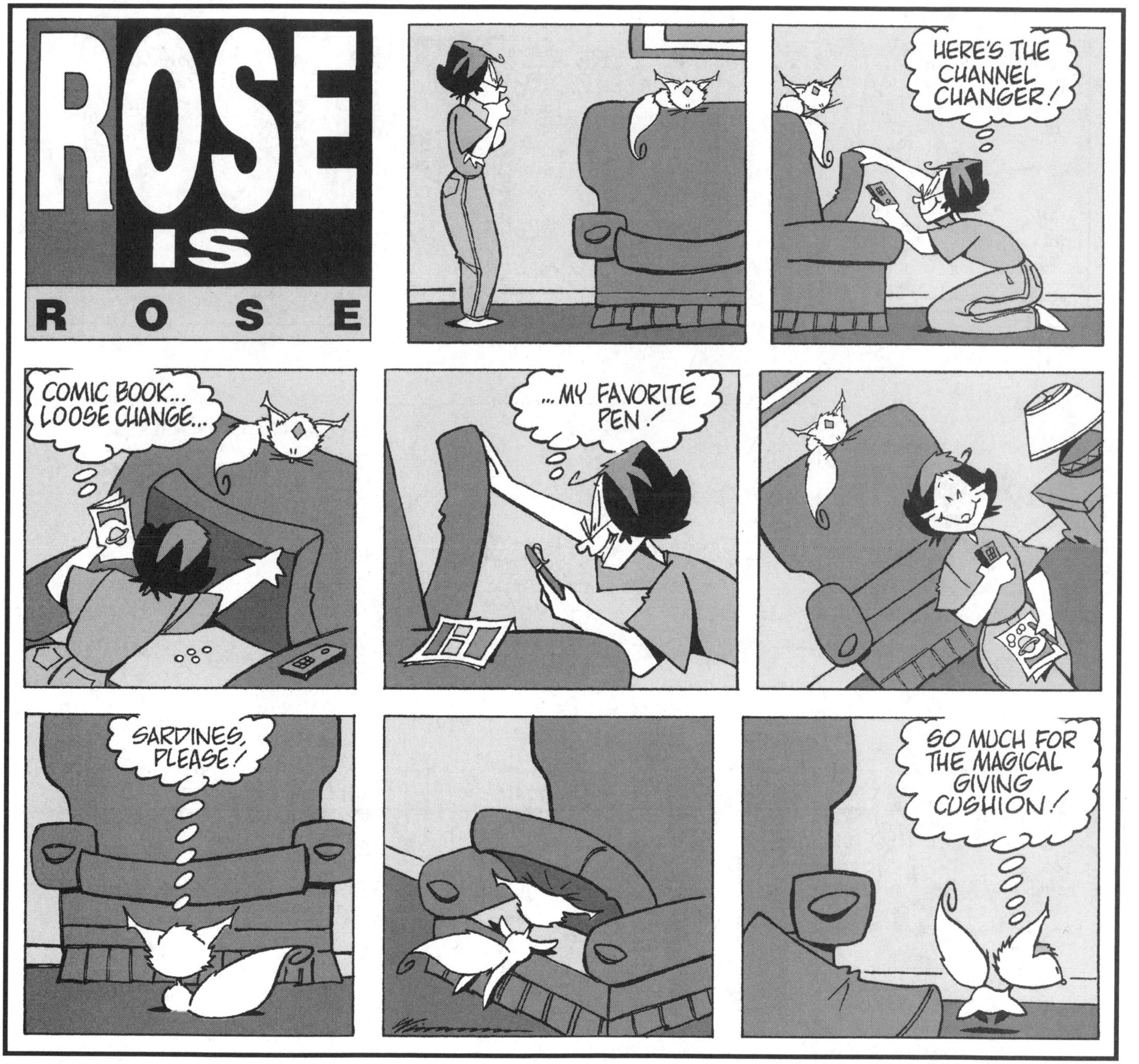
ROSE IS ROSE
HERE'S THE CHANNEL CHANGER!
COMIC BOOK... LOOSE CHANGE...
...MY FAVORITE PEN!
SARDINES, PLEASE!
SO MUCH FOR THE MAGICAL GIVING CUSHION!

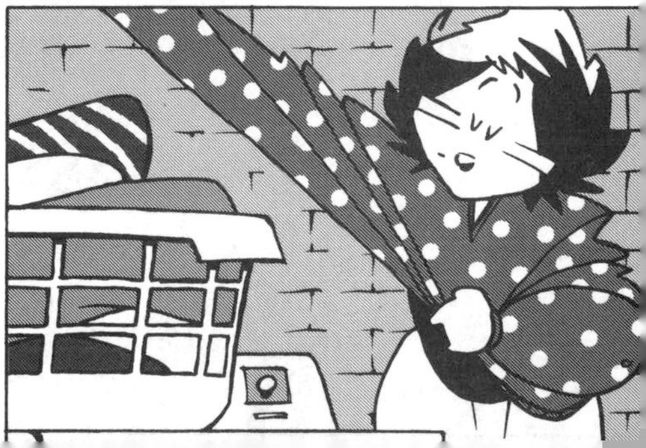

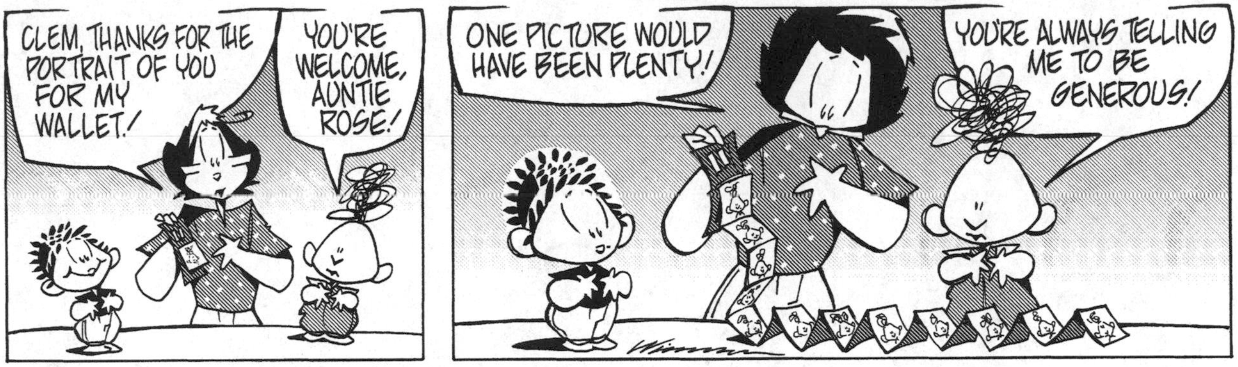
CLEM, THANKS FOR THE PORTRAIT OF YOU FOR MY WALLET!
YOU'RE WELCOME, AUNTIE ROSE!
ONE PICTURE WOULD HAVE BEEN PLENTY!
YOU'RE ALWAYS TELLING ME TO BE GENEROUS!

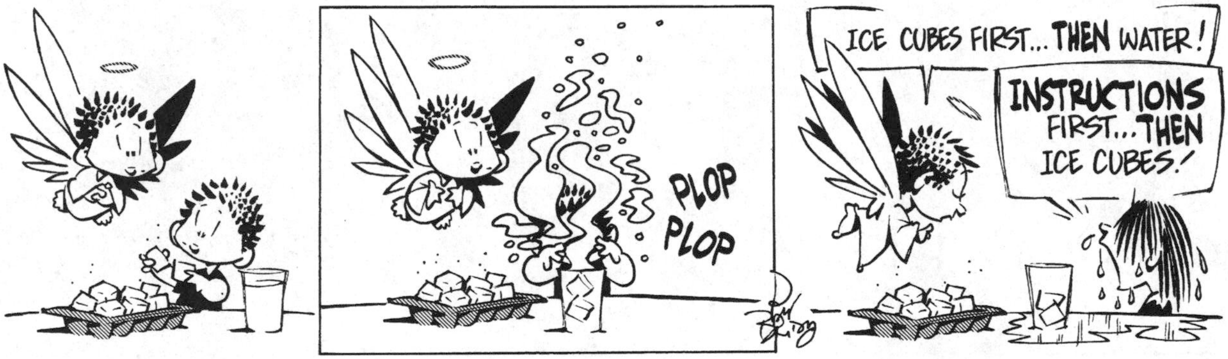
PLOP
PLOP
ICE CUBES FIRST... THEN WATER!
INSTRUCTIONS FIRST... THEN ICE CUBES!

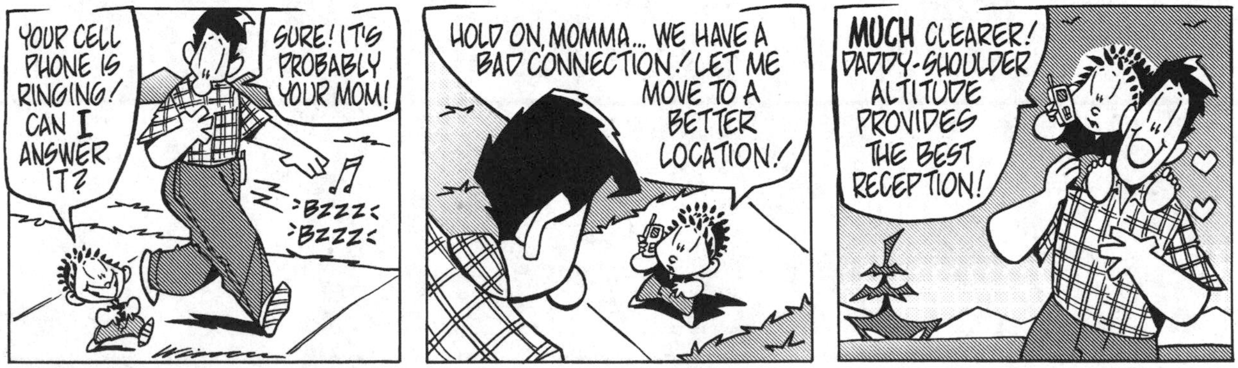
YOUR CELL PHONE IS RINGING! CAN I ANSWER IT?
SURE! IT'S PROBABLY YOUR MOM!
BZZZ
BZZZ
HOLD ON, MOMMA... WE HAVE A BAD CONNECTION! LET ME MOVE TO A BETTER LOCATION!
MUCH CLEARER! DADDY-SHOULDER ALTITUDE PROVIDES THE BEST RECEPTION!

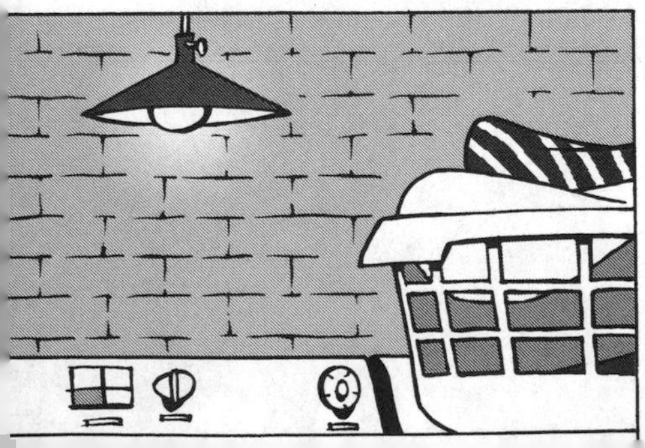

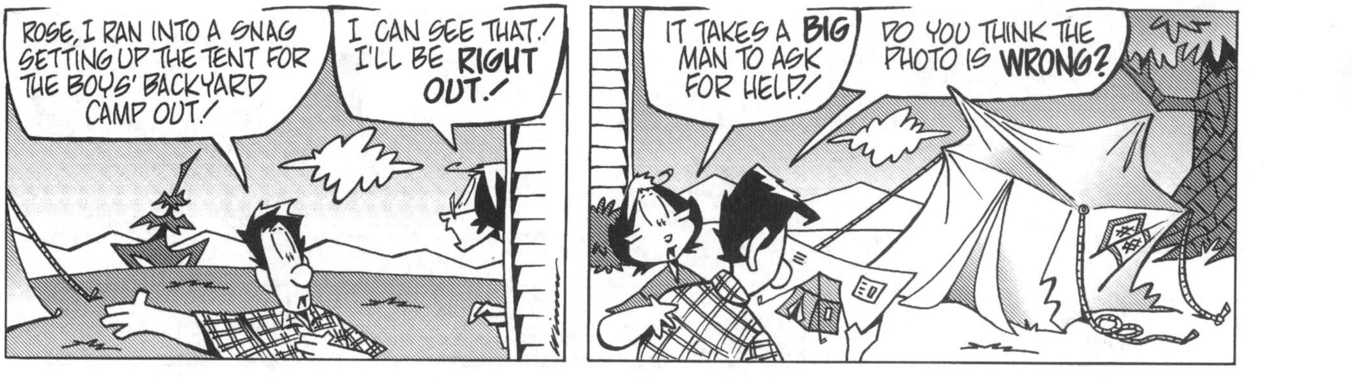
ROSE, I RAN INTO A SNAG SETTING UP THE TENT FOR THE BOYS' BACKYARD CAMP OUT!
I CAN SEE THAT! I'LL BE **RIGHT OUT!**
IT TAKES A **BIG** MAN TO ASK FOR HELP!
DO YOU THINK THE PHOTO IS **WRONG?**

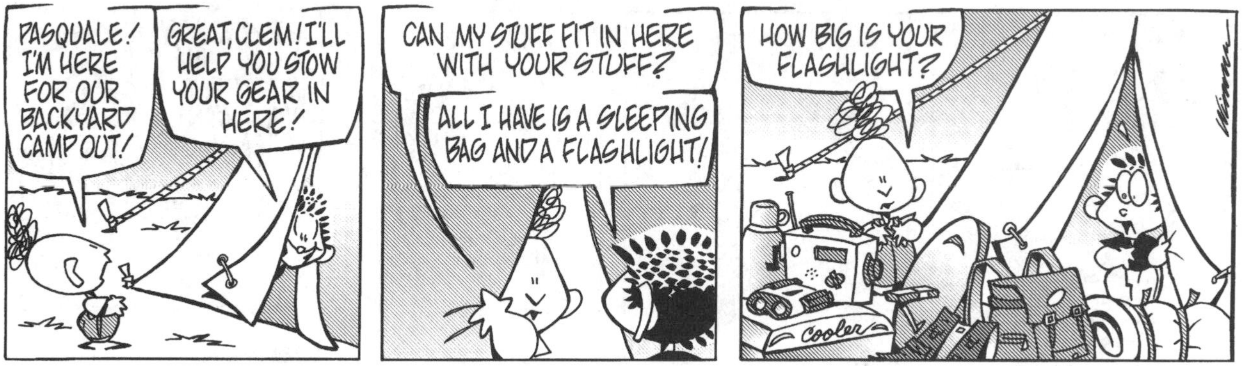
PASQUALE! I'M HERE FOR OUR BACKYARD CAMP OUT!
GREAT, CLEM! I'LL HELP YOU STOW YOUR GEAR IN HERE!
CAN MY STUFF FIT IN HERE WITH YOUR STUFF?
ALL I HAVE IS A SLEEPING BAG AND A FLASHLIGHT!
HOW BIG IS YOUR FLASHLIGHT?
Cooler

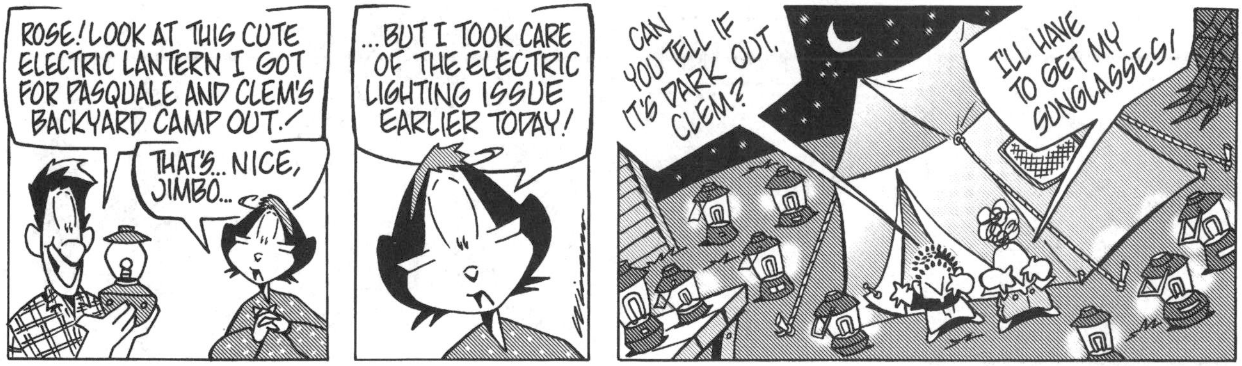
ROSE! LOOK AT THIS CUTE ELECTRIC LANTERN I GOT FOR PASQUALE AND CLEM'S BACKYARD CAMP OUT!
THAT'S... NICE, JIMBO...
...BUT I TOOK CARE OF THE ELECTRIC LIGHTING ISSUE EARLIER TODAY!
CAN YOU TELL IF IT'S DARK OUT, CLEM?
I'LL HAVE TO GET MY SUNGLASSES!

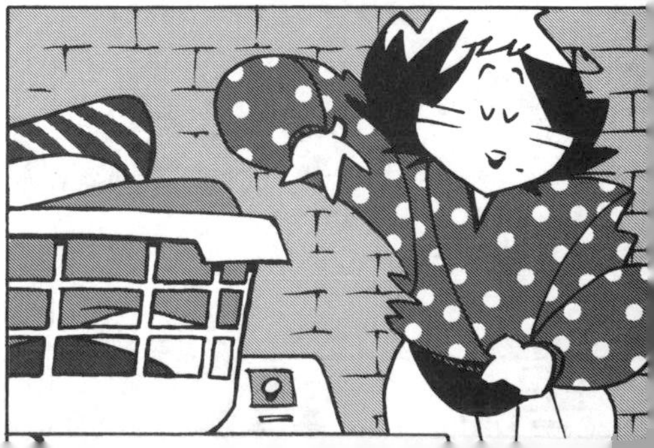

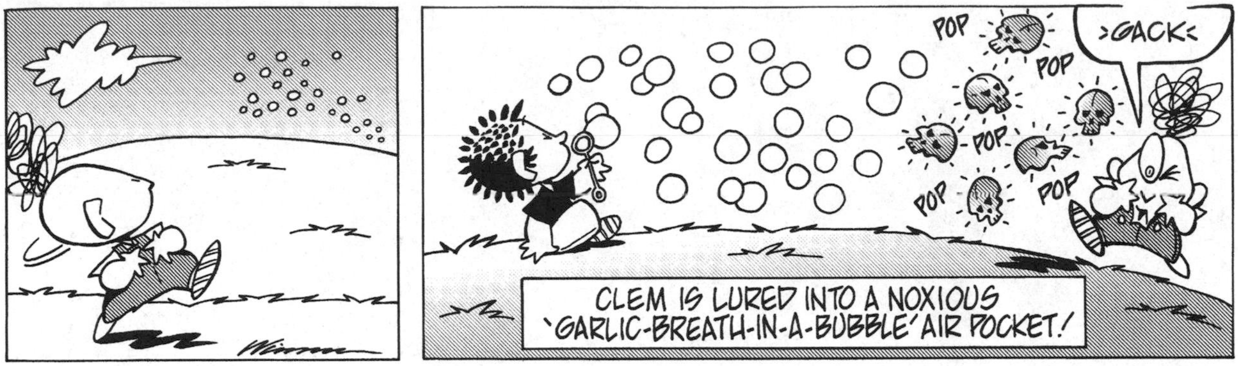
POP
POP
>GACK<
POP
POP
POP
POP
CLEM IS LURED INTO A NOXIOUS `GARLIC-BREATH-IN-A-BUBBLE' AIR POCKET!

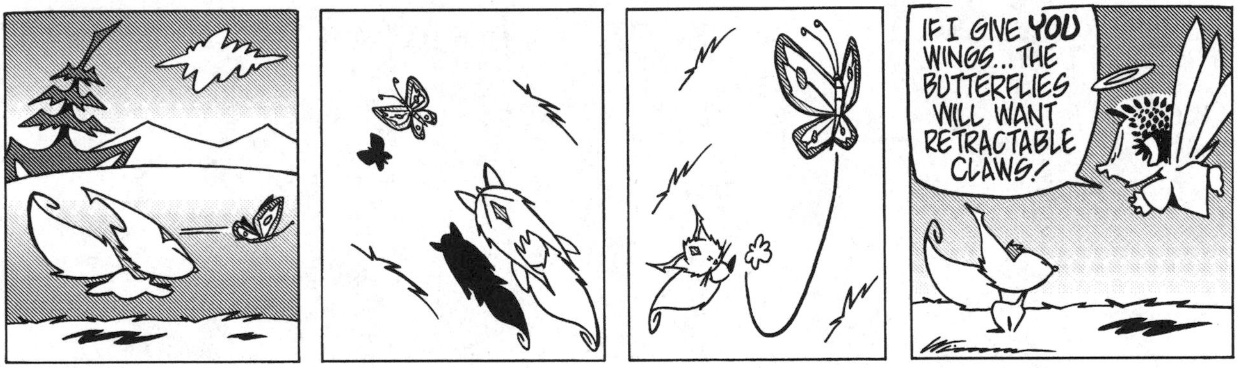
IF I GIVE YOU WINGS... THE BUTTERFLIES WILL WANT RETRACTABLE CLAWS!

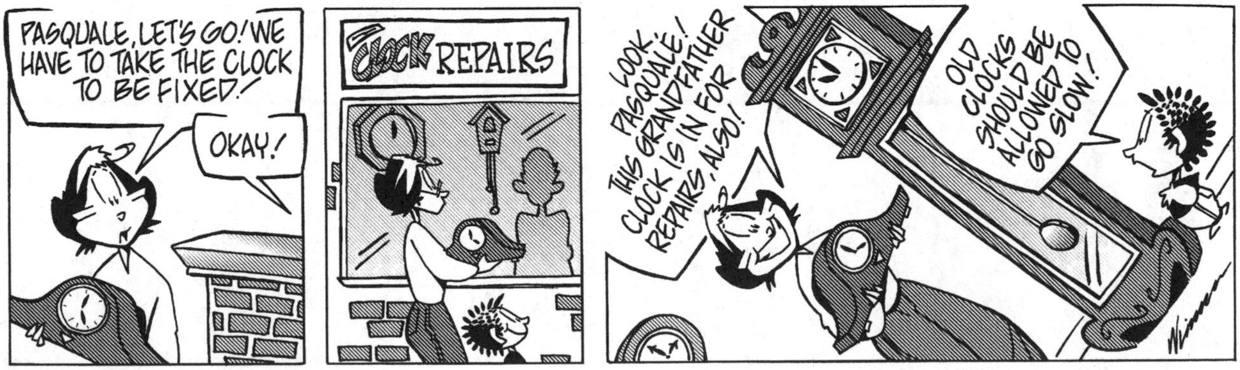
PASQUALE, LET'S GO! WE HAVE TO TAKE THE CLOCK TO BE FIXED!
OKAY!
CLOCK REPAIRS
LOOK, PASQUALE! THIS GRANDFATHER CLOCK IS IN FOR REPAIRS, ALSO!
OLD CLOCKS SHOULD BE ALLOWED TO GO SLOW!

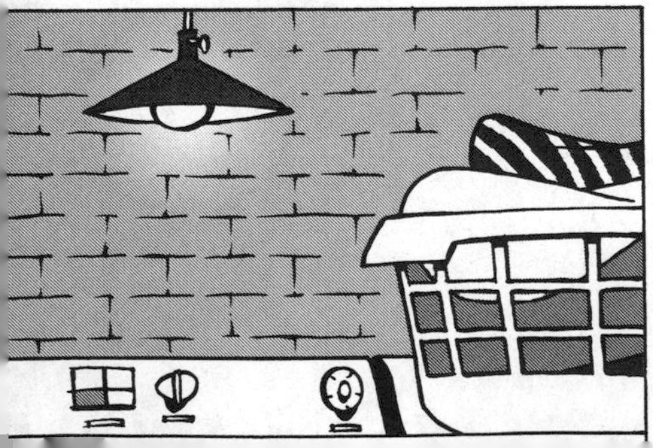

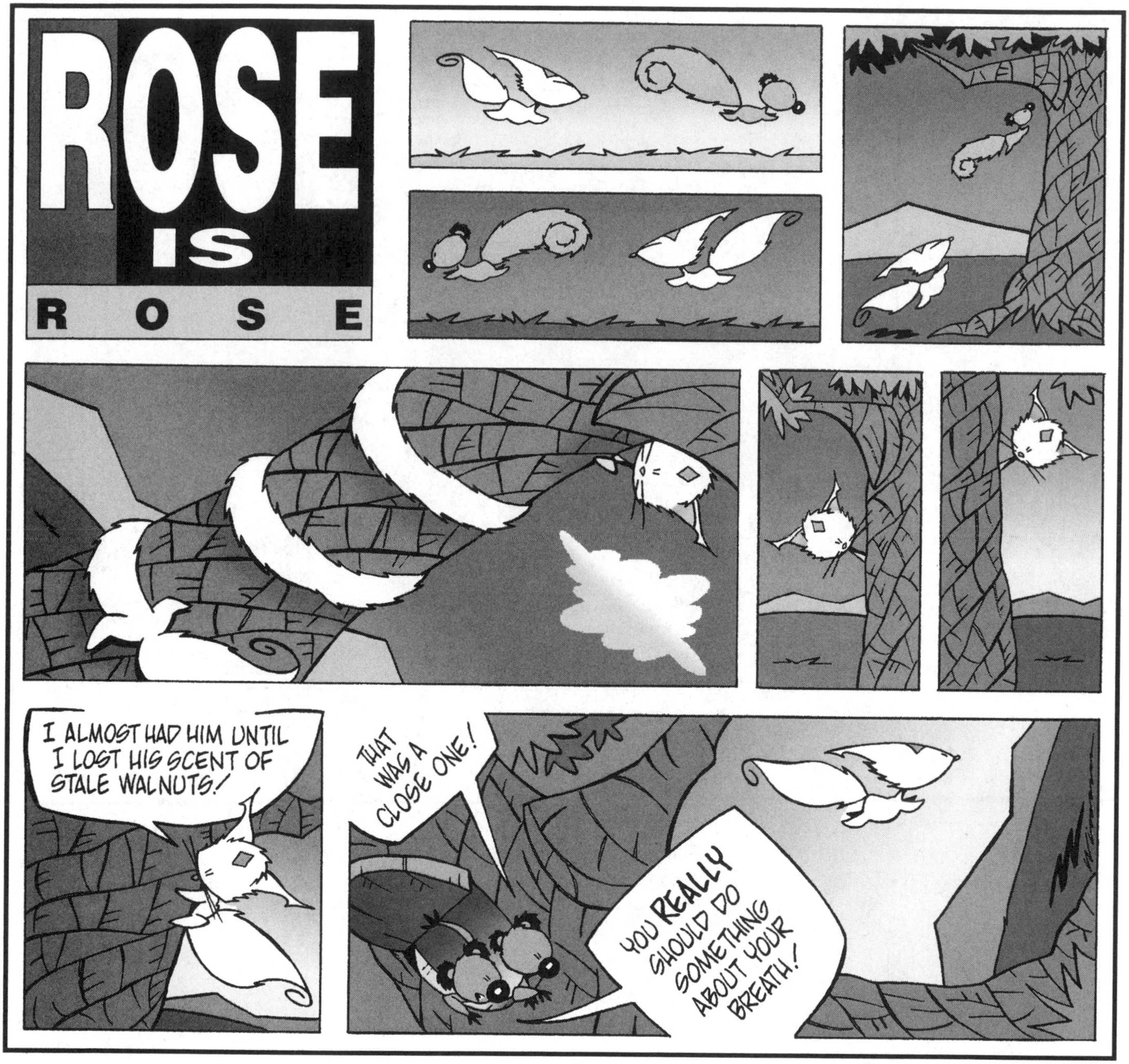
ROSE IS ROSE
I ALMOST HAD HIM UNTIL I LOST HIS SCENT OF STALE WALNUTS!
THAT WAS A CLOSE ONE!
YOU **REALLY** SHOULD DO SOMETHING ABOUT YOUR BREATH!

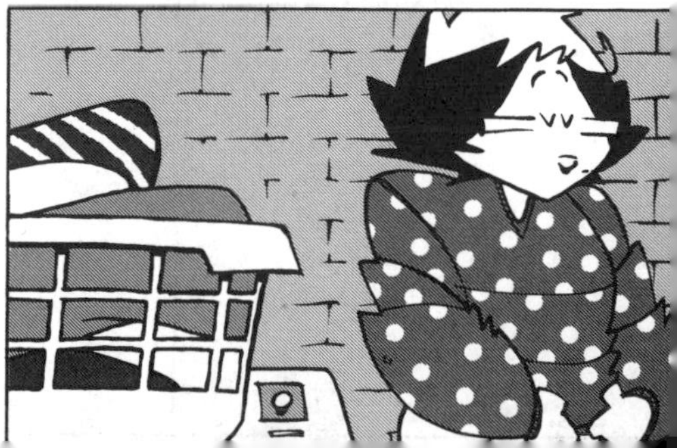

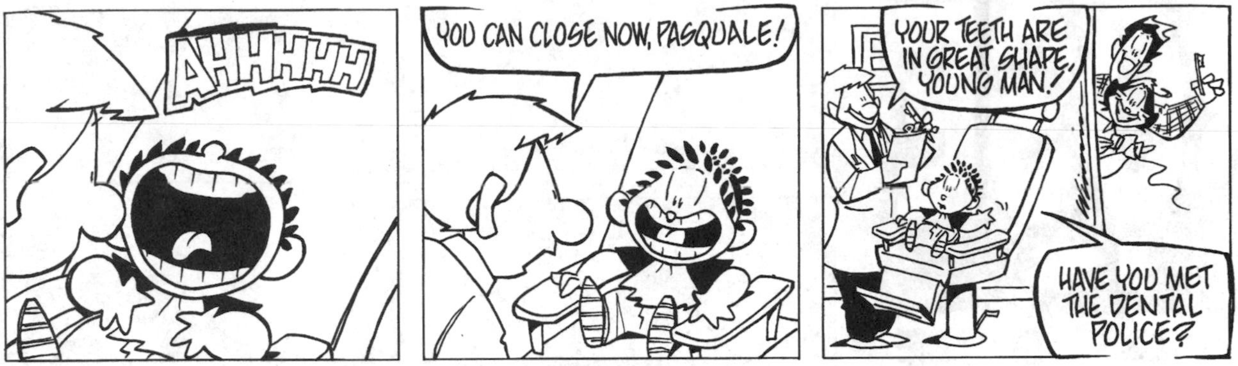
AHHHHH
YOU CAN CLOSE NOW, PASQUALE!
YOUR TEETH ARE IN GREAT SHAPE, YOUNG MAN!
HAVE YOU MET THE DENTAL POLICE?

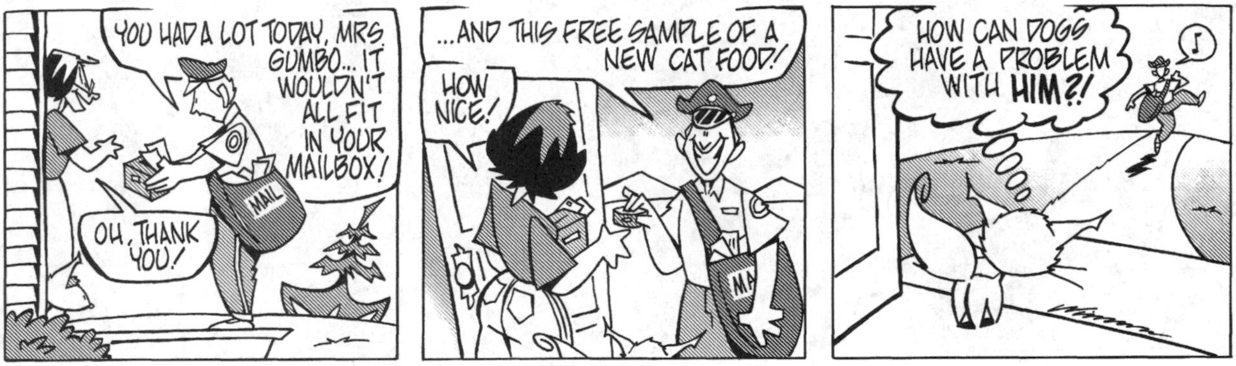
YOU HAD A LOT TODAY, MRS GUMBO... IT WOULDN'T ALL FIT IN YOUR MAILBOX!
MAIL
OH, THANK YOU!
...AND THIS FREE SAMPLE OF A NEW CAT FOOD!
HOW NICE!
HOW CAN DOGS HAVE A PROBLEM WITH HIM?!

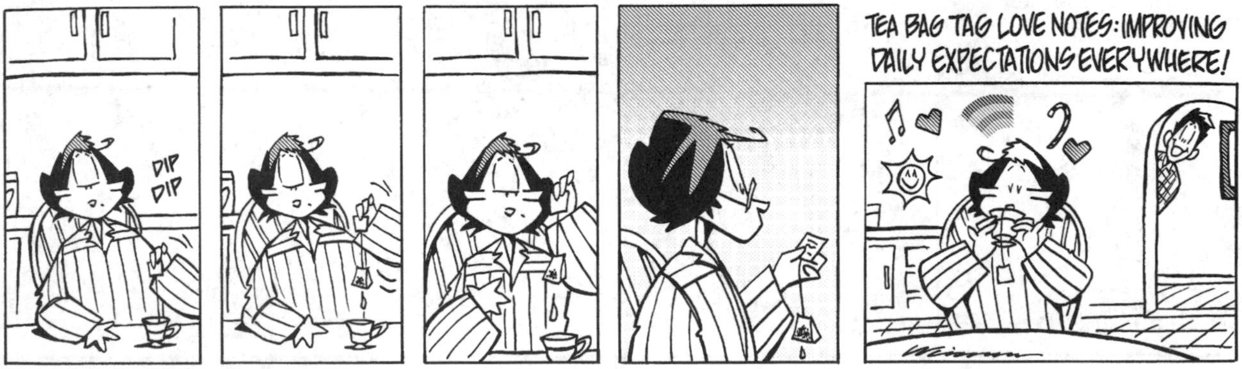
DIP DIP
TEA BAG TAG LOVE NOTES: IMPROVING DAILY EXPECTATIONS EVERYWHERE!

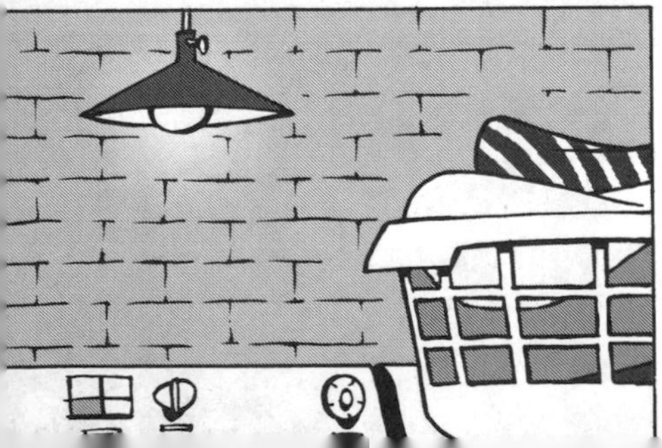

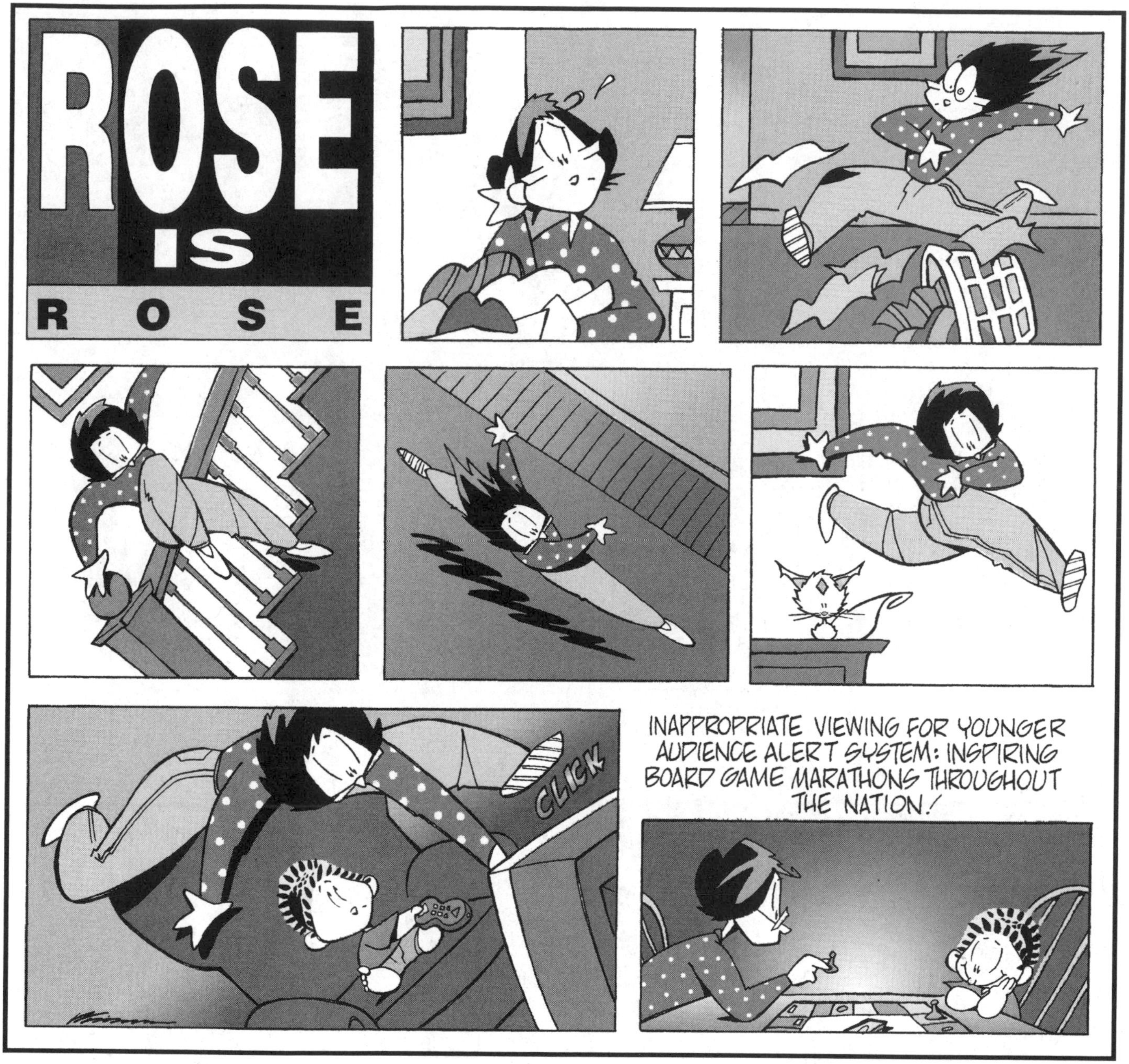
ROSE IS ROSE
CLICK
INAPPROPRIATE VIEWING FOR YOUNGER AUDIENCE ALERT SYSTEM: INSPIRING BOARD GAME MARATHONS THROUGHOUT THE NATION!

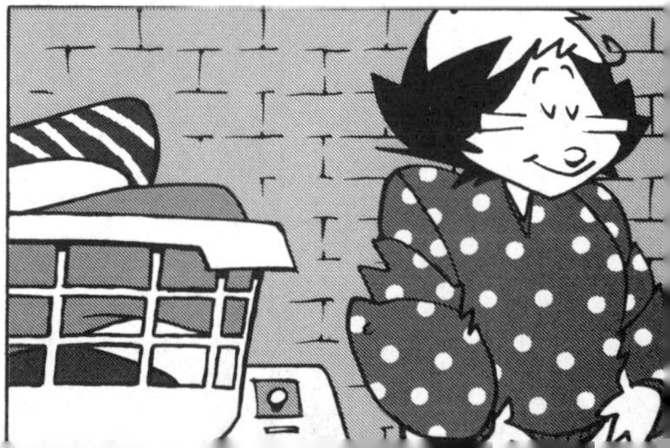

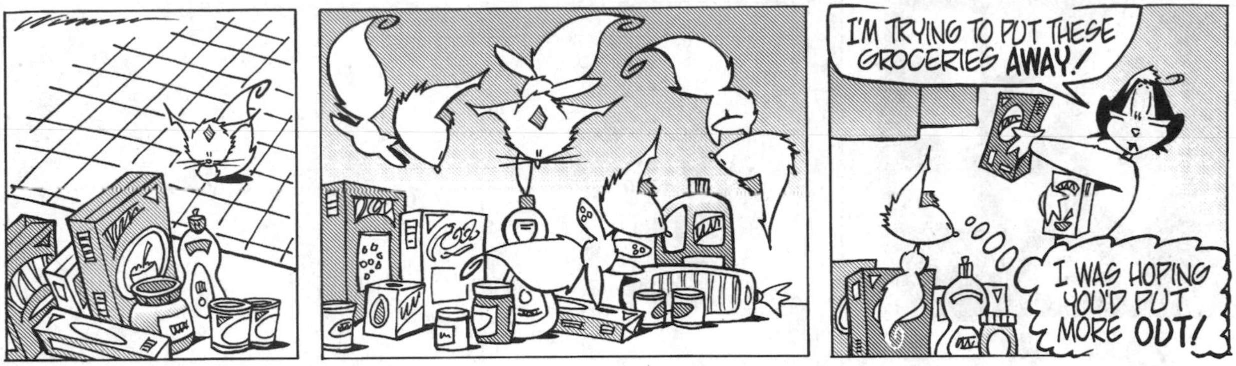
I'M TRYING TO PUT THESE GROCERIES AWAY!
I WAS HOPING YOU'D PUT MORE OUT!

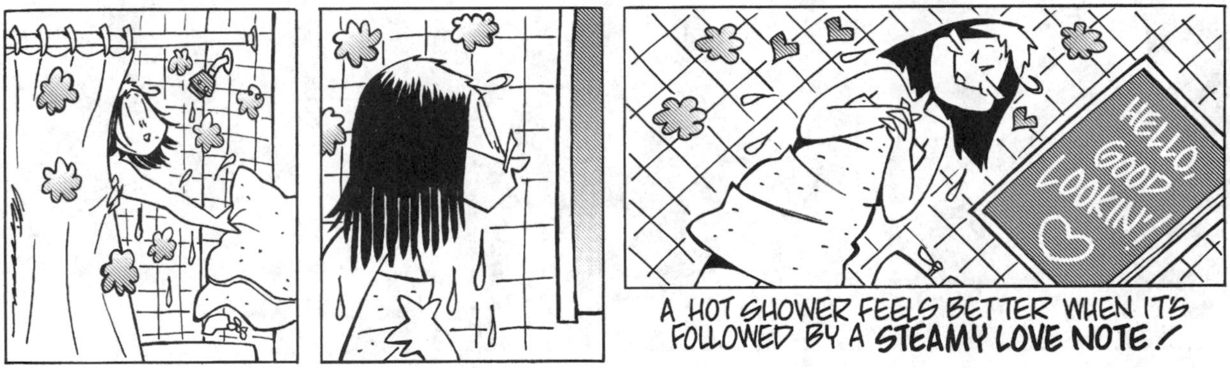
HELLO, GOOD LOOKIN'!
A HOT SHOWER FEELS BETTER WHEN IT'S FOLLOWED BY A STEAMY LOVE NOTE!

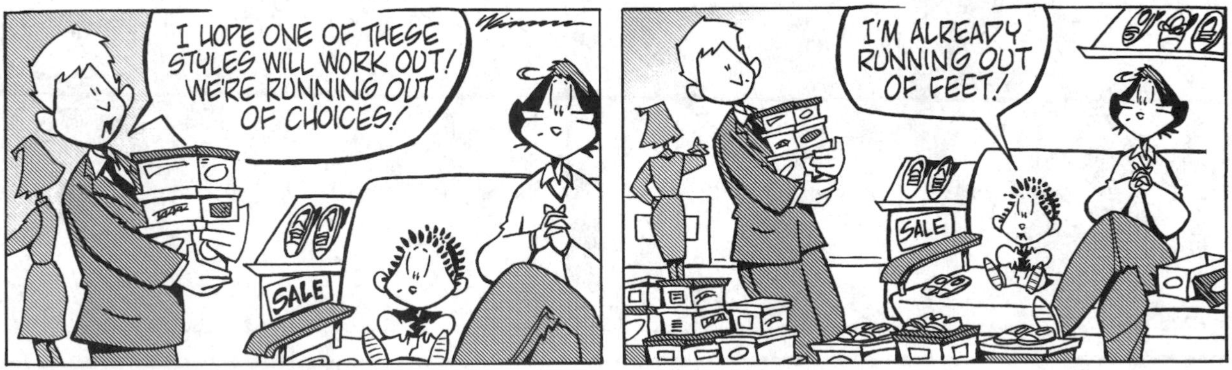
I HOPE ONE OF THESE STYLES WILL WORK OUT! WE'RE RUNNING OUT OF CHOICES!
SALE
I'M ALREADY RUNNING OUT OF FEET!
SALE

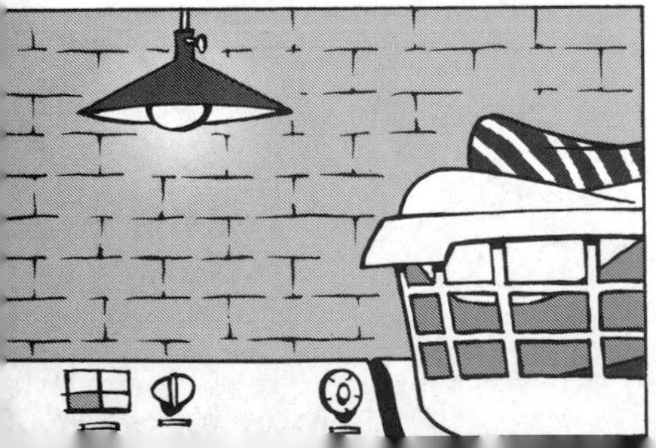

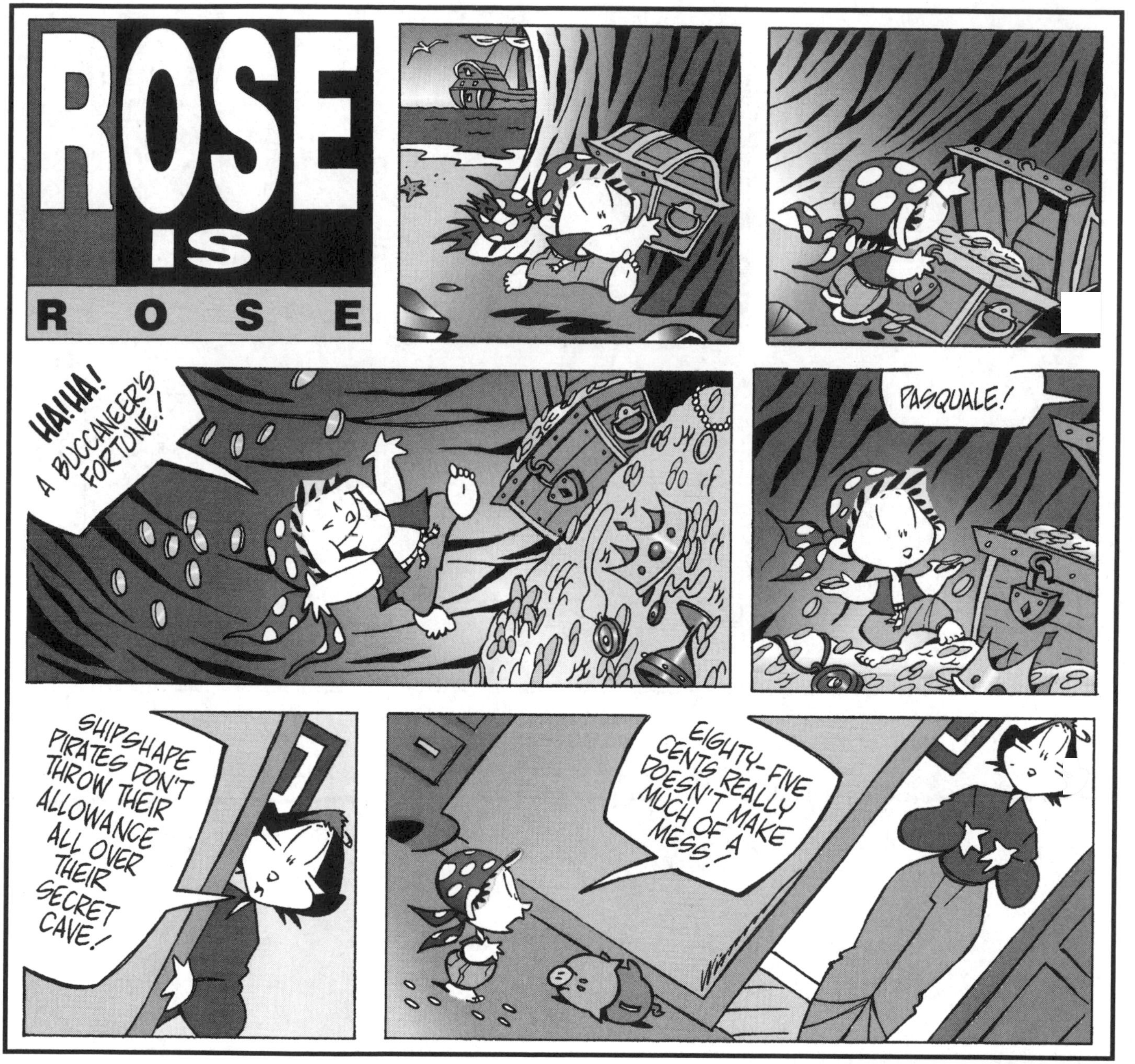
ROSE IS ROSE
HA!HA! A BUCCANEER'S FORTUNE!
PASQUALE!
SHIPSHAPE PIRATES DON'T THROW THEIR ALLOWANCE ALL OVER THEIR SECRET CAVE!
EIGHTY-FIVE CENTS REALLY DOESN'T MAKE MUCH OF A MESS!

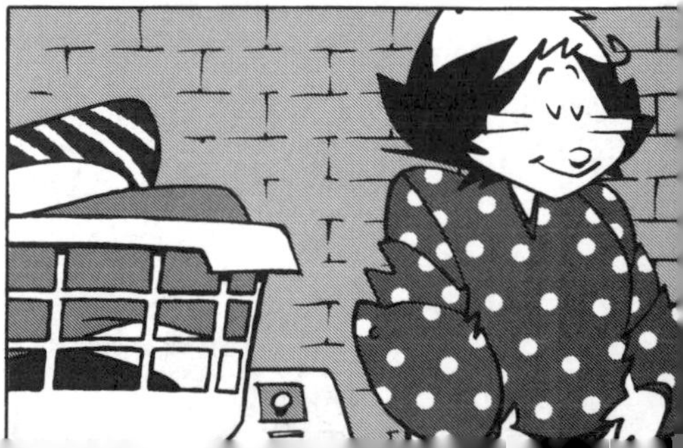

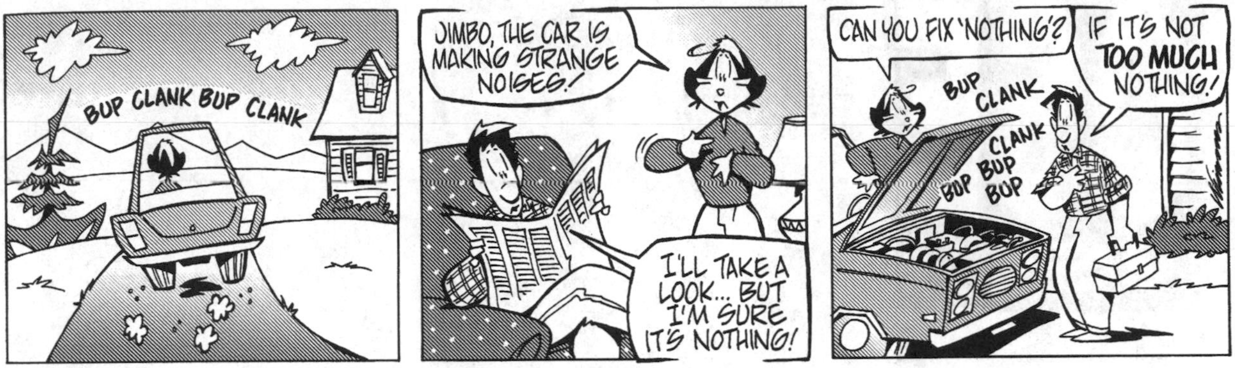
BUP CLANK BUP CLANK
JIMBO, THE CAR IS MAKING STRANGE NOISES!
I'LL TAKE A LOOK... BUT I'M SURE IT'S NOTHING!
CAN YOU FIX 'NOTHING'?
BUP CLANK
CLANK BOP BUP BUP
IF IT'S NOT TOO MUCH NOTHING!

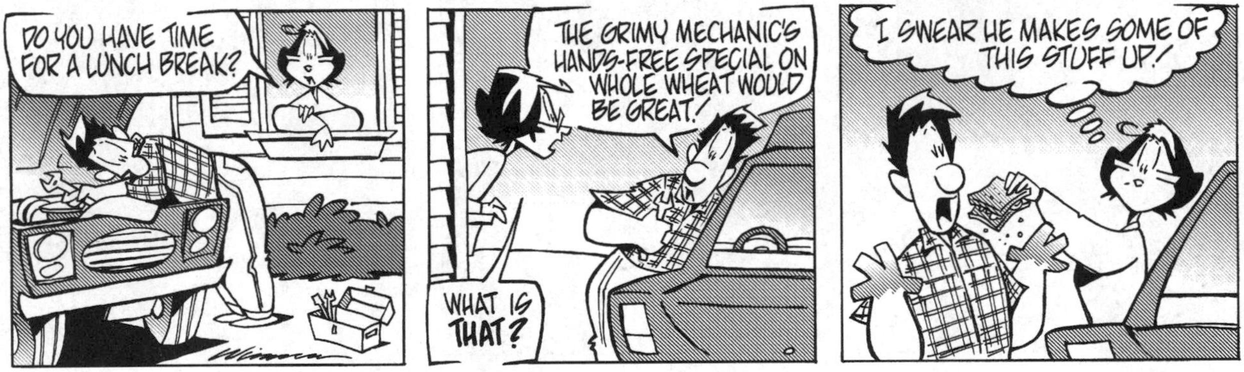
DO YOU HAVE TIME FOR A LUNCH BREAK?
THE GRIMY MECHANIC'S HANDS-FREE SPECIAL ON WHOLE WHEAT WOULD BE GREAT!
WHAT IS THAT?
I SWEAR HE MAKES SOME OF THIS STUFF UP!

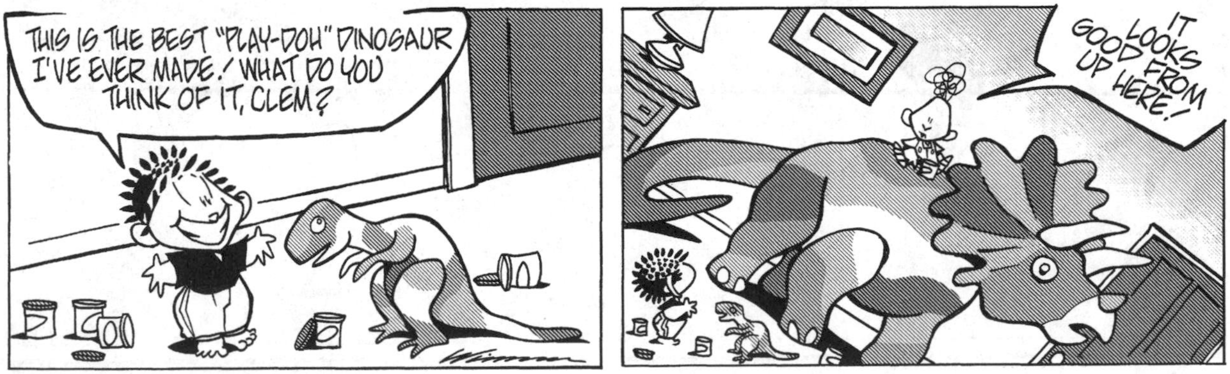
THIS IS THE BEST "PLAY-DOH" DINOSAUR I'VE EVER MADE! WHAT DO YOU THINK OF IT, CLEM?
IT LOOKS GOOD FROM UP HERE!

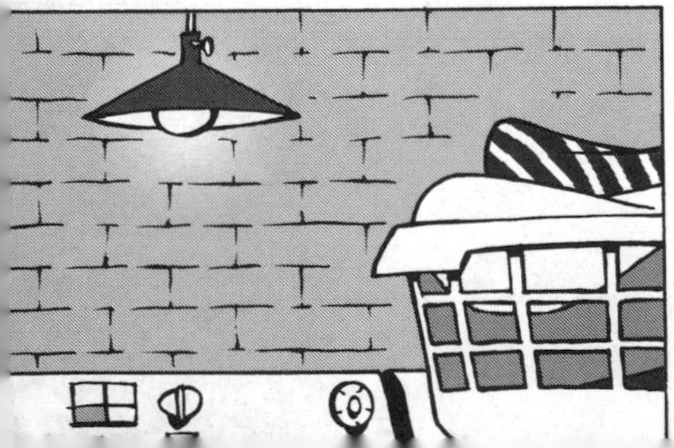

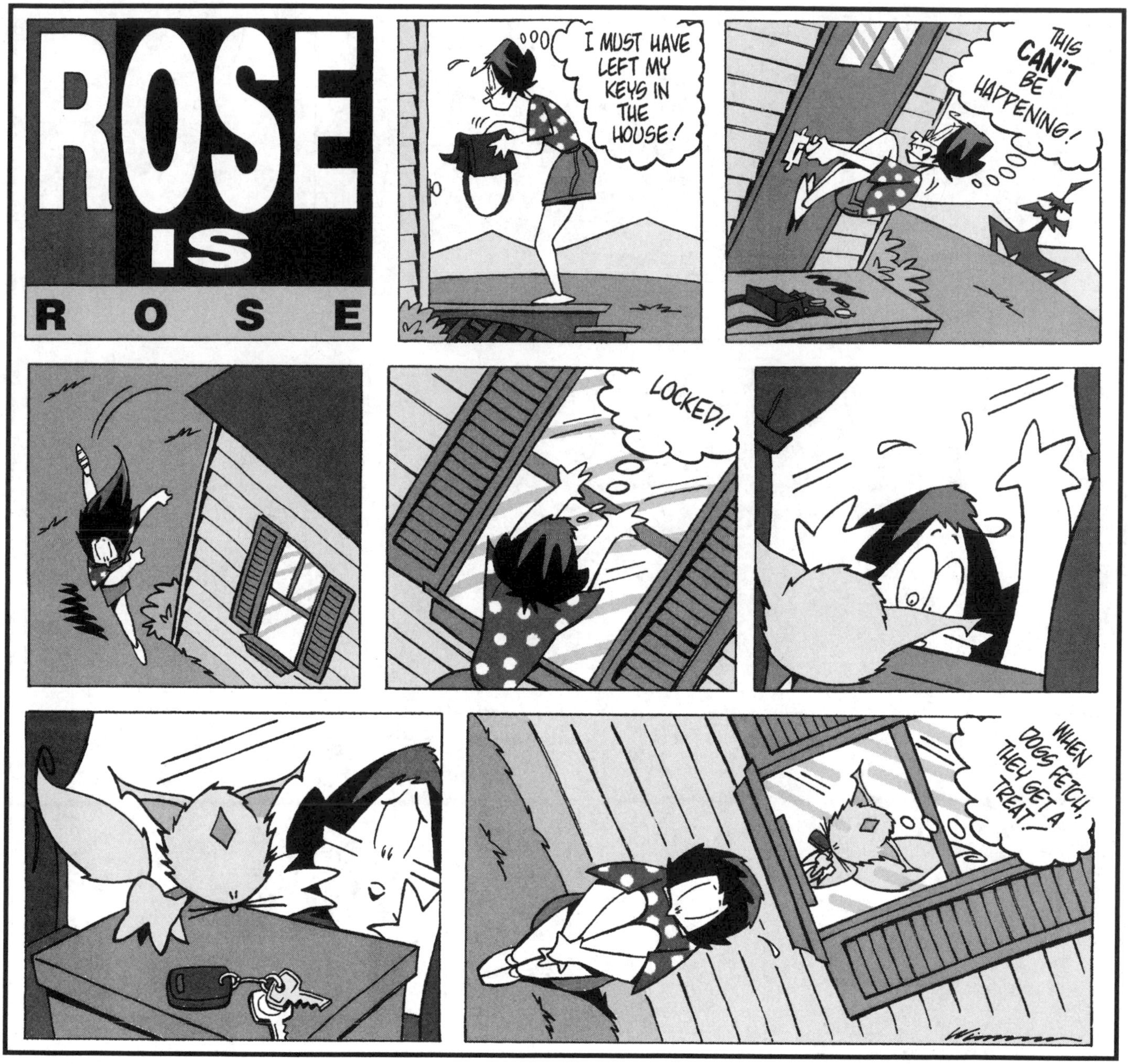
ROSE IS ROSE
I MUST HAVE LEFT MY KEYS IN THE HOUSE!
THIS CAN'T BE HAPPENING!
LOCKED!
WHEN DOGS FETCH, THEY GET A TREAT!

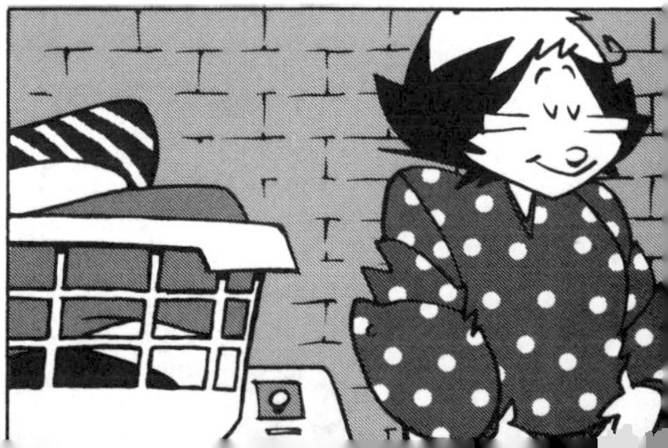

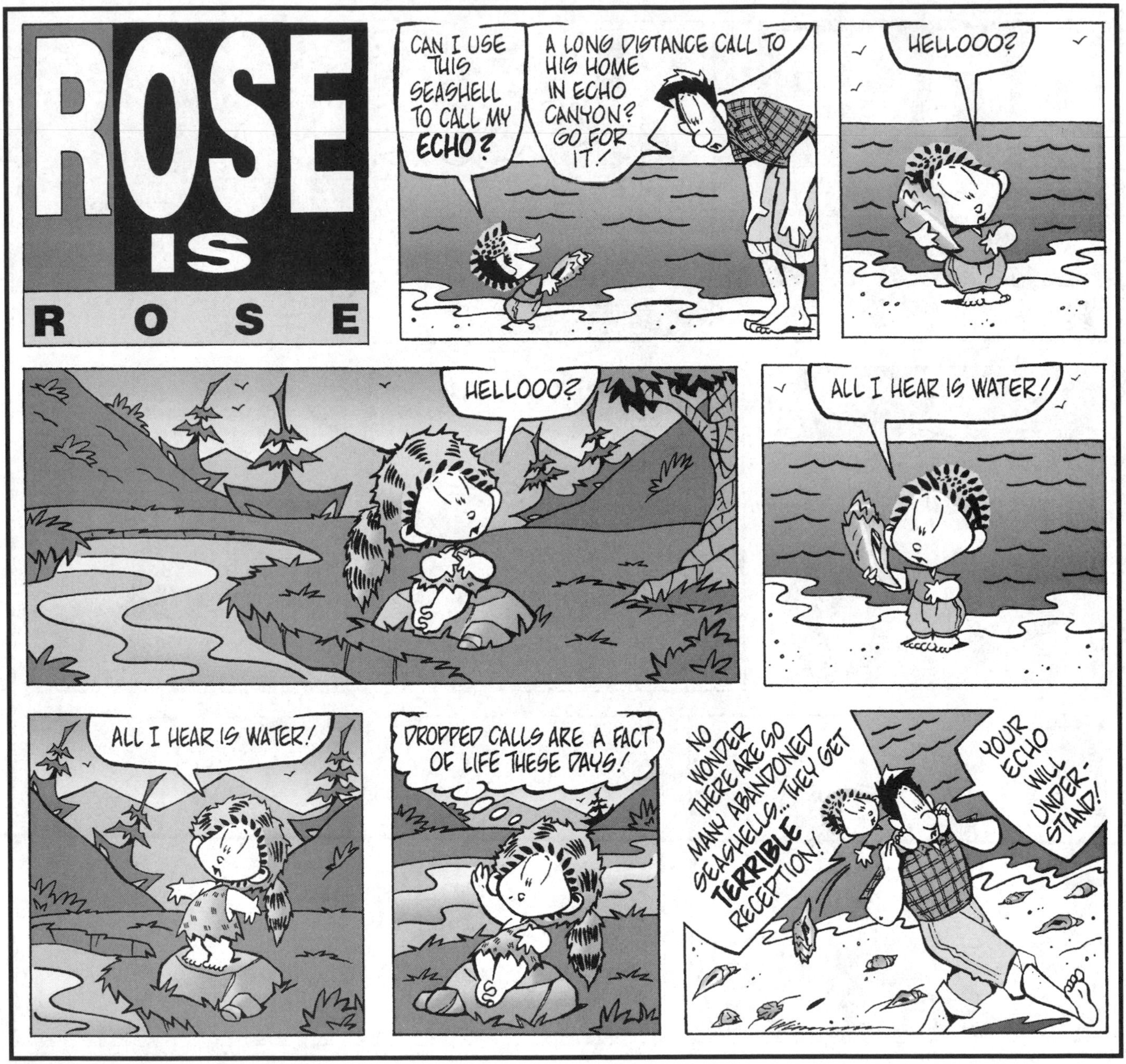
ROSE IS ROSE
CAN I USE THIS SEASHELL TO CALL MY ECHO?
A LONG DISTANCE CALL TO HIS HOME IN ECHO CANYON? GO FOR IT!
HELLOOO?
HELLOOO?
ALL I HEAR IS WATER!
ALL I HEAR IS WATER!
DROPPED CALLS ARE A FACT OF LIFE THESE DAYS!
NO WONDER THERE ARE SO MANY ABANDONED SEASHELLS... THEY GET TERRIBLE RECEPTION!
YOUR ECHO WILL UNDER-STAND!

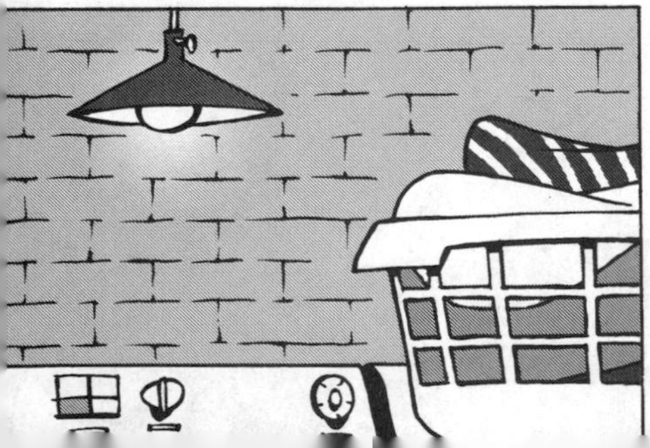

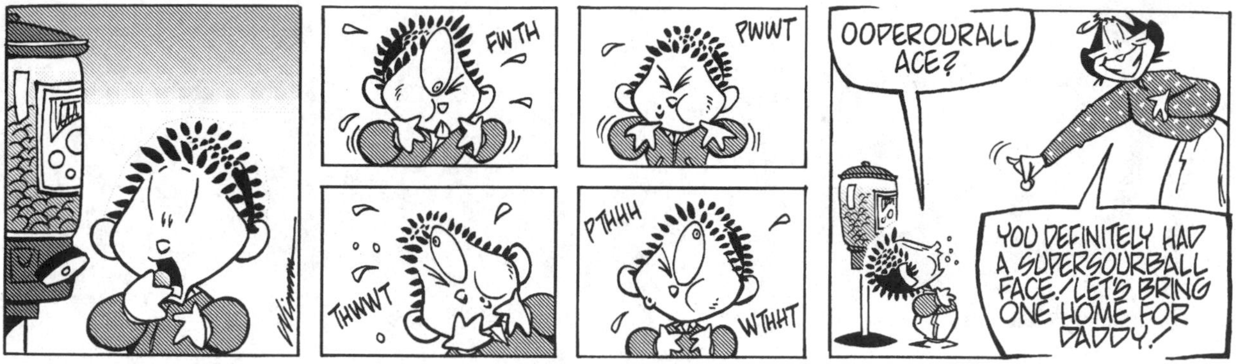
FWTH
PWWT
THWWT
PTHHH
WTHHT
OOPEROURALL ACE?
YOU DEFINITELY HAD A SUPERSOURBALL FACE! LET'S BRING ONE HOME FOR DADDY!

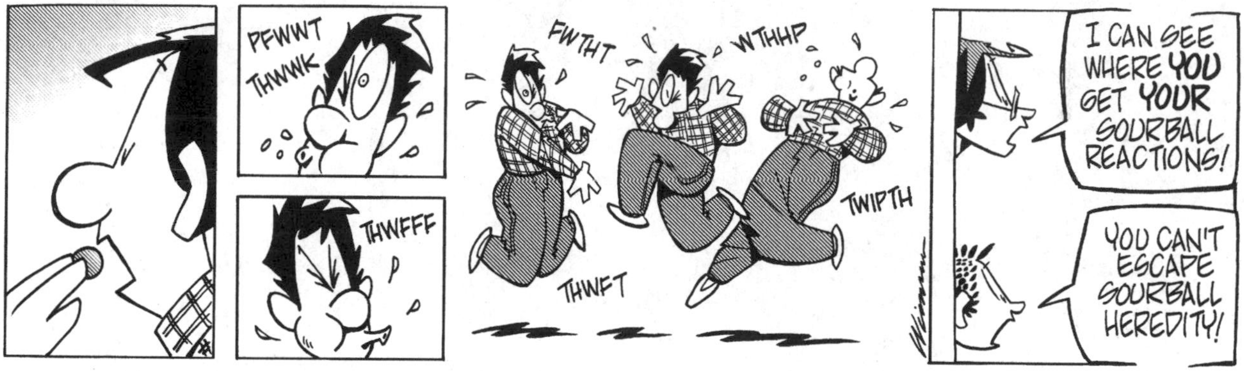
PFWWT
THWWK
THWFFF
FWTHT
WTHHP
THWFT
TWIPTH
I CAN SEE WHERE **YOU** GET **YOUR** SOURBALL REACTIONS!
YOU CAN'T ESCAPE SOURBALL HEREDITY!

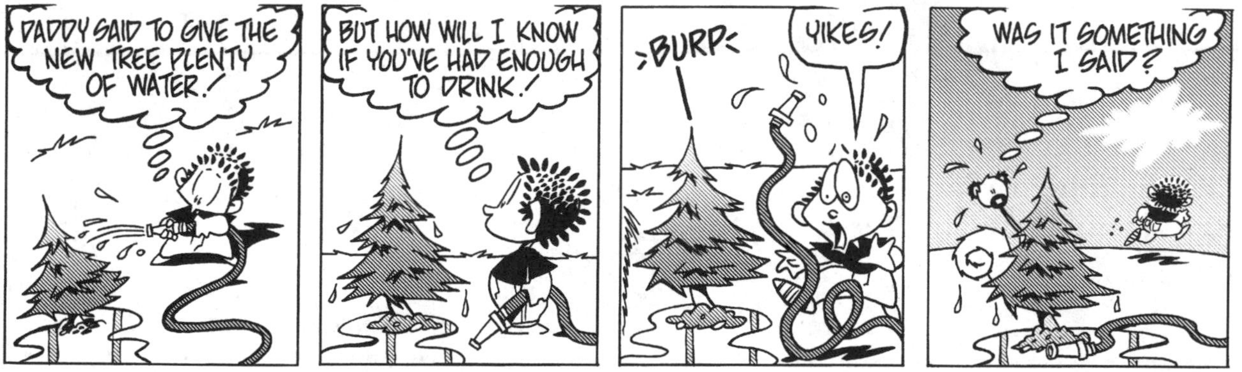
DADDY SAID TO GIVE THE NEW TREE PLENTY OF WATER!
BUT HOW WILL I KNOW IF YOU'VE HAD ENOUGH TO DRINK!
>BURP<
YIKES!
WAS IT SOMETHING I SAID?

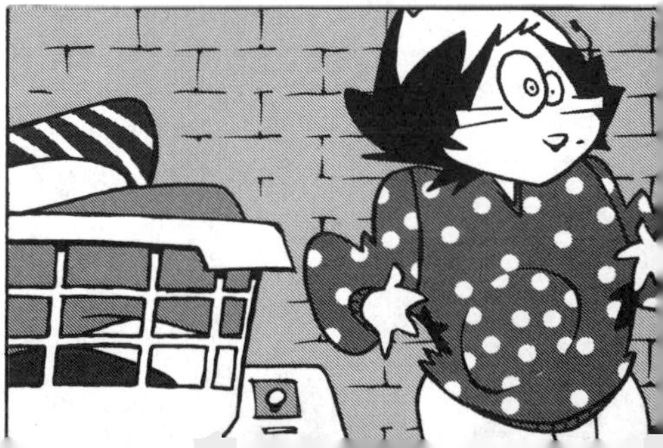

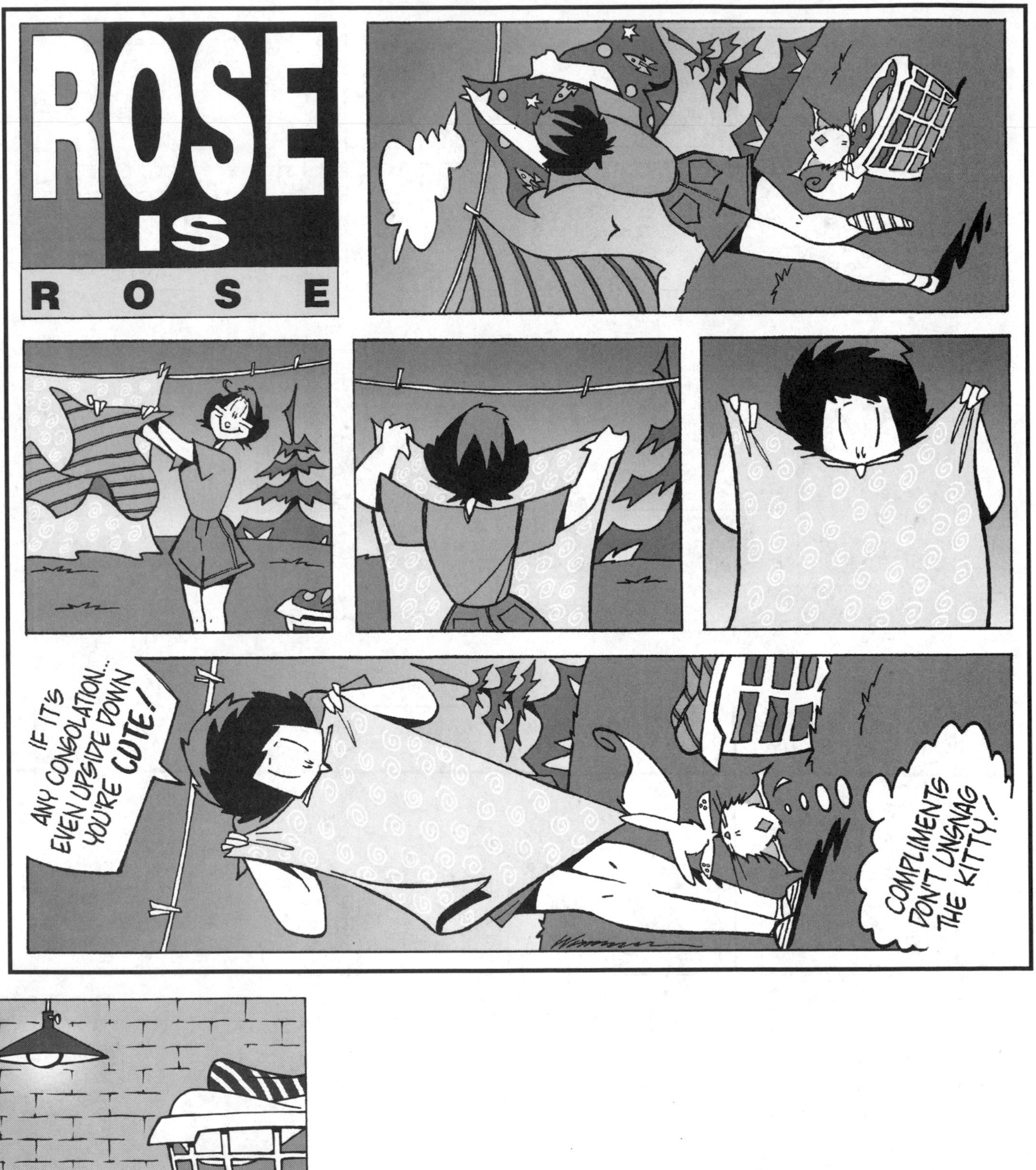
ROSE IS ROSE
IF IT'S ANY CONSOLATION... EVEN UPSIDE DOWN YOU'RE CUTE!
COMPLIMENTS DON'T UNSNAG THE KITTY!

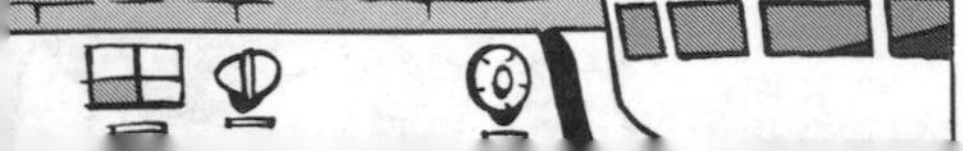

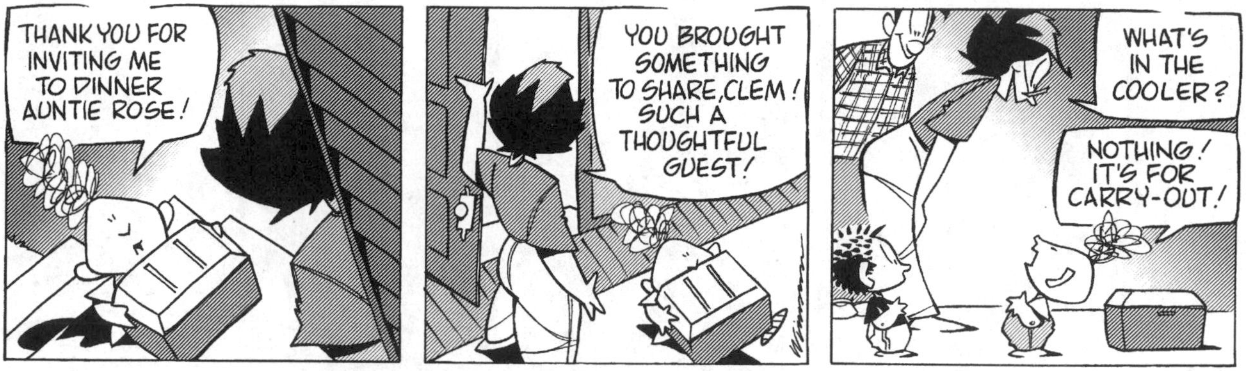
THANK YOU FOR INVITING ME TO DINNER AUNTIE ROSE!
YOU BROUGHT SOMETHING TO SHARE, CLEM! SUCH A THOUGHTFUL GUEST!
WHAT'S IN THE COOLER?
NOTHING! IT'S FOR CARRY-OUT!

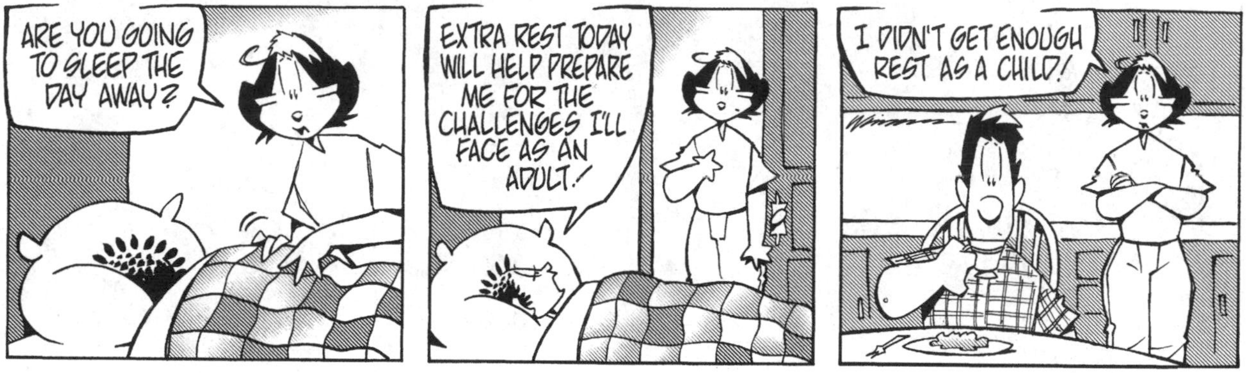
ARE YOU GOING TO SLEEP THE DAY AWAY?
EXTRA REST TODAY WILL HELP PREPARE ME FOR THE CHALLENGES I'LL FACE AS AN ADULT!
I DIDN'T GET ENOUGH REST AS A CHILD!

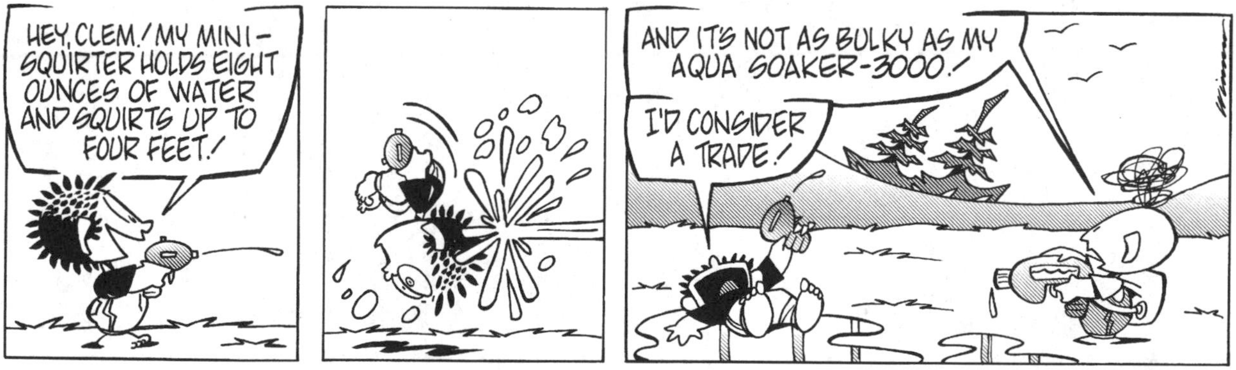
HEY, CLEM! MY MINI-SQUIRTER HOLDS EIGHT OUNCES OF WATER AND SQUIRTS UP TO FOUR FEET!
AND IT'S NOT AS BULKY AS MY AQUA SOAKER-3000!
I'D CONSIDER A TRADE!

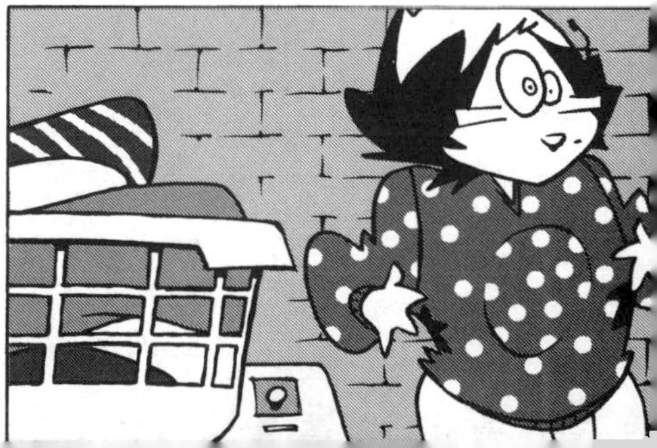

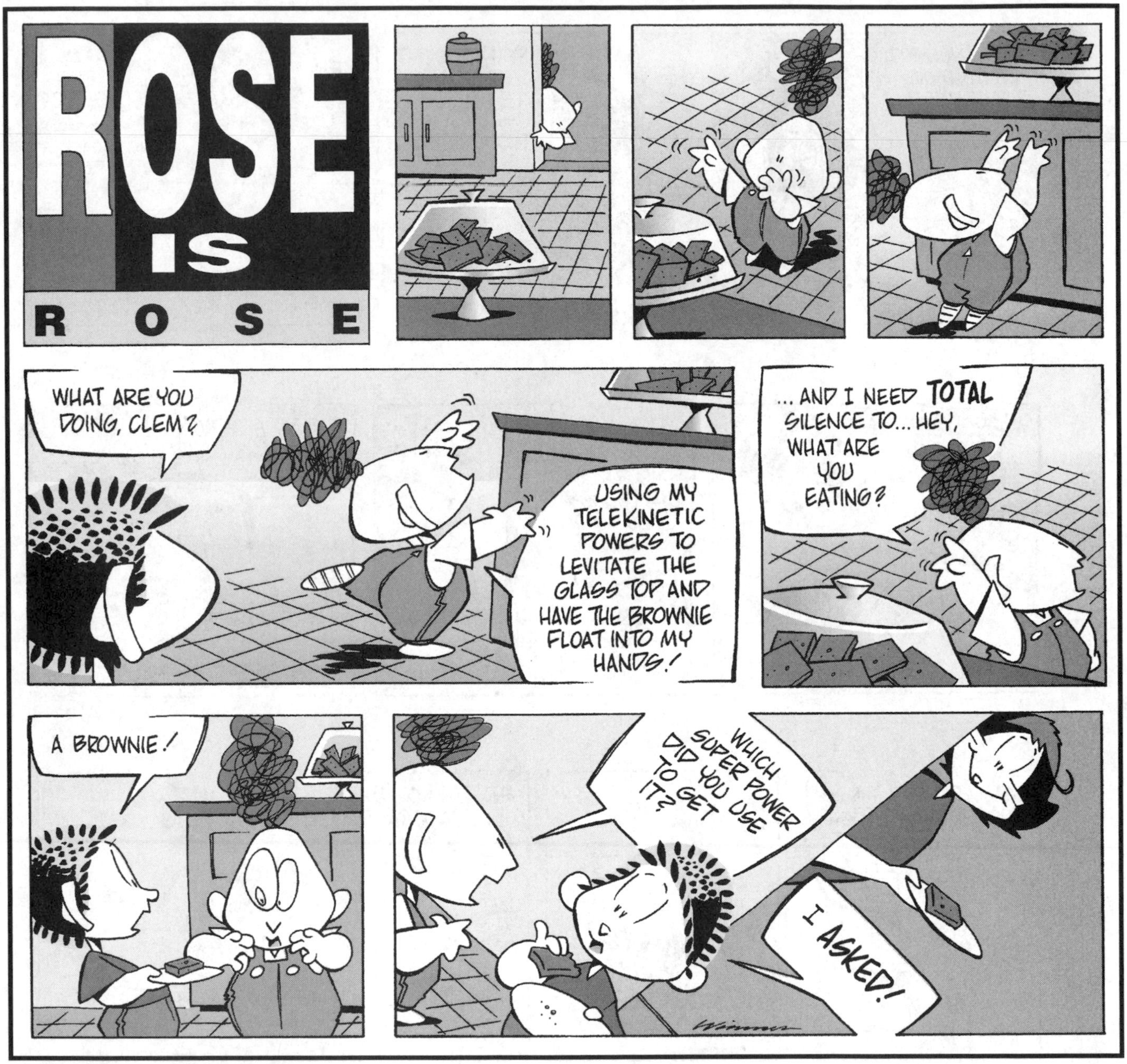
ROSE IS ROSE
WHAT ARE YOU DOING, CLEM?
USING MY TELEKINETIC POWERS TO LEVITATE THE GLASS TOP AND HAVE THE BROWNIE FLOAT INTO MY HANDS!
... AND I NEED TOTAL SILENCE TO... HEY, WHAT ARE YOU EATING?
A BROWNIE!
WHICH SUPER POWER DID YOU USE TO GET IT?
I ASKED!

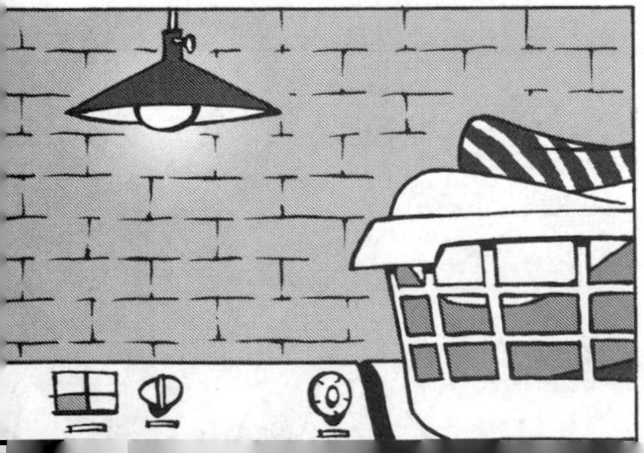

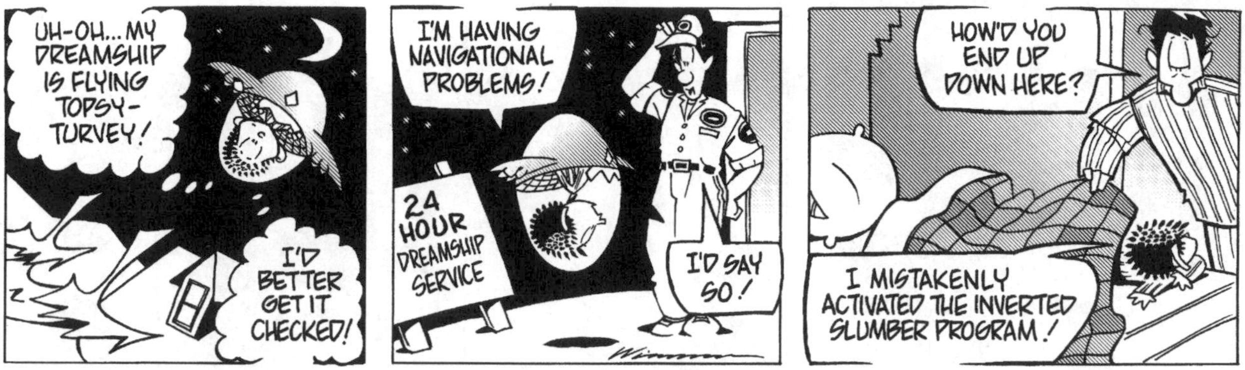
UH-OH... MY DREAMSHIP IS FLYING TOPSY-TURVEY!
I'D BETTER GET IT CHECKED!
I'M HAVING NAVIGATIONAL PROBLEMS!
24 HOUR DREAMSHIP SERVICE
I'D SAY SO!
HOW'D YOU END UP DOWN HERE?
I MISTAKENLY ACTIVATED THE INVERTED SLUMBER PROGRAM!

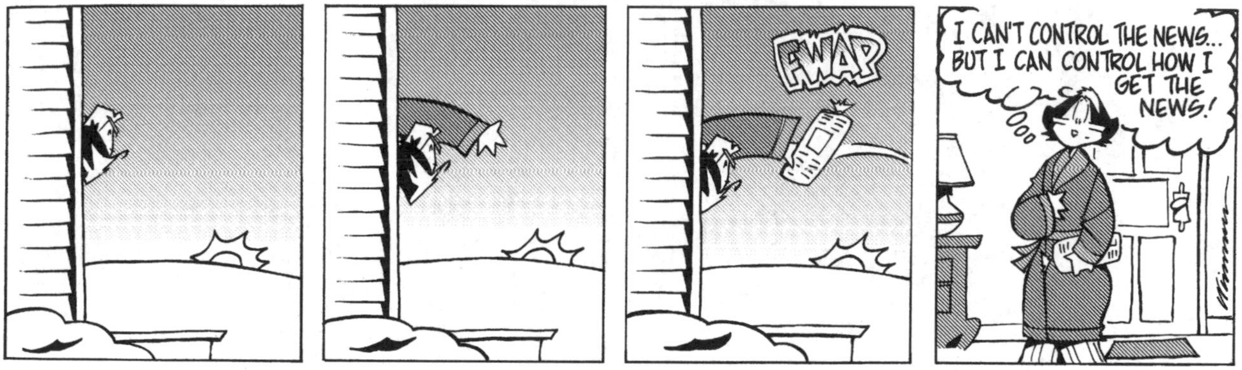
FWAP
I CAN'T CONTROL THE NEWS... BUT I CAN CONTROL HOW I GET THE NEWS!

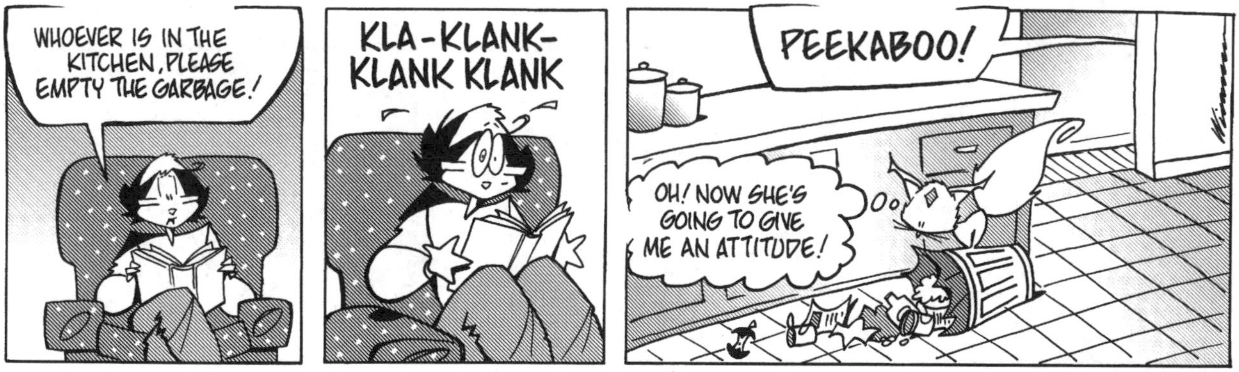
WHOEVER IS IN THE KITCHEN, PLEASE EMPTY THE GARBAGE!
KLA-KLANK-KLANK KLANK
PEEKABOO!
OH! NOW SHE'S GOING TO GIVE ME AN ATTITUDE!

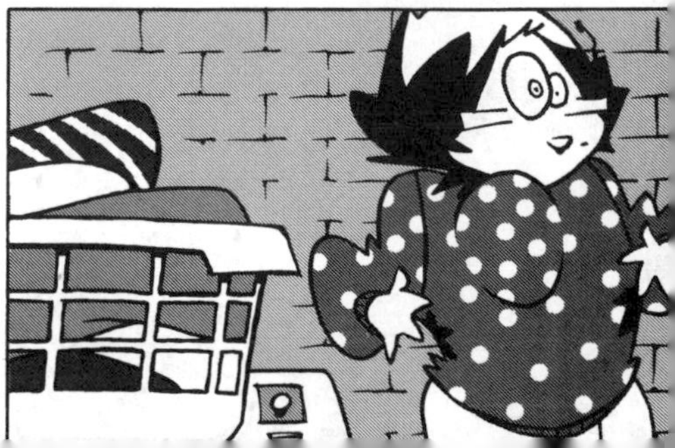

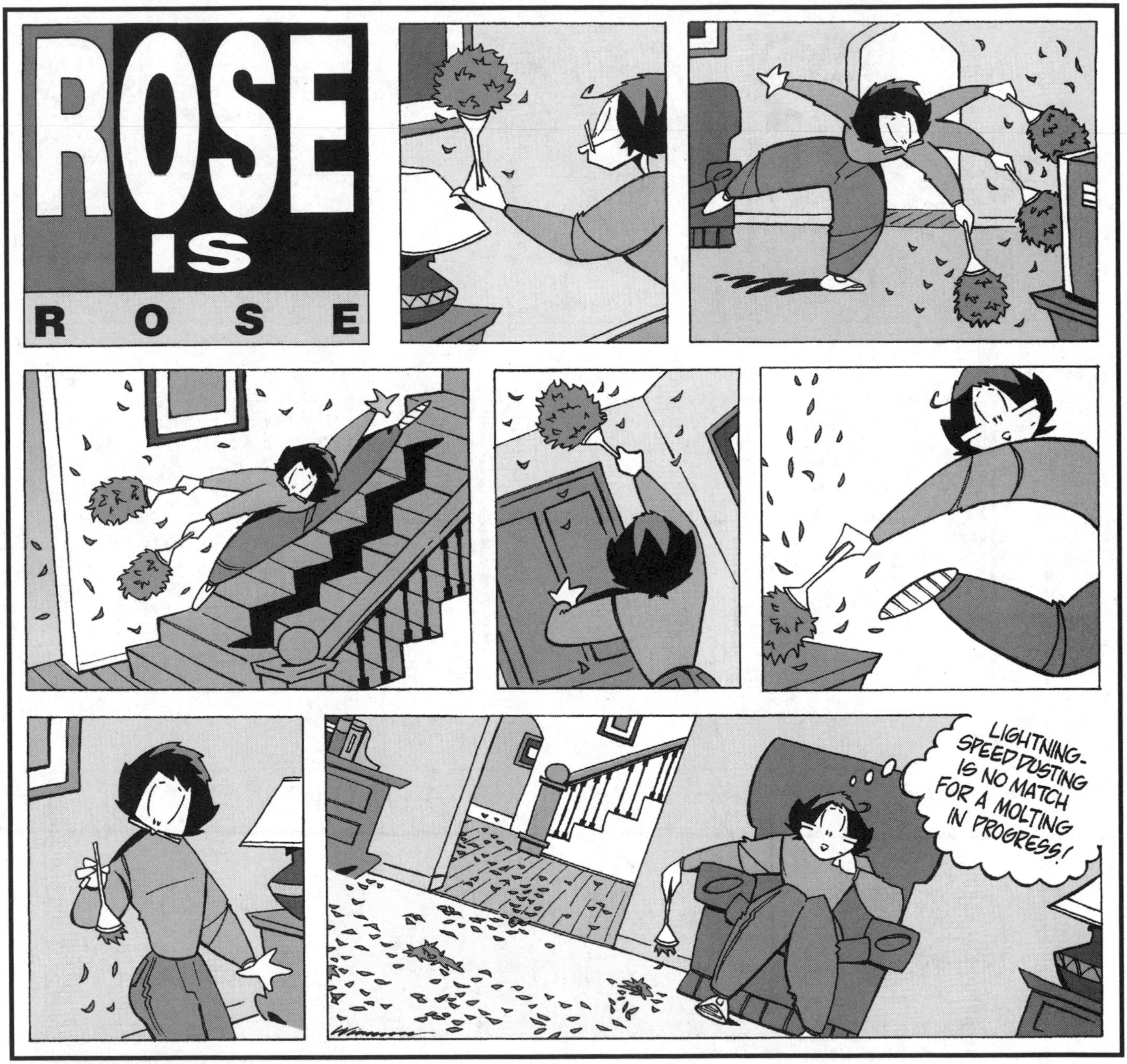
ROSE IS ROSE
LIGHTNING-SPEED DUSTING IS NO MATCH FOR A MOLTING IN PROGRESS!

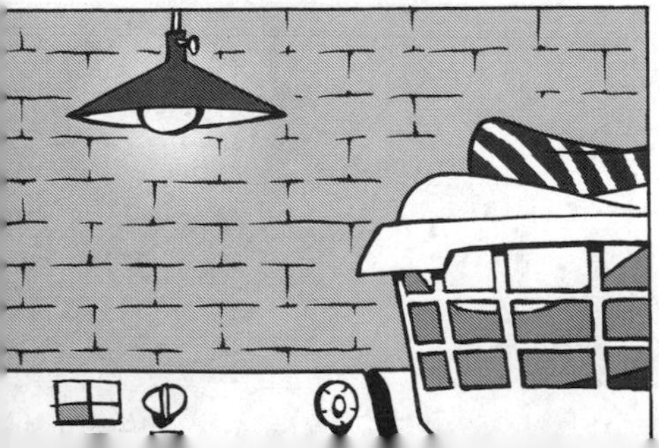

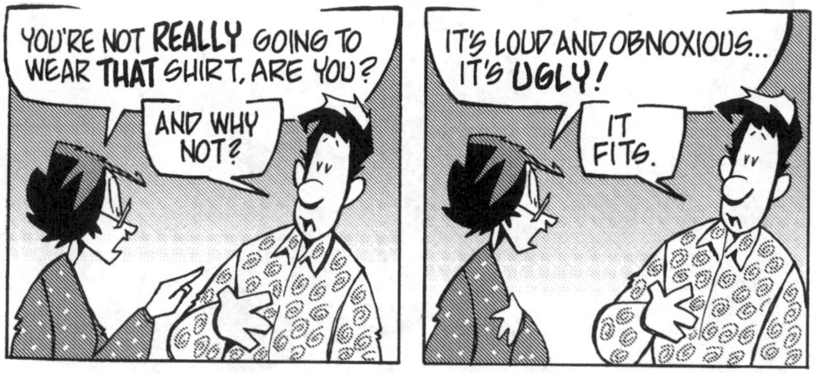
YOU'RE NOT REALLY GOING TO WEAR THAT SHIRT, ARE YOU?
AND WHY NOT?
IT'S LOUD AND OBNOXIOUS... IT'S UGLY!
IT FITS.
UGGGHH! MALE FASHION PRACTICALITY IS SO ANNOYING!
DO STRIPES GO WITH UGLY?

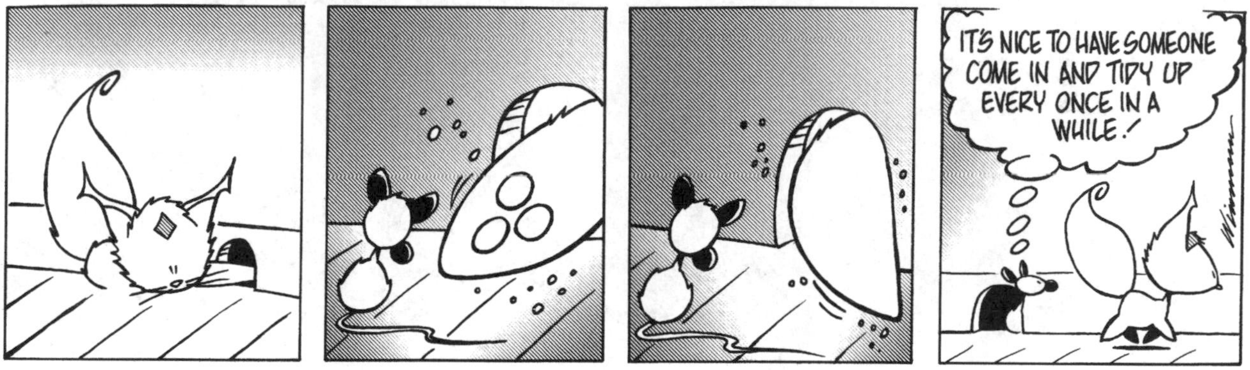
IT'S NICE TO HAVE SOMEONE COME IN AND TIDY UP EVERY ONCE IN A WHILE!

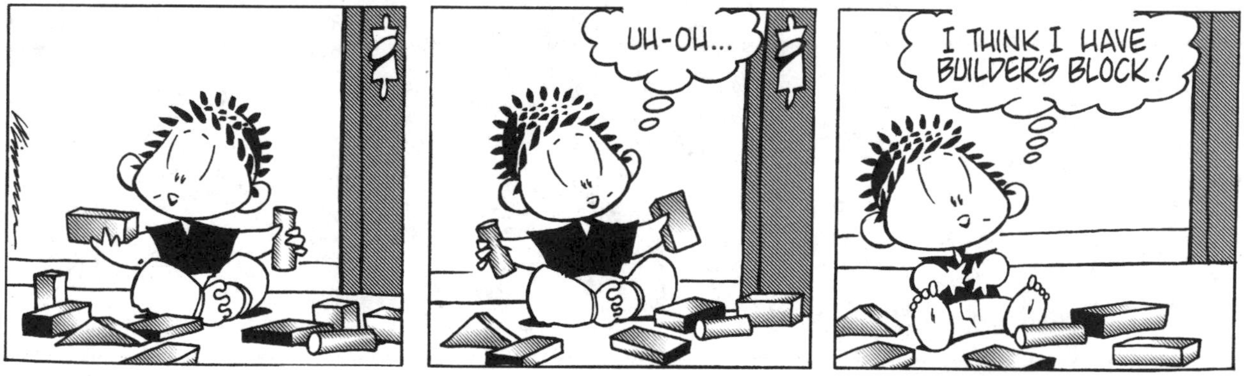
UH-OH...
I THINK I HAVE BUILDER'S BLOCK!

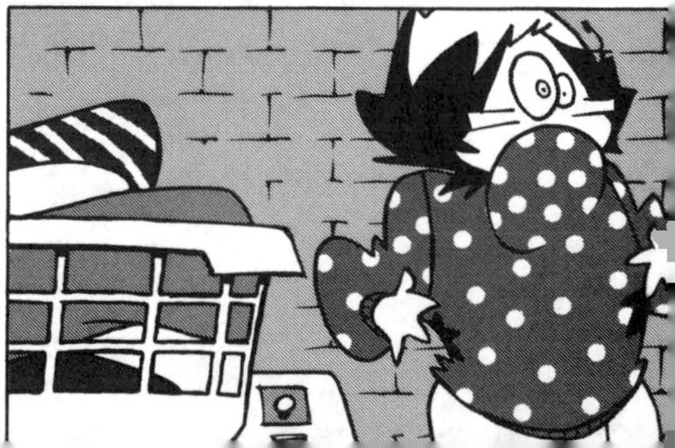

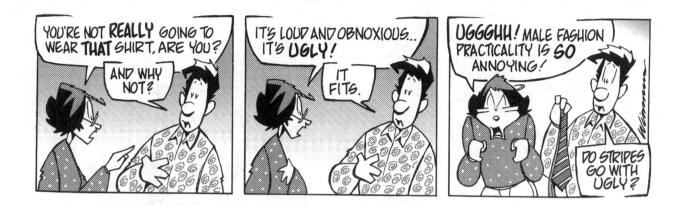

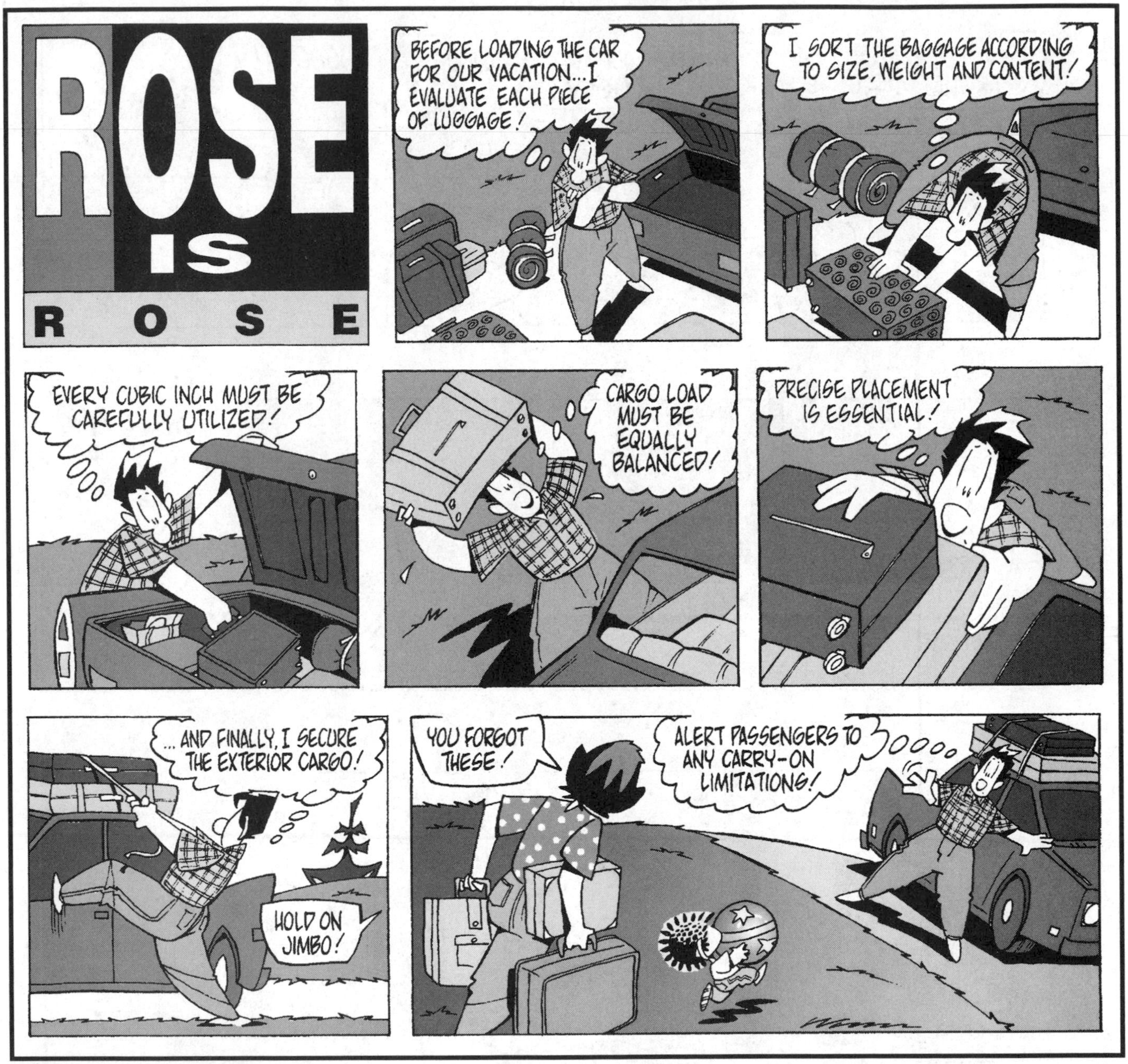
ROSE IS ROSE
BEFORE LOADING THE CAR FOR OUR VACATION...I EVALUATE EACH PIECE OF LUGGAGE!
I SORT THE BAGGAGE ACCORDING TO SIZE, WEIGHT AND CONTENT!
EVERY CUBIC INCH MUST BE CAREFULLY UTILIZED!
CARGO LOAD MUST BE EQUALLY BALANCED!
PRECISE PLACEMENT IS ESSENTIAL!
...AND FINALLY, I SECURE THE EXTERIOR CARGO!
HOLD ON JIMBO!
YOU FORGOT THESE!
ALERT PASSENGERS TO ANY CARRY-ON LIMITATIONS!

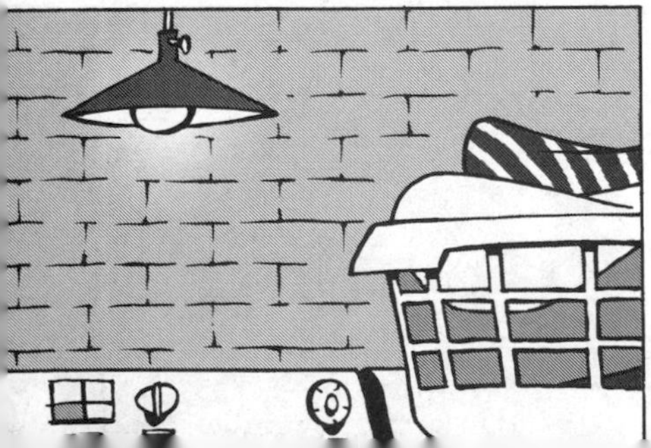

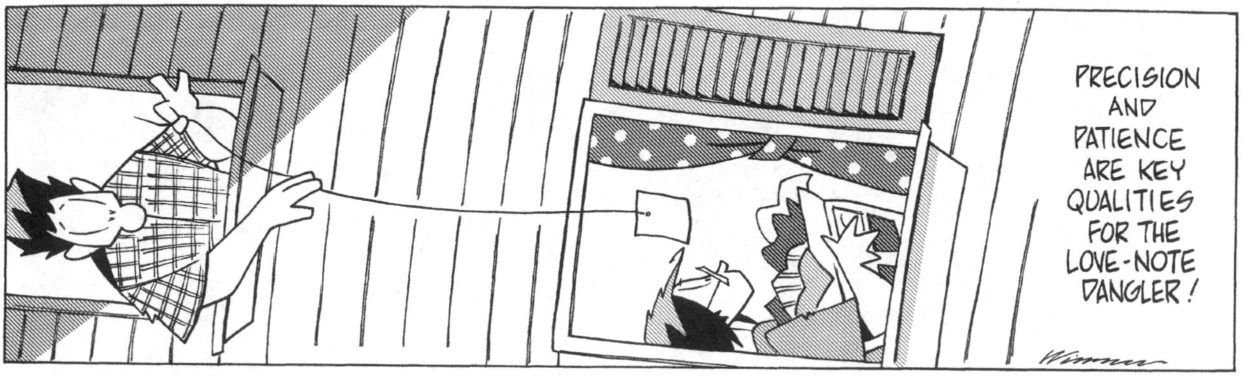
PRECISION AND PATIENCE ARE KEY QUALITIES FOR THE LOVE-NOTE DANGLER!

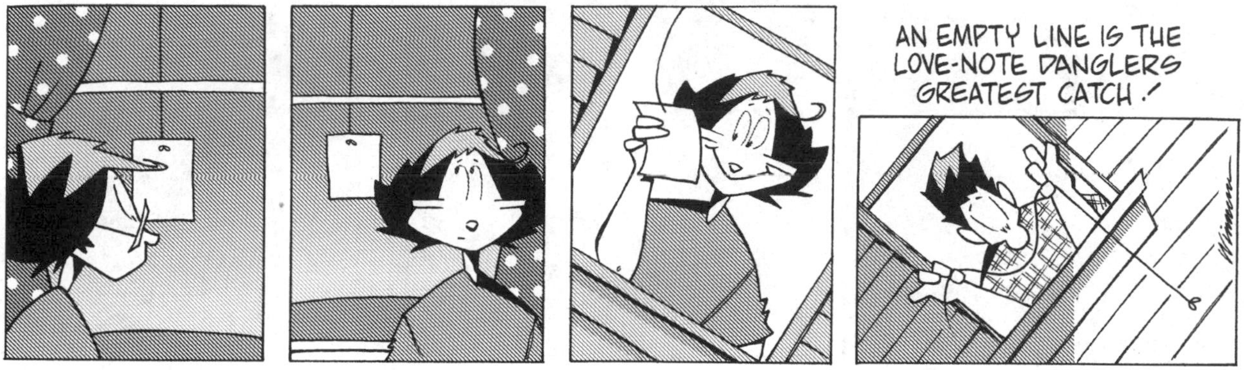
AN EMPTY LINE IS THE LOVE-NOTE DANGLERS GREATEST CATCH!

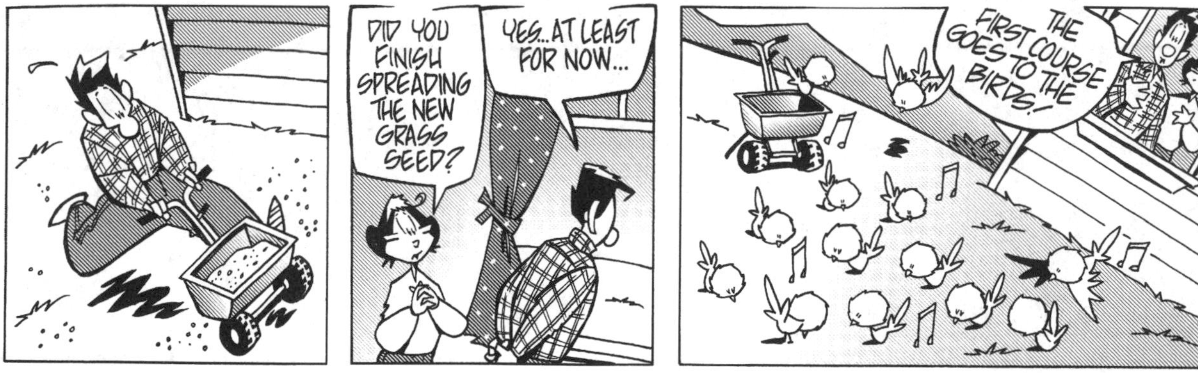
DID YOU FINISH SPREADING THE NEW GRASS SEED?
YES...AT LEAST FOR NOW...
THE FIRST COURSE GOES TO THE BIRDS!

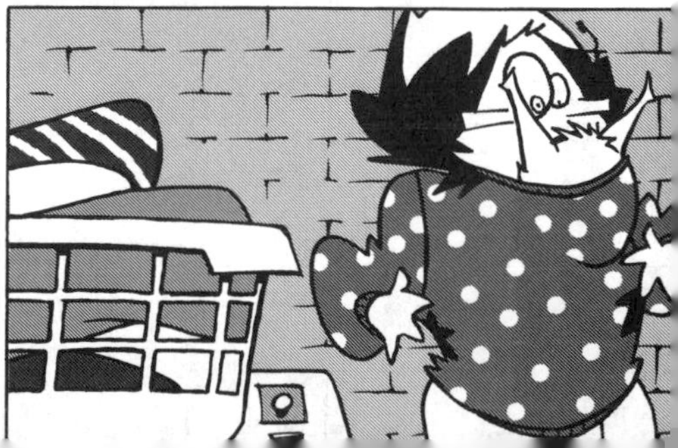

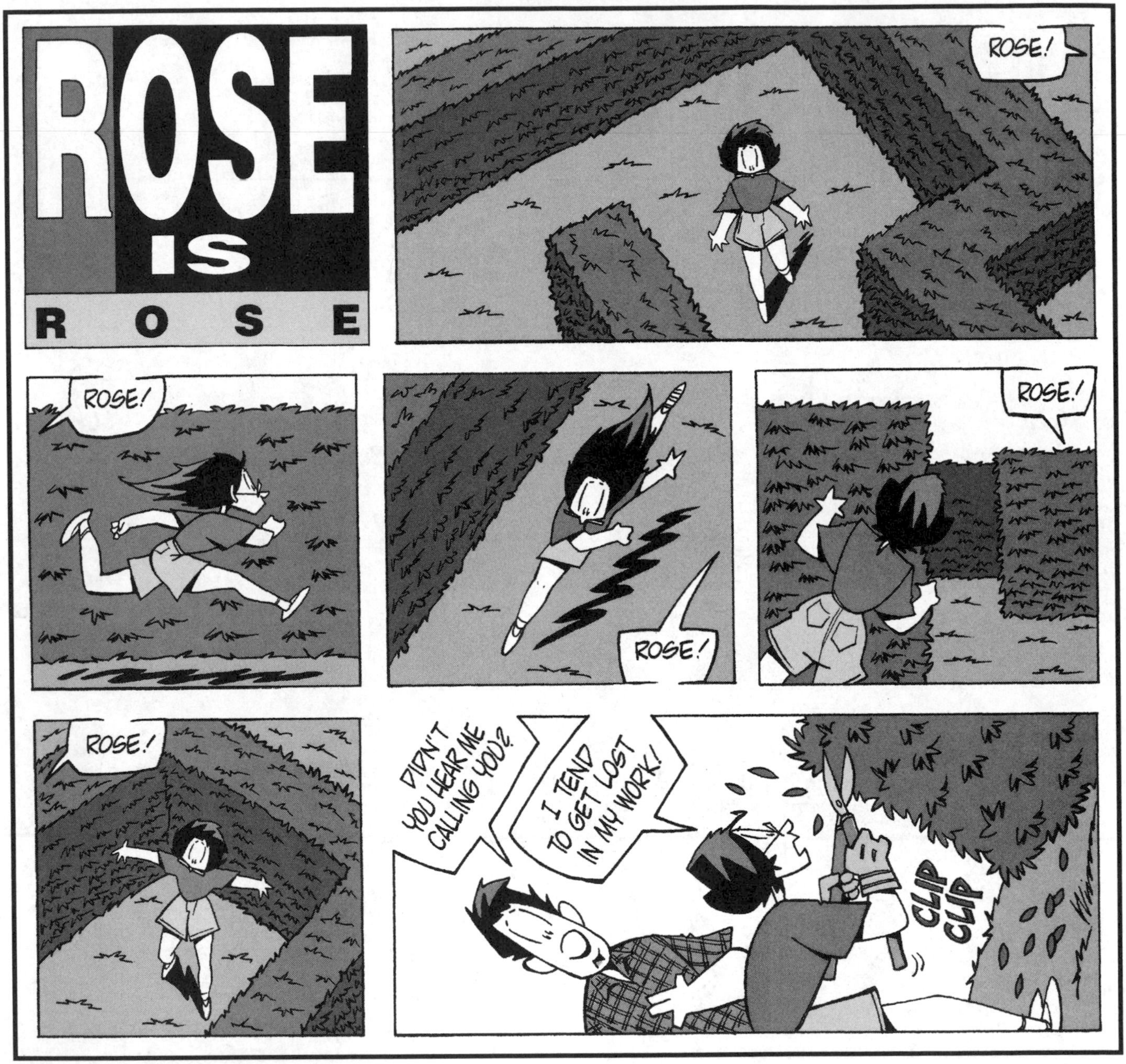
ROSE IS ROSE
ROSE!
ROSE!
ROSE!
ROSE!
ROSE!
DIDN'T YOU HEAR ME CALLING YOU?
I TEND TO GET LOST IN MY WORK!
CLIP CLIP

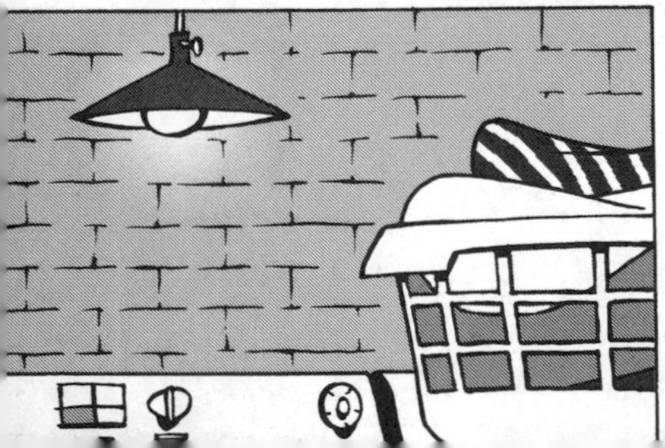

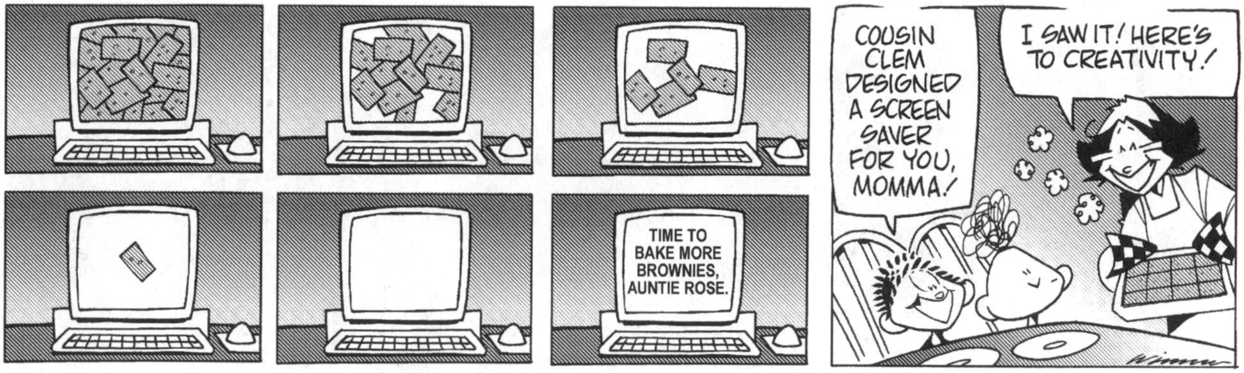
TIME TO BAKE MORE BROWNIES, AUNTIE ROSE.
COUSIN CLEM DESIGNED A SCREEN SAVER FOR YOU, MOMMA!
I SAW IT! HERE'S TO CREATIVITY!

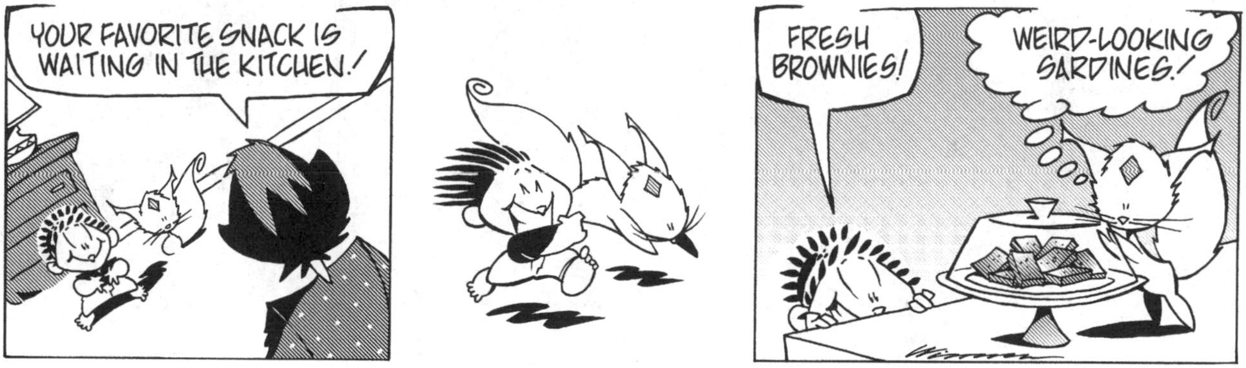
YOUR FAVORITE SNACK IS WAITING IN THE KITCHEN!
FRESH BROWNIES!
WEIRD-LOOKING SARDINES!

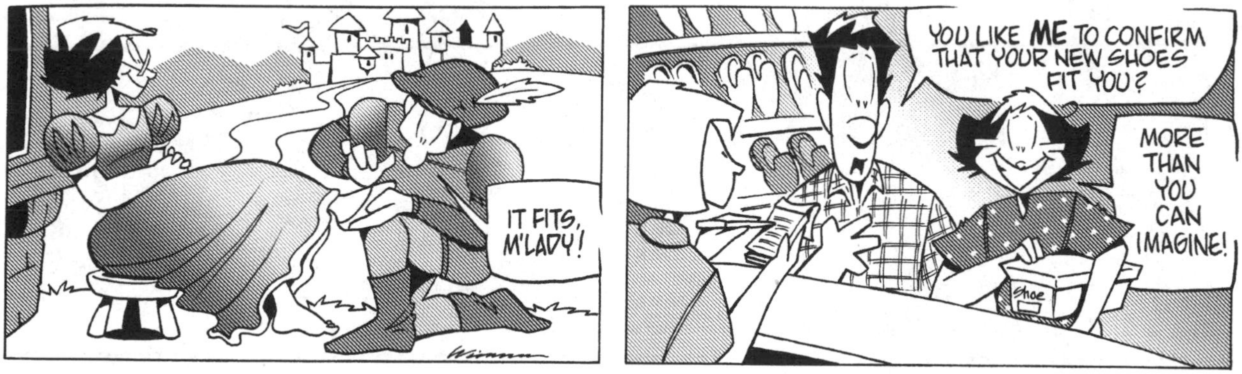
IT FITS, M'LADY!
YOU LIKE **ME** TO CONFIRM THAT YOUR NEW SHOES FIT YOU?
MORE THAN YOU CAN IMAGINE!
Shoe

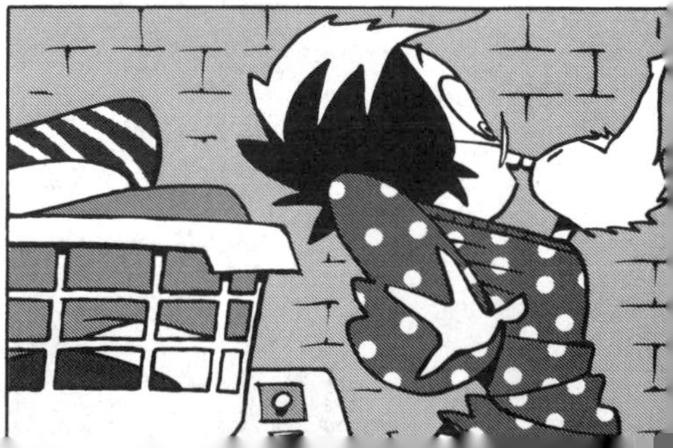

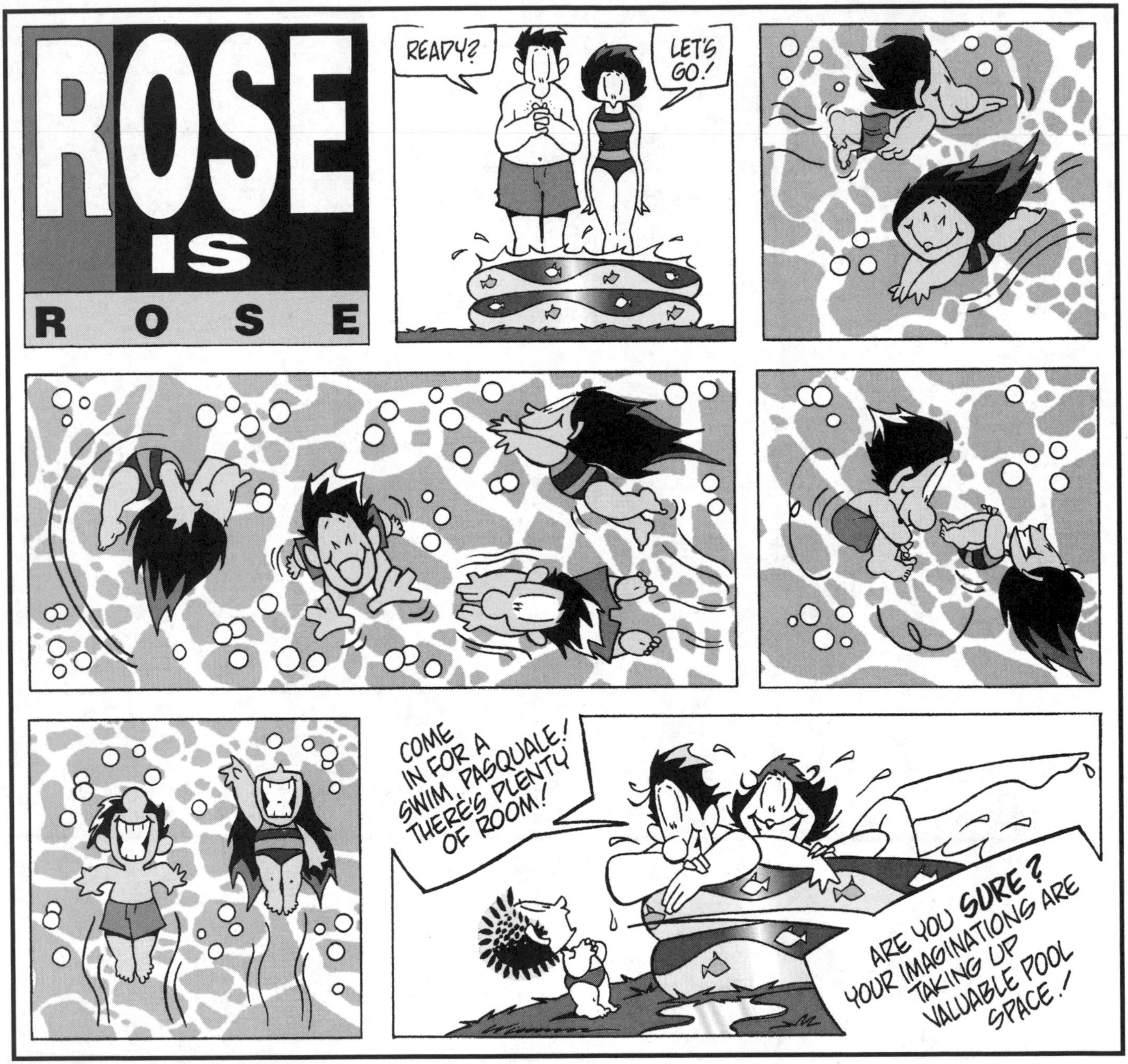
ROSE IS ROSE
READY?
LET'S GO!
COME IN FOR A SWIM, PASQUALE! THERE'S PLENTY OF ROOM!
ARE YOU SURE? YOUR IMAGINATIONS ARE TAKING UP VALUABLE POOL SPACE!

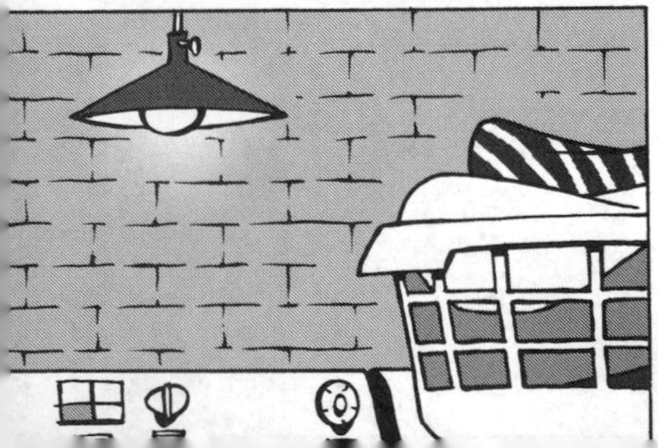

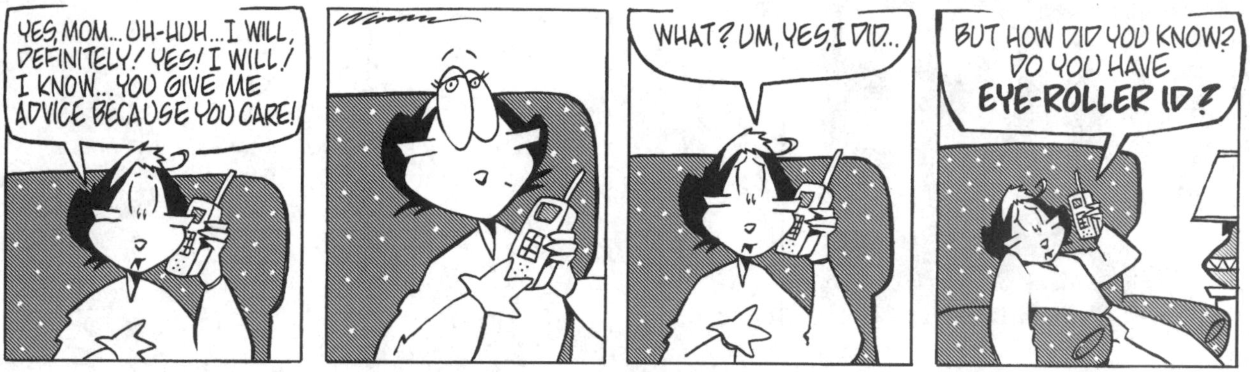
YES, MOM... UH-HUH... I WILL, DEFINITELY! YES! I WILL! I KNOW... YOU GIVE ME ADVICE BECAUSE YOU CARE!
WHAT? UM, YES, I DID...
BUT HOW DID YOU KNOW? DO YOU HAVE **EYE-ROLLER ID**?

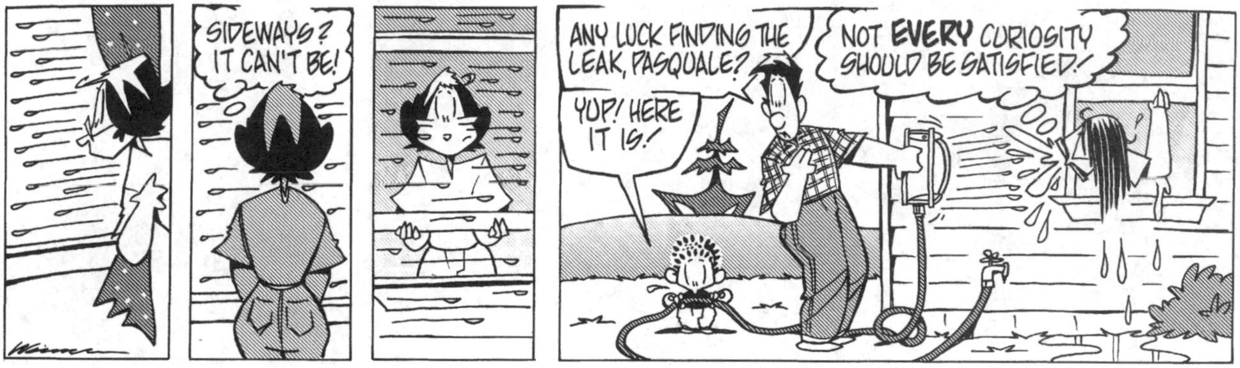
SIDEWAYS? IT CAN'T BE!
ANY LUCK FINDING THE LEAK, PASQUALE?
YUP! HERE IT IS!
NOT **EVERY** CURIOSITY SHOULD BE SATISFIED!

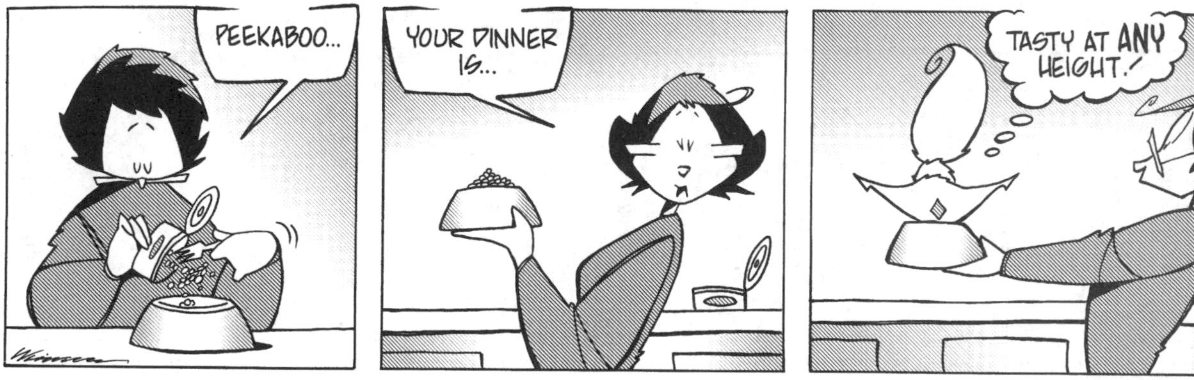
PEEKABOO...
YOUR DINNER IS...
TASTY AT **ANY** HEIGHT!

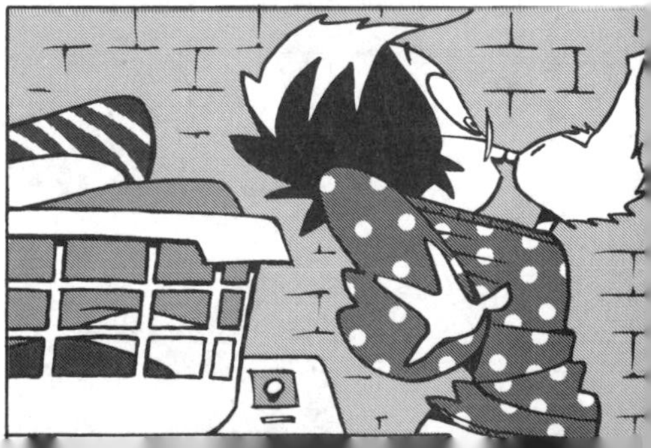

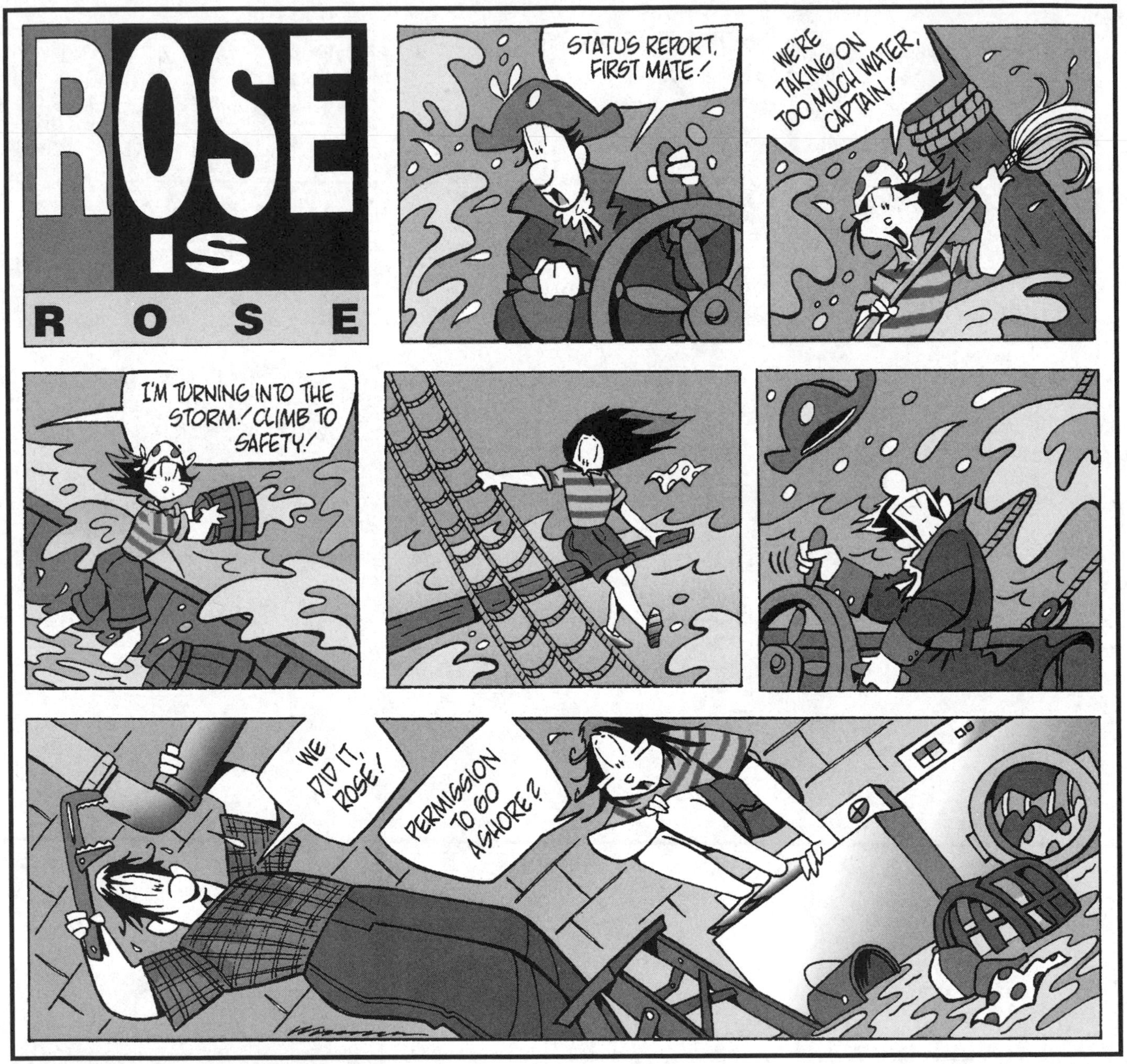
ROSE IS ROSE
STATUS REPORT, FIRST MATE!
WE'RE TAKING ON TOO MUCH WATER, CAPTAIN!
I'M TURNING INTO THE STORM! CLIMB TO SAFETY!
WE DID IT, ROSE!
PERMISSION TO GO ASHORE?

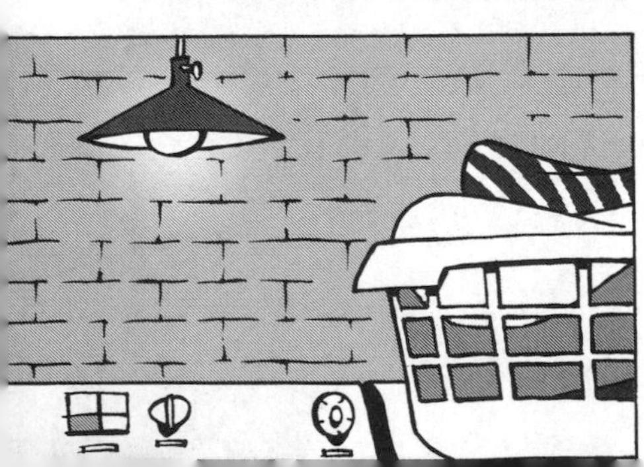

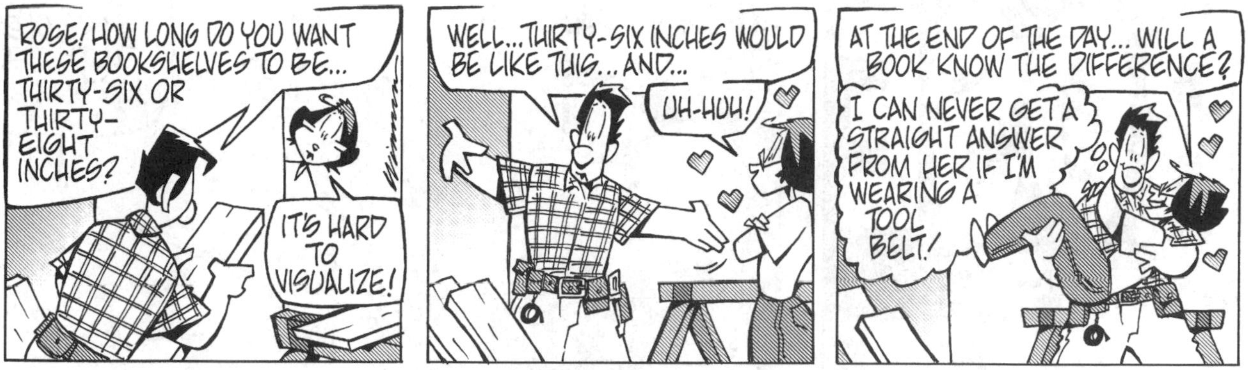
ROSE! HOW LONG DO YOU WANT THESE BOOKSHELVES TO BE... THIRTY-SIX OR THIRTY-EIGHT INCHES?
IT'S HARD TO VISUALIZE!
WELL...THIRTY-SIX INCHES WOULD BE LIKE THIS...AND...
UH-HUH!
AT THE END OF THE DAY... WILL A BOOK KNOW THE DIFFERENCE?
I CAN NEVER GET A STRAIGHT ANSWER FROM HER IF I'M WEARING A TOOL BELT!

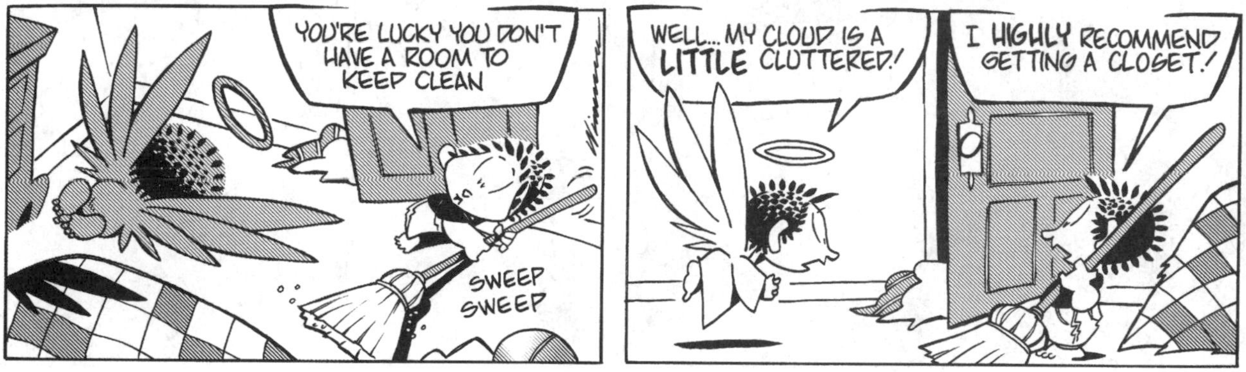
YOU'RE LUCKY YOU DON'T HAVE A ROOM TO KEEP CLEAN
SWEEP SWEEP
WELL... MY CLOUD IS A LITTLE CLUTTERED!
I HIGHLY RECOMMEND GETTING A CLOSET!

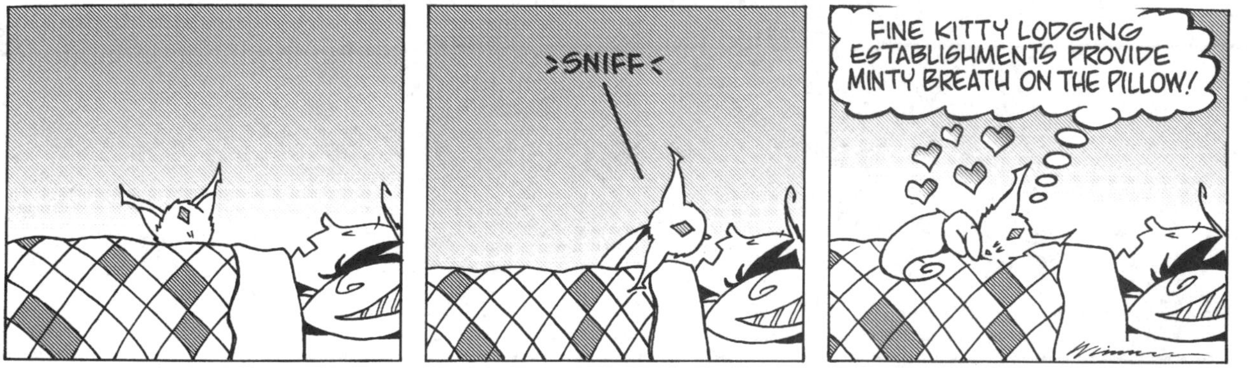
>SNIFF<
FINE KITTY LODGING ESTABLISHMENTS PROVIDE MINTY BREATH ON THE PILLOW!

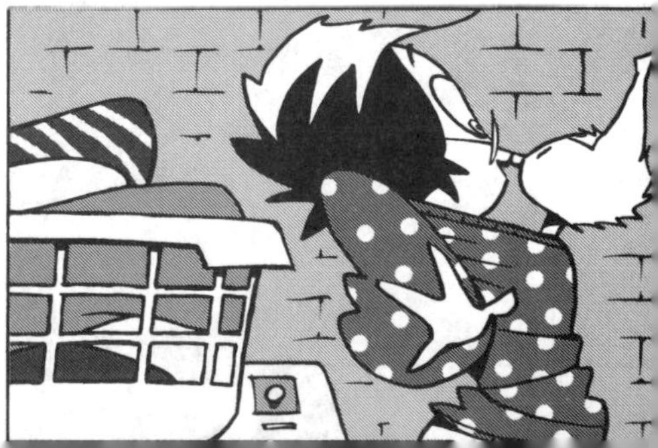

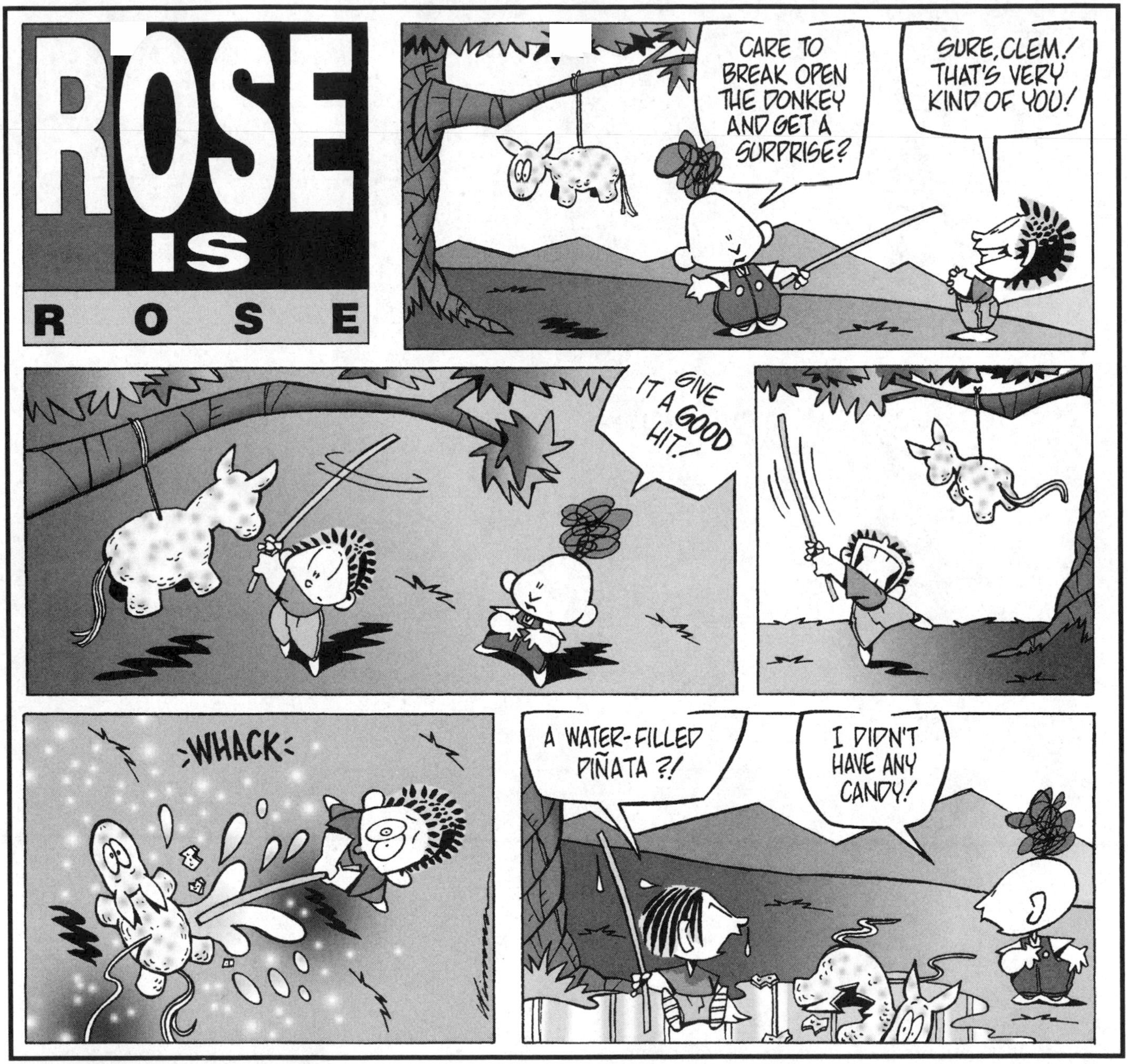
ROSE IS ROSE
CARE TO BREAK OPEN THE DONKEY AND GET A SURPRISE?
SURE, CLEM! THAT'S VERY KIND OF YOU!
GIVE IT A GOOD HIT!
WHACK
A WATER-FILLED PIÑATA ?!
I DIDN'T HAVE ANY CANDY!

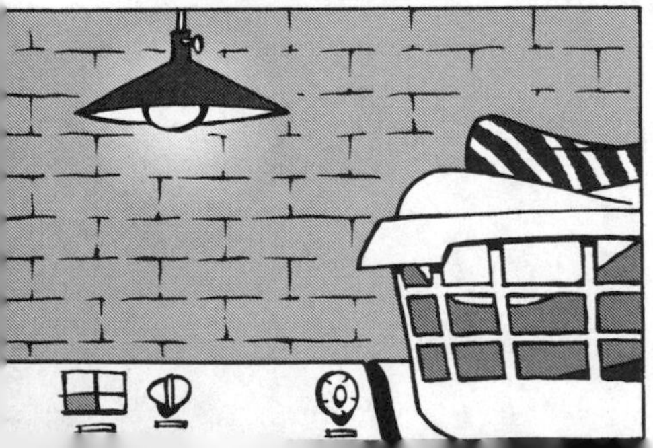

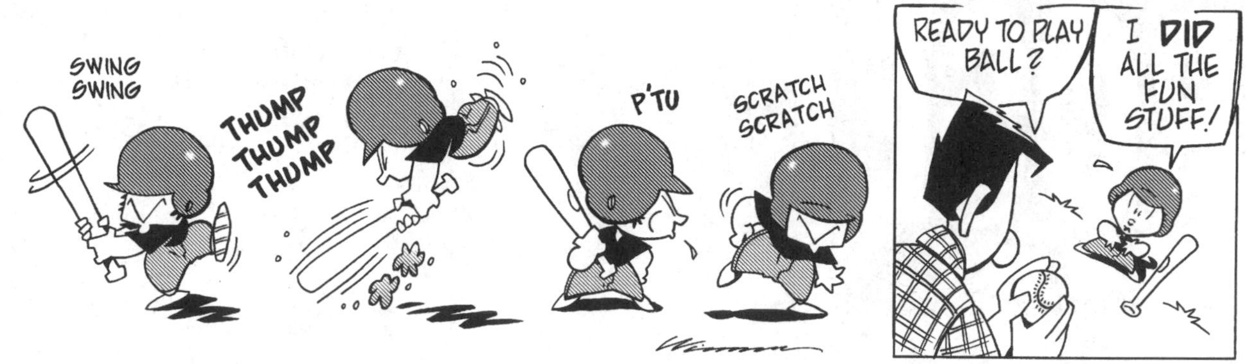
SWING SWING
THUMP THUMP THUMP
P'TU
SCRATCH SCRATCH
READY TO PLAY BALL?
I **DID** ALL THE FUN STUFF!

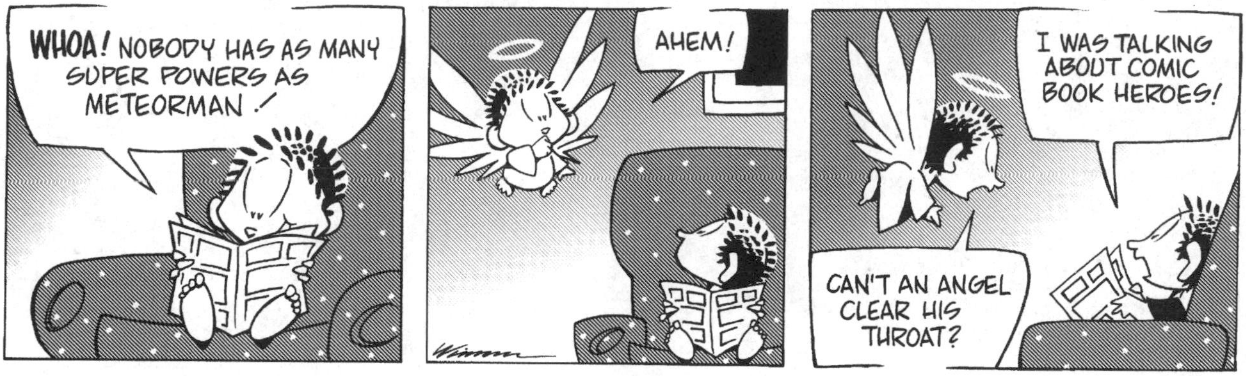
WHOA! NOBODY HAS AS MANY SUPER POWERS AS METEORMAN!
AHEM!
I WAS TALKING ABOUT COMIC BOOK HEROES!
CAN'T AN ANGEL CLEAR HIS THROAT?

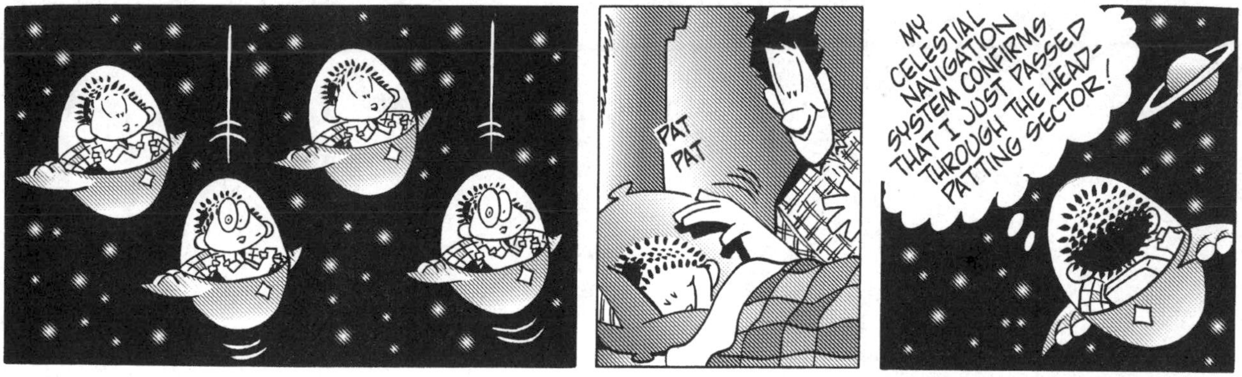
PAT PAT
MY CELESTIAL NAVIGATION SYSTEM CONFIRMS THAT I JUST PASSED THROUGH THE HEAD-PATTING SECTOR!

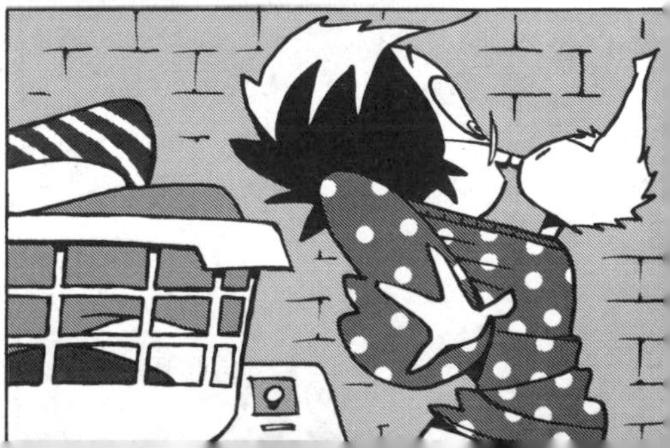

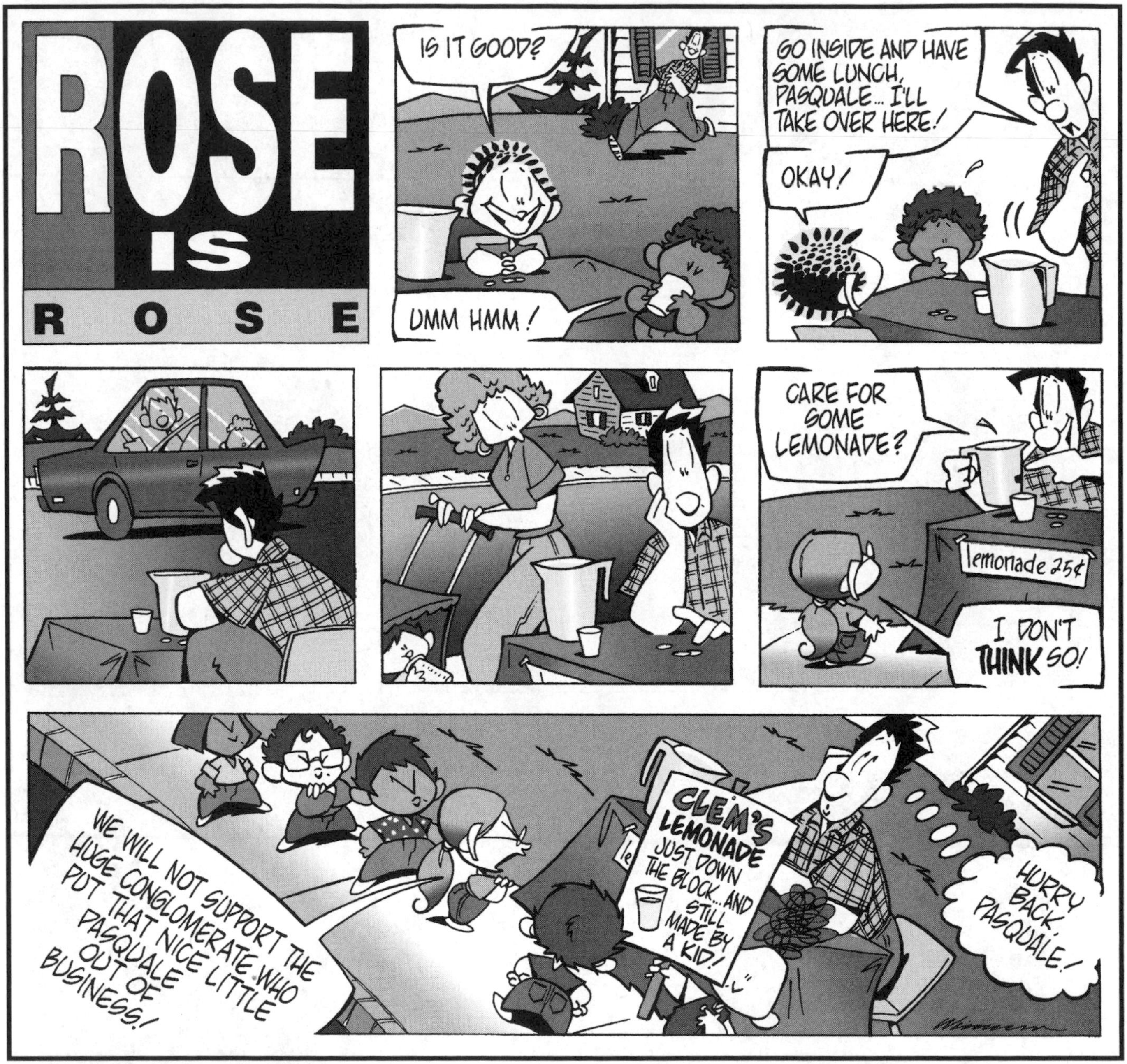
ROSE IS ROSE
IS IT GOOD?
UMM HMM!
GO INSIDE AND HAVE SOME LUNCH, PASQUALE... I'LL TAKE OVER HERE!
OKAY!
CARE FOR SOME LEMONADE?
lemonade 25¢
I DON'T THINK SO!
WE WILL NOT SUPPORT THE HUGE CONGLOMERATE WHO PUT THAT NICE LITTLE PASQUALE OUT OF BUSINESS!
CLEM'S LEMONADE JUST DOWN THE BLOCK... AND STILL MADE BY A KID!
HURRY BACK, PASQUALE!

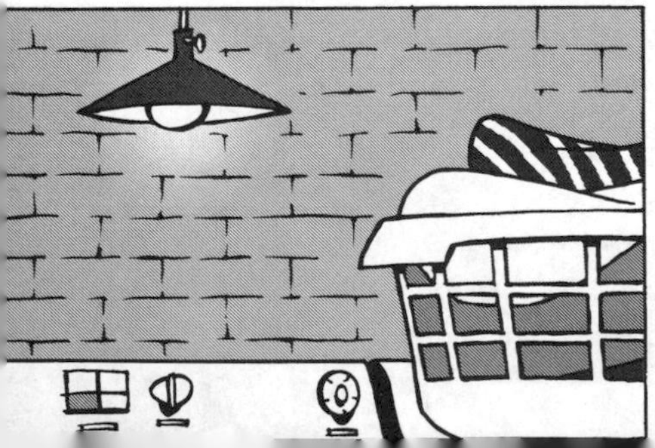

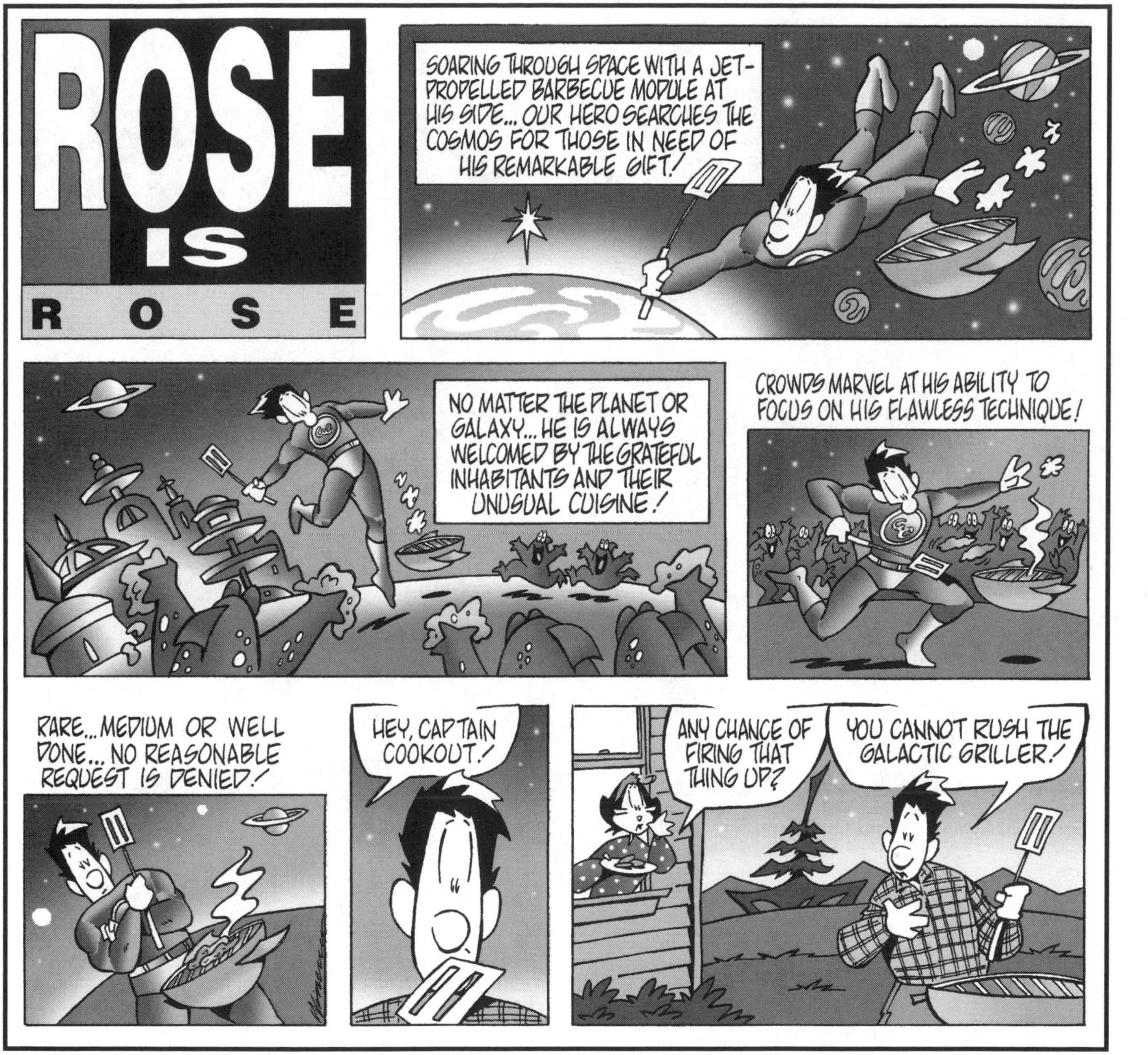
ROSE IS ROSE
SOARING THROUGH SPACE WITH A JET-PROPELLED BARBECUE MODULE AT HIS SIDE... OUR HERO SEARCHES THE COSMOS FOR THOSE IN NEED OF HIS REMARKABLE GIFT!
NO MATTER THE PLANET OR GALAXY... HE IS ALWAYS WELCOMED BY THE GRATEFUL INHABITANTS AND THEIR UNUSUAL CUISINE!
CROWDS MARVEL AT HIS ABILITY TO FOCUS ON HIS FLAWLESS TECHNIQUE!
RARE... MEDIUM OR WELL DONE... NO REASONABLE REQUEST IS DENIED!
HEY, CAPTAIN COOKOUT!
ANY CHANCE OF FIRING THAT THING UP?
YOU CANNOT RUSH THE GALACTIC GRILLER!

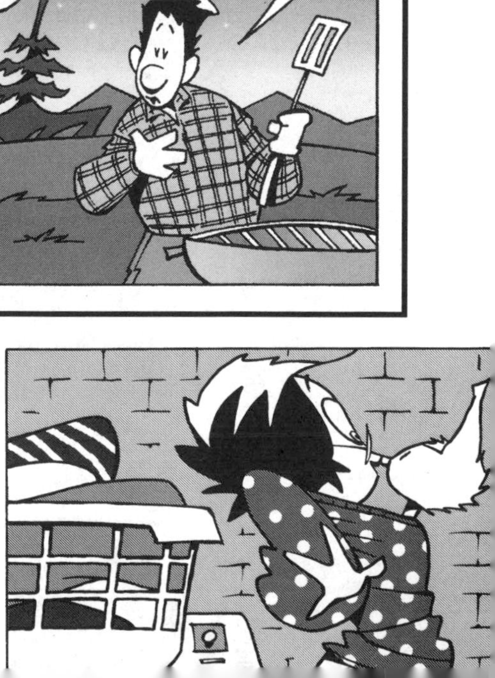

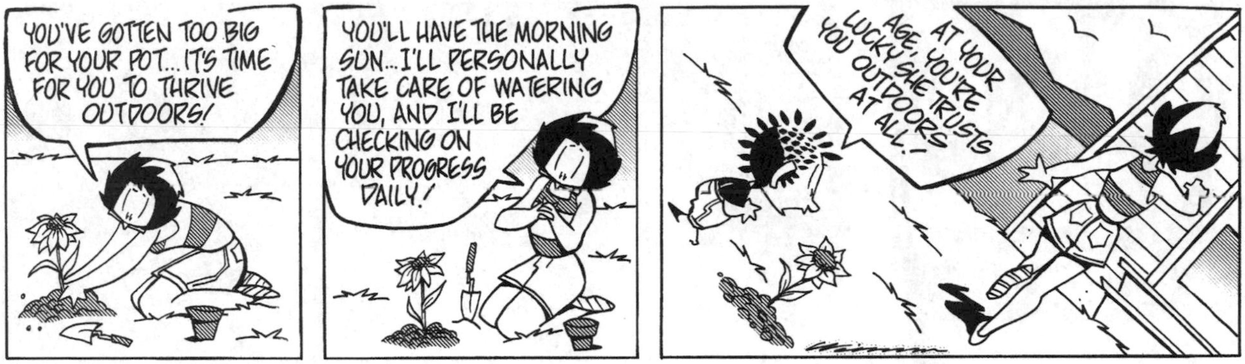
YOU'VE GOTTEN TOO BIG FOR YOUR POT... IT'S TIME FOR YOU TO THRIVE OUTDOORS!
YOU'LL HAVE THE MORNING SUN... I'LL PERSONALLY TAKE CARE OF WATERING YOU, AND I'LL BE CHECKING ON YOUR PROGRESS DAILY!
AT YOUR AGE, YOU'RE LUCKY SHE TRUSTS YOU OUTDOORS AT ALL!

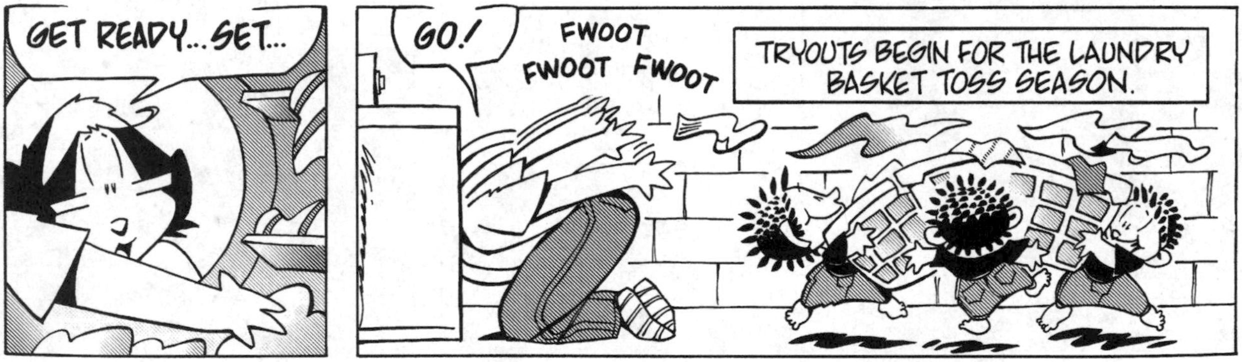
GET READY... SET...
GO!
FWOOT
FWOOT FWOOT
TRYOUTS BEGIN FOR THE LAUNDRY BASKET TOSS SEASON.

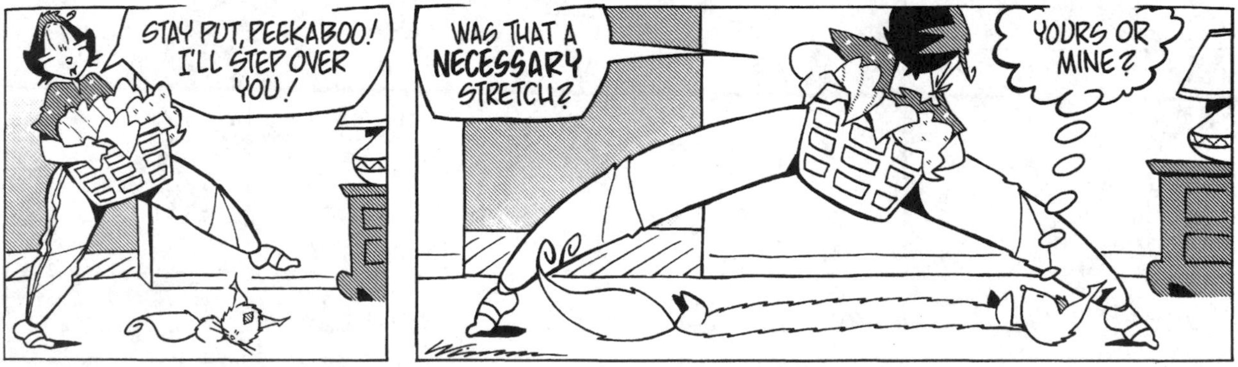
STAY PUT, PEEKABOO! I'LL STEP OVER YOU!
WAS THAT A **NECESSARY** STRETCH?
YOURS OR MINE?

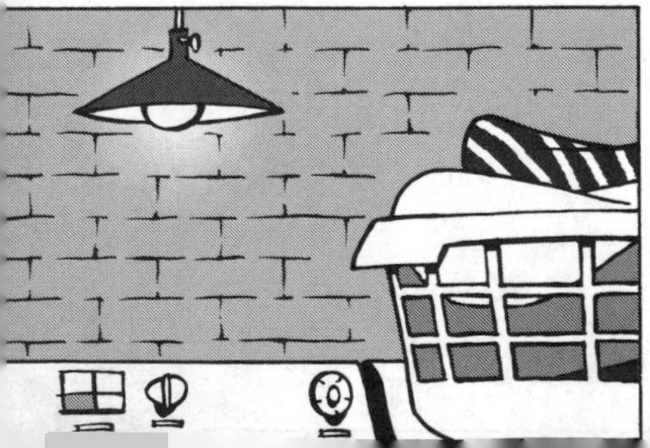

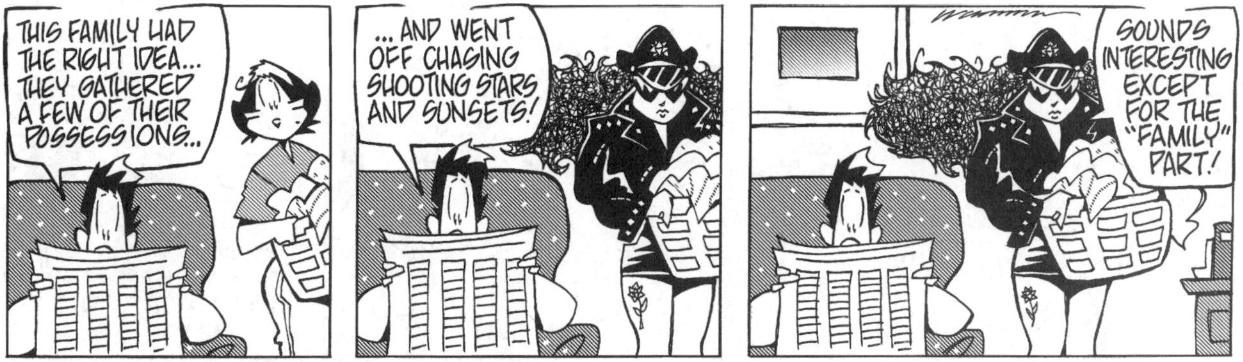
THIS FAMILY HAD THE RIGHT IDEA... THEY GATHERED A FEW OF THEIR POSSESSIONS...
... AND WENT OFF CHASING SHOOTING STARS AND SUNSETS!
SOUNDS INTERESTING EXCEPT FOR THE "FAMILY" PART!

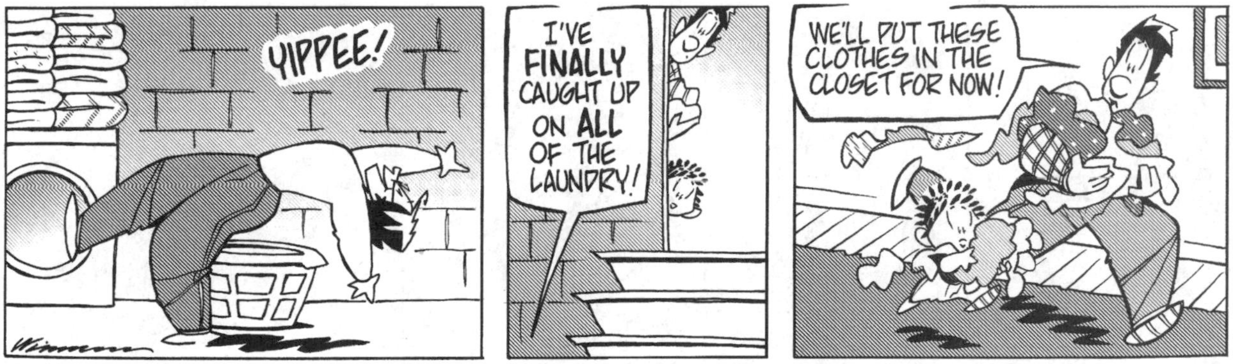
YIPPEE!
I'VE FINALLY CAUGHT UP ON ALL OF THE LAUNDRY!
WE'LL PUT THESE CLOTHES IN THE CLOSET FOR NOW!

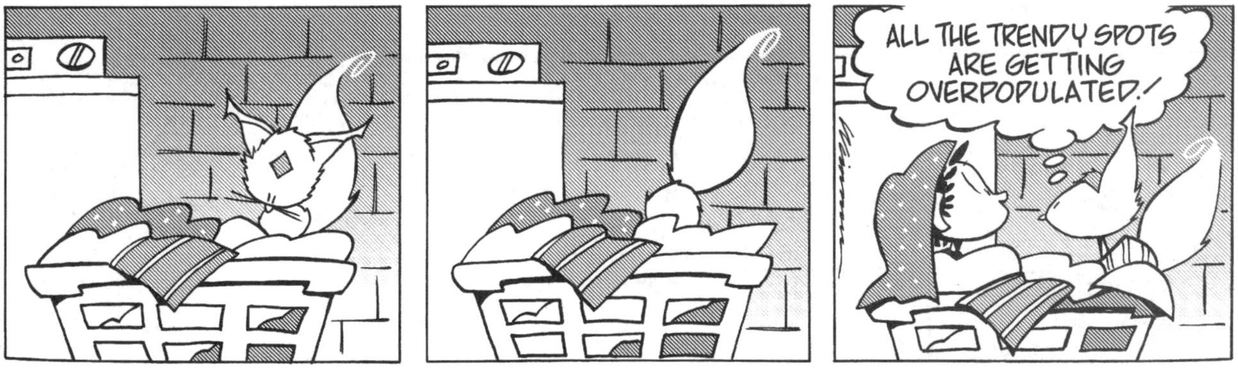
ALL THE TRENDY SPOTS ARE GETTING OVERPOPULATED!

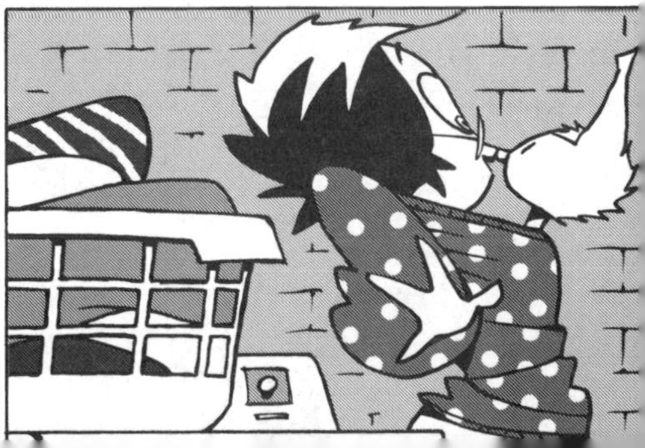

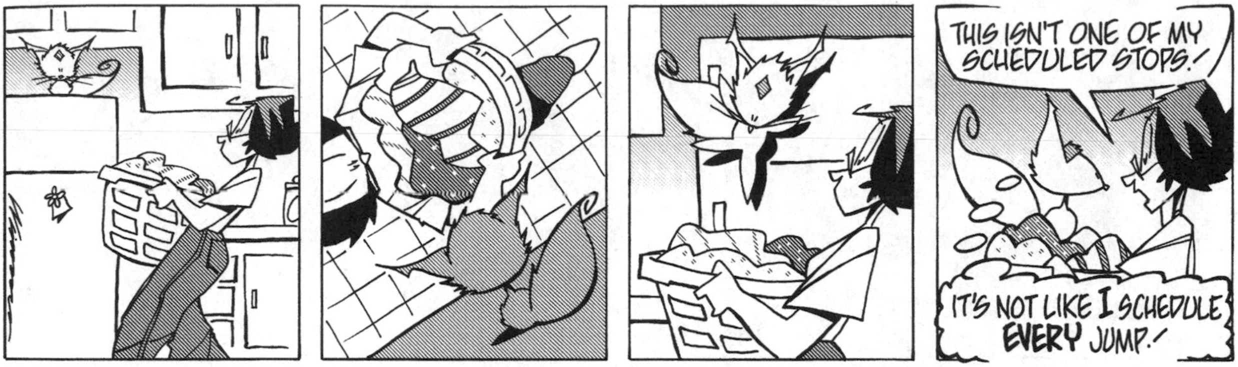
THIS ISN'T ONE OF MY SCHEDULED STOPS!
IT'S NOT LIKE I SCHEDULE EVERY JUMP!

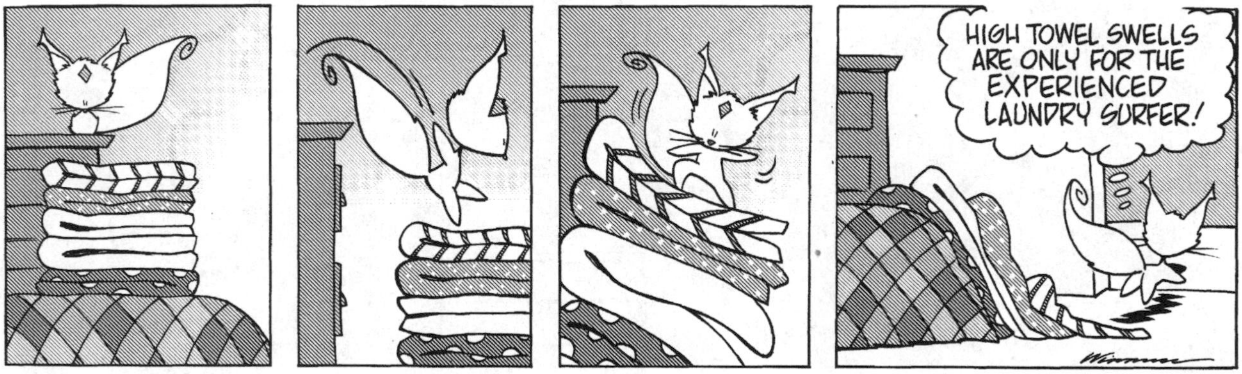
HIGH TOWEL SWELLS ARE ONLY FOR THE EXPERIENCED LAUNDRY SURFER!

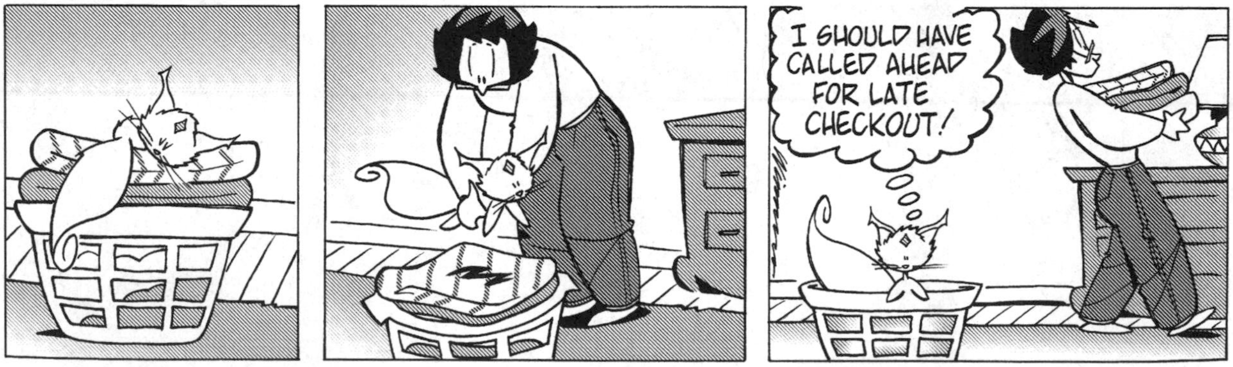
I SHOULD HAVE CALLED AHEAD FOR LATE CHECKOUT!

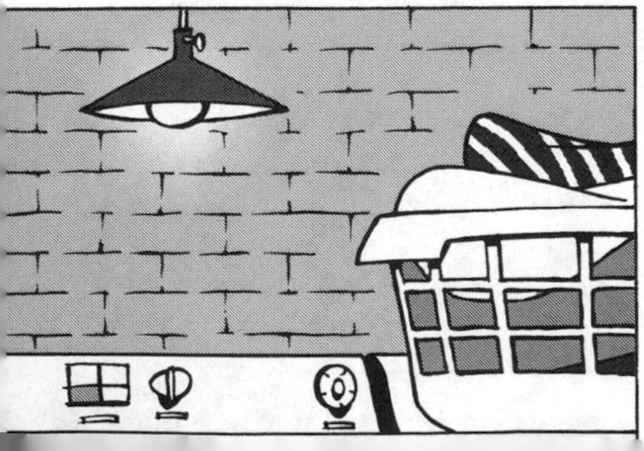

FLIP THE PAGE CORNERS FROM FRONT TO BACK AND WATCH BOTH SIDES TOGETHER!

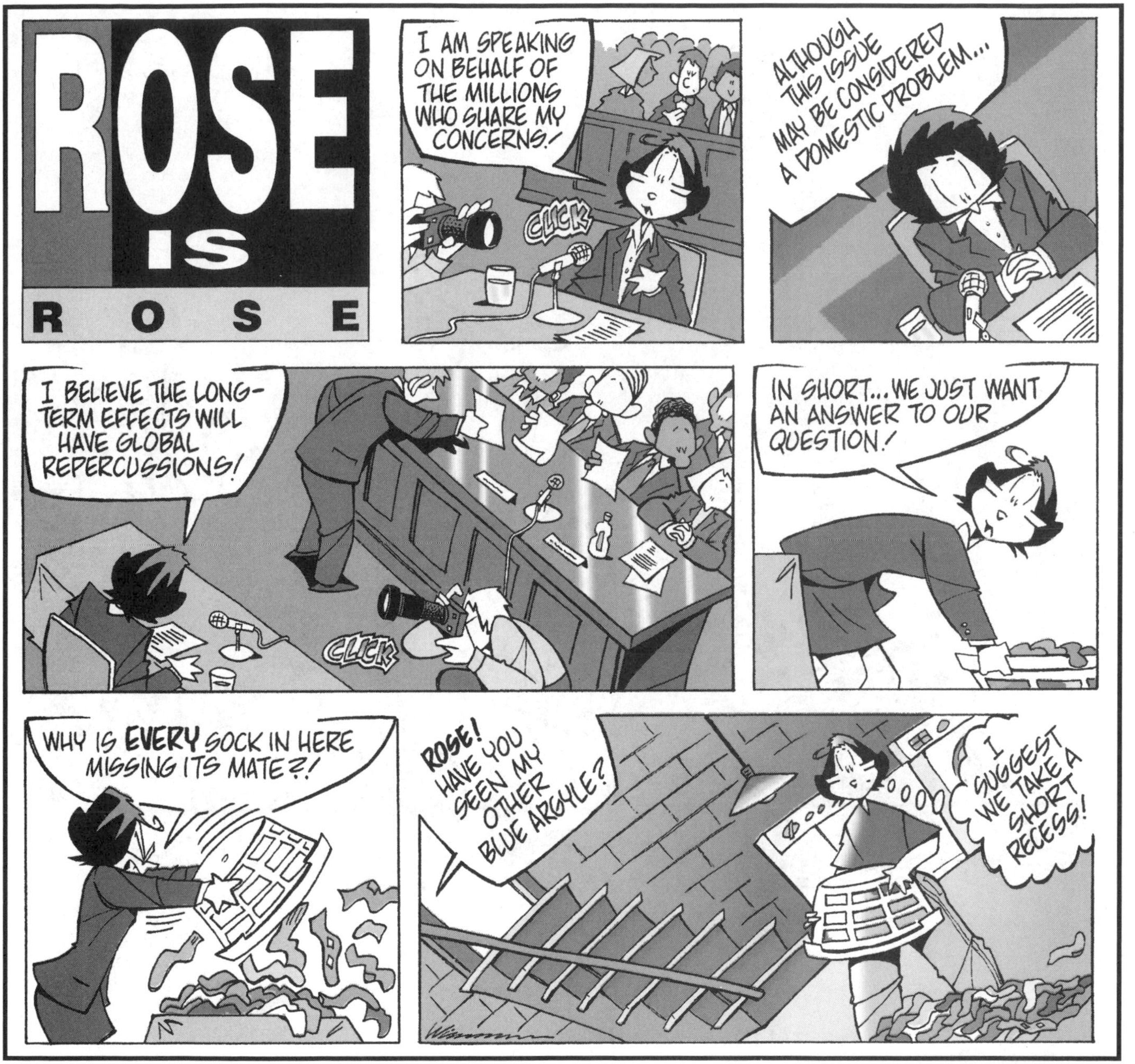
ROSE IS ROSE
I AM SPEAKING ON BEHALF OF THE MILLIONS WHO SHARE MY CONCERNS!
CLICK
ALTHOUGH THIS ISSUE MAY BE CONSIDERED A DOMESTIC PROBLEM...
I BELIEVE THE LONG-TERM EFFECTS WILL HAVE GLOBAL REPERCUSSIONS!
CLICK
IN SHORT...WE JUST WANT AN ANSWER TO OUR QUESTION!
WHY IS EVERY SOCK IN HERE MISSING ITS MATE?!
ROSE! HAVE YOU SEEN MY OTHER BLUE ARGYLE?
I SUGGEST WE TAKE A SHORT RECESS!

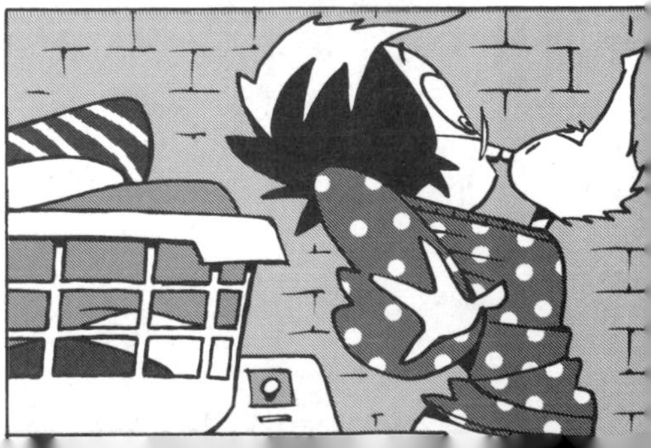